WJEC GCSE Home Economics Child Development

Kate Ford • Susan Gould
Christine Henning • Beverley Parry

Published in 2013 by Illuminate Publishing Ltd, P.O. Box 1160, Cheltenham, Gloucestershire GL50 9RW

Orders: Please visit www.illuminatepublishing.com or email sales@illuminatepublishing.com

British Library Cataloguing in Publication Data

A catalogue record for this book is available from the British Library

ISBN 978-1-908682-15-4

2.16

Printed and bound by CPI Group (UK) Ltd, Croydon, CR0 4YY

The publisher's policy is to use papers that are natural, renewable and recyclable products made from wood grown in sustainable forests. The logging and manufacturing processes are expected to conform to the environmental regulations of the country of origin.

Every effort has been made to contact copyright holders of material produced in this book. If notified, the publisher will be pleased to rectify any errors or omissions at the earliest opportunity.

This material has been endorsed by WJEC and offers high quality support for the delivery of WJEC qualifications. While this material has been through a WJEC quality assurance process, all responsibility for the content remains with the publisher.

Editor: Geoff Tuttle

Design and layout: Patricia Briggs

Image credits:

Cover image: © Shutterstock: serg_dibrova

© Alamy: p8: Wolverhampton City Council – Arts and Heritage; p18: Richard Green; p19(t): Richard Green; p26(b): Jeff Morgan 08; p68: Marmaduke St. John; p69: Imagedoc; p83: INSADCO Photography; p90(tl): A5D3MG; p90(tr): Angela Hampton Picture Library; p193(t): William Yu Photography; p226: I love images / Children; p228(b): Catchlight Visual Services; p245(c): Mitch Diamond; p246: Cultura Creative.

© Fotolia: p1(b): francovolpato; p25(b): Monkey Business; p50left: karandaev; p52(b): Monkey Business; p91(r): Rob Byron; p99(b): WilliV; p100: Anatoly Tiplyashin; p113: GordonGrand; p119: Blend Images; p153: Marc Roche; p196(tl): James H. Pickerell; p197: James H. Pickerell; p204(b): Monkey Business; p211(c): deber73; p225: Marina Dyakonova; p239: Dalia Drulia; p241: coramax; p242(t): masterzphotofo; p245(tr): 3Dmask; p247(r): 3Dmask; p248(t): coramax; p253(r): francovolpato; p253(b): sines; p256: sines.

© Shutterstock: piv(t): michaeljung; piv(l): ifong; piv(r): R. Gino Santa Maria; piv(b): Andrey_Kuzmin; p1(t): Rob Marmion; p2(t): michaeljung; p2(b): glenda; p3(t): Maya Kruchankova; p3(b): michaeljung; p4: Varina and Jay Patel; p6(cl): BlueOrange Studio; p6(r): Pressmaster; p6(b): Juriah Mosin; p7(t): Andrei Zarubaika; p7(r): Larisa Lofitskaya; p9: Danie Nel; p10: ZouZou; p11(t): Monkey Business Images; p11(r): Monkey Business Images; p11(b): paul prescott; p12(t): Naypong; p12(cr): Monkey Business Images; p12(bl): wong yu liang; p12(br): ZouZou; p14(tl): Kzenon; p14(b): Monkey Business Images; p15: Mat Hayward; p16(tr): GVictoria; p16(l): Brian A Jackson; p16(cl): Sam72; p17: Kzenon; p19(b): Monkey Business Images; p20: somchaij; p22: llike; p23: llike; p24(l): auremar; p24(r): CREATISTA; p25(t): auremar; p26(t): Pavel L Photo and Video; p31: Alexander Raths; p40(tl): ifong; p40(b): Africa Studio; p41(t): Mircea BEZERGHEANU; p41(r): Evgenia Sh.; p41(b): Elena Schweitzer; p42(t to b): Jiri Hera, Nattika, Gtranquillity, bonchan, Sam72, Nattika, Stephen Coburn, Robyn Mackenzie, kaband, gillmar, hainaultphoto, Rudchenko Liliia; p43(t to b): Seregam, bonchan, Tim UR, Rudchenko Liliia, Gtranquillity, Yasonya, Kelvin Wong, Alexander Raths, Smileus; p44: ifong; p46(tl): Viktorl; p46(cl): Sandra Caldwell; p46(cr): Svetlana Lukienko; p47(t): Valeriy Velikov; p47(r): Viktorl; p47(b): Valentyn Volkov; p48(t): Blend Images; p49: aboikis; p50(t): Blend Images; p50(r): Venus Angel; p52(tl): Tyler Olson; p53(l): Wiktory; p53(r): Pixel Memoirs; p54(l to r): Ruslan Kudrin, Vladimir Jotov,Madlen, Paul Binet, Stephen Coburn; p54(b): Mariusz S. Jurgielewicz; p55: Tyler Olson; p56(c): Nagy-Bagoly Arpad; p56(b): Wiktory; p57(l): jordache; p57(r): Serhiy Kobyakov; p58: Karen Sarraga; p60(tl): Vudhikrai; p60(b): nd0009; p61(l): Vudhikrai; p61(r): Guy Shapira; p61(b): irencik; p62: ifong; p66(tl): Pablo Scapinachis; p66(r): Pressmaster; p66(b): Aleph Studio; p67: Pressmaster; p68(t to b): ecliptic blue, nito, Z-art, Z-art; p69(t to b): Tomasz Trojanowski, cristi180884, Samuel Borges Photography, areeya_ann; p71: Andy Dean Photography; p72: Hadi Djunaedi; p74(tl): Darren Brode; p76: Monkey Business Images; p77: Ola-ola; p80: udaix; p82(tl): Schweinepriester; p82(r): Biehler Michael; p82(bl): Alexander Raths; p88: Reynardt; p91(c): Andrey_Popov; p92: karen roach; p94: Reynardt; p95: nata-lunata; p97(r): Paul Hakimata Photography; p97(bl): Vereshchagin Dmitry; p98(t): Albert H. Teich; p101: Monkey Business Images; p102: Monkey Business Images; p103: michaeljung; p112: Belinda Pretorius; p114: bikeriderlondon; p115: Brian A Jackson; p116(tl): Shell114; p116(b): paperart; p118(tl): janinajaak; p118(b): SvetlanaFedoseyeva; p120(tl): nrt; p120(l): Oksana Kuzmina; p121: Monkey Business Images; p122: Kiselev Andrey Valerevich; p123(t): Seleznev Oleg; p123(l): Monkey Business Images; p124(tr): Nizzam; p124(b): mayakova; p125: Sergey Novikov; p126(tl): Ana Blazic Pavlovic; p126(b): JMiks; p127: Ana Blazic Pavlovic; p128(tl): Karen H. Ilagan; p128(c): Artpose Adam Borkowski; p129: Karen H. Ilagan; p130(tl): Hriana; p131(c): Levranii; p132(tl): Sergiy Zavgorodny; p132(c): Ermolaev Alexander; p133(t): geniuscook_com; p133(c): MaraZe; p134(tl): Paul Vasarhelyi; p134(b): AlinaMD; p135: arek_malang; p136(tl): hxdbzxy; p136(b): Oleg Mikhaylov; p137: MNStudio; p138(tl): Levent Konuk; p138(b): Tatsianama; p139: Levent Konuk; p140: MNStudio; p141: djedzura; p142: marilyn barbone; p143(l): Michael Pettigrew; p143(r): marilyn barbone; p144(tl): Bombaert Patrick; p144(l): wavebreakmedia; p144(r): etraveler; p145: Andresr; p146(tl): Roman Sulla; p146(b): Renata Osinska; p147: Sarah Dunn; p148(tl): gabczi; p148(b): Kitch Bain; p149: Gina Smith; p150(tl): Martin Haas; p150(b): 2xSamara.com; p151(l to r): Smit, Madlen, SteveWoods, HamsterMan, design56, Sashkin, Todor Rusinov; p152(tl): ronfromyork; p152(b): emin kuliyev; p154(tl): Rob Hainer; p154(b): Tubol Evgeniya; p155: Khamidulin Sergey; p156: Iakov Filimonov; p157: llike; p162(tl): joingate; p162(b): Pete Pahham; p163(t): Jiri Hera; p163(b): szefei; p164(t): Flashon Studio; p164(c): absolute-india; p164(b): Harm Kruyshaar; p165(t): joingate; p165(b): ER_09; p166: BlueOrange Studio; p167: Stuart Miles; p168(tl): Zurijeta; p168(bl): 2xSamara.com; p168(r): Poznyakov; p169(t): Osokina Liudmila; p169(r): Brykaylo Yuriy; p169(c): Michel Borges; p169(b): AnikaNes; p172: MichaelJayBerlin; p172: Maria Uspenskaya; p173(r): alexkatkov; p173(c): Karen Struthers; p174(r): Vitalinka; p174(b): Max Topchii; p175: Gladskikh Tatiana; p176(tl): bikeriderlondon; p176(l): Matthew Cole; p176(br): Jakub Krechowicz; p177(t): Johanna Goodyear; p177(b): arek_malang; p178(c): rSnapshotPhotos; p179: waldru; p180(tl): s_oleg; p182(tl): JordiDelgado; p182(tr): Matthew Cole; p182(r): Klara Viskova; p182(cl): graja; p182(cr): Nenov Brothers Images; p182(b): phototr; p183: alekso94; p188: Olgabo; p189(tr): paul prescott; p189(c): Aleph Studio; p190(tl): Marlon Lopez MMG1 Design; p190(b): OLJ Studio; p191: Marlon Lopez MMG1 Design; p192(l): Francois Loubser; p192(br): Elena Yakusheva; p193(r): DNF Style; p193(b): 2xSamara.com; p194(l): greenland; p194(r): Monkey Business Images; p196(b): Kzenon; p198(tl): Ermolaev Alexander; p198(b): Marcel Jancovic; p199: Ermolaev Alexander; p200(tl): Tubol Evgeniya; p200(c): Blaj Gabriel; p200(r): Tressie Davis; p201: Tubol Evgeniya; p202: 1000 Words; p203: TallyHo Films Inc; p204(t): 2xSamara.com; p205: 2xSamara.com; p206: kaarsten; p208(l): Harm Kruyshaar; p208(r): Tracy Whiteside; p210(tl): ArtFamily; p210(b): Anneka; p211(t): ArtFamily; p212(tl): greenland; p212(c): Igor Sokolov (breeze); p213: greenland; p214(tl): Pedro Monteiro; p214(b): szefei; p215: Pedro Monteiro; p216: Stiggy Photo; p217: Zurijeta; p218: Jandrie Lombard; p219: Aaron Amat; p220: Paul Yates; p222: Tomasz Trojanowski; p223: Tomasz Trojanowski; p224: Gladskikh Tatiana; p228(tl): Hurst Photo; p229: Hurst Photo; p230: llike; p236: wavebreakmedia; p238(c): Pasko Maksim; p238(l): Jacek Fulawka; p238(r): cloki; p242(b): imagedb.com; p243: Andrey_Kuzmin; p244(c): Rob Marmion; p244(b): Sergey Karpov; p247(t): pavla; p248(r): michaeljung; p250: Mega Pixel; p252(tl): Pasko Maksim; p252(r): cloki; p252(l): Jacek Fulawka.

p27: S Santos Photos; p28: Childline, Gingerbread, NSPCC, Relate; p29: Barnardos, Mencap; p45: www.nhs.uk; p170: Peter Burton; p178(l): Bookstart.

Original artwork by Patricia Briggs: pp48(l), 51, 70, 71, 74, 75, 75, 76, 78, 85, 86, 86, 90, 93, 94, 94, 95, 112, 114, 180–1, 221, 130.

Contents

Find out more about the Child Development course by starting here!

What is Child Development?

So, there's the THEORY part of the course ...

Topic 1 looks at the many types of families in which children grow up. Family is one of the biggest influences on the health, growth and development of a child.

In **Topic 2** you will learn about the importance of a healthy diet throughout life and the impact food has on a child's growth and development.

Topic 3 is about planning to be a responsible parent, pregnancy and preparing for the birth. It's important to give the new baby the best possible start in life.

Topics 4–6 are all about PIES. As the child grows you will learn how Physical, Intellectual, Emotional and Social skills are developed. PIES! You will find out about how to look after the child in practical ways and how to provide the right environment for the child to learn the skills needed to become more independent.

Here's what's involved...

You'll study the development and care of children from conception to the age of five years old. You'll look at the physical, intellectual, emotional and social development of children and link these to the family, community and responsibilities for parenthood. You will also need to consider the impact of current trends, technology and environmental issues on the care and development of young children. And the course will ask you to apply your knowledge to a variety of situations in both written and practical work.

So far, so good. Now you also need to do TWO controlled assessments (one in each year of the course). There are plenty of hints and tips on getting the best results in the final examination. And in all topics you'll find suggestions of how you can use the information there to help you with those controlled assessments.

For the **first assessment** you'll **spend time** with a child under 5 years old, and find out how they are developing the skills you covered in Topics 4–6. This is your opportunity to put theory into practice while helping a young child learn something new. To do well in this section it is important that you plan carefully so that you know exactly what information you need to collect.

In the **second assessment** you'll make either food which would encourage a child to enjoy healthy food, or an item to help a child develop specific skills. So, this means you link your theoretical knowledge to a real-life problem. You'll probably develop a few different ideas and choose the best ones to make. The assessment questions are written so that you can select the task which best uses your practical skills – so therefore you can play to your strengths.

And what will you know by the end of the course?

Things like:

- ✓ **Have a good understanding of how children grow and develop.**
- ✓ **Know how to care for a young child.**
- ✓ **Know how to plan and provide the best range of interesting activities to enable them to grow and develop.**
- ✓ **That all children are different and many factors may affect how children learn new skills.**

The book follows the exam spec and content is matched to it throughout, but in some cases we have felt able to go into extra detail on selected topics.

Most importantly, we hope you will have enjoyed the course! We think you'll find that it doesn't matter whether or not you intend to work with children in the future, you'll still gain from all the things you will have learned. They are all excellent skills you will be able to use for the rest of your life, whether it's looking after children of your own or babysitting someone else's.

Kate Ford, Susan Gould, Christine Henning, Beverley Parry

Types of family

What will I learn?

- **The many ways in which people live together as families**
- **The care available for children who cannot live with their own family**

Key Facts

- 2 million single parents in Britain in 2012.
- 8% of single parents (185,000) are fathers in 2012.
- 3 million children living in a single parent household in 2011.
- In 1971 8% of families were single parent families but in 2011 this had risen to 26%.

A family is a usually described as a group of one or two parents and children living together in a household. They could be related to each other by blood, marriage, adoption or arrangement.

Nuclear family

The **nuclear family** is made up of a mother, father and their children. Parents in this type of family can bring up their children without interference from other relatives. They can choose to live in their own way with no rules set by older family members to follow. The family can decide when to visit other family members; therefore children may not see their grandparents often if they live far away. This can sometimes have an effect on the family bonds.

Children might have to be looked after by someone outside the family when parents work or go out for an evening. Childcare therefore needs to be paid for, and in an emergency there may not be any close family members nearby to help out. Parents may struggle to balance the demands of work, family and friendships without outside assistance.

Nuclear family

Key Terms

Nuclear family - parents and children living together

Extended family - parents and other relatives living together or close by

One parent - mother or father looking after children

Extended family

▲ Extended family

The **extended family** is a large family unit which includes grandparents, parents, children, aunts and uncles either all living in the same house or close by. This allows good family bonds to be formed easily. Children can be looked after by family members when parents work or go out for an evening. Therefore the children are being cared for by people they know and they may feel more secure.

There can often be a lack of individual privacy with lots of family members living in the same house or close by. Some of these people may interfere with the upbringing of children, which can cause friction. On the positive side the children may have cousins to play with thus helping to extend **social skills** or even learn new skills themselves.

One-parent family

Key terms in blue are defined on the page.
Glossary terms in green are defined at the end of the book.

In this family children are cared for by only **one parent**. This is usually the mother, but could also be the father. In this family the parent may be happier and more relaxed on their own if their previous relationship was unhappy, and the atmosphere at home may be happier and less stressful for both the parent and children.

However, the parent has to work harder and is under more pressure to support the family by doing everything that is usually shared by two parents. This means paying all bills and other expenses alone, along with dealing with aspects such as household chores, providing food and clothes and teaching children social skills and acceptable behaviour.

Reasons for one parent families

- Surrogacy arrangement
- Adoption by a single person
- Births to single women
- Death of one parent
- Absence of one parent owing to illness, work or imprisonment
- Divorce or separation

Activity

Design and complete a chart to list two of the advantages and two of the disadvantages of each of the different types of family.

Key Terms

Reconstituted – parents with children from a previous marriage

Foster family – adults who temporarily act as parents for children

Adoptive family – children are legally made part of a family

Residential care – care for children who cannot live with their parents

Reconstituted (step-family)

A parent with one or more children marries or lives with a new partner. This may mean that the family may have a better quality of life with more money to spend. However, the children may resent the **step-parent** and not develop a close bond, and step-brothers and -sisters may not get on with each other, causing friction. Discipline issues and expectations may conflict with what the child has been used to.

New relationships can be formed with relatives of the step-parent – such as with grandparents, aunts or uncles – and the family offers both male and female role models.

Foster family

A **foster parent** is someone who temporarily looks after a child who is not their own. Foster carers receive money for the child's care and must be thoroughly checked and approved by **Social Services**. Wherever possible the child is encouraged to visit and have contact with their birth parents, who know their child is being well cared for.

Children know it is a **temporary** measure but they may be unhappy as they feel unwanted and miss their parents. On the positive side, though, **foster families** allow children to have an experience of living in a caring family environment and to develop skills needed for effective family relationships.

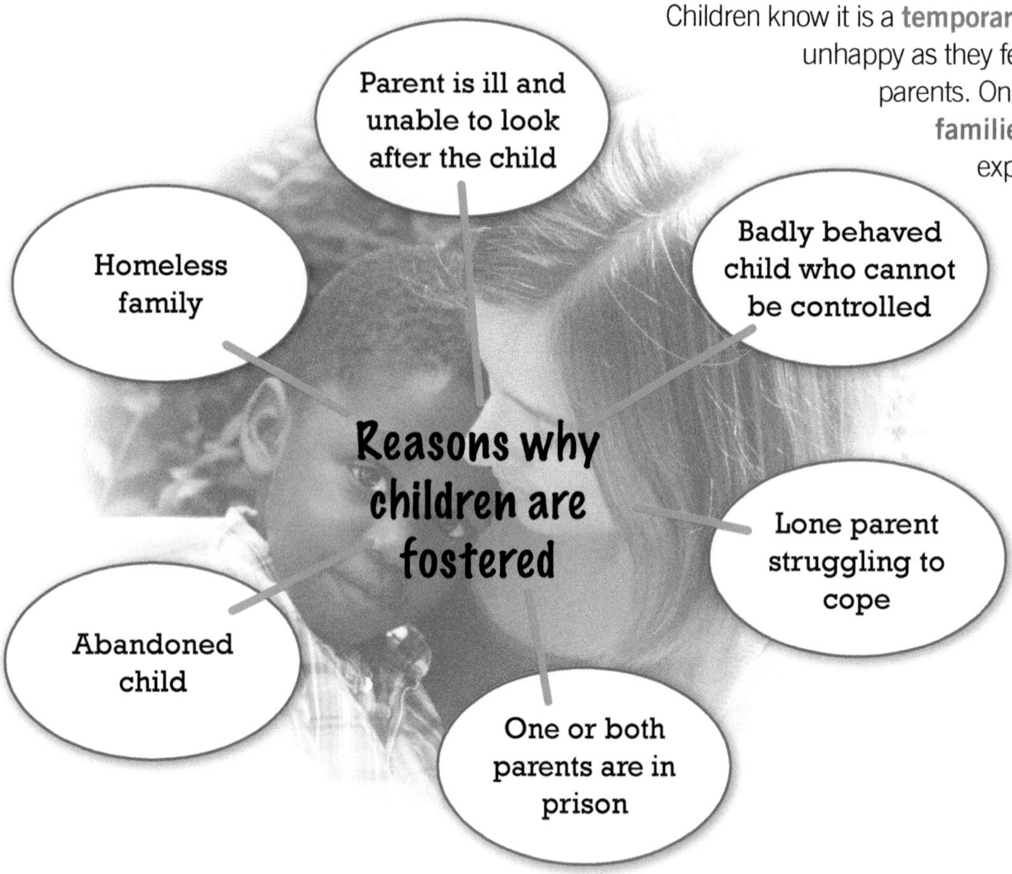

Reasons why children are fostered

- Parent is ill and unable to look after the child
- Badly behaved child who cannot be controlled
- Lone parent struggling to cope
- One or both parents are in prison
- Abandoned child
- Homeless family

Activity

What is the difference between fostering and adoption? Produce a leaflet or PowerPoint that explains what you know about each.

Adoptive family

This is a family where, through a legal process, adults become parents to children who were not born to them. The arrangement is **permanent**; the birth parents give up all rights to the child, with the **adoptive parents** having full legal rights, and give stability and a home life to a child. There is no money provided by any government service, so the adoptive parent pays for the care of the child just as they would had they given birth to the child themselves. The adoptive parents still have to pass rigorous tests and interviews by Social Services.

Residential care

Children without families or whose families are unable or unwilling to look after them may have to live in a residential home that is run by the Local Authority. Children who are 'at risk' and vulnerable are given professional care, including when a court order to remove a child from the care of their family is issued or the child needs sudden immediate care.

Residential homes provide a safe place for children who may find the rules and regulations of the homes different from what they were used to in their own home. Some may experience problems in following those rules, or become unhappy. The physical and emotional **bonding** with parents will also not be experienced in this sort of home.

Child Study

Describe the type of family your study child is part of, e.g. nuclear, extended.

Summary

- In a nuclear family contact with other family members is limited compared with an extended family where there are more people to offer advice, help and emotional support in times of distress.
- Reconstituted families have children living with one natural parent and a step-parent.
- In one parent families there is only one parent and the child/children.
- Foster carers have no legal responsibility for the child; the local authority becomes the child's legal guardian.
- An adoptive family provides stability, a permanent home and gives a child a sense of belonging.
- Residential care homes provide basic and secure care for children in difficult circumstances within the local community.

Watch some TV programmes on any one night and try to identify the different types of families shown in these programmes.

- You should be able to name each different type of family.
- Make sure you can **describe** how the different family structures support or affect the upbringing of children. Include consideration of all aspects such as positive and negative issues.
- When you are asked to **de-scribe** in an essay you must provide a detailed account about the issue in question.

Prove it!

1. **Describe how a nuclear family is different from an extended family.**
2. **List four ways in which members of an extended family can help and support each other.**
3. **Give three advantages of both parents sharing responsibilities within the family.**
4. **State four reasons why a child may be brought up by only one parent.**
5. **What disadvantages could there be for a child in being part of a step-family?**
6. **Suggest why a child may need to be placed in foster care.**

Functions and responsibility of the family

What will I learn?

- How the family should provide for a child's needs

All children have rights and as they are unable to care for themselves, the family is responsible for making sure that the children's rights and needs are met.

Key Terms

Stable environment – constant, consistent care in the home

Praise – give positive comments

Encouragement – support and promote success

Self-esteem – how we feel about ourselves

Role model – a person who is a good example to follow

Communication – verbally sharing information

RIGHT 1

Providing food and drink so that children grow up healthy and have good physical development.

RIGHT 2

Ensuring **suitable clothing** is provided for all types of weather.

RIGHT 3

A clean home that provides warmth and shelter to avoid infection and ill health.

RIGHT 4

A safe environment free from harm and danger.

RIGHT 5

Access to health care including immunisation at appropriate times.

RIGHT 6

A secure and stable environment free from violence and arguments.

RIGHT 7

Providing a loving and encouraging environment that helps to develop good self-esteem in children. Spend time with children and show them affection, as children who experience love become confident and happy.

RIGHT 8

Giving praise and providing discipline so that children have realistic boundaries. Good behaviour should be rewarded: children who are praised will learn more quickly than children who are ignored or constantly corrected. Discipline teaches children what behaviour is acceptable and helps their social development.

Financially supporting children by providing for their needs, e.g. food and clothing, trip money, lunch money.

Teaching social skills such as good table manners, toilet training and hygiene. Opportunities for social development should be provided for children to make friends and talk about their feelings.

Communicating with children, as they need to learn how to express themselves and their feelings.

Being a good role model to guide and support the development of children's morals and values. Parents should model the trait they wish to develop in their children: respect, friendliness, honesty, patience, generosity, forgiveness and the difference between right and wrong.

Supporting children's educational needs by communicating regularly with the school when necessary, helping with homework, celebrating school achievements and talking to their children about school problems.

Providing opportunities for learning to encourage the development of intellectual skills. Make learning skills fun, set realistic expectations and foster an interest in the children's education.

Giving information on spiritual beliefs and maintaining cultural and family traditions whilst living in a changing society.

Summary

- Children should be provided with toys, games, books, opportunities for drawing and painting.
- Children learn a lot about how to behave and act when watching their parents.
- If children are rewarded for doing something, they will want to do it again, so their behaviour improves.
- Encourage children in all things they do and allow them to develop their self-esteem and confidence.
- Children who are not loved are starved emotionally and all aspects of their development slow down.
- Take children to places where they will meet other children to encourage social skills.

Activity

Produce a factsheet that describes how a nuclear family can provide for the basic needs of the child.

Prove it!

1. Every child has certain needs in order to grow and develop.
   a. Identify and list these needs.
   b. Discuss the factors that have the greatest effect on the development of the child. Why have you chosen your particular factors?

Roles

What will I learn?

- **Changing roles in the family**
- **Cultural variations in society**
- **Different child-rearing styles**

Family life and the roles of the individuals within the family have changed considerably over the past 200 years due to changes in legislation, social attitudes and advances in technology.

Changing roles in families

Even as recently as 150 years ago traditional **roles** of men and women were seen as being separate. Men worked or went out, whilst women spent their time at home looking after children.

The men were seen as the main providers for the family. They made the major decisions, were in charge of the money and rarely did any household tasks or looked after the children.

Mothers did the majority of the household tasks whilst caring for the children and preparing the family meals. If women worked, it was usually on cleaning jobs. Mothers were less likely to make decisions affecting the family.

Children's roles were very different from today, as they were expected to earn money at a young age in the mines, factories and as servants. Girls did a lot more household tasks whilst boys were encouraged to attend school.

Key Terms

Role – expected actions or behaviour

Rearing – bringing up children

Discipline – training used to produce appropriate behaviour

Expectations – something hoped for

Compliant – easily follow or obey rules without question

Lenient – easy going and not strict

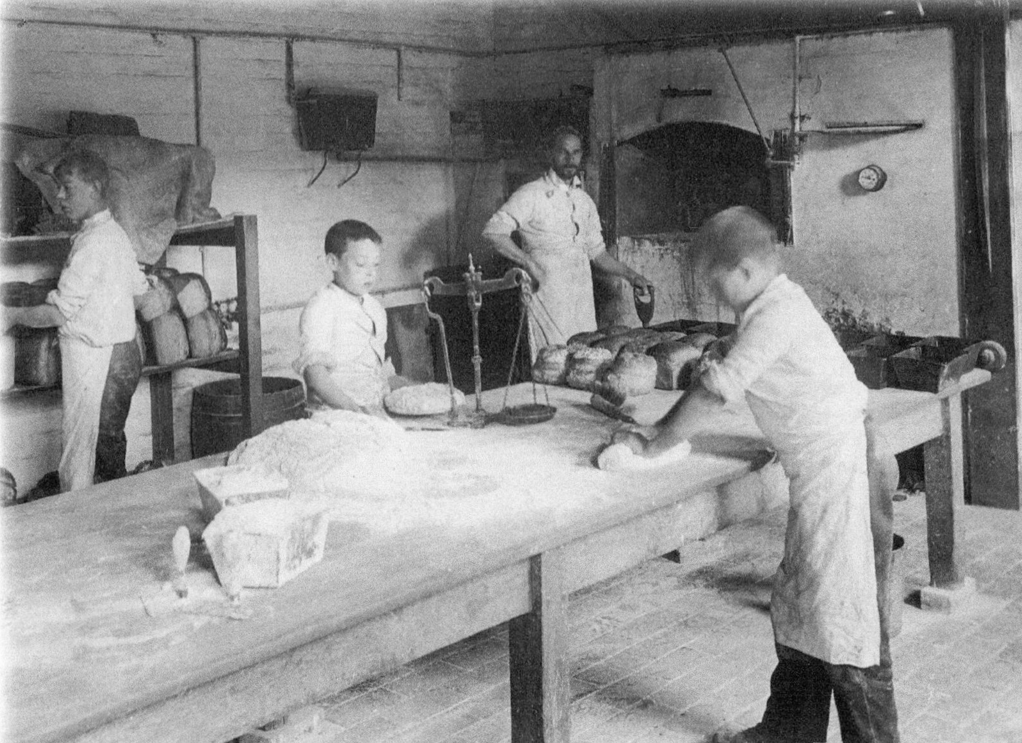

Young boys earning a living by working in a 20th-century bakery

Modern-day families

In today's society all members of the family usually share the household tasks, with older boys and girls caring for younger siblings and preparing some meals. Technological developments in household equipment that save time, e.g. washing machines, vacuum cleaners, allow more women to work outside the home to increase the family income and develop careers. The downside is they may spend less time with their children.

Owing to the increase in income many families go on more holidays together, take part in leisure activities, go out for meals at family-oriented restaurants and run cars. Homes have more amenities such as televisions and electronic equipment so fathers may now be more encouraged to stay at home and share home-centred leisure with their families.

Family decisions are more frequently made jointly by both parents. Both boys and girls have the opportunity to further their education by staying in school or going to higher education. With contraceptives now being readily available, women can choose how many to children to have. More men attend the birth of their babies and play a role in childcare, though the responsibility still tends to rest with the mother. Parents are generally much more involved with their children, spending more time with them and taking an interest in their activities.

Key Facts

- 1.4 million men in the UK are the main carers for their children.
- Research has found that if fathers spend time doing activities with their children, on average, they achieve better results in school.
- Almost 75% of all households in the UK now own a car.

Different child-rearing styles

Every family is different in how they raise and **discipline** their children. Each of the **four** parenting styles has different influences on child development.

1 Authoritarian

Parents set rules and expect children to follow them. The reasoning behind their **expectations** is not explained and children may be shouted at or threatened when they do not follow the rules. Children raised this way tend to be **compliant** to their parents' values, do not learn to think for themselves and may have low self-esteem.

2 Permissive

Parents who use the permissive style of child **rearing** believe children cannot cope with discipline due to feelings of low self-esteem and they therefore treat them **leniently**. Children in turn become good at manipulation to get what they want and do not readily follow routines. Children are allowed to make decisions at an age when they are not capable of doing so.

3 Uninvolved

Parents who are uninvolved in their child's life tend to be more interested in what *they* want and not in the child's needs. Sometimes this happens due to work issues, divorce or if they lack the maturity to care for children. In extreme cases this can be termed neglect.

4 Authoritative/democratic

Parents discuss with the children the rules they are expected to follow and the penalties if they deviate from the expected behaviour. Teenagers will receive guidance to help them meet their parents' expectations whilst very young children will receive **positive reinforcement** for their good behaviour. Parents have firm but reasonable control, and allow more freedom when the child is ready.

Child rearing in other countries

Different **cultures** have different parenting beliefs.

Key Terms

Tradition – practices and beliefs passed down

Community – group of people living in an area

Israel

In some areas of Israel groups of parents and children live together in a kibbutz. Here they work together to provide for all members of the **kibbutz** community. Children live with their parents and move to teenage houses when they are 15 years of age. All children born in the same year are raised by a 'kibbutz mother' and educated together in the children's houses. Meals are eaten together and rotas are made for routine tasks with children expected to do tasks according to their age.

Europe

European cultures tend to use distraction techniques for very young children and the removal of privileges for older children. Some cultures involve the children in making the rules to follow.

Spain

Usually Hispanic families are extended where sharing and co-operation is encouraged. Children are expected to be calm, obedient, polite and to respect adults. Discipline is usually strict.

Middle East

Children are taught to be respectful to their parents and to be obedient. Middle Eastern society has strict codes of conduct and behaviour and children are expected to follow these rules. Parents also believe that their children should do well in school.

Africa

African children are highly valued and the older generation teach the young about their cultural morals. Children are nurtured when young and are expected to learn appropriate social skills based on traditional values. Parents will often disown a child who does not follow cultural standards.

China

Chinese parents believe that children arrive with a good nature and should be respected. The older generation teach, educate and discipline the children. Young children are nurtured and indulged, as parents believe they lack skills to learn. At 5–6 years of age children are disciplined more strictly and emphasis is placed on culturally accepted behaviour and academic success. Parental expectations are high.

To limit the population rate China has a one child policy that allows couples to have only one child. If a woman becomes pregnant again she is possibly fined and often put under pressure to have an abortion. Due to this ruling many families do not want a female child and many are abandoned or neglected as in the Chinese culture a male child is cherished more so parents want a son. This is because a male can inherit the property and obtain work more easily than a female so is able to support parents in their old age. A daughter must give away her property to her husband and care for his parents; responsibility to her own family ends when she marries.

Japan

In order to keep the gods happy, in the Japanese culture children are treated **leniently** and indulged but are also encouraged to be sympathetic and responsive to others. Sometimes it is difficult to tell the difference between being 'spoiled' or 'treated gently'. Mothers tend to discipline the children without anger and by explaining the reasons for the discipline. Grandmothers also play an important role in child rearing and when the child starts school discipline becomes stricter.

India

Parents believe children should be quiet and obedient and that it is possible to shape them whilst young. The environment and parents are seen as being important, so Indian mothers will massage their babies, carry them close to their bodies and spoil them. When children are disciplined at a young age they are taught to obey their parents and physical punishment is used to influence and teach suitable behaviour. Discipline is usually very strict.

Multicultural society

Societies which have different **cultures** living alongside each other are referred to as being **multicultural**. Each culture has traditional features, and families pass their experiences and beliefs to their children. Children are encouraged to follow **traditions** which are sometimes different from those of the wider society.

Key Fact

- Women of the Tiwi tribe on the South Pacific are married as soon as they are born.

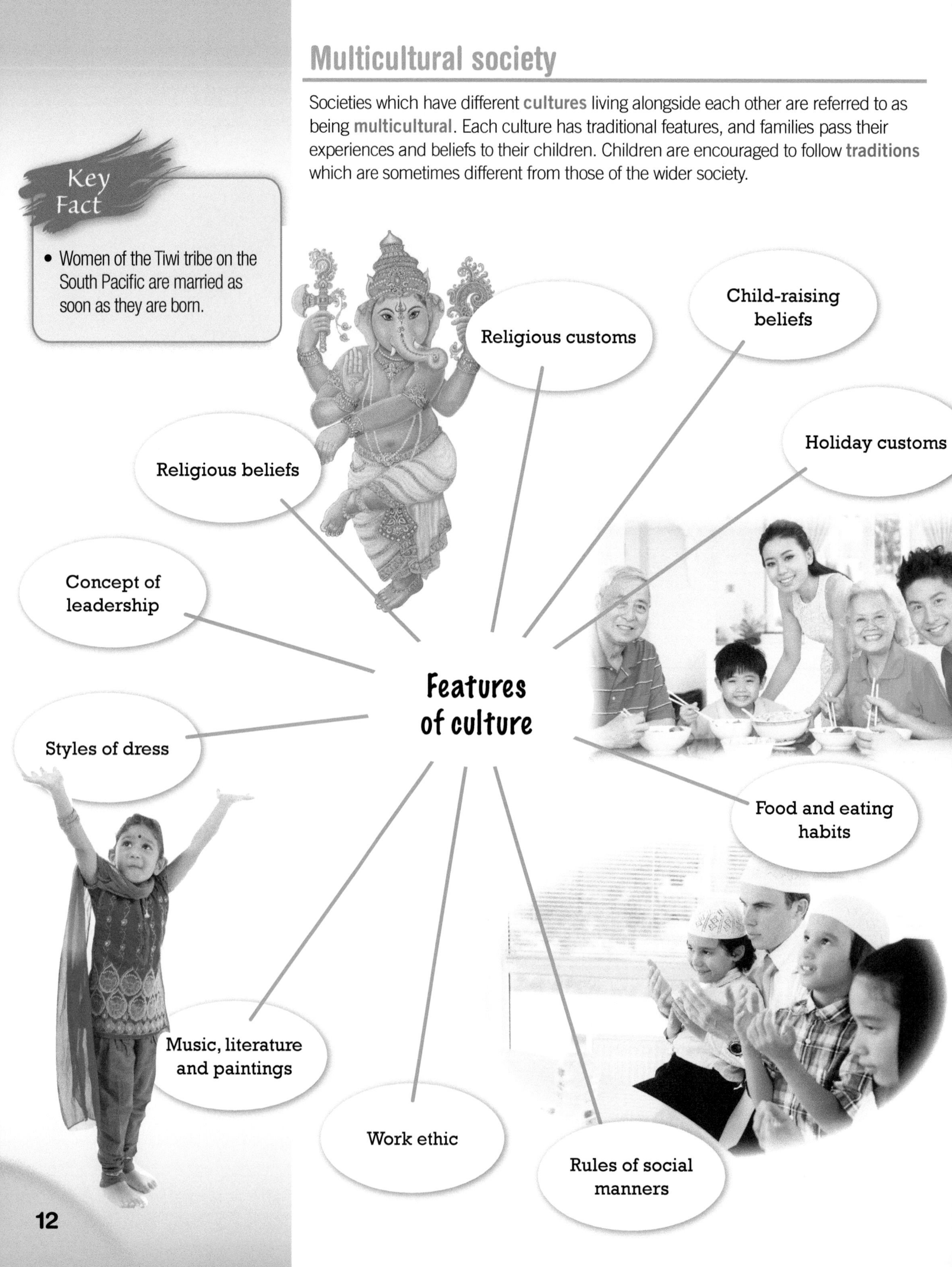

Multiculturalism is seen in the following areas:

- Food from other cultures is found in restaurants, cafes, grocery products and shops
- **Communities** have different accents, languages, styles of dress and appearance
- People take part in cultural festivals.

Through this mixing of cultures there is a better appreciation and tolerance of other cultures and society becomes more interesting and varied.

1. Using the Internet, research and produce a short PowerPoint presentation giving information about family life in four different countries.
2. Using the Internet, investigate family life in the UK at the beginning of the 20th century and how it compares with the present day. What are the key headings that you think you will need to categorise your research? Produce a poster showing the differences.

Summary

- As more women work, their independence and authority in the family has increased as they are no longer as dependent on their male partners.
- Families are smaller so children are given more individual care and attention.
- Different cultures' child-rearing styles give parents ideas about effective alternative discipline methods that could foster good emotional health in children.

Prove it!

1. **Identify two ways that the role of children in the family has changed in the last 100 years.**
2. **What is a multicultural society?**
3. **Identify four cultural differences in a multicultural society.**
4. **Explain three factors that have changed the role of women within the family over the last 30 years.**
5. **Suggest three ways that the roles of men and women in the family have changed.**

If an examination question asks you to explain how roles have changed in the family you must make sure you say how they have changed and why, that is giving reasons to explain a statement.

E.g. the role of man as bread-winner is becoming outdated because more women are successful in the workforce and because mothers are now encouraged to return to work as early as possible after having a child.

Relationships

What will I learn?

- **How adolescence can change relationships**
- **The different pressures that can affect the family**
- **The effects of the identified pressures on the family**

Key Terms

Peers – people of the same age

Role model – someone a person can copy

Self-esteem – how you feel about yourself

Financial – refers to money

Lifestyle – the way people live

Milestones – skills that children can do by a certain age

The relationships we have within our lives can present us with positive and negative feelings that shape our future lives. With support from others within the different types of relationships experienced in life, individuals can work together, share values and cope with pressures.

Different types of relationships

There are **four** basic types of relationship that a person can have with other people:

1. Family
2. Friends
3. Casual
4. Romantic.

Positive family relationships where adults and children care for each other

1 Family

Children are nurtured by the family and develop loving and caring relationships through being part of this family. This enables children to grow up to care for others and develop strong and healthy relationships. However, the relationships between children and family members can vary from harmony to conflict.

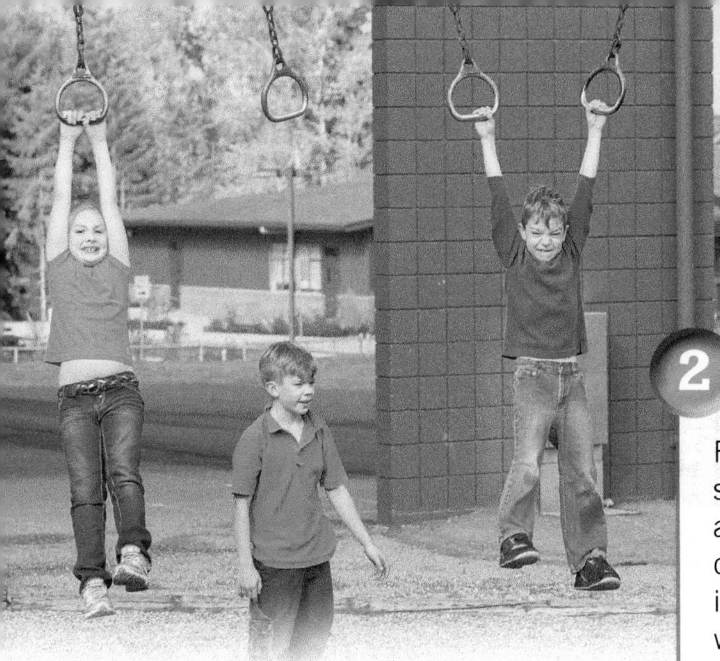

Group of young children playing together that illustrates the typical friend relationship

Friends

Friends are people whom you usually know well, trust and sometimes spend a lot of time with. Younger people's friendships are focused on a group of same sex peers who provide a source of help and company. Relationships with friends become very important and many children prefer to spend more of their time with **peers** than family. Friendships become more stable as children become older but young people become worried about what their peers think of them and what they do. Peer pressure often influences attitudes, values or behaviour, which can be positive or negative.

3 Casual

Casual relationships are those you have with people you meet every day, which could be on a professional level, e.g. teachers, medical staff, or with people you just know in passing. It is important to have a healthy relationship and show respect towards professionals as they will encourage and help you develop skills that can be used in other relationships.

Romantic

In healthy romantic relationships there is respect between both partners but each has their own identity within the relationship. Romantic love is a combination of attraction, closeness and commitment. In mid-teens the relationships do not generally last for long but as teenagers become older the relationships are less about going out and having fun but are more about closeness and sharing and tend to last longer. Sexual feelings can also be part of this attraction. Longer-term relationships prepare teenagers for adult life when they start to think about finding someone they can commit to.

Once individuals have found someone they want to live with and share a life together they may take part in a marriage ceremony, which is a legal contract, or they can live together without a legal contract and this is called cohabitation.

Key Facts

- **Positive peer relationships**
  For teenagers, friends help in the development of many skills and knowledge that is needed for a happy and useful adulthood. Teenagers begin to develop their own identity that is different from their childhood personality. Friends can help them to learn how to co-operate and form relationships with others, find out how to solve problems, share feelings and have fun within a safe place where new values and roles can be tried out with support and encouragement.
- **Negative peer relationships**
  Sometimes friendships with peers can make teenagers feel lonely, unhappy and worried if they have fallen out with their friends. Occasionally teenagers are pressurised by peers to take risks or join in anti-social behaviour, which may leave the teenagers feeling used.

Pressures and their effect on the family

Parental separation and divorce

This can cause a lot of negative effects because family life changes:

- Children become part of a one parent family which could have less income.
- There may be a move to a smaller house in a different area.
- A change of school may be required, causing a loss of friends, school work could suffer and after-school clubs or hobbies may have to be given up.
- The children may become angry, confused, blame themselves or have behaviour problems.

There may only be one parent as a **role model** but if the parents have been arguing and the atmosphere was unpleasant then the child may be relieved and happier living with the one parent.

Low income

Lack of money causing families to struggle to pay for items for the family's basic needs, e.g. food, warmth, clothing, can cause stress within families. When this occurs it can lead to arguments, marriage problems and poor health due to lack of nutrition.

Substance abuse

Relationships within the family can break down as drug and alcohol addicts will give up anything to supply their addiction, often stealing from family members, losing their jobs and not taking part in family activities.

Unemployment

Losing a job can lead to uncertainty within the family causing stress and arguments. Again lack of income may mean basic needs are not met and the parents' **self-esteem** can be affected.

Disabled child in the family

On a negative side the family may have **financial** problems as a result of the cost of specialised equipment needed, appropriate childcare or loss of income as the parent may have to stop working to care for the child. Physical, emotional and social problems can occur because of lack of sleep, tiredness, continuous care and worry about the child and lack of social contact with others.

Bereavement

Loss of a family member can cause families to suffer a lot of stress as it has an impact on physical and emotional health. Children could become withdrawn or may show signs of behavioural problems. There may also be financial worries.

Step-family

Children may not get on with a step-parent or siblings and there may be conflicts with different parenting styles. The quality of life may be better because there is more income.

Ill health

Worry about the ill family member may cause emotional stress with income problems if it is the breadwinner who is ill. Other family members would need to adjust their **lifestyles** because they need to take on some of the roles of the ill person. To make up the salary of the ill person the other parent may need to work longer hours, which means less time spent with the children.

Mother juggling housework with the care of a young child

Working mother

Working mothers are able to have time away from the demands of family life and focus on something else and enjoy the company of other people. They can have a separate identity and use their skills for other challenges. The income earned can be used towards the household expenses or to provide extras such as holidays or activities for the children. Parenting is more positive as the mother tends to be happier and has more confidence.

Children can become more independent and confident if they have experience of being in a childcare setting whilst the mother is working. Fathers generally become more involved in childcare and doing some of the household tasks. Interaction with the children could be increased as fathers may spend more time with their leisure activities, which benefits the children.

Mothers may spend less time with their children but try to make up for it by spending as much time as they can with them after work and at the weekends. Sometimes tiredness can affect the amount of quality time the children are given. The children's nutrition may suffer if the mother has no time to cook meals and relies on ready-made meals. She may worry about the quality of the childcare the children are receiving and that as she is not with them during the day she is missing all their **milestones**.

Activity

Produce a PowerPoint that describes four sources of stress that can affect family life.

Summary

- Having strong relationships with your family is both essential and challenging.
- Families need to encourage and provide support and help to all individuals.
- Peer pressure can influence a change of behaviour, attitude or belief in a child.
- One of the biggest pressures on the family is not enough money to provide for the needs of the family.

When you are asked to explain the effects of pressures on the family you must say how, when and why the factors might affect both the parents and children and give positive and negative reasons to provide a balanced answer.

Prove it!

1. **Explain how divorce could affect children in a family.**
2. **Is it good for children if their mother goes out to work? Discuss possible advantages and disadvantages of mothers working outside the family home.**

Disability

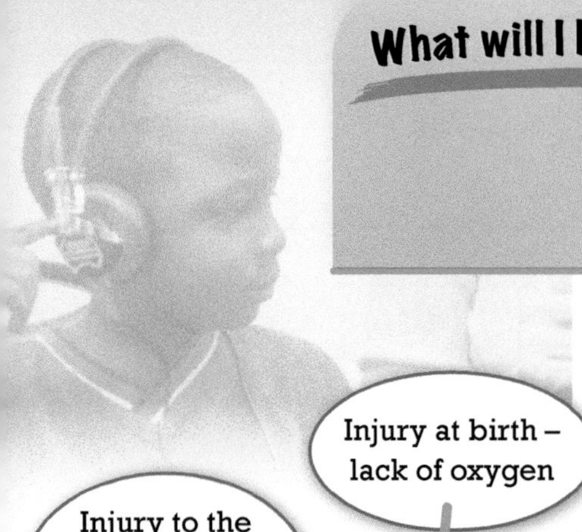

What will I learn?

- Different kinds of special needs
- The effects on a family with a special needs child
- Support available to assist in the care of a child with special needs

Children with special needs are those whose health or development is impaired in some physical, emotional or intellectual way, or they have a learning difficulty. Just like any child, they will still require the same basic needs from parents or carers but will have additional needs according to their disability or special need.

Causes

- Injury at birth – lack of oxygen
- Injury to the foetus – Rubella during early pregnancy
- Disease after birth – meningitis can injure the brain
- Inherited abnormal genes – haemophilia
- Injury after birth – head injury, loss of sight

Special needs can happen in a number of ways

Those disabilities that are present when the baby is born are described as **congenital** disabilities and may be either inherited or as a result of injury in the uterus.

Disability	Condition	Possible causes	Nature of disability
Autism	A disorder of cognition and language development; may be highly intelligent.	25% associated with brain damage, 50% have other disabilities from physical illnesses or injury. More common in boys than girls at a ratio of 4:1.	Children with autism tend to have learning difficulties, language problems and seem to be unable to interpret facial expressions. They are withdrawn and find it difficult to interact socially or develop relationships with others including their families.
Spina bifida	Exposed spinal cord.	Poor maternal diet prior to conception, lack of folic acid.	Children have problems with mobility of the lower limbs. Some can walk without help; others need to use a wheelchair. Bladder and bowel incontinence problems are also present.
Down's syndrome	Eyes slant and eyelids have an extra fold, an enlarged tongue and the head is flatter. Single crease across the palm of the hand.	**Genetic condition** caused by an extra **chromosome** 47 instead of 46. The risk is increased in a woman who has a child after age 35.	Learning difficulties are present and they may develop other health problems, e.g. heart defects and sight problems.
Cerebral palsy	Movement and posture is not good and can range from clumsiness to paralysis.	Birth injury such as being deprived of oxygen, causing brain damage.	Children have difficulties with their fine and gross motor movement. Balance is poor and difficulties are experienced with hand–eye co-ordination. Growth is delayed and they may have incontinence.
Cystic fibrosis	Lungs and digestive system become clogged with thick, sticky mucus.	Defective gene which lets too much salt and water into cells producing a build up of thick, sticky mucus in the body's tubes and passageways.	Children have poor weight gain and growth due to inadequate absorption of food. They also have frequent chest and lung infections and a persistent cough.

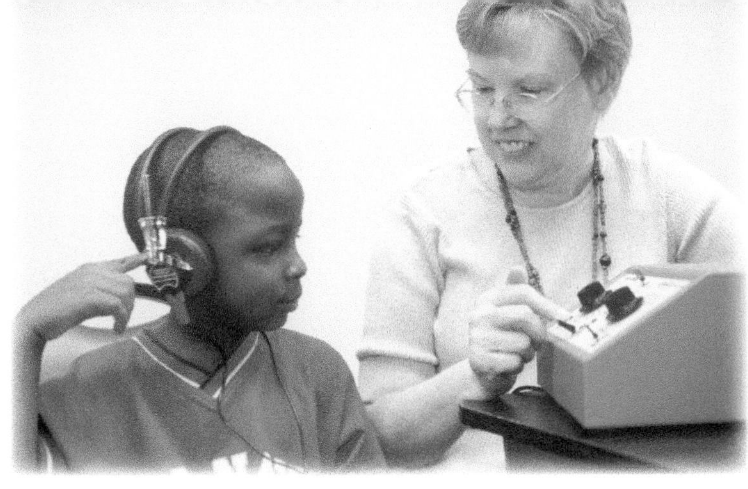

Hearing tests are carried out regularly, usually at 2½ years and between 4 and 5 years, to detect any problems as soon as possible

Hearing impairments

Deafness can be hereditary or caused by any of the following:

- Rubella in pregnancy
- Congenital syphilis
- Head injury
- Meningitis
- Repeated ear infections
- Exposure to high noise levels.

Deafness is usually detected when babies do not respond to noises and look startled when someone unexpectedly stands over them. They fail hearing tests carried out between 6 and 9 months and do not make sounds of their own or develop speech.

Some children may have partial hearing, which may be caused in the same way as deafness or by having problems with the adenoids, sinuses or 'glue' ear.

If hearing **impairments** are not identified then the child has difficulty in understanding what is said and can become confused and frustrated. The child may be wrongly identified as being lazy or having a learning difficulty.

Visual impairments

Blindness may be hereditary or caused by any of the following:

- Rubella in pregnancy
- Optic nerve tumour
- Glaucoma.
- Congenital syphilis
- Cataract

Visual impairments are usually found very early as the baby shows no eye contact and there is no response to stimulation. Opportunities for learning may be significantly reduced.

Vision tests at 2–3 years may indicate that a child is partially sighted and the vision is then improved by spectacles.

Short-sighted children may be unable to see what is written on the board at the front of the classroom and may be identified as being slow learners.

Long-sighted children have difficulty seeing fine detail, therefore writing can be a problem and they may be identified as lazy and lacking in interest.

Some children may have a **squint**, which can be clearly seen from three months. The eyes look in a different direction, so only one eye is used for looking at an object. Children are given eye exercises or wear a patch on the good eye to make the weaker eye work harder and develop.

Congenital – disability present at birth

Disability – problem that can be physical, learning, emotional or behavioural

Autism – disorder that affects communication and social skills

Down's syndrome – genetic condition where there are 47 chromosomes instead of 46

Cerebral palsy – disability that affects movement

Impairment – partial or complete loss of function, e.g. sight

Squint – eyes do not look in the same direction

An eye test can reveal a problem with a child's sight but could also identify more serious eye conditions

Effects on the family

Discovering that a child has a special need is a shock for most parents and can cause much stress in the family. The effects on the family may be varied and include the following issues:

Extra cost – need specially adapted home, equipment, toys and clothing.

Hospital appointments – time needed to attend them, long waiting periods can be physically and emotionally tiring, possible transport problems.

Lack of leisure time – a large proportion of time is spent on care.

Holidays – difficult to arrange as the child needs special facilities.

Practical help needed in the home – assistance welcomed with care or household chores, e.g. shopping.

Parents may be stressed – lack patience and may be feeling guilty.

Extended family or siblings – embarrassed and not wishing to be seen with their sibling. Family members may stay away as they do not know how to deal with the situation.

Babysitters – difficult to arrange so social activities are curtailed, or suitable childcare is hard to find so delaying a return to work.

Parent unable to work – loss of income, and financial worries.

Can bring joy – a special family bond can develop but sometimes family members can be overprotective.

Family members may feel neglected or jealous – parents have less time to spend with each other and siblings.

Insensitivity from the wider community – siblings may be stared at or bullied.

Activity

Choose four different kinds of special need and produce fact sheets that provide the following information:

– A description of the special need
– What causes the special need
– How the special need could be prevented
– Help available to support the parents.

Support for families

Support is available from many areas as illustrated in the table below but will vary from area to area.

	Support
Local Education Authority	• Advice on education • Transport to and from nursery or school • Schools have specialist staff to help children with special needs
Health Authorities	• Provide a Health Visitor to give advice on day-to-day care and development issues • Equipment such as wheelchairs may be available
Children's Services	• Allocate a Social Worker to work with the family • Arrange for aids to assist with the care of the child, e.g. hoists, bath aids • Respite care may be organised for parents to have a break
Housing associations	• May have specially adapted homes available • Provide grants to adapt homes
Department for Work and Pensions	• Financial help is available
Voluntary organisations	• Give specialist information to parents • Support groups where parents can meet other families • Day care centres
Families and friends	• Take out the other children in the family to allow them to have a break and mix with other children

Prove it!

1. **Some newborn babies have congenital disabilities. What is meant by this term?**
2. **Give two possible causes of a congenital disability.**
3. **What is the cause of Down's syndrome?**
4. **Describe how Down's syndrome might affect a child's development.**
5. **Suggest three symptoms of autism.**
6. **What is meant by visual impairment?**

Activities

1. Research the voluntary organisations available that could offer support to families who have some of the special needs identified in this section. Produce a PowerPoint that could be shown in a support centre that describes the services and support available from the different voluntary organisations.
2. Produce a poster that illustrates how a parent may promote the development of a child who has a visual impairment.

Summary

- Foetal development problems can result from the use of alcohol, drugs or cigarettes.
- Foetal alcohol syndrome can affect the development of nerve cells in the foetus's brain causing learning and behaviour problems.
- Some children with special needs require short-term support but if the disability is severe more help is needed.
- Respite care allows families with a special needs child to have a break.

Support for the family and child

What will I learn?

- **Different types of care settings for children**
- **Early years services available for children**
- **Voluntary agencies which provide support for children and their families**
- **Legal support offered to the family and child**

Early years services

To meet the health and educational needs of children and families Local Authorities and the NHS must, by law, provide services to look after the care and **welfare** of people in the community.

Health services

The NHS will have **primary health teams** and hospitals that provide a range of health care services. Examples of two health care professionals from these teams are midwives – who care for mothers before, during and after birth – and health visitors, who visit families with children under 5 years of age to give advice on the health and development of children.

Regular NHS health checks will be offered to help monitor children's development. The first of these are the newborn's hearing test at birth and then at intervals during development. The eyes are also tested within 72 hours after birth. This screening continues until the child reaches 16 years of age to ensure health issues are detected and treated early.

Children's health is also checked before starting Primary School. The height and weight, hearing and vision are checked and if any problems are found the child is referred to a GP, or to an optician if a problem with eyesight is identified.

A Personal Child Health record is given to mothers after birth so that they can check developmental **milestones**, height and weight and **immunisations**. The immunisations offered help to protect children against infectious diseases. They are given at an early age, in combined doses, to reduce the risk of children missing any and to start providing protection when babies are most at risk.

Child Study

- Find out what immunisations your study child has had to date.
- Interview the parent to find out if your study child has had any of the illnesses discussed.

Key Terms

Immunisation – prevention of disease using vaccines

Diphtheria – disease that damages the heart and nervous system

Tetanus – caused by bacteria from soil entering a cut

Pertussis – whooping cough

Polio – muscle paralysis

Haemophilus influenzae – bacterial infection

Immunisation schedule

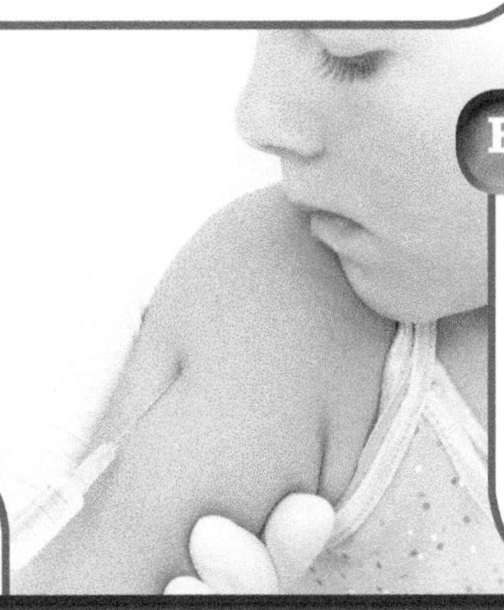

2 months old

- 5-in-1: **Diphtheria, tetanus, pertussis, polio** and **Haemophilus influenzae** type b (DTaP/IPV/Hib)
- Pneumococcal (PCV)

3 months old

- 5-in-1: Diphtheria, tetanus, pertussis, polio and Haemophilus influenzae type b (DTaP/IPV/Hib) second dose
- Meningitis C

4 months old

- 5-in-1: Diphtheria, tetanus, pertussis, polio and Haemophilus influenzae type b (DTaP/IPV/Hib) third dose
- Pneumococcal (PCV) second dose
- Meningitis C second dose

Between 12 and 13 months old

- Haemophilus influenzae type b and meningitis C (Hib/MenC) booster given as single injection
- Pneumococcal (PCV) third dose
- Measles, mumps and rubella (MMR) single injection

3 years 4 months to 5 years old

- 4-in-1: Diphtheria, tetanus, pertussis and polio (DTaP/IPV) pre-school booster
- Measles, mumps and rubella (MMR) second dose

12 to 13 years old (Girls only)

- Human Papilloma Virus (HPV) three injections within 6 months

13 to 18 years old

- 3-in-1: Tetanus, diphtheria and polio (Td/IPV) teenage booster

Source: Immunisation schedule from NHS website.

Dental check-ups should be done at least every 6 months so that any problems can be identified and treated as early as possible. For children to become familiar with visiting the dentist they should be taken as soon as possible but at least once before they are two years old.

Summary

- Children are immunised at 2 months as the antibodies received from the placenta start to wear off.
- Immunisation helps the body build up antibodies to develop resistance to infectious diseases such as measles.
- Immunisation can help prevent epidemics.

Prove it!

1. **Immunisation is important for all children. Name the diseases babies are protected against when they are given:**

   a. MMR vaccine.
   b. DTP triple vaccine.

2. **State two benefits of immunisation.**

Revision Tip

Questions on immunisation could ask you to identify the diseases children are protected from by the acronyms used for the vaccinations, e.g. MMR stands for measles, mumps and rubella. So make sure you know what each one stands for.

Day care settings for children

There has been an increase in the range of **childcare provision** available for working parents. Many mothers wish to continue with their careers after giving birth or their income is needed by the family, so they need other people to care for their children.

Because many employers now offer flexible working arrangements such as job sharing, flexible hours or working from home the childcare used could be part time or full time.

Activity

Investigate day care provision in the local area and produce a guide for parents giving information on what is available. Include a map to indicate where the settings are located.

Childminders

Childminders care for children in their own home and provide a service which may be more flexible for the parents. The registered childminder will be required to go through inspection procedures, and may have qualifications or be a parent, so would be experienced. There are usually other children to play with who may be of mixed ages, which helps children learn to socialise with others. Real-life learning experiences may be enjoyed, e.g. cooking, shopping or going to the library. Continuity of care may be possible if the childminder will do before or after school hours including collecting and returning the children to the family home. If children are ill they may not be allowed to attend in case of passing on infection, or if the childminder is ill then the parents would need to find alternative care.

Key Facts

- In 2007, 599,000 mothers with very young children had full-time jobs. This had risen to 746,000 in 2012.
- There are more mothers who work full time than mothers who stay at home.
- 30% of mothers feel guilty about going out to work and leaving their children.

Day nurseries

Day **nurseries** care for children all day for most of the year but can be costly. They take children from 6 months to 5 years and usually group the children in the setting according to age. Children are prepared for school by becoming used to the routine and taking part in the structured learning programme provided, but they may not get a lot of individual attention.

Their social skills could develop more quickly as they learn to interact and share with other children of the same age. Outdoor play equipment will help develop gross motor skills, and educational activities will encourage intellectual development.

Not all local communities have day nurseries so there may be travelling involved and hours may not be as flexible as parents need.

A Nanny is usually qualified to care for children from birth to 7 years

Nanny

Nannies can work hours to suit the family and could either live in or out depending on circumstances. The child gets personal attention but may become more attached to the nanny than the parent. The child is cared for in the familiar home environment but the total childcare costs can be expensive.

Workplace nursery

Workplace nurseries must be registered and inspected regularly. Costs may be cheaper as they are sometimes subsidised by the employer. It is possible for the parent to visit the child during break times. Children are usually able to attend throughout the year but places may not be available if demand is high. If the parent changes job then another childcare setting will need to be found. A variety of toys and educational activities are usually available so children's physical and intellectual skills are developed.

Playgroups/pre-schools

Playgroups must be registered and are inspected by the local authority to make sure the setting is safe and suitable for children. They are usually run by trained staff with help from parents. Children aged between 2 and 4 years can attend sessions that are organised between two and five times a week and last for about 2–3 hours. Numbers will be limited according to supervision and the size of the setting. There is usually a small charge for each session. As in other settings children have access to different toys and activities to extend their skill development.

Child Study

Discuss what day care provision your study child is attending at present and include information on whether the child enjoys the setting and the child's reaction when the parent leaves. If your study child has attended more than one setting you could include information on those as well.

Some playgroups rely on parents to help, which could allow parents the opportunity to become involved in their child's education

▲ A crèche is good for child care if you require a 'one-off' care session for a specific occasion

Crèches

Crèches are short-term temporary care for children as they are usually found in shopping and leisure centres. Parents can be assured that their children are being cared for in a safe place by qualified staff whilst they are busy. The crèches may accept a wide age range of children and be free of charge or cost per hour depending on the facility.

Parent and toddler groups

Parent and toddler groups allow parents and children to meet others. Parents can share experiences, and children can socialise and gain confidence, making them a good first step towards leaving the child in further day care. Children have the opportunity to play with different toys, take part in activities, listen to stories and sing songs. The groups are usually based in church halls or community centres and are run by volunteers who organise a session of approximately 2 hours once a week during term time. Many groups are free but some may ask for a contribution towards the refreshments provided. Parents do not leave the children; they stay with them and take full responsibility for their care.

EYFS - Early Years Foundation Stage

Nursery and reception classes

Nursery and reception classes are usually part of a primary school or sometimes a separate nursery school. Both are run by the local authority and provide educational experiences through play as part of the **EYFS**.

Both settings will be inspected and are staffed by qualified teachers and nursery nurses at a ratio of 1 staff to 13 children. Children aged 3–4 will attend five days a week during school term time and the session may be full or half days depending on the area of the UK. All 3–4 year olds are entitled to 15 hours of free education a week.

At the age of 4–5, children will start in a reception class, again following the Foundation Stage curriculum.

Out-of-school clubs

Out-of-school clubs include after-school clubs, breakfast clubs, holiday clubs and play schemes. Various activities are provided in the clubs, e.g. drama, sport, art and crafts and homework support. They need to be registered and are inspected regularly. Costs vary according to the type of club.

◄ Out-of-school clubs may help balance work and family commitments, whilst giving children study support and a range of experiences

Grandparents and family members

Children are cared for in a familiar environment, which could be the child's home, by experienced people who are trusted and known. They will develop closer bonds with the grandparents and have one-to-one care but opportunities to mix with other children may be limited. Hours may be flexible and they may be prepared to take and collect the child from school and payment may not be required. If the child is ill the parent will not need to take time off work.

There could be a conflict with discipline and caring issues and the parent may find it difficult to ask the grandparents to care for the child in the way they want it done. The grandparents may find the child physically demanding and not want to look after the child full time.

▲ **Many parents rely on grandparents for child care as they say it is who they trust the most**

Summary

- Childcare may be informal from family or friends, or via formal arrangements, e.g. childminders or nurseries.
- Single parents rely heavily on informal childcare, 34% of them have childcare arrangements with the child's grandparents.
- Day nurseries should be registered and inspected regularly. They open for long hours, e.g. 7.30 am to 6.30 pm.
- After-school clubs are good for extending the care needed for school-age children until parents finish work.
- Childcare settings caring for children from birth to 5 years will register on the Early Years register and deliver the EYFS.
- The Foundation Stage curriculum allows children to develop skills, build ideas, think creatively, interact and communicate effectively with others.
- Many childcare settings can help children's social development when they interact and play with other children.

Prove it!

1. **Name three types of pre-school provision.**
2. **Give three reasons why working parents would choose a childminder instead of a nursery to care for their child.**
3. **Suggest two childcare settings for a working single parent who has a 10-month-old baby and describe the advantages of each one.**
4. **State three ways in which a pre-school group can help with a child's early education.**
5. **Explain the differences between playgroups and parent and toddler groups.**

When answering questions on childcare provision you need to be sure that you know the differences between each of the settings and be able to explain the benefits to both the child and parent.

Voluntary organisations

There is a range of **voluntary** organisations that work to help and support families and children.

Gingerbread

Gingerbread provides support for single parents by providing advice and practical support on a number of issues. Fact sheets and information via email is available on:

- Managing finances – paying bills, receiving the correct benefits, etc.
- Education and employment – information on jobs, training and study options.
- Practical and emotional issues when separating from a partner.
- Childcare – finding and paying for childcare, tax credits, etc.
- Benefits for pregnant teenagers.
- Changes that can affect benefits – moving from benefits to work.

Gingerbread also provides information specifically for single fathers to provide support and try to alleviate isolation when bringing up children on their own.

Key Fact

- In 2010/11 there were 162,177 voluntary organisations in the UK.

Relate

Services provided by Relate include relationship counselling to provide help and support when couples may be considering separation or divorce. Any children or young people can also have counselling if they are experiencing issues with depression, mental health problems, trouble with parents or bullying at school.

Family counselling can help with problems such as conflict between siblings, divorce or separation or becoming part of a step-family.

Workshops are available for parents and children to learn about dealing with difficult issues and to develop relationship skills so that family life becomes better.

NSPCC

The **NSPCC** aims to end cruelty to children in the UK by providing advice and support for adults who are concerned about the welfare of children. They work with other organisations for the protection of children who are deemed to be at risk of neglect, physical or sexual abuse, those who live with violence, alcohol or drug abuse, disabled and looked after children.

ChildLine

ChildLine offers help and advice 24 hours a day all through the year either by telephone (0800 1111) or their website. To meet the needs of children the website has film clips and games to encourage them to speak about their problems and provides opportunities to have support via online chats and email.

Barnardo's

Barnardo's run projects for children and their families which include counselling, fostering and adoption services and vocational training. They believe that children deserve to have a good start in life and to develop their full potential irrespective of who they are, their behaviour or what they have experienced. Barnardo's works in areas such as child poverty, alcohol and drug abuse, homelessness, sexual abuse, domestic violence, parenting support and young carers.

Mencap

Mencap works to support people with a learning disability to live a full life as independently as possible. Advice may be obtained by telephone, from the website or from local groups that are part of the working partnership.

Support may be provided to help the individual to find a job, go to college or find a suitable place to live. Residential and day care services are organised and advice given on transport services, budgeting and respite care.

Activity

Using the Internet, research three voluntary organisations and produce an information leaflet on the work they do to support families.

Key Term

NSPCC - National Society for the Prevention of Cruelty to Children

Summary

- Relate believe in supporting healthy relationships within families by helping couples, families and individuals to make relationships work better.
- ChildLine is free and provided by trained counsellors who offer support on a range of issues.

Prove it!

1. Identify the voluntary organisations from the descriptions given:

   a. Supports lone families
   b. Offers child protection and prevents cruelty to children
   c. Supports people and families with learning difficulties
   d. Offers relationship education and counselling.

2. Describe the support that may be offered by Gingerbread and the NSPCC.

Legal framework for child protection

Children have rights and there is **legislation** to protect their rights.

Rights of the child

The United Nations Convention on the Rights of the Child consists of 54 articles that give information on how children under 18 years of age should be treated.

Create a poster, (minimum size A3) to outline the legal framework relating to the protection of children.

The main principles are as follows:

- Children should be treated fairly irrespective of their race, religion, culture, gender or disability.
- Adults should do the best for children in their care and be given help to make sure they live in an environment that is safe and where they can develop healthily through the provision of good health care and nutrition.
- Children have the right to live and a right to privacy.
- Children should have the opportunity to be listened to and their opinions considered in any decisions that affect them.
- Children should be **protected** from violence, abuse and neglect from care givers.
- Children have the right to free primary education and be encouraged to develop their full potential.

Children Act 1989 and 2004

The 1989 Act changed some of the previous legislation concerning the care and welfare of children. It stated that the care and welfare of children was of utmost importance and that children should be protected from harm by working in partnership with parents.

Part of the change set out in the 2004 Act includes the 'Every Child Matters' document. New duties were identified where there would be closer links and sharing of information with agencies, professionals and practitioners involved in children's care.

Every Child Matters has identified key outcomes for children which state that they should:

- Enjoy a healthy lifestyle with parents, carers and families promoting healthy choices to ensure good physical, emotional and sexual health.
- Be provided with a caring, safe and stable home that is free from maltreatment, neglect, violence, bullying and discrimination.
- Be encouraged to achieve skills for the future and regularly attend and enjoy school.
- Make a positive contribution to society and develop positive relationships and self-confidence, behave positively in and out of school and choose not to bully.
- Be supported to achieve economic well-being by continuing with further education after leaving school or entering the employment market.

Adoption and Children Act 2002

One of the provisions of this Act includes ensuring the child's care and welfare is of utmost importance when adoption decisions are made. This means that the following are considered important:

- The child's wishes and feelings.
- The child's physical, emotional and educational needs.
- Any risk of harm to the child.
- Characteristics of the child, age, gender and background.

A special guardianship order has been introduced for children who cannot live with their birth parents and adoption is not possible. This person will have parental responsibility for the child and must be over the age of 18.

The Act allows for single people, married or unmarried couples to adopt children. The Local Authority must also provide counselling, advice and information, support groups and therapeutic services for adopted children.

Protection of Children Act

This Act states that childcare or education settings, whether employing paid or unpaid staff, must check the Protection of Children Act List for names of prospective employees. This would be done through a **CRB check**. It is a criminal offence if a disqualified person accepts work or continues to work with a child.

CRB - Criminal Records Bureau

Childcare Act 2006

Key provisions of the Childcare Act require local authorities to:

- Provide a Sure Start Children's Centre in the community.
- Work with private, voluntary and independent sectors to provide enough childcare for working parents, including those on low incomes.
- Ensure a free minimum amount of early learning care is available for 3–4 year olds.
- Introduce the EYFS to help support the provision of early education and care from birth to age 5.
- Provide parents with a full range of information needed for their children.

Questions on the legal frame-work may ask you to assess the support legislative acts provide for the family. This type of essay requires you describe or explain how important the acts are and to give both positive and negative aspects.

Summary

- Every child should have the right to live in a loving family environment and be protected from discrimination and punishment.
- The Protection of Children Act List records the names of individuals who are unsuitable to work with children.

Prove it!

1. **Describe the legislation that protects the rights of children.**
2. **Describe the main points of the Every Child Matters document.**

Examination questions

1 **a)** Name **three** different types of families. (3)

b) Complete the following table to name the different types of family. (4)

Description	*Type of family*
A family where the children are brought up by either mum or dad.	
A family where the child or children live with both parents.	
A family where parents, grandparents and other relatives live together or close to each other.	
A family where mum and dad are not the natural parents but they are legally responsible for the child.	

2. In today's society there are many different types of family structure. Discuss the impact of these different structures on family life. (10)

Tip To gain maximum marks for question 2 you need to discuss both advantages and disadvantages for three or four family structures.

This is the first advantage listed.

You need to list both advantages and disadvantages – like this one.

Nuclear family

You can choose when to visit the extended family so there may be no interference from family on a daily basis as they do not live in the same house. Special effort and hard work will be needed to develop close family relationships so children and grandparents may not have such a close relationship. If emergency childcare is needed this may not be available and the grandparents may not be available to look after children so childcare will have to be paid for.

Advantage

Disadvantage

Extended family

Due to the close proximity of family members there will be lots of people to offer help and advice and give childcare support. Unfortunately this could lead to unwanted advice being given, causing conflict over different child-rearing methods. Close family relationships can be formed, with children having relatives to play with, but on the downside there could be a lack of privacy and independence.

Advantage

Disadvantage

Step-family

The family may have a better quality of life as there may be more income. Children will have both male and female role models with the care being shared, but on a negative side the children may not bond with the step-parent or get on with any step-brothers or sisters which could cause friction within the family. Some children may have limited access to their biological parent with the movement between two homes being unsettling. Expectations over behaviour and discipline could be different between the parents.

One parent family
The parent may be happier and more relaxed on their own with the atmosphere at home possibly better as the parent is not in an unhappy relationship any more. The parent may have to work harder to support the family financially, emotionally and physically. The other parent is not available to share worries or the upbringing of the child so the remaining parent feels alone and sometimes very stressed. The child may also be lacking a father or mother figure if there is no or limited contact with the absent parent.

Foster family
Foster care enables a family to stay together long term because the child is cared for, temporarily, in another home when there are difficulties within the family. Children know it is a temporary measure and they can visit their natural parents. The family know their child is in safe hands until they are ready to resume parental care. Sometimes the placement may change and the child may be unhappy in foster care. Variable standards of living may be evident between the foster care and the children's home.

Adoptive family
Adoption gives adoptees a family and a stable home life to a child. The child has a sense of belonging and will possibly have more opportunities. The parents go through rigorous checks before they can adopt a child and when the process is complete they become legally responsible for the child.

Tip To achieve maximum marks for question 4 the answer needs to have at least three to four effects that are discussed.

3 a) What do you understand by the term 'looked after children'? (1)
b) Give **three** reasons why a child might be in local authority care. (3)

4. Fostering involves the care of a child or children within another home.
a) Describe the difference between fostering and adoption. (2)
b) Discuss the effects of foster care upon a child. (5)

Foster care provides stability for a temporary period of time where the child is given a placement in a good home with opportunities that allow the child to succeed when previously this may not have been possible.

This opening paragraph provides both a mention of the effect (provides stability) and then goes on to discuss that effect.

The child can have contact with the birth parents but may be homesick or not settle well with complete strangers. There may be problems with some foster parents' own children as the child may not get on with them. Sometimes the child may become 'attached' to the foster parent and experience a better standard of living in the foster home and not want to go back to their birth parents.

As before, the good answer will mention both the effect AND then go on to a discussion of it within the context of the question.

Occasionally a child may be moved from one placement to another, which can be unsettling for the child and cause further emotional problems.

Tip To answer a question like question 5 you need to give three separate functions. So if you answered 'To provide a safe, secure and stable environment' that would only get you one mark – even though you listed three descriptive words about the type of environment, that is not enough to get you three marks.

Tip Discussing some of these sorts of points – and giving examples and reasons for your answers – will get you best marks. Note that there are more points actually listed here than you'd need to get the 6 marks given in the question, this is to give you the full range of possible points.

Bereavement here is a good example of a factor, but the description afterwards could be expanded. The answer could go into more depth by saying how a death could cause difficulties, and give more examples of what those difficulties could be.

5 **a)** State **three** functions of the family. (3)

b) Outline **two** ways that having a baby might change the parents' lifestyle. (2)

6. A family's culture can affect a child's upbringing.
Assess how all aspects of a family's culture can influence a child's life and development. (6)

- Language
- Religion – provides a set of rules for behaviour, sets special times for worship and festivals
- Traditions
- Education
- Hygiene
- Food, diet and eating habits
- Music, songs, drama, literature and art
- Leisure activities
- Style of dress
- Family relationships – mixed marriages, quarrelling, tension
- Poverty, resources within the home.

7. In today's society there are an increasing number of factors that can cause pressure or difficulties within families.
Discuss the factors which commonly cause difficulties within families. (10)

Your answer here might be a discussion of some of these points, giving examples and reasons for the answer:

- Financial aspects – low income, loss of employment.
- Ill health – of parent, sibling, or member of extended family.
- Bereavement of family member can affect emotional aspects and if it is the loss of a parent financial matters can also be affected.
- Housing – this can be more severe than just 'a move' as if experiencing financial hardship may have to move away from extended family.
- Parental separation or divorce and change of circumstances.
- Step-families and possible relationship problems between the step-parent and step-children or siblings.
- Parents fighting or family arguments with grandparents and other relatives.
- Disabled family member which can put strain on family relationships.
- Both parents working – childcare issues.
- Lack of parental control or lack of consistency of rules.
- Sibling rivalry.
- Single parent family – stress and pressure of supporting the family.

8. Some children have special needs.

a) Explain what you understand by:

i. Spina bifida (1)

ii. Autism (1)

iii. Cerebral palsy (1)

b) What can be done to reduce the risk of a child being born with spina bifida? (1)

c) Children with special needs bring different issues to family life.

i. Explain the effects of a child with special needs on a family (5)

Your answer could be a discussion of some of these points, with examples and reasons:

- Home is the best place for the child as they have the same needs as other children – to be cuddled, smiled at, taken on outings, etc.
- Extra work due to assistance with toilet, eating and movement.
- Specialist equipment needed including adapted car.
- Home adaptations may be required.
- Other children may get bullied or teased by peers.
- Embarrassed to be seen with sibling.
- Parent unable to work, loss of money and social life.
- Special family bond can develop.
- Parents may have little time to play, read or do activities with other children.
- Parents may be too tired and stressed so lack patience.
- Parents could be over protective.
- Other siblings are protective and often gain confidence.
- Other family members may be ignored.

Family members such as siblings may be overlooked because the parents need to spend a lot of time caring for the child with special needs. They have little time to look after the other children who are then left to do a lot more for themselves at a young age. The children could begin to resent their sibling causing family problems.

ii. Describe the types of support that are required for both the child and the family. (5)

For question 8(c)ii, an answer might discuss some of the following points giving examples in order to gain maximum marks:

- Practical advice for day-to-day care and education.
- Advice on helping the child to lead as full a life as possible.
- Contact with other families with similar problems, share experiences and discuss how difficulties can be overcome.
- Financial support for special equipment and other necessary expenses.
- Help with household chores.
- Help to arrange holidays that cater for children with special needs.
- Arrange transport to take the child on outings.
- Childminding help so that parents can have a break and spend time with other children or with each other.
- Respite care to give parents a break and time for themselves.
- Family could take out other children to allow them to get away, play and mix with extended family or friendship groups.

The first part of this point shows you how to answer this type of question. First you give an example of the sort of support that is available, then go on to give a description of the how that support can help the family.

9. a) Voluntary services are available to give help to children and families. What do you understand by a voluntary service? (1)

b) Complete the following table. (5)

Description	*Voluntary organisation*
Supports lone parents	
Offers child protection and prevents cruelty to children	
Supports people and families with learning difficulties	
Offers relationship education and counselling	
Gives confidential support to children	

10 a) Immunisation – the safest way to protect your child.

i) Explain what is meant by immunisation. (4)

ii) Discuss the effect that the vaccination programme has had on the health of children. (5)

b) Name **four** diseases which can be prevented by immunisation. (4)

c) When does the immunisation schedule begin? (1)

d) Some parents choose not to immunise a child. Suggest **two** reasons for this. (2)

You need to list four to get the marks, but there are eight in total you can choose from.

The vaccination programme provides long-lasting protection against diseases which could be fatal therefore lowering the death rate. Epidemics are prevented as it offers protection, not only for your child but for other young babies, children and adults as well within the community.

This is a good discussion because it gives a reason why vaccinations are needed.

Vaccinations are usually quick, simple, safe and combined to allow less chance of children missing any and to give protection from an early age when babies are most at risk. Vaccinations against Haemophilus influenzae (Hib) have decreased early childhood meningitis significantly.

Again this is a good point well made because it describes the specific example (Hib) and gives a reason to help explain the point, that vaccinations reduce childhood illnesses.

Risks are rare, but some concerns over reaction and side effects have resulted in some parents not having their children immunised.

11. There are a number of different types of pre-school provision in the UK. Discuss the variety available and their importance to the child and the family. (10)

Day nurseries – provide care for children aged 6 months to 5 years. They are open for long hours and during school holidays so are good for working parents. They are state or privately run. Children take part in a variety of activities which are not based on structured 'curriculum'.

Workplace nurseries – organised by the employer and are usually on site. They may be subsidised by the employer. Children will participate in a variety of educational activities.

Crèches – care for children for short periods and are often in shopping centres, etc. Staff look after children and keep them safe. Children take part in activities which will be of educational value but there will not be the continuity of learning.

Pre-schools or playgroups – these are usually run by trained staff with assistance from parents. Usually attended by children 2–4 years and sessions are up to 3 hours a day. Children will take part in a variety of educational activities.

Nursery schools – these can be run by the state or privately and are stand alone schools for 3–5 year olds. Children usually attend for five half days. These schools follow a teaching method and have brochures which outline the curriculum and aims of the school.

Early years units or reception classes – these are units linked to state primary schools. As above and often continuity with the primary school, e.g. use of facilities. Children should be prepared for future environment.

Suggested points for discussion on their importance:

- Provide a stimulating and safe, caring environment for the child.
- Actively work to promote a positive self-image of the child.
- Foster physical, social, emotional, intellectual and moral growth.
- Work as partners with the parents for the benefit of the children.
- Allow the child to gain a greater variety of experiences, e.g. diferent cultures.
- Allow the parents to develop their careers and improve their self-worth.

Tip To gain maximum marks, a discussion of 4–5 different types of pre-school provision needs to be provided that includes information on the different opening hours and what the child will be doing when in the setting. Then add a section on how the settings can help the child's development and assist the parents.

12. Assess the factors which need to be considered when choosing childcare provision. (8)

Finding the best possible substitute to take care of the child will give the parent extra reassurance. Different options suit different children but the parent would need to consider the following points if choosing paid care instead of leaving the child with a relative.

The childcare setting should be registered, with a good inspection report which would indicate that it has passed strict rules and complies with child protection laws to safeguard children.

To prevent the spread of disease or infections the place should be clean so that children's health is protected. Good toilet and changing facilities that are clean and large enough should be provided.

All children need to feel happy and secure with the person looking after them. Therefore parents should ensure staff are qualified, CRB checked and trained to handle children, with the correct staff to child ratio so all children are given

Tip A balanced range of factors need to be considered to achieve maximum marks, e.g. safety, good care, qualified staff, welcoming environment that encourages development, location and cost.

This answer would achieve maximum marks as a range of factors are discussed with explanations.

A good start – the answer begins with a proper introduction.

Important – this shows an understanding of the need to ensure the child is well cared for.

Shows consideration of safety.

This shows the student is aware of the issues around the development of the child.

attention and not neglected. The child should be kept safe within the setting by having locked doors, fences around outside areas, etc.

There should be bright and colourful surroundings that are welcoming and stimulating to the child with plenty of toys and activities for amusement and to prevent boredom. To prevent injury these toys should be new and in good condition.

There should be enough space to run around safely whilst taking part in a variety of activities. Outside facilities would provide the opportunity to gain fresh air, run around and experience different toys.

The location of the setting would need to be convenient to the parent or carer for taking and collecting the child on the way to and from work with opening times suiting the parents' or carers' working hours. Linked to this is the cost of the fees to be paid and whether they are affordable.

13. Parents often need to use other people to care for their child. Discuss the advantages and disadvantages of three types of childcare suitable for working parents and their three-year-old child. (9)

Tip The answer given would achieve maximum marks because both advantages (A) and disadvantages (D) have been given with some explanations.

Childminders may have childcare qualifications and will be registered and inspected regularly. They usually live locally and may provide flexible hours of care by being prepared to pick up and drop off children. (A) There will be other children to play with in a home environment with continuity of care, especially if childminder will do after school hours.

Childminders may not look after the child if he/she is ill as there is a risk of infection and if the childminder is ill alternative care needs to be found. There may be worries about health and safety issues in the childminder's home. (D)

When grandparents look after the child, he or she will be cared for in a familiar environment, have continuity of care and develop a close bond with grandparents. (A)

Grandparents may be flexible about hours and be prepared to come to the child's house, drop off and collect from nursery. The care is one to one with less risk of contact with childhood illnesses and the parents do not need to take time off work if child is ill.

Some grandparents may find the child physically demanding and not want to look after him or her full time or may have other commitments which may not fit in with the work hours of the parents. If caring in their home, may not be as child-safe as child's home, also opportunities to mix with other children may be restricted. (D)

Day nurseries will care for children all day on a full-time or part-time basis depending on parents needs. At least half ofthe staff must have early years qualifications and the setting is registered and regularly inspected. They are open all year and for long hours, e.g. 8.00am to 7.00pm (A) but costs can be high. (D)

These settings will take children from 6 months to 5 years though this varies according to area. Children are usually grouped according to age and will follow a structured learning programme.

There may not be one near to the child's home so travelling will be involved and the hours may not be as flexible as needed. (D)

Children may be exposed to illness and infection and not get a lot of individual attention or be bullied.

Tip There are several pieces of relevant legislation that could be discussed. The question asks for three so do not waste time providing more answers. This will not gain you extra marks but waste time that could be spent answering, in detail, the chosen legislation. Remember to choose the legislation you know the most about.

14. Many children experience difficulties during their early years. Assess the support offered by three pieces of legislation in relation to children and their families. (10)

Children's Rights - UN Convention	Children's Act 1989	Childcare Act
• Children should grow up in a family environment with parental love and care • Children should be able to live as individuals in society • Children should be protected and live a life free from all types of discrimination and punishment • Children should be able to express their opinions freely and have their views listened to and respected • Children should be able to develop physically, intellectually, emotionally and spiritually	• The welfare of the child is very important • Whenever possible children should be cared for within their own families • Parents should be offered help if struggling because a partnership with parents is important so that the children's needs are met • Statutory services are offered to children in need • Children should be safe and protected at all times • Children should be kept informed about what happens to them at all times and be allowed to make decisions • If children are not living with parents, they should still be kept informed about their future • The child's race, culture, religion and language must be respected • There should be no delay in child protection cases	• NHS - all authorities to work together for all children - Surestart • Ensure sufficient childcare for all mothers to work • Free early learning care for all 3-4 year olds • Early Years register so all children have Early Years Foundation Phase

Tip For essay-type questions marks are usually awarded following a similar format to the suggested mark range below:

1–2 marks: Essay lacks planning with brief or limited knowledge and understanding of topic.

3–5 marks: Some of the correct answers given showing a reasonable degree of knowledge and understanding.

6–8 marks: Essay planned and well structured showing good knowledge and understanding.

9–10 marks: Essay planned and well structured with comprehensive answers showing excellent understanding and application of knowledge.

Principles of a healthy diet

What will I learn?

- **The nutrients present in food and why they are needed**
- **How to have a healthy balanced diet**
- **Current nutritional guidelines**

A balanced diet contains all the nutrients someone needs to be healthy, in the right amounts for their age, gender and lifestyle.

Key Fact

- All foods contain nutrients so we **should** eat a wide variety of different foods to make sure we get all the nutrients we need.

Nutrients

There are five groups of **nutrients**, all of which are important for good health. These are:

- protein
- carbohydrate
- fat
- vitamins
- minerals.

We also need enough water to keep us hydrated. About 70% of the body is made up of water and it is needed to make blood and tissue fluids. Water is also needed for a number of processes, such as to regulate temperature and to get rid of waste. We also need **dietary fibre** to ensure our digestive system works properly.

Key Fact

- **Macro** means big. This means we need quite a lot of these nutrients, e.g. a toddler needs about 16g of protein per day.

Protein, carbohydrate and fat are known as macronutrients because we need them in large amounts.

Protein

Protein is needed for the growth and repair of the body. It is found in both animal and vegetable foods. Animal sources of protein are: meat, poultry, fish, milk and dairy products. Vegetable sources include beans, peas and lentils (pulses) nuts, tofu and meat replacement products such as Quorn.

Key Terms

Nutrient – the part of food that is used by our body

Dietary fibre – the indigestible part of fruit and vegetables

Protein foods

◀ Sugary foods

▲ Starchy foods

Carbohydrates

Carbohydrates are the body's main source of energy. They can be divided into two groups: sugary foods and starchy foods.

- *Sugary foods* include cakes, biscuits, chocolate and soft drinks.
- *Starchy foods* include potatoes, rice, pasta and bread.

We should get most of our energy from starchy foods. These are harder to digest and release energy slowly. This means that we stay full for longer and are less likely to want unhealthy snacks in between meals. They also contain other important nutrients such as vitamins, minerals and dietary fibre. Sugary foods contain very few other nutrients and are sometimes called 'empty calories'. These foods are linked to tooth decay and obesity and should only be given to children occasionally.

Fats

Fats are also a source of energy. Fats help to keep us warm and provide some vitamins. Fats are found in foods such as butter, margarine and oil, and also in meat, dairy products, cakes and fried foods. Although most people should avoid a high fat diet, because it is linked to health problems like obesity and heart disease, it is not recommended that young children under five have low fat versions of products like milk because they need the energy content. However, a sensible approach is needed because if their fat intake is too high, they will put on weight.

Key Fact

- **Micro** means small, so we only need these nutrients in very small amounts, e.g. toddlers need about 800mg of calcium and 400mg of vitamin A.

▼ Foods high in fat and/or sugar

Try to learn at least two sources of each nutrient. Be specific – don't just write 'fruit', name a type.

Vitamins and minerals are known as micronutrients because we only need them in small amounts. Even though we don't need much of each one, they are still vital for good health.

Vitamins

These are most commonly known by their letter rather than their chemical name. Vitamins A, D, E and K are fat-soluble vitamins. Vitamins B group and C are water soluble. This means that foods containing vitamins B and C must be prepared and cooked carefully so that the vitamins do not dissolve in the cooking liquid so not be consumed.

Vitamin	Function	Sources
Vitamin A	Keeps skin and mucous membranes healthy Helps vision in dim light	Dairy products, eggs, oily fish, liver Red and orange vegetables, e.g. carrots, peppers
Vitamin B group (a number of vitamins with similar functions)	Helps the body use the energy from food Needed for the body's nervous system	Meat, eggs, dairy products, wholegrain cereal products
Vitamin C	Helps wounds to heal Needed for connective tissues Helps the body absorb iron	Citrus fruits, berries (e.g. strawberries), kiwi fruit
Vitamin D	Works with calcium to form strong bones and teeth	Milk, margarine, oily fish The body can also make vitamin D if exposed to sunlight
Vitamin E	Needed for healthy skin	Eggs, nuts, seeds
Vitamin K	Helps the blood to clot	Green vegetables, pulses, meat

Key Fact

- If every woman followed the advice about folic acid, the number of babies born with neural tube defects could be reduced by as much as 70%.

Folic acid is a B group vitamin that is particularly important in pregnancy. Women who are planning a pregnancy are advised to take a supplement of 400mg of folic acid for at least three months before trying for a baby and until three months into the pregnancy. Folic acid is known to help prevent **neural tube defects** such as spina bifida.

Minerals

Mineral	Function	Sources
Calcium	Works with vitamin D to make strong bones and teeth	Milk, cheese, dried fruit, white bread, oranges
Iron	Makes red blood cells, which carry oxygen around the body	Meat, fortified breakfast cereals, green leafy vegetables, e.g. spinach
Fluoride	Helps to make strong tooth enamel	Water, seafood, toothpaste

Key Facts

- Foods which are good sources of iron should be served with foods rich in Vitamin C to help absorption of iron.
- Children need the equivalent of one pint of milk a day to get enough calcium.

Dietary fibre

Fibre is found in all fruit and vegetables. It is also in foods made from **wholegrains** *(see KEY FACT)*, such as some breakfast cereals, wholemeal bread, wholemeal pasta and brown rice. Fibre is important in the diet because it helps the digestive system to work efficiently. Fibre absorbs water and makes **faeces** softer and easier to eliminate. Without enough fibre in the diet, people may become constipatéd and are more at risk of diseases such as colon cancer.

Foods high in fibre can be very filling, so young children should have a mixture of white and wholegrain bread, pasta, etc., to ensure they can eat enough of other nutrients.

Key Terms

Neural tube defects – caused when parts of the brain, spine or spinal cord do not develop properly in the early part of the pregnancy

Wholegrains – foods made from wholegrains use all of the grain rather than processing the grain to get rid of the outer part; they contain much more fibre than those made from white flour and more B vitamins, too

▼ Wholemeal bread is high in fibre

Key Fact

- Foods made from wholegrains use all of the grain rather than processing the grain to get rid of the outer part. They contain much more fibre than those made from white flour and more B vitamins, too.

Key Fact

- In 2010, about 3 in 10 children between the ages of 2 and 15 were overweight or obese. A report by the British Nutrition Foundation in 2011 suggests that by 2050, 70% of school-age girls and 55% of boys could be overweight or obese.

Healthy eating

The UK government sets targets and gives advice to people about how to eat healthily. This is important because many common diseases today are diet-related and could be avoided. In particular the number of children who are overweight or obese is increasing. This will have long-term effects on their health as obesity is linked to higher risks of heart disease and type 2 diabetes.

The eatwell plate

This pie chart shows the proportions of each of the main food groups people should have during the day. The eatwell plate does not apply directly to children under the age of 2. Between the ages of 2 and 5, children should gradually move to eating the same foods as the rest of the family, in these proportions.

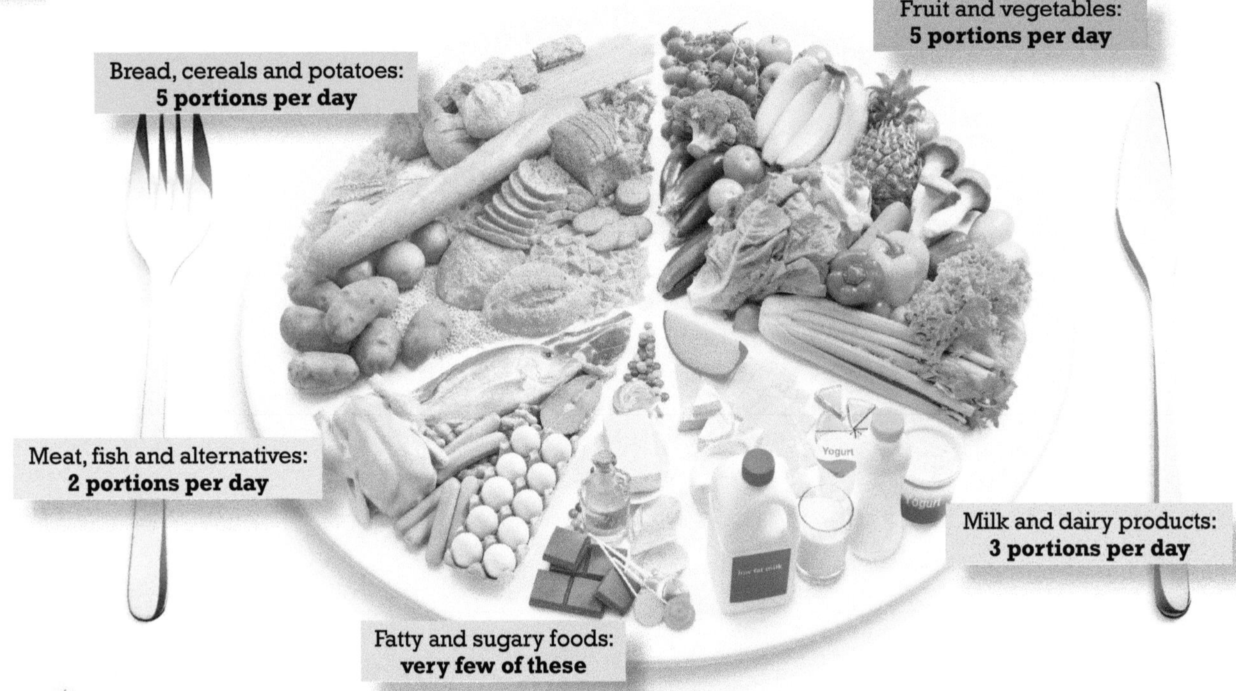

Activities

1 Find out what counts as a portion of fruit and vegetables.

2 Copy and complete the table on the right, showing each of the food groups and which nutrients they contain.

3 Plan a day's meals for a toddler. Give reasons for your choice (tip: you should include the nutritional value and why the dishes would appeal to children). Find out how much the food would cost.

Food group	Main nutrients
Bread, cereals and potatoes	
Fruit and vegetables	
Milk and dairy products	
Meat, fish and alternatives	
Fatty and sugary foods	

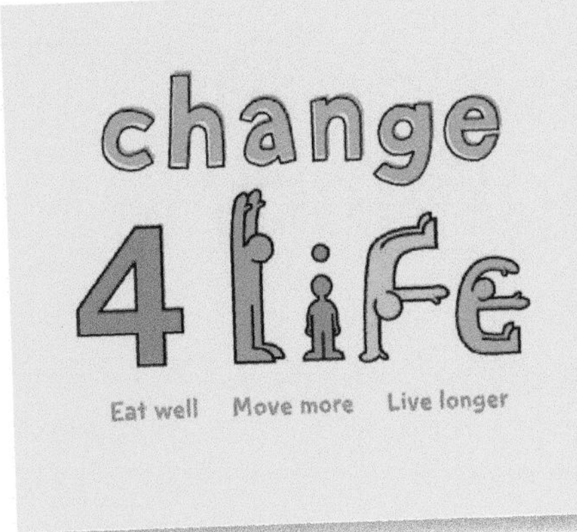

5 A DAY
Getting your 5 portions of fruit and veg a day is easier than you think.

◀ **The 5 a day campaign was launched in the UK in 2002–03: ten years on research suggests that few people are actually changing their eating habits**

The 5 a day campaign

The 5 a day campaign is based on advice from the World Health Organisation, which recommends eating a minimum of 400g of fruit and vegetables a day to lower the risk of serious health problems, such as heart disease, stroke, type 2 diabetes and obesity. Fruit and vegetables are good sources of vitamins, minerals and fibre. They can help reduce the risk of heart disease, stroke and some cancers.

Summary

- Eating a wide variety of different foods is the best way of ensuring we get all the nutrients we need.
- Folic acid is very important for unborn babies, so pregnant women must make sure they get plenty in their diet and should take a vitamin supplement as well.
- Eating five or more portions of fruit and vegetables a day can reduce the risk of several diseases.
- Children should not have salt added to their food because their kidneys cannot cope with large amounts.

Child Study

Find out how healthy your study child's diet is and consider how this might affect their development.

Prove it!

1 **What is a healthy diet?**

2 **List the five main nutrient groups.**

3 **Why is protein needed? Name two animal and two plant sources of protein.**

4 **a) What does the body need fat for?**
b) Why is it important to limit the amount of fat we eat?

5 **What is the main source of energy in the diet?**

6 **Why do children need a good supply of calcium?**

Dietary aims and goals: Diet during pregnancy

What will I learn?

- **How to have a healthy diet during pregnancy**

It is important for a woman who is pregnant to follow the same normal healthy eating guidelines that are given to everyone. This means she should eat foods from the four main food groups every day – you may have heard of the phrase 'eating for two', but there is no need for women to do this. Her body will simply adapt to use whatever nutrients it gets for both her and her baby. Protein requirements for a woman do increase a little during pregnancy. She should make sure she has plenty of fibre, as pregnant women can suffer from constipation and piles. A good intake of folic acid is important too (see page 42). Energy requirements also increase a little in the last three months of pregnancy, and she should have about 200kcal extra per day.

Key Facts

- A healthy diet during pregnancy helps to develop a healthy baby.
- Energy is measured in kilocalories (kcal) although we tend to refer just to calories.

▶ **Foods rich in folic acid**

Foods to avoid

There are some foods that women should avoid when they are pregnant, mainly because they could harm the baby.

Good food hygiene is essential to prevent food poisoning. Food poisoning in pregnancy can have long-term consequences for the unborn baby, even if the mother is not very ill.

Raw or lightly cooked eggs, raw meat and poultry may contain *Salmonella* bacteria. These bacteria can cause food poisoning. This will be unpleasant for the mother-to-be and can cause a **miscarriage** or premature birth. Eggs, meat and poultry must be fully cooked and foods containing raw eggs, such as homemade mayonnaise, and some desserts must be avoided. Unpasteurised milk may also contain *Salmonella*, so it, or yogurt and cheese made from it, should not be consumed.

Link

See also pages 60–61.

◀ **Healthy eating is particularly important during pregnancy**

Soft and blue-veined cheeses (e.g. Brie, Stilton) paté and some ready-meals may contain *Listeria* bacteria. These bacteria can also cause food poisoning in the mother and can harm the developing baby. Possible consequences for the baby are miscarriage, still birth, **meningitis** and sight and hearing problems. Paté and high-risk cheeses should not be eaten. Ready-meals must be very carefully re-heated to ensure they are piping hot all the way through.

Raw and lightly cooked meat and unwashed fruit and vegetables may contain a parasite which causes toxoplasmosis. Toxoplasmosis is rare and if infected, the mother will only suffer from mild flu-like symptoms. However, the infection can be passed to the baby causing miscarriage, stillbirth, **hydrocephalus** and/or eye damage. Meat and poultry must be cooked thoroughly and all fruit and vegetables must be washed to make sure there is no soil on them.

Liver and liver products (e.g. paté) and any supplements that have fish oils all contain high amounts of vitamin A. Vitamin A is stored in the body and a build-up is toxic to the baby, causing birth defects.

Some types of fish, such as swordfish, marlin and shark, contain high levels of mercury, which can harm the baby's nervous system and should be avoided. Tuna also contains mercury, so a pregnant woman should limit her intake to no more than two tuna steaks or four medium cans of tuna a week.

Activity

Plan, prepare and cook a healthy meal containing folic acid that would be suitable for an expectant mother.

▼ **A few of the high risk foods pregnant women should avoid eating**

Summary

- Women who are pregnant should eat a healthy diet and do not need to eat significantly more than before the pregnancy.
- Pregnant women should eliminate all risk of food poisoning from their diet as it would cause harm to the baby. This means there are some foods they should not eat.

Prove it!

1. **Describe how a pregnant woman can make sure she has a healthy diet.**
2. **Identify the foods an expectant mother should avoid. Give reasons for your answer.**

Dietary aims and goals: Feeding the new baby

What will I learn?

- **The different ways of feeding new babies**
- **The advantages and disadvantages of breast and bottle-feeding**

New parents need to decide whether they will breast or bottle-feed their baby, or a mixture of the two. Medical advice is that breastfeeding is best for the baby, but parents should choose whichever they feel will be best for them and their baby. They will need to think about their lifestyle and working patterns and decide who will be spending most time looking after the baby. If it is the mother, then breastfeeding will be easier than if the father was the main carer.

Breastfeeding

During the pregnancy, high levels of the hormones **oestrogen** and **progesterone** work together to stimulate the milk glands in the breasts to produce **colostrum**. This is a yellowish liquid which is designed to feed the new born baby. It contains all the water, protein, sugar, vitamins and minerals the new baby needs, together with **antibodies** which help to protect the baby from infection.

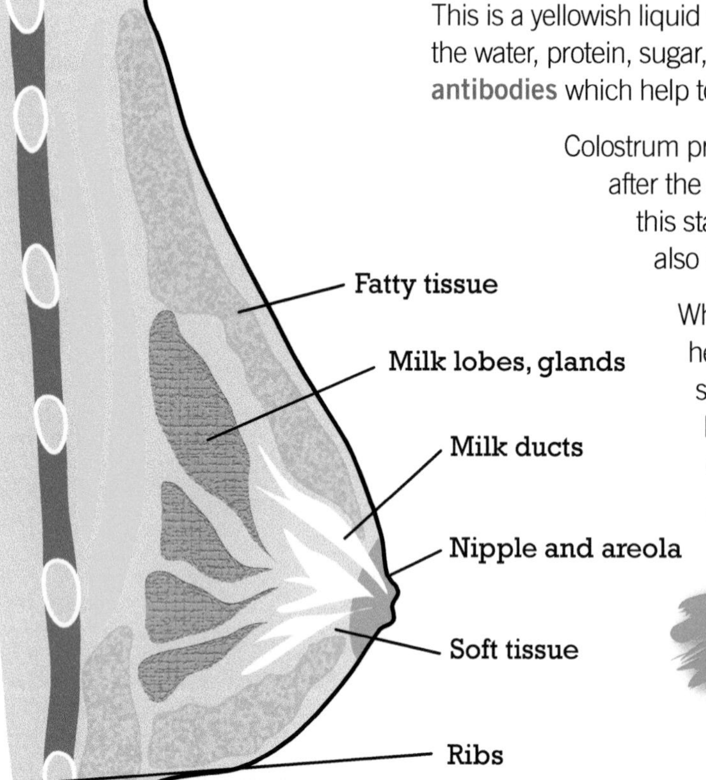

Colostrum production starts when the baby is born. Hormone changes after the birth are the signal for true milk production to begin and this starts three to five days after the birth. Milk production is also known as **lactation**.

While breastfeeding, the mother needs to make sure she has a healthy diet and drinks plenty of liquid to help produce a good supply of milk. Alcohol and some medication can get into breast milk so breastfeeding mothers should limit the amount of alcohol they drink and take advice from their doctor or pharmacist if they need to take any medication.

Key Terms

Colostrum – the first 'milk' produced by the mother

Antibodies – substances produced by the immune system which fight diseases

Lactation – the name given to the production of milk

Advantages and disadvantages of breastfeeding

Advantages:

- Breast milk contains all the nutrients and antibodies needed to give the baby a good start.
- Breast milk does not need any preparation and is the right temperature.
- Babies who are breastfed are less likely to suffer from nappy rash, eczema and other allergies than those who are bottle-fed.
- There is less chance of the baby having diarrhoea and vomiting and also chest and ear infections.
- Babies are less likely to become obese and therefore develop type 2 diabetes and other illnesses later in life.
- Breastfeeding helps with bonding between mother and baby.
- It helps the mother to lose the weight she put on in pregnancy.

Disadvantages:

- The mother may feel uncomfortable about feeding her baby in public.
- It can be tiring as breastfed babies tend to want feeding more often than bottle-fed babies.
- The mother may find it more difficult to leave the baby, for example to go back to work.

▲ **Breastfeeding can encourage the bonding process between mother and child**

Summary

- Babies are born with a natural instinct to suck. This is called the **sucking reflex**.
- Breast milk contains all the nutrients a baby needs for the first six months of life.
- Most women can breastfeed, but if they are HIV positive or on some types of medication they may be advised not to.
- Over 70% of women in the UK breastfeed for a time.

Some mothers find the idea of breastfeeding in public uncomfortable or embarrassing.

1 Interview some parents to find out how they decided to feed their baby and what influenced their decision.

2 Carry out research to find items that can be purchased to make breastfeeding more discrete and comfortable for the mother.

Prove it!

1 **Why is colostrum important to the new baby?**

2 **What key factors will a mother need to think about when choosing how to feed her baby?**

3 **Why do health professionals say 'breast is best'?**

Bottle-feeding

Mothers who choose not to breastfeed will need to use formula milk. This is cow's milk that has been modified by diluting it and adding extra vitamins and minerals to make it suitable for human babies. Soya milk versions are also available if the baby cannot tolerate cow's milk. These should only be given after consultation with medical professionals because babies who are allergic to cows' milk may also be allergic to soya milk.

The baby will be given infant formula for the first 4–6 months and then move on to follow-on milk until 12 months, when they can be given ordinary cows' milk.

Advantages and disadvantages of bottle-feeding

Advantages:

- The mother knows how much milk the baby has taken.
- The milk is unaffected by anything the mother has consumed.
- Other people can help with feeding, so it relieves some pressure from the mother.
- It is useful when the mother wishes to leave the baby, for example to go back to work.

Disadvantages:

- Formula milk does not contain any antibodies found in breast milk, so the baby does not have the same protection against infection.
- There is a lot of preparation involved in sterilising bottles and making up the feed.
- Using formula milk is more expensive than breastfeeding as both equipment and milk have to be bought.
- Babies tend to swallow more air when bottle-fed and then need to be winded more often.
- Bottle-fed babies are more likely to suffer from constipation.

▲ Bottle-feeding

Feeding equipment

Bottles, **teats** and sterilising equipment will all be needed.

Bottles come in a variety of shapes and sizes. The type chosen is a matter of personal preference, but well-designed bottles have a wide neck for easy cleaning, are made from a clear material, have measurements on the side to help with mixing the feed and have a cap to protect the **teat**.

Teats also come in a range of shapes and sizes to suit different babies. Finding one that suits the baby can be trial and error. The most important feature of the teat is the size of the hole. It should allow the milk to drip rapidly when the bottle is held upside down. A hole which is too small will mean that the baby swallows a lot of air, one which is too large means the milk will flow too quickly and could cause the baby to choke.

▲ Baby bottle

There are different types of **steriliser** available. Cold water sterilisers work with sterilising tablets and water. Equipment must be fully submerged for at least 30 minutes. Steam sterilisers can be electric or used in the microwave. Cold water is added and then the steriliser is either switched on or put in the microwave. Both take about 10 minutes, depending on the model.

▶ Steriliser

Making up a feed

1. Good hygiene is vital at every stage. Hands and nails must be washed thoroughly and all equipment must be sterilised.

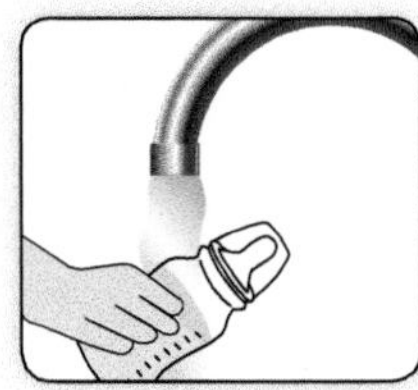
2. Cooled, boiled water is used to make up the feed. Pour the correct amount into a graduated bottle.

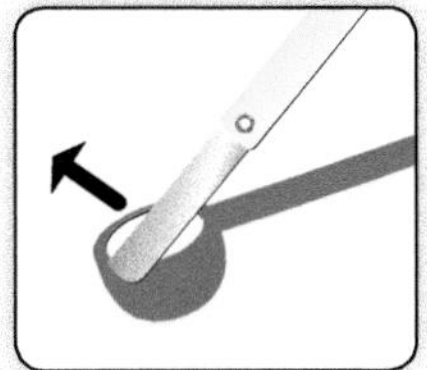
3. Put the required number of scoops of formula powder into the bottle. Each scoop must be levelled with a knife.

4. Fill the bottle and attach the teat and cap.

5. Shake the bottle well to make sure the milk powder has all dissolved.

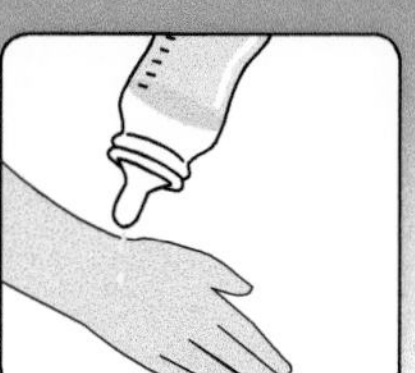
6. If the milk is to be used immediately, test the temperature on the inside of the wrist.If the milk is to be stored for later, place it in the fridge until needed. Prepared milk should not be stored for more than 24 hours.

Bottle-feeding with breast milk

It is possible to **express** breast **milk** into a bottle that can then be given to the baby at another time. Hand or electric breast pumps can be used to fill a bottle which has been sterilised as above. This means that the baby has the advantages of breast milk, but that the mother does not have to do all the feeding.

Summary

- Cows' milk should not be given as a main drink to babies under the age of one because it does not contain the right proportion of nutrients and their digestive system cannot cope with the high protein and salt content.
- Most formula milk is purchased in powder form and needs to be reconstituted before use. Formula milk can also be purchased in cartons ready mixed, but this tends to be more expensive.
- Babies must never be left alone to feed with the bottle propped up as they could choke.
- Cleaning and sterilising are very important. If hands and equipment carry any germs, the baby may get **gastroenteritis**.
- Gastroenteritis causes vomiting and diarrhoea. A young baby can get dehydrated very quickly and may need hospital treatment.
- Infant formula must be prepared using the exact proportions of milk powder and water. If it is too strong it could make the baby put on too much weight or became seriously ill from too much sodium. If it is too weak the baby will not have the nutrients needed.

Activities

1 Describe and compare the range of sterilising equipment available to new parents.

2 Write an article for a parenting magazine giving advice to an expectant mother who is not sure how to feed her baby. What reassurance or tips can you give her on how to find out what is best?

Prove it!

1 What is infant formula milk?

2 Why is good hygiene so important when preparing infant formula?

3 Write preparation instructions that could be included on the packaging of infant formula.

Key Terms

Sterilisers – used to ensure that no micro-organisms are on equipment used to feed the baby as this could make the baby ill

Express milk – to extract milk from the breast so it can be stored and used later

Dietary aims and goals: Weaning

What will I learn?

- **When a baby usually starts weaning**
- **How to introduce solid foods**
- **The range of weaning foods available**

Weaning starts when the baby is showing signs that they are not satisfied on just a milk feed.

When to start weaning

Usual signs are that the baby:

- Is still hungry after a milk feed
- Wakes up hungry before the next feed is due
- Can co-ordinate their eyes, hands and mouth so that they can look at the food, pick it up and put it in their mouth, without help.

Weaning – the gradual introduction of solid foods into the baby's diet

Department of Health guidelines are that babies are introduced to solid food from 26 weeks (6 months). By this time, the supply of iron the baby was born with will be starting to run out so iron will need to be provided by the baby's diet.

Babies younger than six months are unable to properly digest food and have not developed the ability to swallow foods with a thick consistency. **Weaning** too early can also cause some **allergies**.

▶ **Solid food should be introduced from 6 months**

Key Fact

- Babies don't need three meals a day to begin with, so solid foods can be given at a convenient time, e.g. when the baby is not too tired.

The purpose of weaning

The main purpose of weaning is to get babies used to eating a wide range of solid foods and provide all the nutrients they need to grow. Weaning does have other functions though:

- It develops **fine motor skills** by handling cutlery, etc.
- It develops independence as babies can start to feed themselves.

▲ **As this child learns to hold a spoon and feed himself, he is developing his fine motor skills too**

Stages of weaning

Weaning usually happens in three main stages.

Stage 1 (from 6 months)

At this stage, milk is still the most important food. Food must be pureed to a smooth consistency similar to milk. A small amount should be given on a spoon usually before or halfway through the usual feed. Parents need to be patient because the baby has to get used to new tastes and textures as well as learning to swallow new foods. The baby may spit the food out or refuse to try it at first, so parents should persevere, but not force the baby to eat food they do not want.

Foods to try:

- Baby rice mixed with the baby's usual milk.
- Pureed fruit and vegetables.

- Give the child a soft spoon and feeding cup from about 6 months so they can practise feeding themselves.

Stage 2 (about 7–9 months)

This is the time to increase the range of foods being offered, although the food must still be pureed at first, progressing to mashed, as the baby gets used to more variety.

Foods to try:

- A wider selection of fruit and vegetables.
- Beans, lentils chicken and fish (no bones).
- Well-cooked egg yolk.

Stage 3 (9–12 months)

Lumpier foods can now be introduced as the baby will be able to cope with chewing and swallowing. Finger foods (e.g. breadsticks, slices of fruit and vegetables) can also be given to encourage the baby to be independent.

Foods to try:

- Foods with more lumps.
- Cheese and yogurt.
- Pasta.
- Bread.

Key Fact

- Honey should not be given to children under one year old. Honey has not been pasteurised (heat treated to kill bacteria) and may contain *clostridium botulinum*. These bacteria can cause a rare, but serious illness called infant botulism because the baby's intestines are not developed enough to fight off the infection. Infant botulism causes muscle weakness and breathing problems often needing treatment in hospital.

Foods to avoid

- Some foods should be avoided during weaning because they may cause harm to the baby or because they are not needed in a healthy diet.
- Salt should not be added because the baby's kidneys cannot get rid of it.
- Sugar can cause tooth decay and start to develop a preference for sweet foods.
- The baby could choke on whole nuts, so nuts must be chopped.
- Fatty and fried foods are difficult for the baby to digest and are not needed in the diet.
- Cows' milk can be given as a drink from 12 months. Before then, cows' milk can be used in small quantities mixed with other food, but breast milk or formula milk should be given as a drink.

▶ **Foods to avoid when weaning**

▼ **Babies enjoy feeding themselves**

Tips for success

In order to make the process of weaning go smoothly, parents should try to make mealtimes an enjoyable experience, without worrying about the mess. If the baby is able to enjoy touching the food and attempt to feed themself, they are more likely to try different foods. Plenty of time for eating is needed, especially at first. Rushing or forcing the baby could lead to problems later on, so it is best to go at the baby's pace and stop when they have had enough.

Hot food must be cooled and tested before giving it to the baby and the baby should never be left unsupervised when eating in case they choke.

Weaning foods

There is a wide range of commercially prepared baby foods suitable for weaning when parents are unable to make their own food. These are quick, easy to use, and convenient when away from the home. The ingredients and nutritional value are clearly labelled, so parents know what they are giving to the baby. However, these foods are more expensive than homemade versions and there may be wastage if the baby only has a small amount.

▲ **Ready-made baby food**

Activities

1 Try a range of baby food for different ages and comment on the flavour and texture.

2 Design a new recipe for a savoury or sweet baby food. Draw the packaging, including all the information someone purchasing the food would want to know.

Summary

- Weaning should be done slowly so the baby's digestive system can develop.
- Weaning should start at around 6 months.
- Salt must never be added to weaning foods because the baby's kidneys cannot process it.
- Food for weaning should be bland to start with and stronger flavours introduced slowly.
- Food should be pureed until smooth at first and more texture added as the baby gets used to solid food.

Prove it!

1 Describe the three stages of weaning.

2 Why should new foods be introduced gradually?

3 There are some foods that should not be given during weaning. Identify these foods and explain why they are not suitable.

4 Compare the advantages and disadvantages of homemade and commercially prepared baby food.

Dietary aims and goals: Feeding young children

What will I learn?

- **How to encourage children to eat healthily**

By the time they are about a year old, babies are usually eating the same food as the rest of the family. They should be having three meals a day with healthy snacks in between if they are hungry. This is the best time to develop healthy eating habits that will, hopefully, remain into adulthood. Children like the food they get used to, so it is best to follow the appropriate healthy eating guidelines from a very young age. Children will develop their own likes and dislikes and these should be respected with suitable alternatives being offered. However, children's tastes do change over time, so foods that have been rejected should be tried again another time.

Carry out research into the variety and cost of equipment for feeding young children. You could include highchairs, bibs, cutlery, plates and cups.

Encouraging children to eat

Children need to be taught to develop good eating habits. Many children happily eat a wide range of foods, but most will go through periods of being fussy eaters. Tips to encourage children to eat well include:

Set a good example. Children learn by copying what they see, so they need to be shown to eat a wide variety of healthy foods.

2 **Eat as a family if possible, with the child having the same food as everyone else so they can develop social skills.**

Encourage children to feed themselves by providing suitable plates, bowls and cutlery and by making the food easy to eat.

Present food attractively so it is appealing to eat.

Give small portions and offer more when it is finished. A large plateful can be overwhelming.

Get children involved in choosing and preparing meals. They are more likely to eat food if they have been involved.

Do not use food as a punishment or reward or bribe; for example, sweets after finishing vegetables, as this gives the message that healthy foods are something to be endured rather than enjoyed.

Do not give too many snacks between meals.

Do not make a fuss if the child refuses to eat. Healthy children will not starve themselves and refusing to eat may be about seeking attention and testing boundaries, or they may just not be hungry. If the child is active and gaining weight, then they are probably eating enough for their needs.

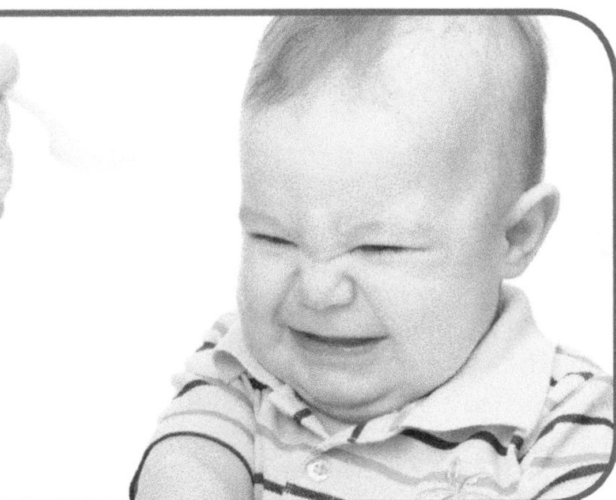

Summary

- Mealtimes are an important time for young children. The habits they acquire in early childhood are likely to stay with them for the rest of their lives.
- Meals are a good opportunity for children to learn and practise fine manipulative and social skills.
- It is normal for children to be fussy about foods at times, but this should be ignored as paying attention is likely to make it worse.

Activity

Plan a day's meals for a young child. Give reasons for your choice. Use a nutritional analysis program to compare your menu to the nutritional requirements for a child.

Prove it!

1 What advice would you give to a parent whose child was refusing to eat?

2 Why do you think there has been an increase in childhood obesity?

Special dietary needs

What will I learn?

- **The types of special dietary needs children may have**
- **How these needs can be met**

Children may have special dietary requirements for health or other reasons. Some may have a food allergy or diabetes, which means their food intake must be carefully monitored. Children may also have to follow a special diet for religious, cultural or environmental reasons.

Food allergies and intolerances

Food intolerance is an unpleasant reaction to a food, which happens every time the product is consumed. This may be because the body is unable to digest a particular food, for example lactose, which is the sugar found in milk.

A food **allergy** is a reaction by the body's immune system to eating a particular food. Symptoms include rashes, eczema, vomiting, diarrhoea, cramps, wheezing and difficulty breathing. In rare cases, a food can cause **anaphylaxis**. Anaphylaxis is a serious condition where breathing becomes restricted and parts of the body (e.g. the mouth and throat) swell. It can cause death very quickly, so urgent medical help is needed.

The food the child is allergic to must be avoided and food labels need to be carefully checked for ingredients. Many children grow out of food allergies as they get older, but professional advice should be sought before attempting to reintroduce foods that have previously caused a reaction.

There are also medical conditions or diseases which mean children may not be able to eat certain foods. **Coeliac disease**, for instance, is a condition where the body cannot digest **gluten**, a protein found in wheat and some other cereals. The only way to control this disease is to avoid all products containing gluten, including bread, pasta, cakes and biscuits. Special gluten-free products are available in supermarkets, but again care needs to be taken with checking food labelling if a child is known to have coeliac disease.

Diabetes

Diabetes is a condition where the body is unable to produce enough **insulin**. Insulin is a **hormone** that controls the amount of glucose (a type of sugar) in the blood. People with undiagnosed diabetes often feel very thirsty, tired and lose weight quickly.

There are two types of diabetes. Type 1 is most common in children and is treated with insulin injections and by following a healthy diet. Blood glucose levels need to be tested regularly and the amount of food or insulin adjusted accordingly. Otherwise the child should be able to lead a normal lifestyle. Type 2 diabetes is more likely to be found in older people and those who are overweight. It can be controlled by following a healthy diet.

Key Facts

- Children who are known to have a severe reaction to an allergen may be prescribed an **epipen**, which contains an injection of adrenaline and is given to reverse the symptoms of anaphylaxis.
- The most common foods causing allergies are: peanuts, soya, tree nuts, wheat and gluten, cows' milk and its products, shellfish, eggs and fish.
- About 1 in 700–1000 children under the age of 17 has diabetes. Of these 97% have type 1.

If you are answering an exam question about special diets, remember that the information about nutrition and healthy eating may apply too.

Vegetarian and vegan diets

There are many reasons people choose to follow a **vegetarian** or **vegan** diet. For example:

- Animal welfare: objections to the way animals are farmed or slaughtered.
- Environmental: meat production is expensive in terms of money and land compared with crops.
- Health: some animal products are high in saturated fat, which is linked to heart disease and other health conditions.
- Some religious groups also follow a vegetarian diet.

There are several different types of vegetarians. One of the most common are lacto-vegetarians who avoid eating meat, poultry or fish, but will eat dairy products and eggs. Vegans do not eat or use any animal products at all.

It is possible for a child to have a healthy diet as a vegetarian or vegan, but good nutritional knowledge and careful planning are needed to ensure that all the nutrients are provided. A vegan diet can be high in fibre and therefore very filling, making it harder for the child to eat enough nutrients, so supplements may be needed.

Religion and food choice

Many religions have dietary rules that affect food choice. It is important to be aware of these rules when working with children, for example in a nursery, as the child is unlikely on their own to be able to identify foods that they should not eat.

The most common food choices are shown below:

Religion	Foods to avoid
Islam	Pork, fish without scales, shellfish and meat which is not **halal**.
Hinduism	Beef. Many Hindus are vegetarian.
Judaism	Pork, fish without scales, shellfish and meat that is not **kosher**. Meat and dairy products cannot be cooked or eaten together.
Sikhism	Beef.
Buddhism	Many Buddhists are vegetarian as the religion prohibits killing.

Prove it!

1 **What nutrients are contained in:**

a) **Meat?**

b) **Dairy products?**

2 **What alternatives to these foods should a vegetarian or vegan child be given to ensure they have all the nutrients they need?**

3 **Why is it important to know about the special dietary requirements children may have?**

Child Study

Find out what foods your study child eats over several days. Comment on how healthy their diet is and how it may affect their development.

Do they have any special diet?

Ask the parents if they are a fussy eater and how they overcome it.

Activity

Investigate the range of foods available for children with a food allergy or intolerance.

Allergy – abnormal reaction to a substance that is usually harmless

Vegetarian – a person who excludes meat, poultry and fish from the diet; some also do not eat eggs

Vegan – a person who excludes all animal products from the diet

Food safety

What will I learn?

- **The most common causes of food poisoning**
- **The importance of good hygiene practices when preparing food**

Food must be carefully stored, prepared and cooked to ensure that it is safe to eat. This is particularly important for babies and young children as they are more vulnerable to infection than adults because their immune systems are immature.

Key Facts

- Bacteria can stay alive on our hands for up to three hours.
- Even after washing, bacteria can be found under nails and jewellery.

How does food poisoning occur?

Bacteria need warmth, moisture, food and time to grow. In the right conditions, they will multiply rapidly and are hard to detect because they usually cannot be seen or smelled.

Food poisoning is caused when **pathogenic** bacteria grow in food that is then consumed. High-risk foods are those that bacteria grow on easily, for example meat and poultry, dairy products, eggs and shellfish. However, most food can harbour harmful bacteria if good hygiene rules are not followed.

Key Facts

The main causes of food poisoning are:

- Undercooking
- Poor personal hygiene
- Food being stored at the wrong temperature, e.g. chilled food not refrigerated properly, or hot food not kept hot enough
- **Cross-contamination**.

Symptoms of food poisoning

The most common symptoms of food poisoning are vomiting and diarrhoea. They may begin anywhere from one hour to five days after eating the contaminated food. People with food poisoning need to rest and drink plenty of water. This is particularly important in young children who can become dehydrated very quickly. Medical help should be sought if the symptoms are severe or persist.

Activity

Identify the food safety risks in the picture on the right.

Preventing food poisoning

Good hygiene is vital to prevent food poisoning. Following these simple rules should ensure that food is safe to eat.

Personal hygiene:

- Wash hands thoroughly after using the toilet and before and after preparing and eating food.
- Cover cuts with a waterproof dressing.
- Never cough or sneeze on food.
- Wear clean, protective clothing.
- Tie long hair back.

Kitchen hygiene:

- Ensure that all surfaces and equipment are thoroughly clean, particularly after handling raw meat.
- Use separate chopping boards for raw meat, vegetables, etc.
- Ensure that dishcloths, tea towels, etc., are clean and changed regularly.
- Empty waste bins regularly and clean them frequently.

Storing and preparing food

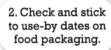

1. Follow storage instructions
2. Check and stick to use-by dates on food packaging.
3. The temperature of a fridge should be between 1 and 5°C and a freezer should be –18°C
4. Store high-risk foods in the fridge, with raw food at the bottom and cooked food above.
5. Cover or wrap all food.
6. Defrost frozen food completely before cooking, unless the food label says it can be cooked from frozen.
7. Never re-freeze food that has begun to thaw.
8. Make sure food is piping hot all the way through.

Key Terms

Pathogenic – harmful

Cross contamination – occurs when bacteria get into food products from people, surfaces, equipment or other food, this is especially dangerous if the food is not going to be cooked before eating.

Prove it!

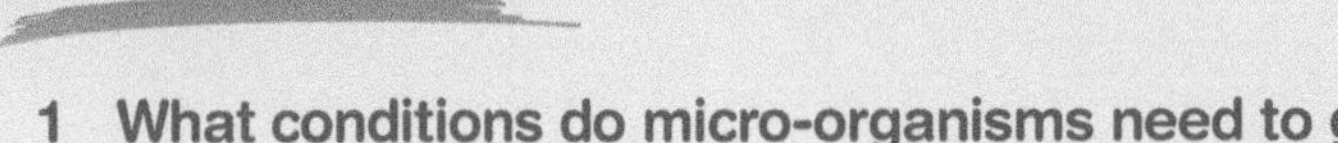

1 What conditions do micro-organisms need to grow?

2 Explain how following each of the rules above will help to prevent food poisoning.

Examination questions

1. Healthy eating is extremely important for an expectant mother. Complete the following chart. (6)

Nutrient	*Function in the diet*	*Example of food*
Protein	Growth and development	Fish
Iron		
Folic acid		
Calcium		

Think about advantages for the mother as well as the baby.

2. Many mothers choose to breastfeed during the first months of a baby's life.
   a) What is *colostrum*? (1)
   b) What is lactation? (1)
   c) Give **four** advantages of breastfeeding. (4)
   d) Suggest **two** reasons why a mother may be unable to breastfeed her baby. (2)

3. If properly bottle-fed, a baby should thrive, grow and develop in the same way as a breastfed baby.
   a) Suggest **three** reasons a mother may choose to bottle-feed. (3)
   b) State **three** guidelines that should be followed when bottle-feeding. (3)

4. Weaning is the stage between the time babies drink only milk and that time when they eat solid foods.
   a) Weaning can be divided into **three** stages. Identify the age at which each stage occurs. (3)
      (i) Stage 1
      (ii) Stage 2
      (iii) Stage 3
   b) Suggest **four** guidelines that should be followed during the **first** stage of weaning. (4)
   c) Identify **two** pieces of equipment and explain how they make self-feeding easier for a young child during the second stage of weaning. (2)

This question is about things that help the child to feed themselves, not the parents feeding them.

5. Eating a well-balanced diet is important for a young child.

   a) What is meant by a *balanced diet*? (2)
   b) Explain why it is important for a child to eat a well-balanced diet. (4)

This needs more detail than 'healthy' for 2 marks.

c) A recent survey found that one in twenty children refuses to eat, which can cause great anxiety. Suggest ways in which this problem can be overcome. (6)

Think about how to make food fun.

6. a) To ensure a child's health and safety there are certain foods a parent should avoid giving their child. Complete the chart below, giving reasons why these foods should be avoided. The first one has been completed for you. (4)

Food	*Reason to avoid*
Salt	Can affect a child's kidneys
Nuts	
High fibre food	
Sugary foods	
Uncooked eggs	

b) Explain what is meant by the following conditions and suggest how they may be controlled through diet:
(i) Type 2 diabetes (2)
(ii) Coeliac disease. (2)

This is a two-part question. Often candidates miss out the second part and can only get half the marks.

7. Healthy eating in childhood is very important for development.
a) Complete the chart below. (3)

Vitamin	*Function*	*Food source*
Vitamin A		Butter, carrots
Vitamin B	Releases energy from food	
Vitamin C		Citrus fruits

b) Give **one** reason why a child might become obese. (1)
c) Suggest **three** risks of a child being obese. (3)

8. Study the following diet given to a four year old:

Breakfast	*Scrambled egg and toast*	*Orange juice*
Mid-morning	Packet crisps	Blackcurrant squash
Lunch	Ham sandwich	Apple juice
Snack	Chocolate mini roll	Orange squash
Tea	Fish fingers, chips and peas	Strawberry milk shake

a) Name **one** food that will give the child energy. (1)
b) Name **one** food that will be used to help the child grow. (1)
c) Suggest how the menu may be improved to ensure a healthy balanced diet. Give reasons for your choices. (4)

Don't forget to say why your idea is better.

9. Milk is an essential part of a child's diet.
a) At what age can children drink cows' milk? (1)
b) Suggest **two** reasons why children should not be given cows' milk earlier. (2)
c) After six months, milk alone is insufficient for children. Suggest a reason. (1)
d) Name **two** nutrients found in milk that are important for a child's growth and development (2)
e) Suggest **two** ways a child may be encouraged to drink more milk. (2)

10. a) What is meant by the term *weaning*? (1)

b) Suggest **three** advantages to a parent/carer of using commercially prepared baby foods. (3)

c) Discuss the reasons for the different stages of weaning. (8)

Stage 1: by the age of 6 months the baby needs more nutrients than are in milk alone. At this stage the baby cannot chew, swallow or digest lumps so all food must be smooth but a thicker consistency than milk. Parents should start with very small quantities of bland foods so the baby gets used to the new experience. A wider variety of flavours and textures can be introduced slowly.

Stage 2: begins between 7 and 9 months. The baby is now able to chew, so more lumps and finger foods can be given. The baby should be encouraged to feed themselves as they need to become more independent. It is important not to worry about the mess at this stage. They should be given their own spoon, but will need help with feeding as well. If a new food is rejected, then it should be tried again at a later date.

Stage 3: by 9–12 months the baby can have the same meals as the rest of the family, although the food will still need to be mashed or cut into small pieces as the baby will not be able to manage larger pieces. As the amount of food the baby is eating increases, milk can be reduced. Cows' milk should not be given until after 12 months as the baby may not be able to digest it properly. Babies at this age should be given three meals a day with healthy snacks in between as they only have a small appetite.

This answer would get 6 marks. The stages are described and some reasons given. It could be improved by giving examples of foods that would be suitable and those that should be avoided.

11. Discuss factors which should be considered when feeding toddlers. (6)

Toddlers need to eat a healthy diet but often have small appetites and are easily distracted. Mealtimes need to be occasions that children look forward to so they will eat well. Children need routines, so regular mealtimes and eating the same meal together as a family will help them to develop good habits. (1) Providing small portions stops children becoming overwhelmed by too much on the plate as this might make them give up. (2) If food is colourful and attractively presented then it is more appealing to eat. (3) Toddlers also like to be independent so should be encouraged to feed themselves. (4) Children need a wide variety of foods to make sure they get all the nutrients they need. (5) Water and milk are good choices of drinks as fizzy and sugary drink can cause tooth decay. They also fill children up so they don't want to eat meals. (6)

This answer looks quite short, but if you look to see where the marks have been given, there are 6 points and each one has an explanation. 'Discuss' questions need more than just a list of suggestions. The answer shows understanding of toddlers' likes and knowledge of healthy eating.

12. Healthy eating habits should be established in early childhood. Discuss this statement. (10)

Children need a healthy diet to ensure they get all the nutrients they need to grow and develop properly. If they have a wide range of foods in sensible amounts, they should have the right proportions of nutrients. The eatwell plate is a good example of the type of balanced diet that most people should aim for. Children should be encouraged to eat three meals a day, with healthy snacks in between. They should aim for five or more portions of fruit and vegetables every day to make sure they get all the vitamins and minerals they need for growth and to prevent illnesses. Fruit and vegetables also contain fibre to prevent constipation. Main meals should contain protein which the child needs for growth, and enough carbohydrate to give the child energy to play. They also need calcium to develop strong bones and teeth while they are still growing.

Introduction shows you understand why healthy eating is important.

Show understanding of the different nutrients and why *children* need them (it doesn't matter what adults need for this question).

Children under 5 do not need to have reduced fat foods such as skimmed milk, because they need the fat to give them energy. However, high fat foods such as crisps and chips should be limited as they do not provide other valuable nutrients. Sweets and sugary drinks should only be given occasionally because of the risk of developing tooth decay. A diet which is high in fat, sugar and salt puts the child at greater risk of developing food-related illnesses as they get older. For example, too much fat and sugar can lead to obesity, heart disease and type 2 diabetes. Too much salt can lead to high blood pressure. All of these can result in reduced life expectancy.

Identify the problems caused by poor eating habits.

If a child gets used to eating healthy meals and snacks from a young age, they are more likely to continue to have a healthy diet in later life. If they are given the opportunity to try lots of different foods when they are young, they should be willing to eat a wide range as they get older. Bad habits are difficult to break so it is best to give healthy food as soon as a child begins weaning so that they don't develop a taste for foods which could do them harm if eaten in large quantities.

Make sure the end of your answer links back to the question.

This answer would get full marks because it contains all the relevant information in a logical order.

In high-mark questions like this you will be assessed on your ability to write clearly and follow rules of spelling, punctuation and grammar, so it is a good idea to plan before starting to write.

Preparation for pregnancy

What will I learn?

- **The factors to consider before becoming a parent**
- **The different methods of contraception available**
- **The importance of both partners being healthy before the woman becomes pregnant**

Becoming a parent involves a major life-change where couples need to prepare themselves emotionally, physically and financially. Therefore before deciding to have a baby there are a number of factors to consider before becoming pregnant.

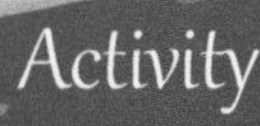

Activity

Produce a leaflet to be given to prospective new parents informing them of the changes to their lives that will occur when they become parents.

Parents' relationship

The decision to have a baby should be made jointly otherwise if a woman becomes pregnant and her partner does not want a child then there could be feelings of resentment and a lack of trust within the relationship. If the relationship is poor then having a baby in the hope that it will improve is not a suitable decision because it often makes the relationship deteriorate further.

Young couple discussing family matters and the possibility of having a baby

Babies are hard work and need a great deal of attention so couples need to consider whether the relationship they have with each other is stable. Are they able to support each other through the new experience of caring for a baby? Do they have the **maturity** to accept the **responsibility** of caring for another person?

Parents should be able to work together to bring up the baby and avoid having arguments and resentments over issues like money and a restricted social life. Couples need to allow time to adjust to each other within the relationship, and make sure they are both emotionally stable.

Changes in lifestyle

Babies are totally dependent on parents for their basic care needs, so it is important that they consider whether they are able to put the baby's needs before theirs. Parents will have less independence as it will not be possible to go out whenever they want as the baby's care needs to be considered. A visit to a friend or going shopping will require planning and packing the baby's equipment or arranging for a babysitter.

Parents need to think if they can change their way of life to meet the needs of a child. They need to be ready to support and enjoy a baby's development, not be resentful that the baby has taken over areas of their life.

Money

Couples will need to discuss whether they are financially stable to care for and support a child. Sacrifices may need to be made as it may be necessary for one parent to take a career break or give up work, which could mean having less income. This means any money has to stretch further, which can limit a couple's social life, holidays and hobbies.

Money may also not be available to purchase all the equipment needed for the baby and as the baby grows the costs will increase. Childcare costs could be an issue if the mother wants to return to work after the birth. Will they be able to afford the childcare costs as well as providing for the baby's needs? If parents are worried by money problems then the baby can also become emotionally affected by this.

Environment

Prospective parents need to consider whether their accommodation is suitable for the child:

- Does it have enough bedrooms?
- Is the environment safe, both inside and outside the home?
- Is it near facilities such as parks and schools?
- Is there enough space to grow?

When answering a question on the impact of parenthood on a couple's lives it is important to provide a balanced answer that includes the social, emotional and physical effects on their lives.

Summary

- Children are hard work and demand a lot of time, care, attention, commitment and money for many years.
- Children make many changes to people's lives so it is important that the decision to have children is well thought out and planned.

Prove it!

1. **Give some examples of the decisions and choices that a young couple would need to consider before having a baby.**
2. **Below are some possible ways a new baby can affect a couple's life. Write an explanation on each one explaining how this may happen.**
   - **Parents feel stressed.**
   - **Parents argue more frequently.**
   - **Parents happier than before.**
   - **Social life changes.**

Contraception

It is not a good idea to have a baby to prove you are grown up or to try to improve a relationship that is going through a difficult time. Sometimes pressure from friends or family affects a person's choice about having a baby. It is important that a baby is welcomed into a loving, caring family, therefore it may be necessary to delay having a baby until a good **nurturing environment** can be provided.

Method	Image	How it works	Advantages and disadvantages
Male condom		Placed over the penis to prevent sperm entering the vagina. 98% effective.	Purchased in chemists and supermarkets but free from Family Planning Clinics. These can protect both partners from contracting sexually transmitted infections (STIs) and AIDS. The condom may split or slip off if not put on correctly.
Female condom		Placed inside the vagina to prevent the sperm entering the vagina. 95% effective.	Can protect both partners from contracting STIs including AIDS. To work effectively the penis must be placed to enter the condom, not between the condom and vagina.
Diaphragm		Prevents sperm from meeting an egg by placing it as a barrier over the cervix. 92–95% effective.	Can be fiddly to use and must be fitted by a doctor the first time to check for correct size. Spermicide jelly or cream should also be used to make sure the sperm is made inactive and it must be kept in place for 6 hours after intercourse.
IUD **(Intrauterine device)**		Prevents the implantation of a fertilised egg. 98% effective.	Also known as the coil and must be inserted by a doctor. Once in place it works straight away and may be kept in the uterus for 3–10 years. Not suitable for all women and may cause painful, heavier periods.
IUS **(Intrauterine system)** **Mirena coil**		Prevents implantation of a fertilised egg and releases the hormone **progestogen** which prevents sperm from meeting an egg 99+% effective.	Must be inserted by a doctor, works immediately and prevents pregnancy for 5 years. Possible side effects include tender breasts and acne.

Part of the decision-making process about whether to have a baby, and when to get pregnant involves a discussion around **contraception**. This means the deliberate prevention of pregnancy.

Several methods of contraception are available and advice is provided by GPs and Family Planning Clinics on the most suitable type for each individual's needs.

Method	Image	How it works	Advantages and disadvantages
Contraceptive patch		A patch that releases **oestrogen** and progestogen and is placed on the buttocks, abdomen or arm once a week for 3 weeks. No patch on week 4. 99% effective.	Not affected by vomiting, diarrhoea or antibiotics.
Combined pill		Taken orally, it contains oestrogen and **progesterone** and stops the ovaries from releasing eggs. 100% effective.	Must be prescribed by the doctor and is suitable for healthy non-smokers. If taken 12 hours late or if suffering from vomiting or diarrhoea or taking antibiotics it becomes unreliable. Often reduces period pain.
Mini pill		Taken orally, it contains progesterone making it difficult for sperm to swim to meet the egg and prevents a fertilised egg being implanted. 99% effective.	Must be prescribed by the doctor. If taken more than 3 hours late or you are suffering from vomiting or diarrhoea it becomes unreliable. Can be used when breastfeeding. May cause irregular periods and does not work as well if the woman weighs more than 70kg.
Contraceptive implant		Slow release of progestogen which prevents the egg and sperm meeting due to the thickening of the cervical mucus. Implantation of the egg is also prevented. 99% effective.	The small implant is placed under the skin in the upper arm and can prevent pregnancy for up to 3 years. It may be difficult to remove and can cause side effects of headaches and weight gain. Fertility returns straightaway after the implant has been removed.
Contraceptive injection		Releases progestogen which prevents a woman from releasing an egg and thickens cervical mucus making it difficult for sperm to enter the uterus. 99% effective.	Must be given by a doctor and can last for 2–3 months. It may cause irregular bleeding, weight gain, tender breasts and acne. The hormone cannot be removed from the body so fertility can take one or two years to return to normal after the injections are stopped.

Natural methods of contraception

Natural methods of contraception are sometimes preferred by couples due to religious beliefs but it is important that both partners understand how these methods work. No side effects or chemicals are involved but the effectiveness is unreliable especially if periods are irregular.

One method involves the woman keeping daily records of her temperature and cervical secretions. These allow the woman to identify when she is most fertile so that intercourse is avoided during this time. The woman's temperature rises after **ovulation** and cervical secretions change in texture and amount during different times of the menstrual cycle.

The second natural method is termed the 'withdrawal method' and involves the male removing the penis before ejaculation. Semen can leak at anytime during intercourse making this an unreliable method.

Saying no to intercourse is 100% effective. This is called abstention.

Sterilisation

A permanent form of contraception is **sterilisation** and should only be considered by women who do not want more children. Advice and counselling is important prior to the procedure as it is generally considered to be irreversible.

For women, the sterilisation process involves the fallopian tubes being cut or sealed so that the egg is unable to travel through the tubes to meet the sperm.

Key Fact

- Of 100 couples who use natural family planning methods each year, anywhere from 1 to 25 will become pregnant.

Key Terms

Contraception – *prevention of pregnancy*

Oestrogen – *female sex hormone*

Progesterone – *female sex hormone*

Ovulation – *release of mature egg from the ovary*

Female sterilisation

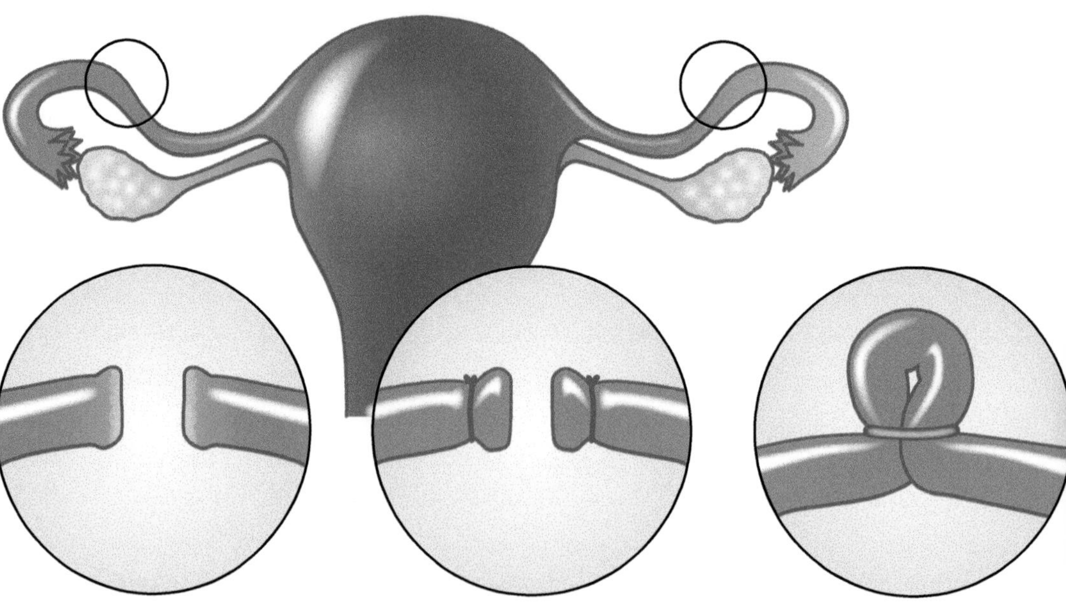

Cauterised

a) A small portion of the fallopian tube is divided and sealed with heat

Tied and cut

b) The fallopian tube is cut and tied; 3–4cm of the tube is destroyed

Banded

c) A small loop of the fallopian tube is pulled through a silicone ring then clamped shut

Key Facts

- On the whole, female sterilisation is more than 99% effective. There is a small possibility that the blocked tubes can rejoin immediately or years later but only one woman in 200 will become pregnant in her lifetime after having it done.
- Condoms should be used as protection against sexually transmitted infections, as female or male sterilisation does not protect against STIs.

Male sterilisation involves the sperm tube being cut or blocked so that it is not possible for the sperm to pass through to the testes. Ejaculated semen therefore contains no sperm.

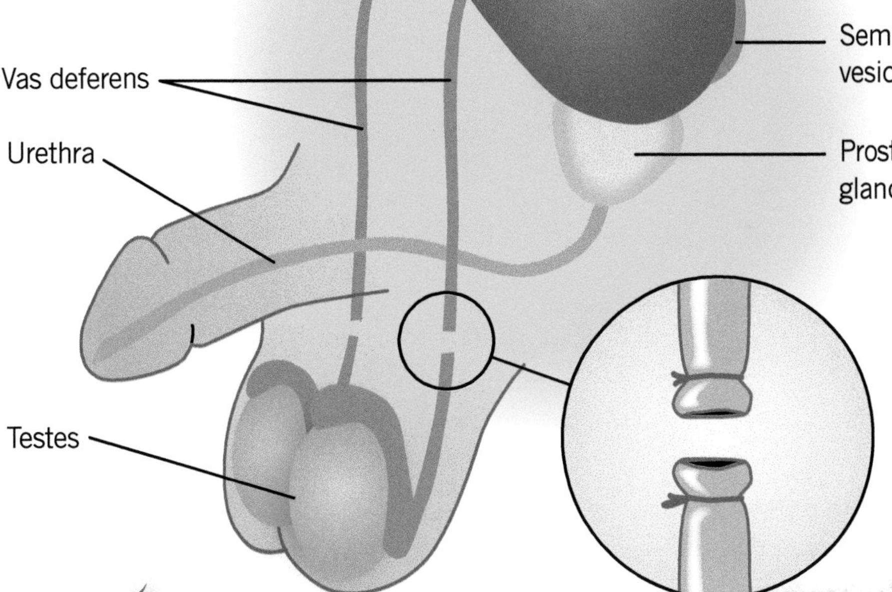

Male sterilisation

The tubes that carry sperm from the testicles to the penis are cut, blocked or sealed with heat

Activities

1. Produce a PowerPoint or a web page giving teenagers information about the different types of contraception, to include how they work and their effectiveness.
2. Write a magazine article outlining natural methods of birth control.

Emergency contraception

Emergency contraception is available if unprotected sex has taken place or if there is a strong risk that the normal form of contraception has failed. Emergency pills – usually called 'the morning after pill' – must be taken within 72 hours of unprotected intercourse. The pill works by starting a period so that the uterus lining comes away preventing the egg from being implanted.

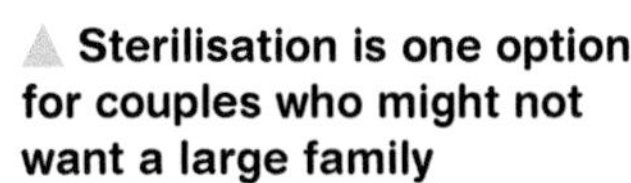

Sterilisation is one option for couples who might not want a large family

Summary

- Contraception must be used correctly if it is to prevent a pregnancy.
- Choice of contraception depends on personal preference, religious belief, health, age and if it is required for long- or short-term use.
- It is important that the morning after pill is only used in an emergency and not used as a regular form of contraception.

Pre-conceptual care

To make sure the baby will be as healthy as possible from the very first moment of conception, it is important that for at least 3 months before conception women should prepare their bodies for pregnancy. Men should also be in good physical health. This is termed **pre-conceptual care**.

Contraception

Discuss stopping contraception, e.g. stop taking pill, remove IUD as the return of fertility varies according to the type of contraception used.

Drugs

Women should avoid using illegal substances to increase fertility. Some drugs may prevent the ovulation process and when taken prior to conception could lead to a higher risk of **birth defects**. In men, drugs have been found to lower sperm count and reduce sperm mobility while increasing the number of abnormal sperm.

Genetic counselling

If there is a concern about **hereditary diseases** such as **cystic fibrosis**, haemophilia or sickle-cell anaemia, then couples should have genetic counselling.

Immunity

Important to check if the woman is immune to **Rubella** and Polio. If the mother becomes infected with Rubella during pregnancy it can cause **abnormalities** in the unborn baby.

Alcohol

Should generally be avoided as this can affect fertility by reducing the amount of sperm in men, and disrupting the ovulation and menstrual cycles in women.

Sexually transmitted infections

STIs should be checked for, especially Chlamydia, which can cause blocked fallopian tubes. Gonorrhoea can block sperm ducts and fallopian tubes reducing fertility. During pregnancy syphilis can pass from mother to baby and can cause blindness, deafness and even death.

Exercise

To ensure the mother is fit and healthy before and during pregnancy she should take some exercise regularly.

Diet

It is important to eat a generally healthy diet, but in particular one that is rich in **folic acid** to prevent spina bifida where the brain and spinal cord fail to develop properly. Folic acid is a B vitamin and is found in broccoli, leafy green vegetables, wholegrain cereals and wholemeal bread. It may also be taken as a supplement in tablet form.

Smoking

Should be stopped as the cigarette smoke and **toxins** damage the unborn baby's health. This also includes avoiding passive smoking from any smoky atmospheres. A study has shown that compounds in cigarette smoke affect the ovaries and contribute to infertility.

Activities

Pre-conceptual care discussions should include information from both the male and female perspective. Design an information leaflet or fact sheet for prospective parents outlining the importance of pre-conceptual care.

Fathers

To produce good quality sperm men need to be healthy. Smoking and drinking alcohol should be given up and they should eat a healthy diet. This will support and encourage their partners and improve their own well-being.

Key Terms

Pre-conceptual care – changes a woman should make in her life before pregnancy

Rubella – German measles

Folic acid – vitamin B taken to prevent spina bifida

Medication

If the mother has a medical condition that involves taking medicines (for instance diabetes, epilepsy or heart disease), then she needs to visit her GP to discuss an adjustment to her medication. This would avoid the baby being harmed, as it is possible for medicines to cross the placenta and reach the baby.

Key Facts

- Folic acid has a 72% protective effect against spina bifida but should be taken before conception to make sure it is effective in the first stages of growth.
- In 2010 it was found that 26% of mothers in the UK smoked at some point in the 12 months before or during their pregnancy, only 54% of them gave up at some point before the birth.
- The likelihood of developing gestational diabetes is reduced by 55% if the mother regularly exercises before pregnancy.

Summary

- Pre-conceptual care involves a woman preparing herself physically, socially and emotionally before becoming pregnant.
- Couples can increase their chances of becoming parents if they have a healthy lifestyle.

Prove it!

1. What do you understand by the term pre-conceptual care?
2. Why is folic acid important in pre-conceptual care?

Foetal development

What will I learn?

- **The process of conception**
- **Details of the male and female reproductive systems**
- **Growth and development of the foetus**
- **Factors that affect the development of the foetus**

The human reproduction process, when a baby is created, requires two types of sex cells, the female egg and the male sperm. The process therefore involves both the male and female reproductive systems, which are different in shape and structure but are able to make, nourish and transport either the egg or the sperm.

Key Terms

Vagina – muscular tube that leads to the uterus

Cervix – neck of the uterus

Uterus – womb, place to hold the foetus

Ovaries – produce egg cells

Fallopian tubes – tubes connecting the ovaries to the uterus

Ovum – single female egg

Menstrual cycle – monthly cycle in females causing some blood to flow from the vagina

Conception – egg is fertilised and implants itself in the uterus

Embryo – name given to fertilised egg until 8 weeks old

Foetus – name for unborn baby from 8 to 28 weeks

Female reproductive system

Fallopian tube (oviduct) – Carries the **ovum** (egg) from the ovary into the uterus.
Uterus – Pear-shaped organ where the baby develops, it enlarges as the baby grows.
Ovary – Glands where the ova (eggs) are produced, usually one each month.
Vagina – Passage that allows menstrual flow to leave the body, sperm is placed at the top of the vagina during intercourse.
Cervix – Entrance to the womb, this stretches during labour.

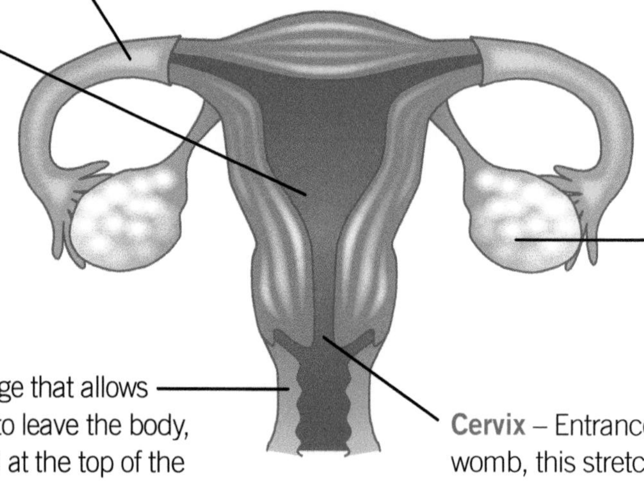

Menstrual cycle

The **menstrual cycle** is the process where the uterus is prepared to receive a fertilised egg, and then the thickened uterus lining detaches if the egg is not fertilised.

Menstruation usually begins between 10 and 17 years of age and the average cycle takes place over 28 days. However, this can be different for each individual as the cycle is affected by factors such as stress, diet and age.

The first half of the cycle begins by the uterus lining thickening to prepare for the implantation of a fertilised egg. At approximately day 14 of a usual cycle, the egg is released from the ovary and travels down the fallopian tube. Hormone levels rise. When the egg is not fertilised hormone levels drop and the uterus lining breaks down. This is removed from the body through the menstrual bleed which lasts for about 4 to 6 days.

Male reproductive system

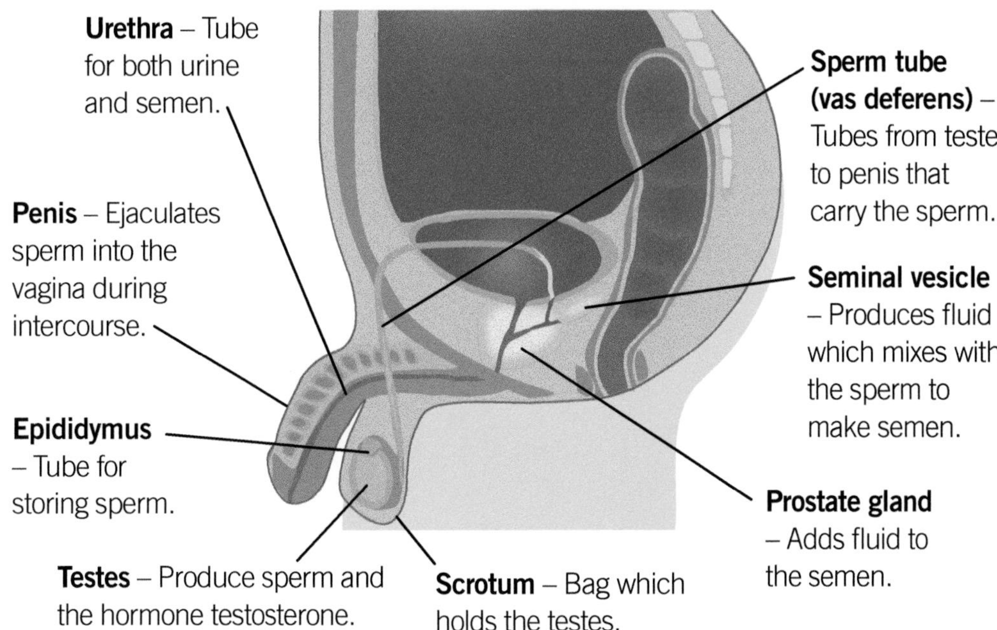
Urethra – Tube for both urine and semen.
Penis – Ejaculates sperm into the vagina during intercourse.
Epididymus – Tube for storing sperm.
Testes – Produce sperm and the hormone testosterone.
Scrotum – Bag which holds the testes.
Sperm tube (vas deferens) – Tubes from testes to penis that carry the sperm.
Seminal vesicle – Produces fluid which mixes with the sperm to make semen.
Prostate gland – Adds fluid to the semen.

Revision Tip

Diagrams could be provided in an examination and you will be expected to label them accurately. So it's a good idea to practise this.

Conception

During sexual intercourse **sperm** from the male meets an **egg** from the female and a baby is conceived. This is the process of **conception**, which begins by semen being ejaculated into the vagina. Sperm in the semen are shaped like tadpoles with a head and a long tail which allows them to swim towards the fallopian tube to meet the egg. When this happens only one sperm will **fertilise** the egg. This then continues to the uterus dividing into cells as it travels along the fallopian tube.

The fertilised egg reaches the uterus where it will become implanted in the prepared uterus lining. An **embryo** begins to form, which becomes a **foetus** after 8 weeks.

Activities

1. Make a set of Domino cards on the functions of the male and female reproductive organs, which can then be used as a revision game.

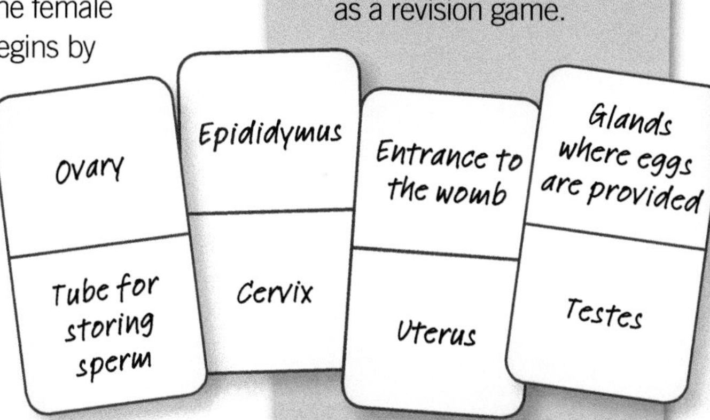
Ovary
Tube for storing sperm
Epididymus
Cervix
Entrance to the womb
Uterus
Glands where eggs are provided
Testes

2. Produce a leaflet explaining the menstrual cycle for 10–11 year olds.

Summary

- Ovulation is the process where the egg is released into the fallopian tube.
- Sperm meets the egg in the fallopian tube and fertilisation takes place.

Prove it!

1. Describe the menstrual cycle.
2. Describe how conception takes place.
3. Describe the function of the following:
   a) Fallopian tubes. b) Uterus. c) Ovaries.

Multiple pregnancies

If the fertilised egg splits into two parts then each part develops into a baby which becomes identical twins. In the uterus they will share the same placenta.

Non-identical (fraternal) twins are formed when two eggs are fertilised by two different sperm. They each have their own placenta.

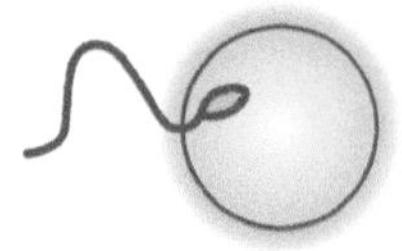

1 egg +
1 sperm

2 eggs +
2 sperms

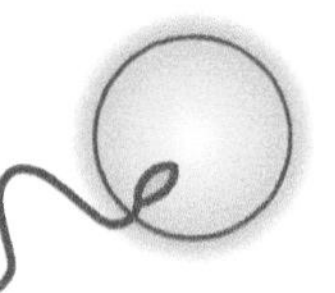

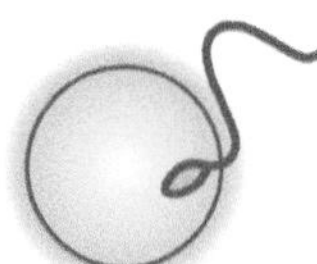

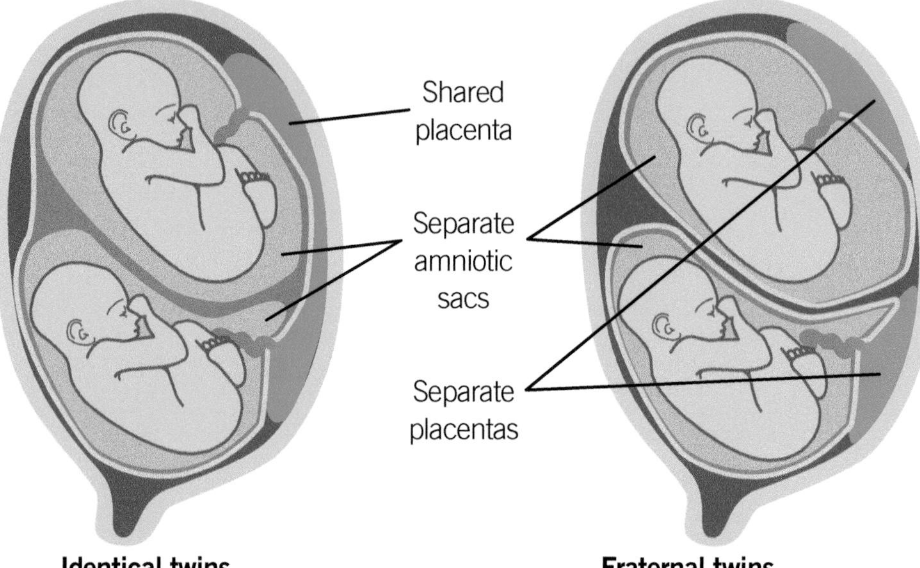

Infertility

Sometimes conception does not happen for many reasons. This is termed **infertility** and could be caused by problems with the male or female.

Causes of infertility

- Ovulation does not take place so no eggs are produced by the ovaries
- Low sperm count due to contracting mumps or medical conditions
- Cervical mucus limits the sperms' movement as it is too thick
- Cancer treatment can make male or female infertile
- Fallopian tubes are blocked so sperm cannot reach the egg
- Sexually transmitted infections – chlamydia and gonorrhoea

Key Facts

- Latest data on multiple births in the UK shows twins and triplets are becoming more common. Around 98.5% of all multiple births in the UK are twins and in 2011, 12652 women gave birth to twins in the UK.
- Almost half of all twins are born prematurely and/or have low birth weight. Full term for twins is considered 37 weeks and low birth weight below 2.5kg (5.5lbs). The average time between the delivery of the first and second twin is 17 minutes.

▶ **Conceiving twins**

Key Term

Infertility – inability to conceive a baby

Key Facts

- One in seven couples in the UK – approximately 3.5 million people are affected by fertility problems.
- Every year in the UK there are 31,000 IVF cycles with 10,000 IVF babies born each year. 25% cycles are done within the NHS whilst 75% are done privately, with couples paying privately for their own treatment.

Possible signs of pregnancy

- Period is missed.
- Sickness, which can occur any time of the day even though it is called 'morning sickness'.
- Metallic taste in the mouth.
- May need to pass urine more frequently.
- Constipation possible.
- More vaginal mucus is discharged.
- Breasts are tender and the nipples and areola around them become darker.
- Tiredness occurs more frequently with possible fainting spells.
- May crave new foods and dislike foods usually eaten.

NOT PREGNANT

PREGNANT

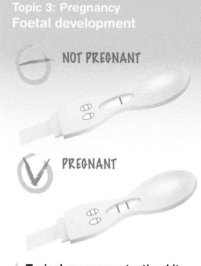

Typical pregnancy testing kit; several different brands are available

To confirm pregnancy, testing kits may be purchased from chemists or supermarkets; however, it is important that the instructions are followed closely to make sure the result is accurate. Testing can also be done by a GP or Family Planning clinic.

As soon as pregnancy is confirmed an appointment is made for the woman to attend her GP antenatal clinic where her care will be planned. One task will be to calculate the **Estimated Delivery Date** (EDD). This is done by adding 9 months and 7 days to the first day of the last period, but a GP will use special charts to work out the most likely date. A typical pregnancy is 40 weeks but could be anywhere between 38 and 42 weeks.

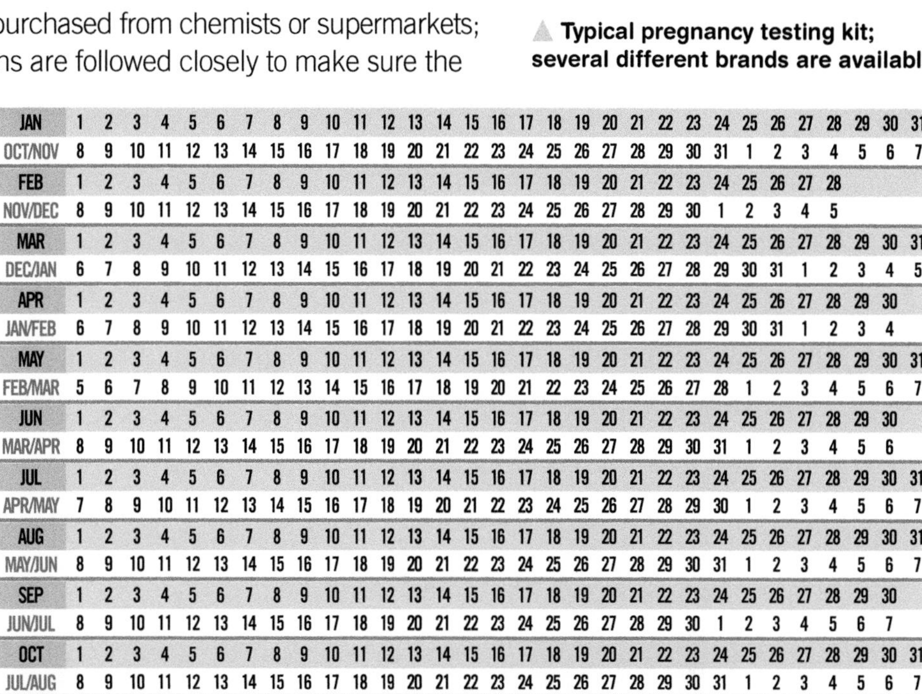

JAN	1	2	3	4	5	6	7	8	9	10	11	12	13	14	15	16	17	18	19	20	21	22	23	24	25	26	27	28	29	30	31
OCT/NOV	8	9	10	11	12	13	14	15	16	17	18	19	20	21	22	23	24	25	26	27	28	29	30	31	1	2	3	4	5	6	7
FEB	1	2	3	4	5	6	7	8	9	10	11	12	13	14	15	16	17	18	19	20	21	22	23	24	25	26	27	28			
NOV/DEC	8	9	10	11	12	13	14	15	16	17	18	19	20	21	22	23	24	25	26	27	28	29	30	1	2	3	4	5			
MAR	1	2	3	4	5	6	7	8	9	10	11	12	13	14	15	16	17	18	19	20	21	22	23	24	25	26	27	28	29	30	31
DEC/JAN	6	7	8	9	10	11	12	13	14	15	16	17	18	19	20	21	22	23	24	25	26	27	28	29	30	31	1	2	3	4	5
APR	1	2	3	4	5	6	7	8	9	10	11	12	13	14	15	16	17	18	19	20	21	22	23	24	25	26	27	28	29	30	
JAN/FEB	6	7	8	9	10	11	12	13	14	15	16	17	18	19	20	21	22	23	24	25	26	27	28	29	30	31	1	2	3	4	
MAY	1	2	3	4	5	6	7	8	9	10	11	12	13	14	15	16	17	18	19	20	21	22	23	24	25	26	27	28	29	30	31
FEB/MAR	5	6	7	8	9	10	11	12	13	14	15	16	17	18	19	20	21	22	23	24	25	26	27	28	1	2	3	4	5	6	7
JUN	1	2	3	4	5	6	7	8	9	10	11	12	13	14	15	16	17	18	19	20	21	22	23	24	25	26	27	28	29	30	
MAR/APR	8	9	10	11	12	13	14	15	16	17	18	19	20	21	22	23	24	25	26	27	28	29	30	31	1	2	3	4	5	6	
JUL	1	2	3	4	5	6	7	8	9	10	11	12	13	14	15	16	17	18	19	20	21	22	23	24	25	26	27	28	29	30	31
APR/MAY	7	8	9	10	11	12	13	14	15	16	17	18	19	20	21	22	23	24	25	26	27	28	29	30	1	2	3	4	5	6	7
AUG	1	2	3	4	5	6	7	8	9	10	11	12	13	14	15	16	17	18	19	20	21	22	23	24	25	26	27	28	29	30	31
MAY/JUN	8	9	10	11	12	13	14	15	16	17	18	19	20	21	22	23	24	25	26	27	28	29	30	31	1	2	3	4	5	6	7
SEP	1	2	3	4	5	6	7	8	9	10	11	12	13	14	15	16	17	18	19	20	21	22	23	24	25	26	27	28	29	30	
JUN/JUL	8	9	10	11	12	13	14	15	16	17	18	19	20	21	22	23	24	25	26	27	28	29	30	1	2	3	4	5	6	7	
OCT	1	2	3	4	5	6	7	8	9	10	11	12	13	14	15	16	17	18	19	20	21	22	23	24	25	26	27	28	29	30	31
JUL/AUG	8	9	10	11	12	13	14	15	16	17	18	19	20	21	22	23	24	25	26	27	28	29	30	31	1	2	3	4	5	6	7
NOV	1	2	3	4	5	6	7	8	9	10	11	12	13	14	15	16	17	18	19	20	21	22	23	24	25	26	27	28	29	30	
AUG/SEP	8	9	10	11	12	13	14	15	16	17	18	19	20	21	22	23	24	25	26	27	28	29	30	31	1	2	3	4	5	6	
DEC	1	2	3	4	5	6	7	8	9	10	11	12	13	14	15	16	17	18	19	20	21	22	23	24	25	26	27	28	29	30	31
SEP/OCT	7	8	9	10	11	12	13	14	15	16	17	18	19	20	21	22	23	24	25	26	27	28	29	30	1	2	3	4	5	6	7

An example of a chart that may be used by GPs in antenatal clinics to calculate the Estimated Date of Delivery (EDD)

Summary

- A fertilised egg contains 23 pairs of chromosomes.
- Identical twins have the same genes, are the same gender and look exactly alike.
- Non-identical twins have different genes, look different and one could be a boy and one a girl.

Key Facts

- The average duration of a regular pregnancy is 40 weeks. In a twin pregnancy, the average is 37 weeks, for triplets 34 and quadruplets 32 weeks.
- Only 58% of women have given birth by the time they're 40 weeks pregnant.

Prove it!

1. **Describe the causes of infertility.**
2. **State four possible signs of pregnancy.**
3. **Explain the differences between identical and non-identical twins.**

Foetal development

Pregnancy is divided into three **trimesters**. The first trimester is between weeks 1 and 14 and it is during this period that the development of the foetus can be affected by drugs, smoking alcohol and medicines.

The second trimester is from 14 to 28 weeks and the third from 28 weeks to delivery.

When the egg is fertilised by the sperm it becomes a **zygote** which divides into cells and after 7 days implants itself into the thickened uterus lining.

Weeks 3–5

The spinal column and nervous system form, liver, kidneys and intestines take shape whilst the heart begins to beat with the embryo's own blood. The eyes, legs and hands begin to develop. The embryo is about the size of an apple seed.

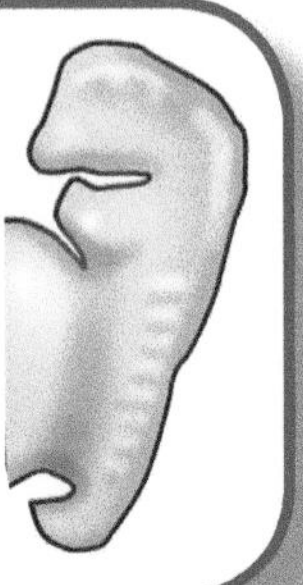

Weeks 6–7

Brain waves are present, the mouth, lips, eyelids and toes form and the nose is distinct. The placenta and amniotic sac have developed. The embryo is now 1.5cm.

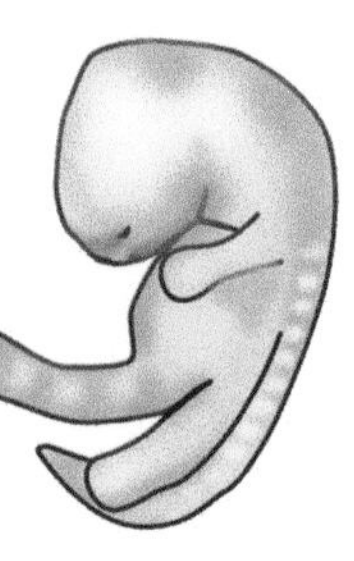

Week 24

The fused eyelids are separated allowing the foetus to open and shut its eyes. The skin is covered in fine hair (**lanugo**) and protected by a layer of waxy secretion (**vernix**). This will almost disappear by birth. The foetus is 22cm and 700 grams and is considered to be **viable** if born **prematurely**. This means it has a chance of survival although it would need to be cared for in a Special Care Baby Unit.

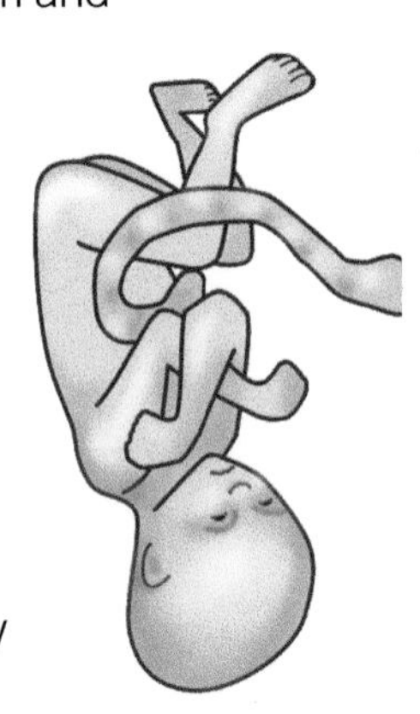

Weeks 25–28

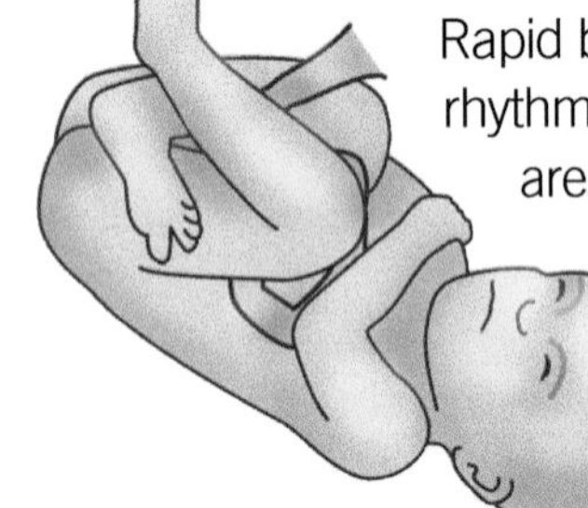

Rapid brain development occurs, rhythmic breathing happens but lungs are not yet mature. The foetus sleeps for most of the day. It has now grown to 37 cm and weighs between 1 and 1.3kg.

Weeks 30–40

The baby can open and close eyes and knows the difference between waking and sleeping. A layer of fat is produced and stored beneath the skin. By 32 weeks the head will be lying downwards in preparation for birth and by 36 weeks the head will be nestled in the pelvic cavity ready for birth. The size can now be 48–53cm in length and between 2.2 and 3.2kg in weight.

Summary

- Babies born before 37 weeks are considered to be premature.
- Average babies weigh between 3.2 and 3.5kg (7 and 7.5lbs) and are 51 to 55cm (20–22 inches) in length.

1. Complete a table with changes in the foetus and mother during pregnancy.

Stage of embryo/ foetal development	Embryonic/foetal facts	Pregnant woman facts

2. Using images and research produce an illustrated timeline of the development of the foetus.

It is important that you know what happens at different weeks of foetal development as you could be expected to match descriptions with the correct week.

Week 8

The embryo is now known as a foetus and is more human like in appearance and is 2cm in size, which is about the size of a grape. Every organ is now in place.

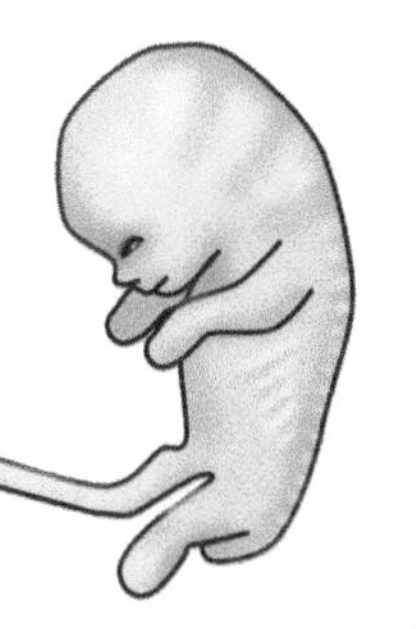

By week 12

The foetus can turn its head, which is almost half the length of the body, frown and suck its thumb. It now begins to swim about more vigorously and can feel pain. The foetus is 5–7cm and weighs 15 grams.

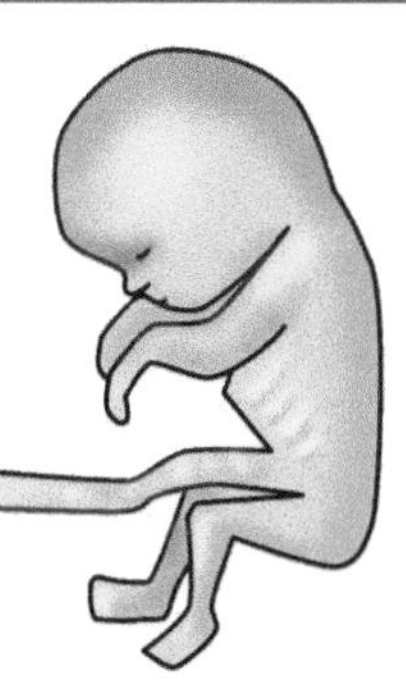

Week 20

The foetus is now 16cm and will grow about 1cm per week. Ears are fully functioning and the foetus can recognise its mother's voice. Genitals can be seen on an ultrasound scan and hair on the scalp is growing. The weight is now 25 grams.

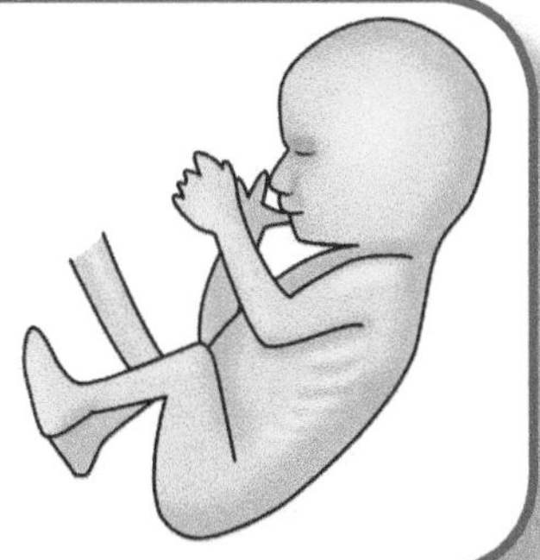

Prove it!

1. What do you understand by the following terms:
   a. Zygote?
   b. Embryo?
2. Describe the development of the foetus at 20 weeks.
3. Identify the age of the foetus from the descriptions given:
   a. Fully formed with closed eyes and developed sex organs, arms and legs constantly move.
   b. Development complete except for the lungs, only weighs 700g and could survive if born.
   c. Positioned for birth with head well down in pelvic cavity.

Key Terms

Lanugo – soft hair covering the foetus

Vernix – substance that protects the skin of the foetus

Viable – a baby born early that can survive with medical assistance

Premature – baby born before 37 weeks

The baby's support system

The foetus needs a support system for nourishment, oxygen and protection and this is provided by the **placenta**, **umbilical cord** and **amniotic sac**.

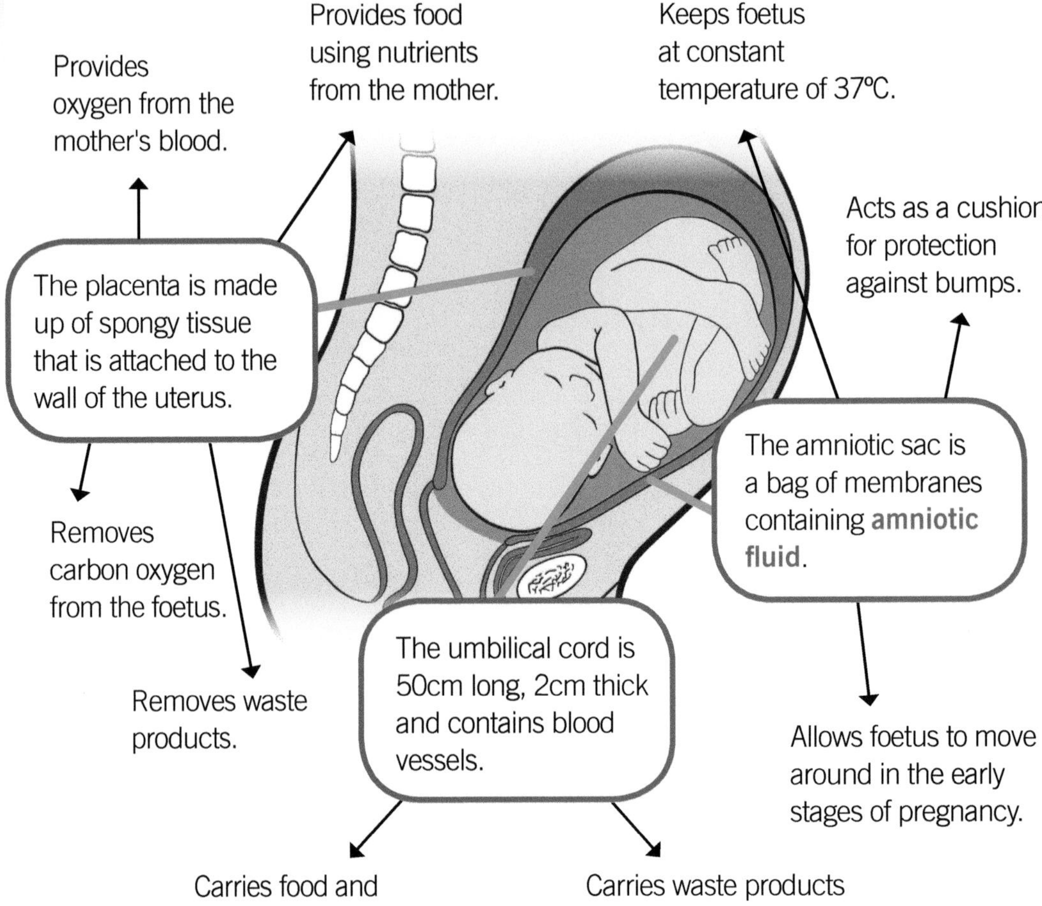

Provides oxygen from the mother's blood.
Provides food using nutrients from the mother.
Keeps foetus at constant temperature of 37°C.
Acts as a cushion for protection against bumps.
The placenta is made up of spongy tissue that is attached to the wall of the uterus.
Removes carbon oxygen from the foetus.
Removes waste products.
The amniotic sac is a bag of membranes containing amniotic fluid.
The umbilical cord is 50cm long, 2cm thick and contains blood vessels.
Allows foetus to move around in the early stages of pregnancy.
Carries food and oxygen to the foetus.
Carries waste products away from the foetus.

Key Terms

Placenta – afterbirth, tissue that nourishes the foetus

Umbilical cord – attaches the foetus to the placenta

Amniotic sac – bag holding the amniotic fluid

Amniotic fluid – water that surrounds the foetus in the uterus

Foetal alcohol syndrome – condition that affects the baby's development

Toxoplasmosis – disease caused by undercooked meat and cat faeces

Listeriosis – food poisoning bacteria

Foods to avoid

Some other foods can also cause problems with foetal development and should not be eaten in large amounts:

- Liver has too much vitamin A.
- Tuna has small amounts of mercury.
- Too many peanuts can cause the baby to have a peanut allergy.

Key Facts

- Despite advice which warns of the effects of smoking whilst pregnant, such as miscarriage and premature birth, 12% of mothers still smoked during pregnancy.
- Women who smoke during pregnancy also double the risk of stillbirth.
- Research has found that the risk was increased by 26% for having a baby with missing or deformed limbs, 28% for clubfoot, 27% for gastrointestinal defects, 33% for skull defects, 25% for eye defects, and 28% for cleft lip/palate.
- The number of babies born with low birth weight could be reduced by approximately 20% if women did not smoke during pregnancy.
- Pregnant teenagers need to make sure they have a good intake of calcium as their own bones are still growing.

Factors affecting foetal development

Damaging substances can cross the placenta to the foetus, which can cause problems with the development of the foetus.

Factors affecting foetal development

Smoking

Nicotine and other harmful chemicals in cigarettes are absorbed in the mother's bloodstream which then travel to the foetus. The foetus has a poor supply of oxygen due to the effects of carbon dioxide on the foetus' blood. The foetus does not grow and develop properly and the foetal heart beats too fast. Therefore there is an increased risk of:

- A premature birth.
- A baby who has a low birth weight.
- A miscarriage or stillbirth.
- A baby who has learning difficulties in later life or physical abnormalities.
- Sudden Infant Death Syndrome

Drugs

Illegal drugs, e.g. cannabis, cocaine, heroin, can damage the foetus by causing physical abnormalities. The baby is born addicted, with a low birth weight, high pitched cry and is difficult to settle. After birth the baby suffers from withdrawal symptoms.

Alcohol

There is an increased risk of a baby being born with a condition called **foetal alcohol syndrome**, the baby may also be addicted to alcohol and have a low birth weight. The development of the brain and nervous system is affected, which could result in learning difficulties.

Other diseases

Toxoplasmosis, which is caught from cat faeces or contaminated soil, can cause the embryo's nervous system and eyes to be affected. To avoid this, pregnant women should not change cat litter trays unless gloves are worn and hands thoroughly washed. Fruit and vegetables should also be thoroughly washed before use.
Listeriosis can cause a miscarriage, still birth or a very ill baby. This disease can be found in certain food which should not be eaten by pregnant women. These foods include:

- Paté
- Undercooked meat
- Soft cheeses, e.g. Brie, Camembert, Stilton
- Unpasteurised milk
- Cook chill foods unless reheated properly.

Infectious diseases

If a pregnant woman develops Rubella (German measles) in the first 3–4 months of pregnancy it may cause the baby to be born blind or deaf, or have heart defects or brain damage. If she contracts chickenpox this could result in the baby having brain damage.

Summary

- The placenta, or afterbirth, which weighs 500 grams is the only disposable organ in the body.
- Alcohol, viruses, medicines and nicotine pass through the placenta to the foetus.

Activity

Produce a PowerPoint or leaflet for parents outlining the factors that affect the development of the foetus.

Prove it!

1. State three functions of the placenta.
2. List two functions of the amniotic sac.
3. Identify and explain four factors that may affect foetal development.
4. Suggest three reasons why a baby may have a low birth weight.

As the development of the foetus is seriously affected by alcohol, drugs, etc., it is important that you can explain the effects and what a pregnant woman needs to do to minimise the risks to the developing foetus.

Antenatal care

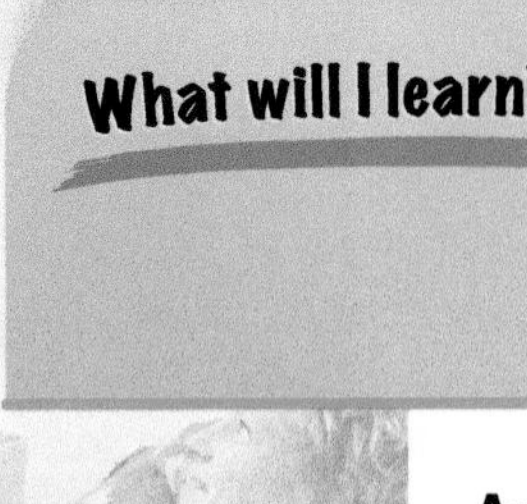

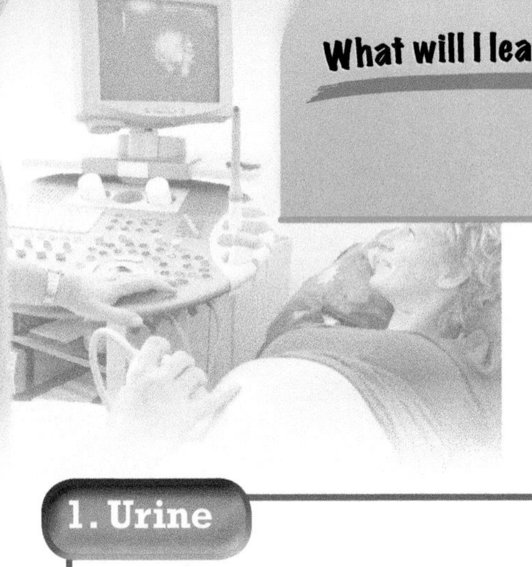

What will I learn?

- **The importance of antenatal care**
- **The routine and specialised tests that are offered in antenatal clinics**

As soon as the pregnancy has been confirmed a woman will be cared for by a team of health professionals. The first phase of this care is termed antenatal care, which means care given before birth.

Monitoring

The health of the mother and foetus is carefully monitored through regular check-ups and routine tests. There are usually **SIX** types of test:

1. Urine

- If ketones are detected, this could indicate the mother is dehydrated.
- Glucose may be a sign that the mother has gestational diabetes. This could cause the baby to be larger than is healthy for the mother or baby.
- Protein would mean the mother may have an infection in the bladder and kidneys, which could start a premature birth. More seriously, protein in the urine can be an early indicator of **pre-eclampsia**, the high blood pressure disease of pregnancy.

2. Uterus

This is examined by the **midwife** or doctor who presses on the outside of the abdomen so that the position, movement and size of the foetus can be determined.

3. Weight

The mother is weighed to make sure the baby is growing. Also this allows a check of the mother's BMI because there is more risk of developing gestational diabetes if, in early pregnancy, the BMI is over 30.

4. Legs

Legs are checked for varicose veins and any swelling especially in the ankles. Swollen ankles could just be a sign that the mother is retaining too much fluid or it may be a symptom of pre-eclampsia.

5. Blood pressure

At the mother's first check-up the blood pressure is taken and used as an indicator of what is normal for the mother. It is checked again at each further visit because increasing blood pressure is an early sign of pre-eclampsia.

6. Blood

- Low haemoglobin levels indicate iron deficiency (**anaemia**).
- Blood group is noted in case a transfusion is needed.
- **Rhesus factor** is noted – rhesus negative women will be given an anti-D injection during weeks 28 to 30 of pregnancy or within 72 hours of giving birth.
- Any infectious diseases – such as syphilis, HIV and hepatitis B – can be found.
- Immunity to Rubella, if this is not found a vaccination will be offered after the baby is born, in the postnatal period.

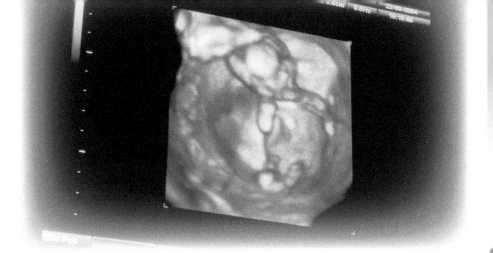

A baby scan which allows the baby to be seen in colour and 3D – these can cost approximately £130 and are not available everywhere

Ultrasound scans

The first **ultrasound scan** takes place between 10 and 18 weeks into the pregnancy. It measures the baby's size, checks the heartbeat is present, and confirms the length of pregnancy to calculate the due date. It is also used to see if there is more than one baby and the position of the placenta in the uterus.

Another scan (called the **anomaly scan**) is carried out between 18 and 21 weeks to determine that the baby is developing and growing as would be expected. If there are problems, the type of care given can be changed. This scan will check the major organs such as the brain, heart, stomach, kidneys, bladder, limbs and genitals. The spine will also be checked for signs of spina bifida.

Growth and well-being scans may be carried out after 26 weeks when measurements of the head, waist and thigh bone of the foetus are taken to estimate the baby's weight. An examination of the amount of fluid around the baby and the function of the placenta using Doppler ultrasound assesses the overall well-being of the baby.

New technology now allows 3D and 4D scans, usually carried out between 26 and 32 weeks. These are popular with parents as they are able to see life-like images of the baby's face that they can share with family and friends. These often show the baby smiling, yawning or sucking depending on whether the baby is awake or sleeping.

Key Terms

Antenatal – before birth

Pre-eclampsia – medical condition that can occur in late pregnancy

Midwife – health professional who cares for pregnant women

Anaemia – lack of iron in the blood

Rhesus factor – protein in red blood cells

Ultrasound scan – routine screening test

Anomaly scan – mid pregnancy screening test

Summary

- Antenatal care takes place in the GP's surgery, the hospital or health centre.
- During pregnancy a woman can gain an average of 12kg (2 stone) in weight.
- Pre-eclampsia is a dangerous condition than can lead to premature labour, organ failure and death of mother and/or foetus.
- Antenatal care includes attending classes to learn about breathing and relaxation exercises, the birthing process and the needs of the newborn.

Activity

Make a chart that explains why the following tests carried out during pregnancy are important:

a. Blood tests
b. Urine tests

Prove it!

1. **Eclampsia is a serious condition. What are the symptoms of pre-eclampsia?**
2. **Name four key things an ultrasound scan does.**

Screening tests

Screening tests are offered during pregnancy to see if the baby is at risk of certain birth defects. They are a combination of ultrasound scans and maternal blood testing carried out during the first and second trimester of pregnancy. They may be used alone or with other tests.

Nuchal translucency

Nuchal translucency screening is carried out at 11–14 weeks and combines the woman's age, a measurement of two proteins in the mother's blood and an ultrasound test to examine the area at the back of the foetal neck for increased fluid. This test is used as a prediction for a baby with Down's syndrome.

Blood tests

Blood tests measure two substances found in the blood of all pregnant women:

- **Pregnancy-associated plasma protein screening** – a protein produced by the placenta in early pregnancy.
- **Human chorionic gonadotropin (hCG)** – a hormone produced by the placenta in early pregnancy.

Abnormal levels of these substances indicate an increased risk of chromosome abnormality.

Alpha-fetoprotein screening (AFP)

AFP is a blood test, taken between 15 and 20 weeks, that measures the level of alpha-fetoprotein in the mother's blood during pregnancy. AFP is a protein produced by the foetal liver and is present in the amniotic fluid, which crosses the placenta into the mother's blood. Abnormal levels of AFP may indicate the following:

- Spina bifida
- Down's syndrome
- Defects in the abdominal wall of the foetus
- Twins because more than one foetus is making the protein.

Screening – tests to identify if a person is at risk of a certain condition or disease

Nuchal translucency – scan that measures fluid at the back of the baby's neck

Diagnostic – tests that confirm the baby has the condition being screened for

Amniocentesis – test to see if baby has Down's syndrome

It is important to note that abnormal results of ANY screening tests may suggest that additional testing is required, and genetic counselling would also be recommended.

Produce a PowerPoint presentation that may be used on an information screen in antenatal clinics to explain the screening and diagnostic tests available to pregnant women.

When answering questions on antenatal care it is important that you are able to identify and know the difference between routine, screening and diagnostic tests and can explain why each test is carried out in pregnancy.

Diagnostic tests

These additional tests are called **diagnostic** tests**.** They will give a definite answer if the baby does have a specific medical condition. As the tests are **invasive** there is a risk of miscarriage.

Amniocentesis

An **amniocentesis** is offered to women who have an increased risk of having a baby with Down's syndrome, such as women who are over 35 years of age at delivery, those with a family history of chromosomal abnormalities or those who have had abnormal screening test results.

The test is carried out between 15 and 20 weeks of the pregnancy. Ultrasound is used to help guide a hollow needle through the mother's abdomen into the amniotic sac to withdraw a small sample of the amniotic fluid for examination. The amniotic fluid contains cells shed by the foetus, which contain genetic information.

Alpha-fetoprotein, a protein made by the foetus that is found in the fluid, is also measured to rule out spina bifida. Test results can take two to three weeks.

Key Fact

- Down's syndrome affects around one in every 1,000 babies born. In 2011, just under 724,000 babies were born in England and Wales, and 725 of these were born with Down's syndrome.

Placenta

Foetus

Uterus (womb)

Amniotic fluid

Cervix

Amniocentesis test procedure

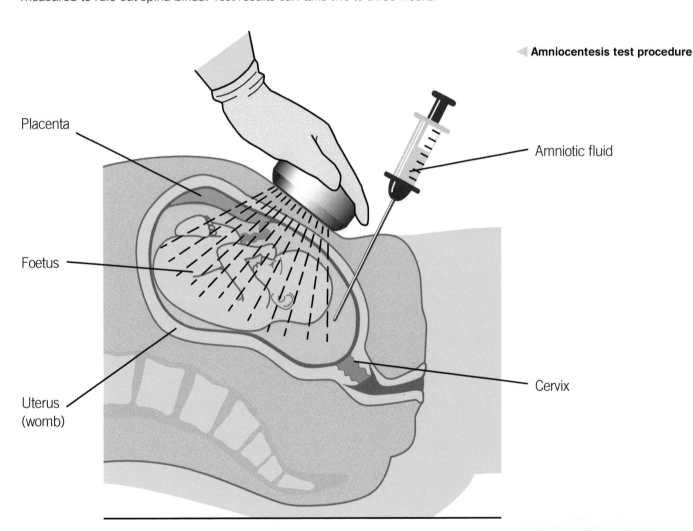

Chorionic villus sampling (CVS)

Chorionic villus sampling may be offered to women who have an increased risk for chromosomal abnormalities or have a family history of inherited diseases such as **sickle-cell anaemia** or **thalassaemia**. CVS is usually carried out between weeks 10 and 12 of pregnancy and involves inserting a needle through the woman's abdomen and into her uterus to obtain a small sample of the placenta. Ultrasound is used to guide the needle into place near the placenta. Results are usually available in 3–4 days.

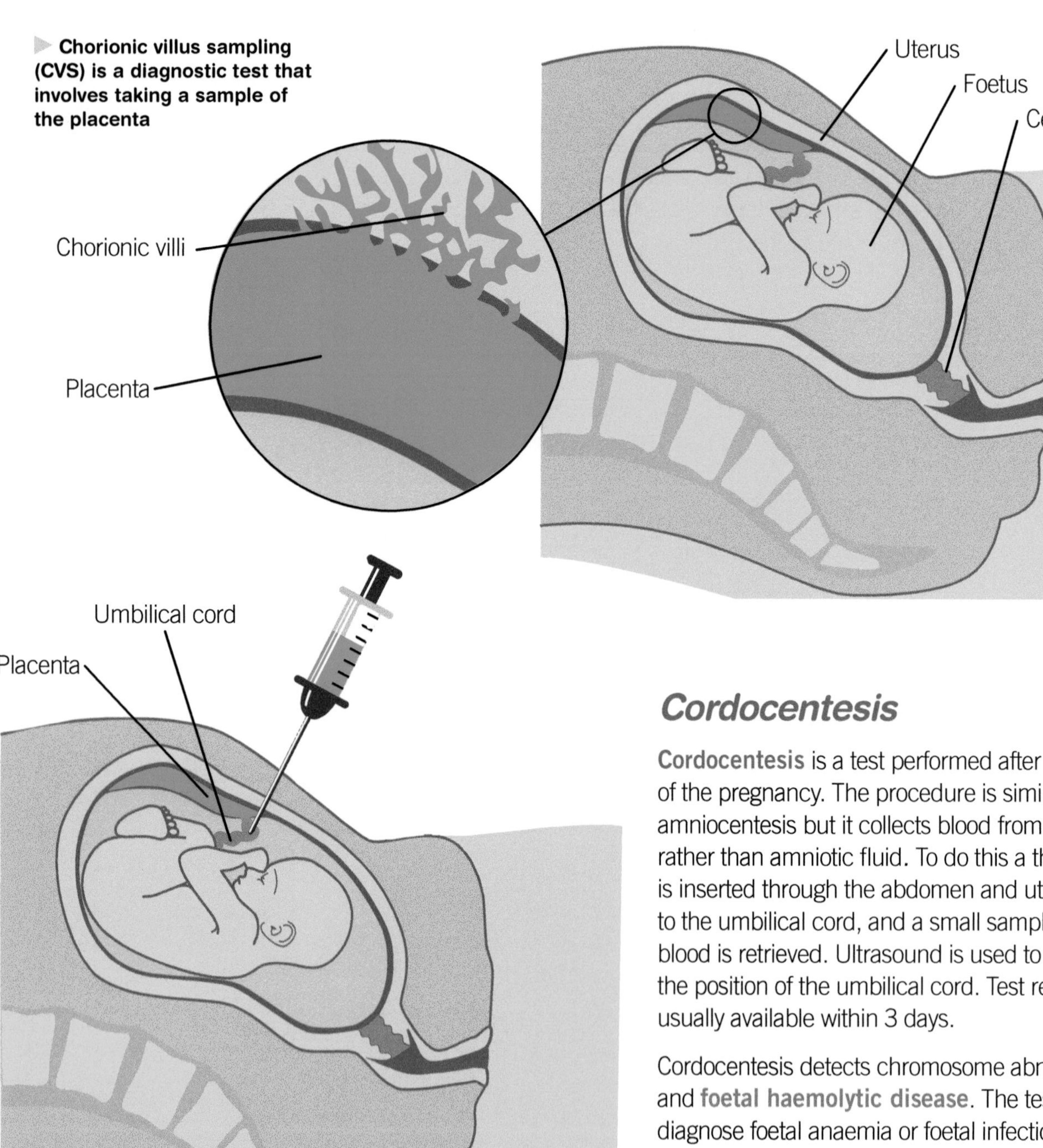

Chorionic villus sampling (CVS) is a diagnostic test that involves taking a sample of the placenta

Cordocentesis

Cordocentesis is a test performed after 17 weeks of the pregnancy. The procedure is similar to amniocentesis but it collects blood from the foetus rather than amniotic fluid. To do this a thin needle is inserted through the abdomen and uterine walls to the umbilical cord, and a small sample of foetal blood is retrieved. Ultrasound is used to identify the position of the umbilical cord. Test results are usually available within 3 days.

Cordocentesis detects chromosome abnormalities and **foetal haemolytic disease**. The test may help diagnose foetal anaemia or foetal infections, e.g. toxoplasmosis.

Cordocentesis test procedure

Making the decision to have any of the available tests varies for each individual. However, if a mother or couple take the tests to confirm an initial diagnosis then this has some benefits. They can:

- Begin planning for a child with special needs.
- Start considering anticipated lifestyle changes.
- Identify support groups and resources.
- Decide to abort the pregnancy.

Some women choose not to have any additional tests because they are comfortable with the results no matter what the outcome is, or they may feel that for personal, moral or religious reasons, the choice of not carrying the child to term is simply not an option for them. Due to the possibility of miscarriage with some of the tests, many women choose not to have any testing that could risk harming the developing baby.

It is important to discuss the risks and benefits of testing thoroughly to evaluate whether the benefits from the results could outweigh any risks from the procedure.

Chorionic villus sampling – diagnostic test using a sample of the placenta

Cordocentesis – umbilical cord blood sampling

Key Facts

- The risks related to antenatal testing depend on the procedure being carried out.
- Blood tests: minimum risk, the mother may experience discomfort, bleeding from the puncture site or infection.
- Ultrasound: no risks when having an ultrasound scan.
- Amniocentesis: less than 0.5% risk of miscarriage when the amniocenteses is done between 15 and 20 weeks. Maternal infection, injuries to the foetus and premature labour may be other possible risks.
- Chorionic villus sampling: less than 2% risk of miscarriage when CVS is carried out between 9 and 11 weeks.

Summary

- Screening tests assess the risk of having a baby with a particular condition, whilst diagnostic tests will tell you if the baby does have a specific condition.
- An amniocentesis is a procedure used to collect a small sample of the amniotic fluid that surrounds the foetus to diagnose chromosomal disorders and spina bifida.
- Chorionic villus sampling involves taking a sample of the placental tissue which is tested for chromosomal abnormalities and some other genetic problems.

Prove it!

1. **Antenatal care provides important information about the health of the mother and unborn baby.**
   a. **Identify and explain the routine check-ups an expectant mother receives during pregnancy.**
   b. **Discuss two of the routine screening or diagnostic tests an expectant mother may receive during pregnancy.**
2. **Explain the importance of attending regular antenatal appointments.**

Birth of the baby

What will I learn?

- **Choices available for the delivery of the baby**
- **Pain relief available when giving birth**
- **Stages of labour and methods of delivery**
- **The role of the birth partner**
- **The needs of premature babies**

People have different opinions on the best place for giving birth – some choose hospital, while others prefer a home birth. Whatever she chooses, the mother will be provided with all the information she needs about the choice of birth place and pain relief available to her. This will allow her to make an informed decision that is suited to her own personal needs, and ensure the safe delivery of the baby.

Activity

Investigate the most appropriate type of birth for the following:

a. A teenager expecting her first baby.
b. A mother expecting twins.
c. A mother having her third baby.

Delivery options – hospital or home?

Hospital birth

Sometimes the place of delivery is chosen for the mother as she is advised to have her baby in hospital. This may be for the following reasons:

- The mother or unborn baby may require medical assistance because of health problems.
- It is a first baby.
- The mother is under 17 or over 35.
- The mother has previously had a Caesarean.
- There is more than one baby.
- The mother has had three or more babies.
- The mother has rhesus negative blood.

Home birth

Mothers who make the decision to have their baby at home know that the midwife will care for her there. If there are complications or further medical help is required then the mother is usually transferred to a hospital.

Water birth

Water births can be beneficial in labour as the mother feels more relaxed and secure. Gas and air can still be used if extra pain relief is required.

Domino scheme

The **domino scheme** combines home and hospital care. The mother is visited at home by a midwife who looks after her during the early stages of labour. Close to the delivery time the midwife accompanies the mother to hospital where she will give birth. After a few hours, if the mother and baby are well enough, they may return home. The midwife continues caring for the mother and baby for the first 10 days, after which the health visitor will take over.

Revision Tips

- When a question asks you to 'evaluate' you will be expected to make statements giving an opinion on the quality, usefulness or suitability of something.
- Place of birth is important so you will need to discuss the advantages and disadvantages of each one and provide a balanced answer to show your understanding of the topic.

Summary

- Most women give birth in hospital.
- Not all women can have a home birth.

Hospital birth

Positive reasons	Negative reasons
✓ Specialist baby care, if required, from neonatologists or paediatricians ✓ No domestic chores so the mother may rest when the baby is sleeping ✓ Assistance from **obstetricians** if required and 24-hour assistance from midwives for the care of the baby ✓ Epidurals can be given for pain relief ✓ Other mothers to talk to and discuss problems and experiences ✓ Restricted visiting hours limits numbers of visitors enabling mother to rest	✗ Birth partner may need to leave soon after the birth and may be less involved ✗ Moved to a ward with other mothers and babies so less privacy ✗ Cared for by a different midwife ✗ May not feel relaxed and comfortable ✗ Risk of infection is higher than in mothers who give birth at home ✗ Sometimes the mother doesn't get much rest

Home birth

Positive reasons	Negative reasons
✓ Familiar surroundings make the mother more relaxed ✓ Other family members can enjoy the experience and help care for the baby ✓ The baby maybe more settled as the mother can set her own routines and look after the baby in her own way ✓ The midwife will be known to the mother ✓ No restrictions on visitors and the mother can choose when to see them ✓ No transport required	✗ No specialist equipment or staff if anything goes wrong ✗ Range of pain relief not available as epidurals require an anaesthetist ✗ May be a delay in getting medical help if the hospital is far from the home ✗ Mother may still have household responsibilities and other children so becomes tired ✗ Lots of visitors may restrict rest periods for the mother

Water birth

Positive reasons	Negative reasons
✓ Less stressful birth experience for babies as they have spent their life in the womb ✓ Being upright in the birthing pool allows gravity to assist with the birth ✓ Warm water can help if contractions are strong and frequent ✓ Encourages the release of endorphins ✓ Birth partners can feel more involved as they can go in the birthing pool	✗ A midwife trained in water births must be at hand when the mother is in the water ✗ Does not take away all of the pain ✗ Temperature must be kept between 35 and 37°C otherwise if the mother becomes overheated the baby can become distressed ✗ The mother will need to leave the pool for a vaginal examination which checks the labour progress and if there are concerns with the mother or baby

Prove it!

1. **Give three reasons why a woman might be advised to have her baby in hospital.**
2. **Describe the domino delivery system and discuss why it is beneficial for both mother and baby.**
3. **Give three advantages of:**
   a) a home birth b) a hospital birth.

Obstetrician – doctor who specialises in pregnancy and childbirth

Questions relating to pain relief will need to evaluate both drug free pain killers and ones that use drugs to relieve pain so make sure you know the difference and that you can explain how they work to benefit the mother.

Pain relief

Labour is painful so it is important that the mother is given information about the different ways to relieve pain. Some forms of pain relief use drugs but some women prefer not to use drugs and will consider alternative methods. Not all of these are effective and it is quite normal to use different methods at different stages during labour.

Pain relief using drugs

Entonox

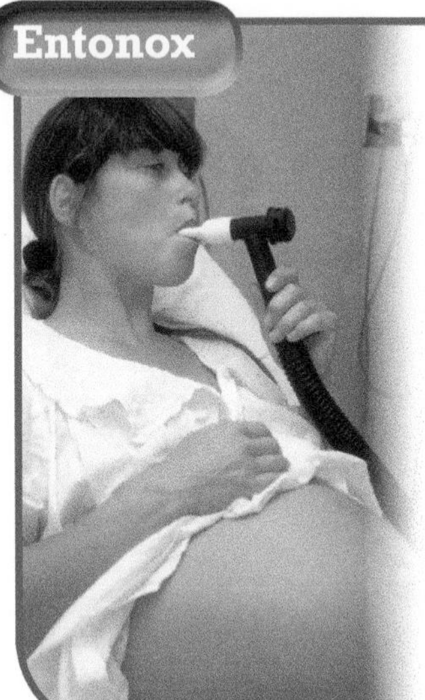

Entonox – sometimes just called 'gas and air' – is a combination of oxygen and nitrous oxide. The effect of it is to dull the pain of labour but it does not remove it completely. The mother can use gas and air at any time during labour and it is administered by breathing it in through a mouthpiece or mask. It is usually fast acting, easy to use and the mother controls how it is used to relieve pain. Gas and air does not affect the baby and it may be used during a water birth. The mother may feel drowsy, light headed, and nauseous and if used for long periods, a dry mouth may develop.

Pethidine

Pethidine is given as an injection into the thigh and takes about 30 minutes to start working. The mother may feel dizzy, nauseous and occasionally drowsy. Even though it is a pain killer, it doesn't take away all of the pain. It is given by a midwife in the first stage of labour when the cervix is dilating and may be used in hospital or home births.

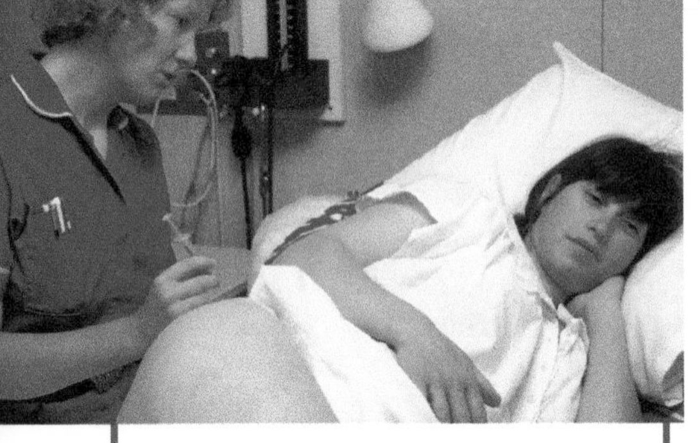

Pethidine can cross the placenta and can affect the baby's breathing, make them drowsy and cause problems with rooting and sucking reflexes which can cause difficulties starting breastfeeding.

Epidural

An anaesthetist must give an **epidural**, so it is not available for a home birth. A thin tube is placed in the epidural space at the side of the spinal cord and the anaesthetic is administered through this tube. The mother's lower half becomes numb unless she is offered a mobile epidural which allows more movement in the legs. The baby's heart beat and the mother's contractions are regularly monitored.

The second stage of labour may be longer than the first, so the midwife will need to tell the mother when to push if she cannot feel the contractions. The baby's head may need to be delivered with the help of forceps or a ventouse. After birth, a catheter may be put in the bladder if the mother has problems passing urine.

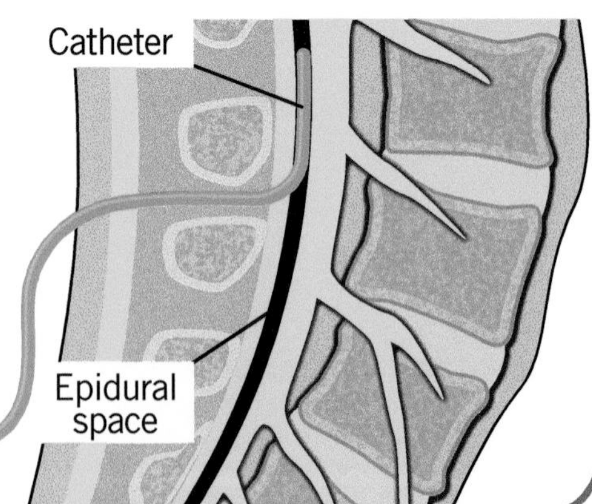

Activity

A drug-free childbirth is ideal from the baby's point of view. On the other hand, drugs ease the pain for the mother. Investigate three methods of pain relief available to the mother during childbirth. Produce a PowerPoint that can be used in the antenatal classes.

Pain relief without drugs

Massage

A slow firm massage to the back can help to soothe the mother's muscles by releasing **endorphins** to ease the labour pains.

Homeopathy

Advice needs to be obtained on the most suitable remedy to be used during labour as each one deals with a different problem, e.g. arnica is used for soreness and aconite for strong labour pains.

Aromatherapy

Scented oils can create a calming atmosphere and may be placed in a diffuser if the hospital allows it or in a bowl of warm water. Sage, neroli, ylang ylang and lavender may help keep the mother calm.

Hypnotherapy

It has been suggested that self-hypnosis during labour can relieve some of the pain and reduce feelings of fear and worry. Studies also say medical assistance is reduced and labour is shorter.

TENS

TENS stands for Transcutaneous Electrical Nerve Stimulation. It is a hand-held battery operated machine linked by wires to pads that are placed on the mother's back. The stimulation affects the way pain signals are received by the brain so the body is encouraged to produce more endorphins. TENS works best in the early stage of labour and has no side-effects on the mother or baby. The mother can move around freely and pethidine or gas and air can still be used. If the mother wants a water birth, TENS cannot be used and it needs to be removed if the baby's heart needs electronic monitoring.

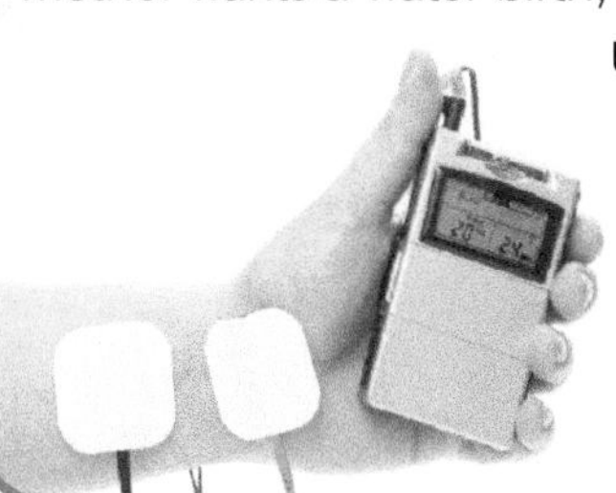

Reflexology

Pressure is applied to parts of the soles of the feet to affect other parts of the body so that muscle tension is lowered and the mother feels relaxed during labour.

Acupuncture

Can help with pain relief and have a calming effect on the brain so that the mother is more relaxed during labour.

Summary

- An epidural is the most effective form of pain relief.
- Many pain relief methods do not take away all the pain, the mother is just made to feel more relaxed and more in control.

Prove it!

1. **Name two different types of drug-free pain relief.**
2. **Describe the advantages and disadvantages of using Entonox as pain relief when giving birth.**
3. **Discuss the types of pain relief available to a pregnant woman during labour.**

Key Terms

Pethidine – pain relief drug given as an injection

Entonox – gas and air, provides pain relief when inhaled

Epidural – anaesthetic injected into a space around the spinal area

Endorphins – pain relieving hormones

Birth plan

The **midwife** or GP will provide information about preparing for labour and birth and discuss the **birth plan** with the mother. The reason they do this is so that they know what is important to the mother during labour and birth. A special birth plan form may be provided to write down the decisions made. Birth plans are personal but need to be flexible because labour does not always go to plan.

Birth plans can include information such as:

- **Where the birth will take place, at home or hospital.**
- **Who the birth partner will be.**
- **During labour what position will be preferred – lying on the bed, kneeling.**
- **What pain relief will be used, if any – pethidine, epidural, or gas and air.**
- **If labour slows down, whether the midwife uses interventions to speed it up again.**
- **Whether an injection is given to speed up delivery of the placenta.**
- **Who cuts the baby's umbilical cord.**
- **Choice of forceps or ventouse for an assisted delivery.**
- **Thoughts on having a Caesarean section if required.**
- **Choice of having an episiotomy or not.**
- **Views on having the baby's heart rate monitored continuously.**
- **Whether the baby is placed straight onto the mother's stomach before or after being cleaned.**
- **Whether the baby will be breastfed or bottle-fed.**
- **If vitamin K is to be given to the baby.**
- **Whether student nurses, midwives or doctors can be present during labour.**

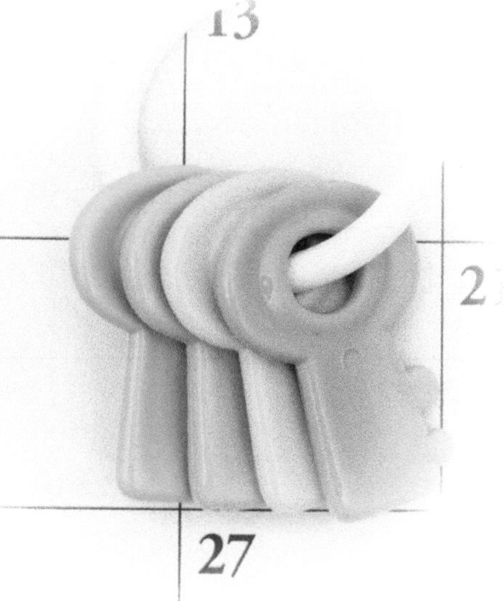

Key Facts

- In Holland, around 32% of births take place at home. In the UK, it's only 2%.
- Babies don't drown if they are born under water as they continue to 'breathe' through their umbilical cord, as they do in the womb, until they feel air on their face, at which point they open their lungs to breathe.

Activity

Work in groups and prepare a possible birth plan for the following women:

a. A first-time mother who wants a reasonably pain-free labour.
b. A mother who is having her third child and wants a home birth.
c. A second-time mother who had a difficult first birth.

Prepare a mini presentation to explain your choices to the rest of the class.

Birth partner's role

- Make sure everything is ready for the hospital – bag, camera, phone, etc.
- Remain patient and calm
- Be supportive of the mother and listen to what she wants
- During the birth help the mother to get into a comfortable position
- Encourage the mother during contractions
- Repeat the midwife's instructions if necessary
- Remind mother about breathing techniques
- Provide a hand to hold, a drink or a massage
- Sponge face and neck
- Remind the midwife of what is in the birth plan
- Talk and entertain to pass the time
- Cut the umbilical cord

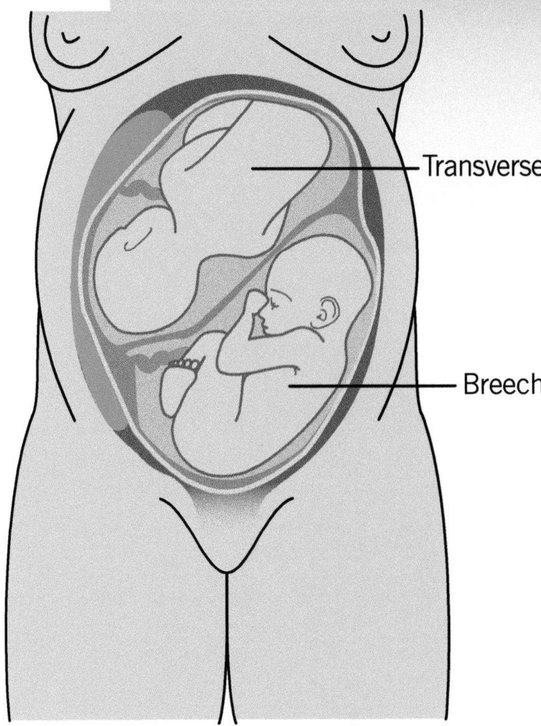

Breech and transverse twins

Positions of the baby

By week 38 of pregnancy the baby is usually engaged in the birth position where the head is facing down. Sometimes this does not happen and the baby is lying in either a **breech** position or **transverse**. In these two cases a Caesarean is usually recommended.

Before labour starts the mother may experience some of the following signs that labour is approaching.

Signs of labour approaching

- Vaginal discharge increases
- The plug of slightly bloody mucus comes away from the cervix
- Painful contractions 30 minutes apart, which are different from the Braxton Hicks contractions previously experienced
- The amniotic sac breaks and 'water' rushes out of the vagina
- May have nausea, backache or diarrhoea

Key Terms

Umbilical cord – lifeline that connects the foetus to the placenta

Forceps – metal instrument that look like tongs

Ventouse – vacuum tool that is used in an assisted birth

Caesarean – cut made in the abdomen for the baby to be lifted out

Episiotomy – cut made in the vagina to ease delivery

Breech – baby born bottom or feet first

Transverse – baby lying across the uterus

Summary

- Breech position babies are born bottom or feet first.
- Transverse position means the baby is lying across the uterus.

Prove it!

1. **Suggest five ways the birth partner can help during labour and birth.**
2. **What is a birth plan and what are four key pieces of information contained in it?**
3. **What is a transverse presentation?**

What happens in the first stage of labour?

Contractions become longer and more frequent – about every 10–30 minutes – as the **cervix** opens so that the baby can be born. During early labour the cervix goes from closed to 3 or 4 centimetres **dilated**, and the labour pains may only be mild like period cramps. As labour progresses the contractions last longer and are more frequent and the cervix will open to 10 cm. The uterus, cervix and vagina are now the **birth canal**. Contractions are more painful, last 60–90 seconds and happen every 3–4 minutes. There may be the need to use the breathing and relaxation techniques learnt in antenatal classes, other pain relief will also be available.

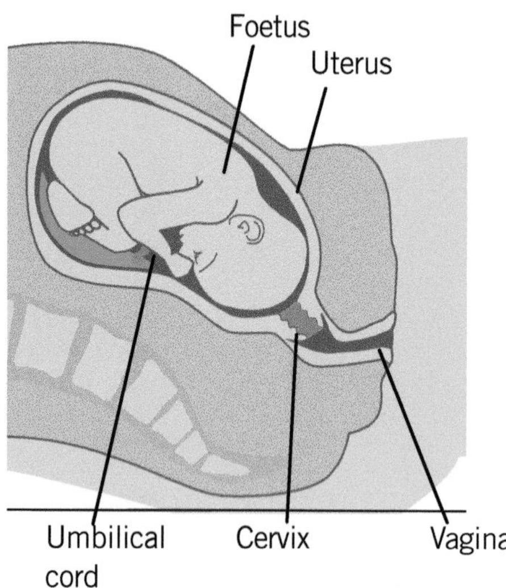

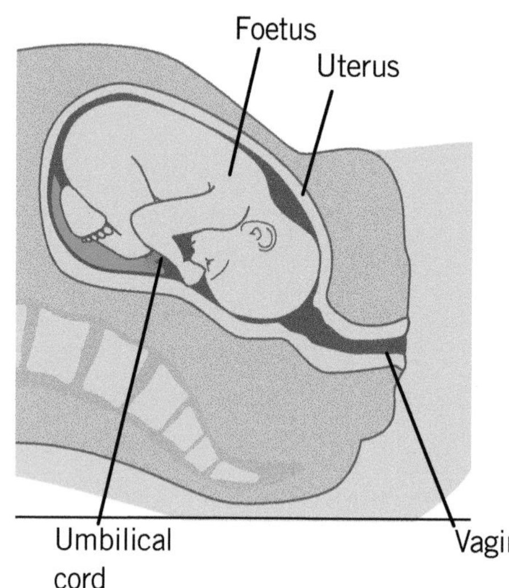

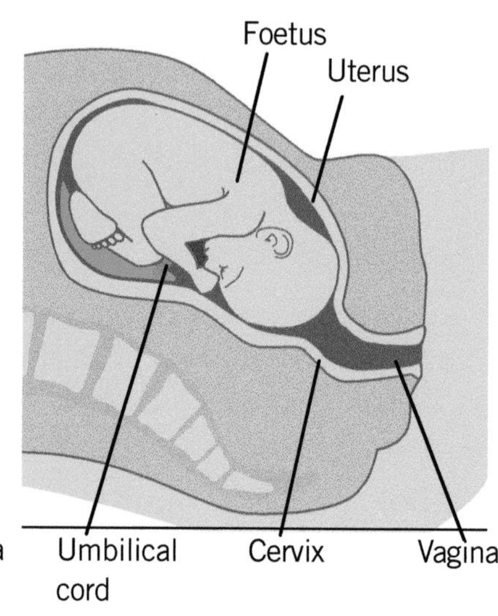

What happens in the second stage of labour?

Contractions become very strong and powerful and the mother feels the urge to push the baby. The midwife will guide the mother when to push with each contraction. With each push the baby moves down the birth canal until the head can be seen at the opening of the vagina. This is called **crowning** and there may be a hot stinging sensation as the vagina stretches. An episiotomy may be required if the skin is in danger of tearing.

After the head is born the midwife delivers the shoulders one at a time then the rest of the baby. The umbilical cord is clamped and cut, the baby now becomes a separate person. The baby is given to the mother as soon as possible after birth for the bonding process to begin.

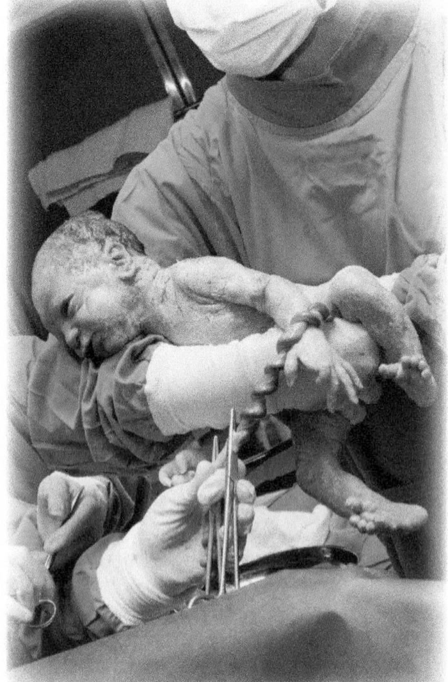

A newborn baby is held by a doctor whilst the umbilical cord is cut

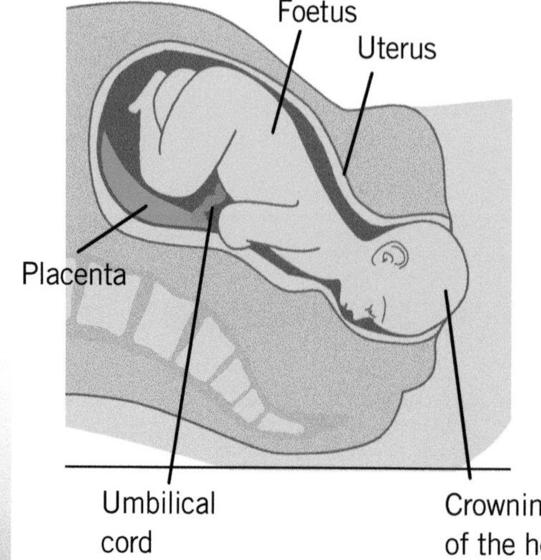

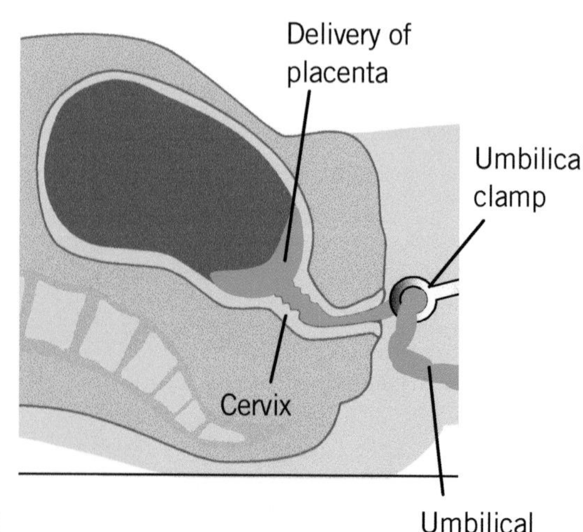

What happens in the third stage of labour?

Contractions are weaker now but cause the **placenta** or afterbirth to come away from the uterus wall. The mother may feel the urge to push and with assistance from the midwife, the placenta and membranes from the amniotic sac will slide out of the vagina. The mother may be given an injection to speed up this process. The placenta and membranes will be checked to make sure nothing has been left inside the mother as this can cause an infection.

After birth, the placenta is examined by a midwife or doctor

Key Facts

In 2011 approximately,

- 40% of mothers had 'normal deliveries' with no use of instruments, induction, epidural or general anaesthetic.
- 33% of women had an epidural during child birth.
- 27% of births were by Caesarean section, 12% were planned C-sections, 15% were emergency C-sections.
- 13% are assisted deliveries, 8% involving forceps and 5% using ventouse.
- 22% of births are induced.

Assisted delivery

Approximately one in eight women needs to have an **assisted birth** because the baby is in distress, the mother is tired or the contractions are not strong enough. Forceps or a ventouse suction cap may be used to help the baby out of the vagina.

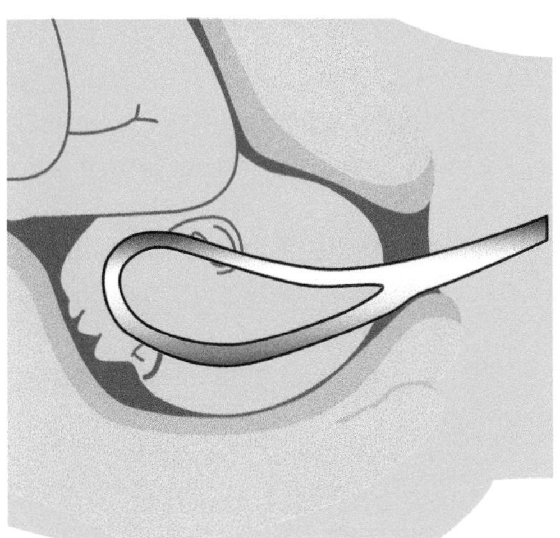

(a)

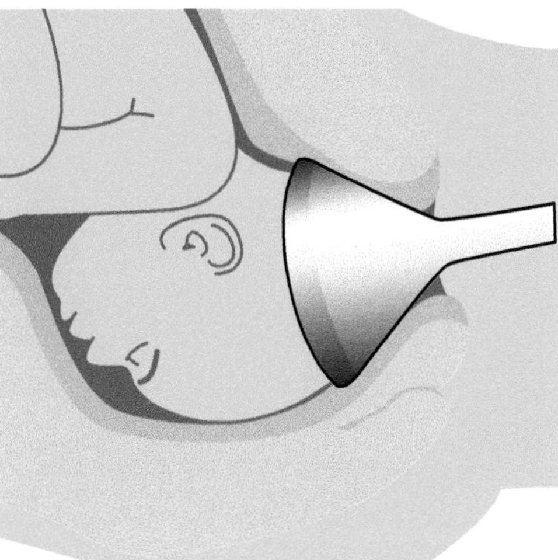

(b)

Assisted delivery using:
a) forceps, and
b) a ventouse suction cap

Revision Tip

You may be shown an illustration of a stage of labour, so make sure you can describe what happens at each stage. Practise describing illustrations by annotating them in detail.

Forceps

Forceps are curved, smooth metal instruments that are similar to tongs or large spoons. By placing the forceps carefully around the baby's head and pulling gently during a contraction the midwife helps ease the baby's head out of the vagina. An episiotomy is needed for a forceps delivery.

Ventouse

A plastic or metal cup is attached by a tube to a suction device and when the cup is attached to the baby's head and the mother has a contraction the midwife gently pulls to help deliver the baby.

Both forceps and ventouse can leave small marks on the baby's head.

Key Terms

Dilation - Cervix opening during labour

Crowning - Appearance of the baby's head at the entrance of the vagina

Placenta - The afterbirth, the organ through which the baby ate, breathed and excreted waste matter

Caesarean section

Sometimes the best option for the mother or baby is a Caesarean section, which may be planned (elective) or done as an emergency. The procedure involves a cut first through the abdomen, below the bikini line, then into the uterus; the baby is then lifted out. This may be done under general anaesthetic or more often using an epidural. The mother will feel a little pulling as the baby is delivered when an epidural is used but no other pain and because she is awake she can hold the baby straightaway.

Elective Caesareans are carried out 2–3 weeks before the estimated delivery date (EDD) to make sure it is done before the mother goes into labour.

Caesareans occur for the following reasons:

Elective Caesareans	Emergency Caesareans
The placenta is either lying across the cervix or has come away from the uterus wall.	Foetal distress.
The baby is lying across the uterus in the transverse position or is breech.	Pre-eclampsia develops.
The mother has had a previous caesarean.	**Haemorrhaging** from the uterus.
There is more than one baby.	Mother's health is at risk.
The mother has a medical condition such as HIV or genital herpes.	Long labour that is not progressing.

Use some modelling materials to represent the three stages of labour (remember a model doesn't have to look exactly the same as the real thing).

Some things you could use: bag, balloon, pipe cleaners, sponge, newspapers, and straws.

Make sure you can explain how your models show the different stages of labour.

Summary

- **Elective Caesareans** are planned in advance for medical reasons, whereas emergency Caesareans occur if complications develop and the baby is in distress and needs to be born quickly.
- Braxton Hicks contractions are practice contractions of the uterus as the muscles of the uterus start to tighten in preparation for labour.
- Labour and childbirth move forward in three stages.
- At 10 cm a cervix is termed as being fully dilated, which signifies stage one of labour is over.
- First stage labour, especially with a first baby, can last a long time.
- To assist the head emerging from the vagina a small cut, called an episiotomy, is made in the vagina.
- Stage two of labour ends when the baby is born.

Prove it!

1. **Discuss the term Caesarean section, referring to both an elective and an emergency Caesarean.**
2. **Sometimes a pregnant woman might need to have an assisted delivery. Give two examples of an assisted delivery.**
3. **Describe what happens during a Caesarean birth.**

Induced births

Some women may need to have labour artificially started for the following reasons:

- The EDD has passed by one to two weeks.
- The baby is not growing as the placenta is not working.
- The mother has high blood pressure.
- Contractions started but then stopped.
- Mother has pre-eclampsia.

The procedure may involve the mother being given a pessary in the vagina to soften the cervix, a drip containing the hormone syntocin to stimulate contractions, or the waters will be broken using an instrument that ruptures the membranes around the baby.

Key Fact

- In England alone 54,000 babies are born prematurely each year. More premature babies are surviving because problems in pregnancies are identified during antenatal care so many issues can be treated early. Developments with technology and treatments mean that doctors are willing to deliver babies early before problems deteriorate. Intensive care is now accessible to babies who years ago would not have received it; so greater numbers of very small babies are being born alive and surviving.

Premature babies

All babies that are born before 37 weeks, or those born with a low weight or who need breathing support, or are suffering from a medical condition are cared for in Special Care Baby Units (SCBU) or **Neonatal** Intensive Care Units (NICU). The length of a baby's stay varies according to their needs.

Babies that need care in the SCBU have many of the following features:

Weak immune system
Small size and a low birth weight
Problems with feeding as they are unable to suck and swallow
Low calcium, iron and blood sugar levels
Wrinkled thin skin that could be red or tinged with yellow due to jaundice
Unable to regulate body temperature as little body fat under the skin
Problems breathing due to under-developed lungs
Sealed eyes

Premature baby in an incubator

Special equipment

In the womb, a baby receives oxygen from the mother's blood and once born, all babies have to get their own oxygen by breathing. This can be a problem for very **premature** babies as their lungs are not fully developed as these are the last organs to mature.

Ventilators

Ventilators inflate the lungs and blow oxygen-enriched air into the baby's lungs through tubes via the nose or mouth. Rate of breathing is regularly adjusted to meet the baby's needs.

Incubator

A baby needs to be kept warm, so placing a baby inside an incubator will help regulate the baby's temperature. Incubators control the humidity around the baby to prevent moisture being lost from their immature skin and help keep the baby in a germ-free environment. Hand-sized holes at the side enable nurses to provide care.

Neonatal – newborn

Ventilator – machine that supports breathing

Premature – born before 37 weeks

Modern neonatal incubator

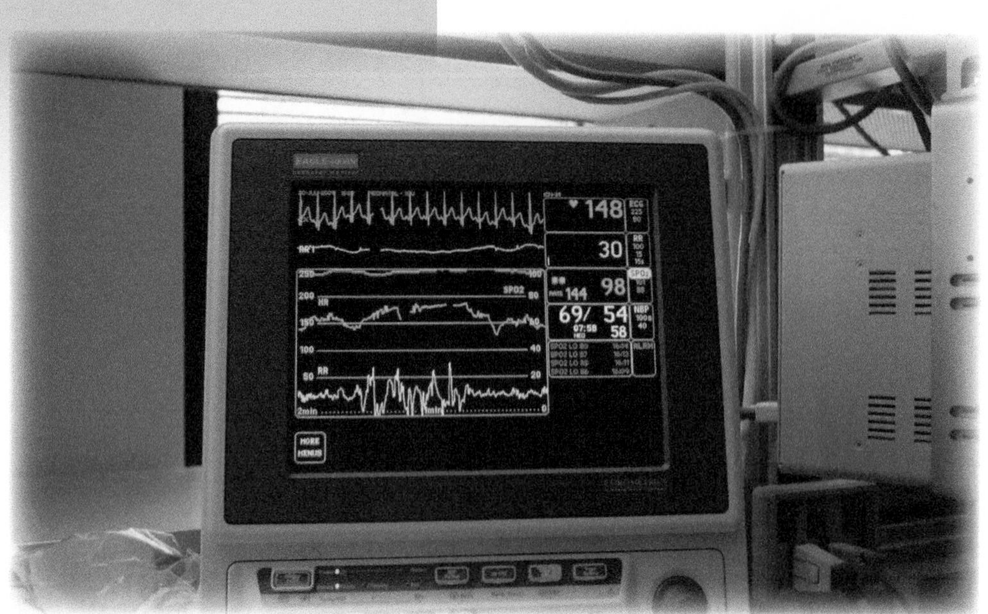

▲ **Vital signs monitor used with premature babies in NICU**

Monitors

Monitors are used to check the baby's vital signs. They are very sensitive and are programmed to go off when the smallest change is detected. Monitors check:

- The heart is beating properly.
- If there are changes in breathing.
- If the baby forgets to breathe – common in premature babies.
- The level of oxygen concentration in the baby's blood.

Intravenous lines

Premature babies only have a small amount of blood and fragile skin. Fine tubes are inserted into a blood vessel so that they can be given medicines, fluid and nutrition to help them grow.

Nasogastric tube

Very early babies have difficulty feeding so are fed through special feeding tubes that go via the nose or mouth direct to the stomach. Babies are able to be fed expressed breast milk this way.

Light therapy

To treat jaundice a light therapy unit is placed above the incubator. Before being placed under the light, baby's eyes must be covered to protect them from the ultraviolet light.

Seeing a baby for the first time in a neonatal unit can be distressing and frightening. Produce a leaflet that explains how the equipment helps in the care of premature babies. Remember that not all babies need all the equipment.

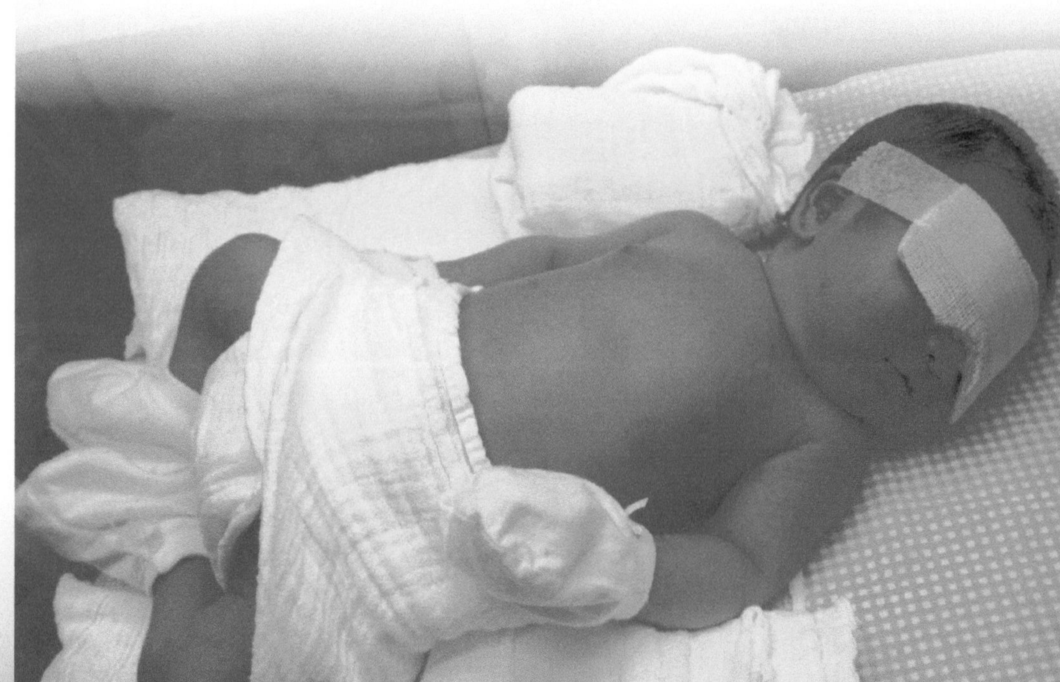

▶ **Newborn baby in an incubator, being treated with ultraviolet light**

Effects on the parents having a baby in SCBU

Parents may experience stress after the birth of a premature baby. Factors may include:

- Became parents earlier than expected.
- Parents are tired and exhausted.
- Baby is tiny and very ill.
- Baby's appearance is worrying – small, surrounded by wires and tubes and on a ventilator.
- Baby may seem to be suffering, constant highs and lows as the baby struggles to survive.
- Separated from the baby soon after birth, unable to bond.
- Baby seems to be disturbed by parents' attempts to touch and talk to it.
- Feel more like a visitor than a parent.
- Jealous of the nurses' ability to handle and care for the baby.
- Mother unable to breastfeed.
- Demands of other siblings to care for.
- No time for 'normal life' as parents juggle work and hospital.

To help with the **bonding process** parents can:

- Gently stroke the baby.
- Sing and talk quietly to the baby, this is reassuring as the baby would have heard the mother's voice in the womb.
- Work with the team of nurses and make decisions.
- Express breast milk as this is the best milk for premature babies.
- Help with washing, and changing nappies.
- Kangaroo skin to skin contact helps if the baby is well enough and the hospital offers it.
- If the baby cannot be held then they may find comfort in holding the parent's finger.
- Make eye contact, smile and play with the baby.
- Show the baby toys, though not ones that are too noisy
- Learn about baby's needs, when rest is required or gentle stimulation.

Child Study

As part of the introduction and background information of the study child you could interview the mother for information about the study child's birth.

Possible questions could relate to the type of birth – natural, assisted or Caesarean, type of pain relief used, if the baby was born to date, early or late, birth weight and length, baby received vitamin K or not.

Summary

- Skin-to-skin contact after birth helps the baby regulate body temperature and provides reassurance from the mother's heartbeat.
- Many babies in the neonatal units are extremely tiny and immature.
- Equipment in Special Care Baby Units keeps babies warm, monitors their body functions and supports their breathing.
- The more you can interact with your premature baby in the SCBU the more confident you will feel in caring for your baby at home.

Having a baby in SCBU can be stressful for parents. You will need to understand how this affects both parents and the rest of the family and explain what can be done to help parents cope with the situation. E.g. mother cannot breastfeed the baby but she can express her breast milk for feeding to the baby, as breast milk is beneficial for premature babies. This would make her feel more involved in the baby's care.

Prove it!

1. **Some babies may be placed in a special care unit after birth.**
   a. **Explain the importance of an incubator for a newborn baby.**
   b. **Discuss the effects on the family of having a baby placed in a Special Care Baby Unit.**
2. **Explain how the process of attachment (bonding) can be encouraged immediately after birth.**
3. **Sometimes labour needs to be induced. What does this mean and why might it be needed?**

Postnatal care

What will I learn?

- **The importance of postnatal care for the mother and baby**
- **The role of the health visitor in supporting a mother with a new baby**

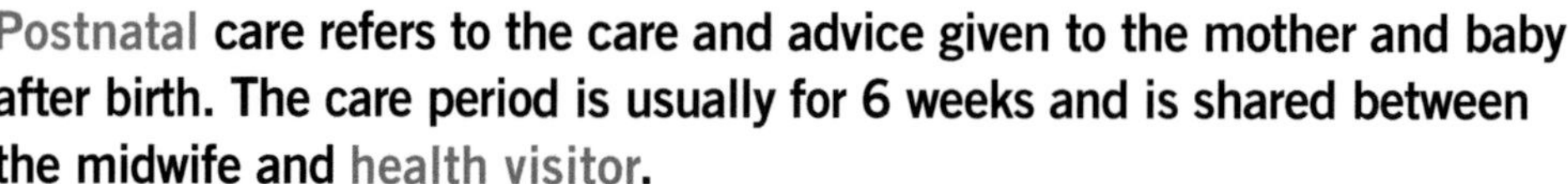

Postnatal care refers to the care and advice given to the mother and baby after birth. The care period is usually for 6 weeks and is shared between the midwife and health visitor.

Examination of the baby

The newborn baby is checked immediately at birth, and a more detailed physical examination of the baby is done within 24 hours by a **paediatrician** (if mother and baby are still in hospital) or by a midwife or GP if at home.

Area of the baby	Checks
Appearance	Colour of skin in case of **jaundice**, presence of birth marks – strawberry mark, Mongolian spot
Head including the **fontanelle**	Symmetry of the head, a squashed head is common, which rights itself in 48 hours
Ears and nose	Checks for any abnormal discharge
Eyes	Uses an ophthalmoscope to look for cataracts
Fingers and toes	Counted and checked for webbing
Heart rate and rhythm	To rule out heart murmurs
Abdomen including umbilical cord	For signs of swelling and to check the kidneys, liver and spleen are in the correct place
Genitals	Undescended testes in males
Hands	A single straight crease across the palm of the hand can indicate Down's syndrome
Hips	For signs of **congenital hip dislocation** so that early treatment may be given
Spine	Assessed for straightness and spina bifida
Nervous system	Overall activity and reflexes
Lungs	Breathing pattern observed
Weight	It is normal for some of birth weight to have been lost

Newborn blood spot screening

Before the baby is a week old a heel prick test is carried out. This involves a tiny amount of blood taken from the heel and placed on a special card. The blood is then analysed for the following:

- **Phenyl-ketonuria (PKU)** if detected, further tests are given to confirm the baby has the condition. The baby will require a special diet to help them develop normally.
- **Cystic fibrosis**, which is an inherited disorder that affects the lungs and digestive system.
- **Sickle-cell anaemia**, an inherited blood disorder.

Vitamin K

Vitamin K is needed to help blood clots form but some babies are born without enough vitamin K to prevent internal bleeding problems. This risk is highest in the first 13 weeks of life.

If a baby's blood does not clot easily then any bleeding might lead to a **haemorrhage** into their brain which can cause brain damage. In many of these cases the baby will die. The condition itself is quite rare. Babies most at risk seem to be those born before 37 weeks of pregnancy, those whose birth involved the use of forceps, ventouse or Caesarean and babies who had difficulty breathing and did not get enough oxygen when they were born.

All babies are therefore given:

- A single injection of vitamin K shortly after birth.
- Or two doses of vitamin K by mouth given during baby's first week. If breastfeeding, another dose is recommended when baby is a month old since bottle-fed babies receive enough because vitamin K is added to formula milk.

Key Terms

Postnatal – after birth

Health visitor – health professional who looks after the health of children

Congenital hip dislocation – born with a hip problem

Jaundice – yellow tinge to the skin

Phenyl-ketonuria – rare disorder where the body cannot break down protein

Paediatrician – a doctor who provides specialist care to infants, children and young people

Role of the health visitor

The health visitor takes over from the midwife and continues to provide support to the mother and baby either at home or in baby clinics. Health visitors are qualified nurses who have been trained in family health and child development, so they are able to give advice on baby care. This includes feeding, sleep patterns, nappy changing issues and teething problems. The health visitor will also carry out developmental checks at various stages, and discuss and provide the mother with a timetable for the baby's immunisations.

Health visitors can also give the mother advice on keeping herself healthy, and this can also include emotional help and guidance. Information on support groups that could be attended to meet other parents and children, share ideas and discuss worries is also possible via the health visitor.

The health visitor will provide encouragement for the mother to continue with postnatal exercises so that she regains her pre-birth body-shape to boost self-esteem and improve overall health.

Postnatal examination for the mother

Six weeks after giving birth, the mother must have a postnatal examination where her well-being and body's return to pre-pregnancy state is checked. This includes:

Urine sample – no infection present and kidneys are working properly.

Blood pressure check.

Weight measured – weight loss advice is given and information on a healthy diet.

Abdomen – no tenderness present.

Postnatal exercises discussed.

Cervical smear test may be done.

Advice given on contraception.

Internal pelvic examination – feel uterus to check if it is back to normal size.

Emotional state is checked.

Checks on vaginal discharge and if bleeding has ceased.

Vagina and cervix examined – to see if the episiotomy and any bruises have healed and stitches dissolved.

Registering the birth

A baby's birth must be registered within 42 days of the child being born in England, Wales and Northern Ireland but within 21 days in Scotland. A birth certificate is then issued.

Postnatal exercises

To help the woman's body to recover from the pregnancy and birth gentle exercise in the first few weeks is to be encouraged.

For the first few days after birth, the perineum or pelvic floor muscles may feel uncomfortable, swollen or very heavy so it is important to start gently with short walks of about 10 minutes, building to 20 minutes.

Pelvic floor exercises can be also be done which will help the perineum and vagina to heal more quickly through improving the circulation to the area, helping to reduce swelling and bruising.

Lower tummy muscles work with the pelvic floor muscles to support the back and pelvis so it is important to exercise the lower tummy muscles. This may also assist in losing the post-pregnancy belly.

Pelvic tilts are useful because they gently move and stretch the back and exercise the tummy muscles whilst helping to alleviate back pain.

Bonding with the baby

A good attachment bond helps the baby to trust, to communicate their feelings, and eventually to trust others. As the mother and baby bond, the baby learns how to have a good feeling of self and how to be in a loving relationship.

It is important to react to the baby quickly when upset or happy, this will assist in building strong bonds of trust. Showing this love, attention and affection will help the baby to develop.

To help the baby's brain to grow and develop and to assist in the bonding process the mother should interact with the baby whilst doing the caring tasks. This can be done by giving lots of eye contact, talking and smiling plus holding the baby close.

Revision Tip

When discussing postnatal care remember to provide a balanced answer that shows you know to include the care of the baby AND mother.

Role of the father

A newborn baby can bring joy to the parents but they often feel anxious and tired as they try to cope with providing full-time care. Newborns are dependent on their parents for their every need, so parents need to be in good health.

Breastfeeding mothers especially need to eat a nutritiously balanced diet, and all new mothers should get more rest than they usually do. Fathers are now entitled to two weeks paternity leave, which can be used to support the mother in any way possible, such as helping with household chores, looking after other children or by caring for the newborn while she rests. Emotional support can be given by being prepared to listen and discuss any worries the mother may have.

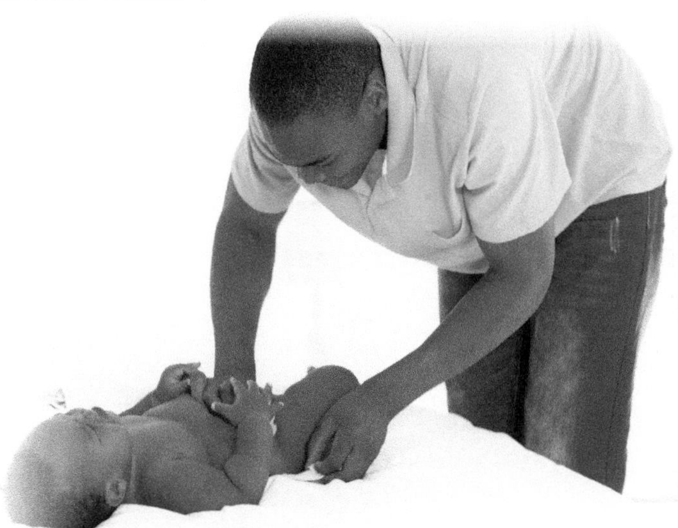

Summary

- Postnatal care supports parents in giving their new baby a healthy start in life.
- If PKU is not screened and left undetected without treatment then irreversible brain damage will gradually take place.
- A midwife visits the mother during the first 10 days after the birth of the baby.
- The health visitor takes over supporting and advising the mother 10 days after birth.
- Fathers should be as supportive as possible towards the needs of the mother and baby.

Activities

1. Produce an information leaflet that outlines the checks carried out on a day-old baby.
2. Prepare a job advert for a health visitor outlining the roles and responsibilities.

Prove it!

1. **When does a health visitor start to visit a new mother?**
2. **a. Describe how the PKU test is carried out on a newborn baby.**
   b. Explain what would happen if the test were positive.
3. **Postnatal refers to the first days and weeks after the baby is born. Discuss the importance of this time for the baby and parents.**

Examination questions

Suggestions here should refer back to practical health-related steps they can take, for example for overweight women to try and lose weight.

1 (a) Give **two** reasons why pre-conceptual care is important for a couple planning to have a baby. (2)
(b) Give **two** reasons why a couple planning to have a baby might need to have genetic counselling. (2)
(c) State **five** ways a couple could increase their chances of conceiving a baby. (5)

2 (a) Give **two** ways in which the foetus can easily be damaged between conception and twelve weeks. (2)
(b) Describe how the baby might be affected if the mother drinks alcohol regularly during pregnancy. (3)

Tip This answer requires at least two or three factors that have been described. This response would achieve full marks.

Alcohol crosses the placenta causing harm to the foetus which could result in the baby having a heart defect or foetal alcohol syndrome. The baby may have a small head and facial abnormalities, learning difficulties or brain damage and behavioural problems. The mother has more of a risk of miscarriage and the baby's growth rate is lower so the birth weight will be small. When born, the baby can suffer from withdrawal symptoms.

Here is the first reason.

This second reason actually lists a few physical and physiological factors.

Here is the last – third – reason.

3 (a) State why folic acid needs to be in the diet before and during pregnancy. (2)
(b) Describe how folic acid can be obtained in the diet. (2)
(c) State, with reasons, **four** foods that should be **avoided** during pregnancy. (4 × 2)

4. Pre-conceptual care and the first stages of pregnancy are vitally important for the development of a healthy baby. Assess the importance of both parents' lifestyles at this time. (10)

Tip To achieve the second mark in 3b, examples of foods that contain folic acid need to be given. For 3c, one mark will be given for the correct food and the second mark for the reason. Valuable marks will be lost if you do not know why the food should be avoided.

A possible answer to this might include:

Parents should stop drinking alcohol because it can affect fertility making it more difficult to become pregnant. The amount of sperm in men is reduced and it can change the ovulation and menstrual cycles in women.

- Stop drinking alcohol
- Both parents should stop smoking to avoid passive smoking and avoid all smoky places
- Stop taking recreational drugs
- Both parents should be checked for sexually transmitted diseases

- Mother should check if she has immunity to rubella and polio
- Exercise regularly
- Try not to be overweight
- Discuss stopping contraception and the implications
- Eat a healthy diet, especially one rich in folic acid, and take folic acid supplements for 3 months before conception
- Medication taken for epilepsy, diabetes, etc., may need adjusting so that the baby is not harmed
- Limit the amount of caffeine taken
- Avoid any X-rays
- Health checks
- Avoid foods that can cause problems – soft cheeses, undercooked eggs and meat
- Take extra care with food hygiene
- Do not handle animal faeces.

Tip You will need to give a balanced answer that describes more than drugs, alcohol and smoking. For maximum marks – Essay must be well structured with comprehensive answers that show an excellent understanding of the factors that parents need to consider.

5. Describe the advice that may be given to a woman to ensure she has a healthy and comfortable pregnancy. (10)

Your answer could cover the following points:

- Not to smoke – nicotine makes the baby's heart beat too fast, carbon monoxide stops haemoglobin in the baby's blood carrying oxygen, baby lacks oxygen to grow, and develop risk of miscarriage and stillbirth. Babies of smokers tend to grow slowly once born, and are more likely to have learning difficulties.
- Alcohol – crosses the placenta, interferes with growth of foetus and can severely affect development of the brain.
- Drugs – cross into the baby's blood stream and damage the foetus. The baby can be born addicted to drugs.
- Rubella – baby may be born deaf, blind, have heart disease or learning disability.
- Chickenpox – baby may have brain damage and skin problems.
- Toxoplasmosis – caught from cat faeces and can damage the nervous system of the baby.
- Avoid soft cheeses – can result in miscarriage, stillbirth or severe illness in the newborn baby.
- Diet – needs to contain extra protein, vitamins (folic acid), iron, calcium and fibre to prevent constipation.
- Rest – helps to prevent problems like backache, varicose veins and over-tiredness.
- Visit dentist – teeth more prone to decay and gums a little swollen and spongy.
- X-rays – can damage the baby so they should be avoided.
- Pelvic floor exercises – muscles around the vagina, bowel and openings need to be strengthened to cope with strain of pregnancy.
- Posture – good posture avoids backache which is common in pregnancy.
- Attend all appointments – to ensure baby is developing and mother is healthy.
- Appropriate conditions – safe, clean, warm home that is also free from damp and cigarette smoke.

6. Name the following that are described here.
   (a) The place where the baby develops. (1)
   (b) The opening of the female reproductive system where sexual intercourse takes place. (1)
   (c) The pouch where the testes are stored. (1)
   (d) The place where seminal fluid is produced and stored. (1)

7 **(a)** How many days does a woman's menstrual cycle usually last? (1)
   (b) Name **one** female hormone that controls the menstrual cycle. (1)
   (c) State **three** possible causes of female infertility. (3)

8. What do you understand by the following terms?
   (a) Fertilisation (1)
   (b) Implantation (1)
   (c) Zygote (1)
   (d) Ectopic pregnancy (1)

9 **(a)** Where in the body does conception take place? (1)
   (b) How many sperm fertilise one egg? (1)

Tip For question 10, there are probably six or seven signs from which you can choose any four.

10. State **four** early signs of pregnancy a woman would notice. (4)

11. How many **weeks** is a normal pregnancy? (1)

12. **(a)** What causes anaemia in pregnancy? (1)
   (b) Give **two** ways in which anaemia affects a pregnant woman. (2)
   (c) State **two** ways in which anaemia can be treated. (2)

13. A pregnant woman should not smoke, drink alcohol or take drugs whilst she is pregnant. Explain the effects these can have on the foetus. (10)

This is a good start because it immediately identifies a factor.

Good – the answer relates the explanation of how the baby is affected to the factor identified at the start.

Effects of alcohol

Alcohol crosses the placenta so the baby takes in alcohol, therefore the baby can be born addicted to alcohol and is usually very unsettled. Frequent drinking can interfere with the growth and development of the foetus causing malformations to the heart and limbs with facial disfigurements. If mother is an alcoholic the baby can be born with foetal alcohol syndrome. There is an increased risk of miscarriage and stillbirth and when the mother is drunk she could fall and harm the unborn baby.

Tip For maximum marks for question 13 – Essay must be well structured with comprehensive answers on each factor that show an excellent understanding of how the foetus can be affected by these products.

Effects of smoking

Harmful chemicals from the cigarettes cross the placenta into the baby's blood. Nicotine increases the baby's heart rate and the baby receives less oxygen as carbon monoxide takes the place of oxygen in the blood. Baby's growth is slower and development is affected so is born with a low birth weight. Lung capacity of the baby is affected, may have problems with breathing, be prone to bronchitis and asthma. There is a greater risk of developing ADHD and behavioural problems and the baby may have facial disfigurements. Smoking may be a contributory factor in SIDS (Sudden Infant Death Syndrome).

The mother is more likely to have a miscarriage, stillbirth or premature birth and there is a possibility that the mother could develop lung cancer in the future.

As before, this is a good approach to take – identify the factor first, then explain how the baby is affected by it.

It's a good idea to add further information – if relevant – if you know it.

Effects of drugs

Drugs cross the placenta into baby's blood so the baby may be addicted to drugs and have withdrawal symptoms when born. The baby could be born with low blood sugar and internal bleeding in the head. The risk of the baby having abnormalities is higher.

Money is used for drugs not food, lack of nutrients will affect baby's development and the baby may be born prematurely, with a low birth weight. There is an increased risk of miscarriage or stillbirth and if the mother shares needles the baby is at risk of contracting HIV.

14 **(a)** What is the difference between a screening test and a diagnostic test. (2)
(b) Name **one** screening test. (1)
(c) At what stage of the pregnancy would an amniocentesis test usually be carried out? (1)
(d) Give **two** reasons why an amniocentesis test might be carried out. (2)

15. Discuss why it is important for a pregnant woman to attend her antenatal appointments. (10)

There are about five different tests you can choose from. You only need to list one to get the mark.

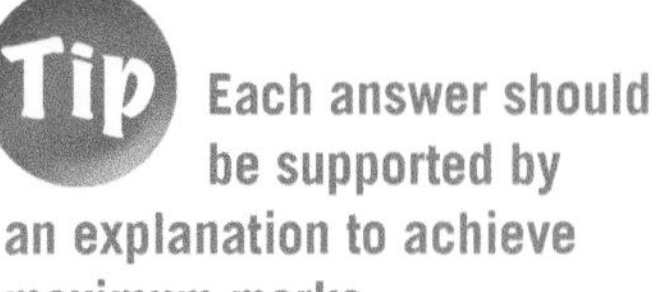

Each answer should be supported by an explanation to achieve maximum marks.

Your answer could cover these sorts of points:

- Tests carried out, e.g. blood tests – anaemia, urine test – protein
- Blood pressure checked at each visit – pre-eclampsia can be detected
- Advice on diet, nutrients needed, folic acid, listeriosis, toxoplasmosis
- Advice on minor problems during pregnancy
- Opportunity to meet other mothers
- Ultrasound scan checks the baby is developing correctly and if there is more than one baby
- Discuss types of birth available, visit delivery rooms
- Discus pain relief available and the effectiveness of each one
- Write birth plan
- Monitor baby's heartbeat
- Mother's weight is checked, increase could be of pre-eclampsia, loss could mean baby not growing.

There are lots of reasons you can list here but make sure they are acceptable medical ones – such as the baby is too large to easily go through the pelvis, or the foetal heart rate drops indicating that the baby is in distress. Social reasons are not valid.

16. What is a transverse presentation? (2)

17. Describe the following types of delivery:

(a) A ventouse extraction (2)

(b) A Caesarean section (3)

(c) Give **three** reasons why a mother might need a Caesarean section. (3)

18. The second stage of labour begins when the cervix is fully dilated and the vagina and cervix have formed the birth canal.
Explain what happens during the second stage of labour. (5)

Tip As question 18 is worth 5 marks a detailed answer is expected. This response could achieve the 5 marks.

The mother's contractions become quicker and stronger. The baby's head moves slowly down the birth canal and the mother has the urge to push with each contraction. The baby's head can be seen, which is termed 'crowning', and the mother is told to stop pushing and to pant with contractions to reduce the risk of the perineum tearing. If necessary an episiotomy may be given. The baby's head is born followed by the shoulders then the body. At this stage the umbilical cord is cut and clamped.

19. Suggest **five** ways the birth partner can help during labour and birth. (5)

20 **(a)** What do you understand by a premature (pre-term) baby? (1)

(b) Premature babies are usually cared for in a neo-natal or special care baby unit.
Explain how this will help them to survive. (5)

Tip Question 20b is worth 5 marks so a detailed answer is expected. This response could achieve 4–5 marks.

This could be improved if you mention the type of specialist staff available – for instance a neonatal nurse.

The baby will have 24-hour care and monitoring by a high ratio of specialist staff. Specialist equipment such as incubators will be available to maintain the baby's temperature, filter air and protect against infection. If the baby has trouble breathing a ventilator will be used to help breathing.

Monitors continually check breathing, heartbeat and oxygen levels whilst IV lines maintain fluid levels, give drugs and food if needed.

If the baby is unable to swallow, nasogastric tubes are used to aid feeding and light therapy used to treat jaundice.

Hygiene levels are high as the baby is prone to infection.

Another good point – not only does the answer comment on the type of problem, but it also suggests how the baby can be helped.

Although hygiene is important to mention, the answer does not develop it fully enough here.

Good point – it mentions a specific type of equipment.

(c) Explain how the following pieces of equipment in a special care baby unit can help in the care of premature babies:
(i) An incubator. (2)
(ii) A nasogastric tube. (1)

21. Newborn babies are given an APGAR test at birth.
(a) Why is the test important? (1)
(b) Explain when and how it is given. (4)

The midwife gives the APGAR test immediately at birth and again 5 minutes after birth. She checks the Appearance, Pulse, Grimace, Activity and Respiration of the baby. This means the colour, heartbeat, breathing, muscle tone, lungs, responses and reflexes are given a score between 0 and 2. If the total is 7+ the baby is in excellent condition but below 4 the baby may need resuscitation or medical help.

These are what the word APGAR represents, and to gain maximum marks you will need to show what each of them means.

22. A newborn baby will be examined by a paediatrician soon after the birth. Identify **two** checks carried out by the paediatrician during this examination. (2)

There are many different checks, but to help you remember some a good idea is to think about checks on the external and internal physical health of the baby.

23. Six weeks after the birth the mother will have a postnatal examination. Identify **four** checks which will be carried out at a postnatal examination. (4)

24. The health visitor is a key health care professional.
Assess the role of the health visitor in relation to both the mother and the baby. (6)

Your answer could cover the following points:

- Call on the mother and baby ten days after the birth – taking over from the midwife to support mother and baby.
- Visit the mother from time to time to complete development tests.
- Be available on the telephone for advice and support.
- Gives mother advice on how to keep herself and baby healthy.
- Check the baby is making normal progress – discussion of tests at relevant times.
- Advise on feeding – breast and bottle feeding.
- Advise the mother to attend a baby clinic.
- Discussions regarding teething.
- Discuss timetable for immunisation.
- Give help and guidance on emotional problems.
- Put the mother in touch with other mothers and postnatal groups.

25. Postnatal refers to the first days and weeks after the baby is born. Discuss the importance of this time for the baby and parents. (10)

A good start – this straightaway mentions the first health professional.

The midwife will visit for 10 days after birth to examine the mother and baby to check the baby is gaining weight and the mother is recovering from the birth. She will also provide advice on caring for the baby, e.g. breastfeeding or bathing.

Here is the second professional that is involved in postnatal care. Remember, we are only talking about care given by professionals after the baby is born – postnatal!

The health visitor will take over from the midwife after 10 days and will also check the baby is making normal progress. Advice may be given on health for mother and baby, feeding (which would include weaning) and immunisation will be discussed.

The mother will be encouraged to attend the local baby clinic and she may be put in touch with other mothers or groups. Help and guidance on emotional problems will also be offered.

This is perhaps slightly brief in describing care of the baby, and could be expanded slightly.

During this period the baby is examined and this usually takes place a day after birth. Important health checks on the eyes, heart, mouth and hip joints are done. A few tests will also be done and these include the PKU (Phenylketonuria) test where a sample of blood is taken from the heel of the baby to test for high phenylalanine levels. If detected, the child is put on a special diet to prevent brain damage and future learning difficulties. A second

Tip To gain maximum marks, you will need to provide a balanced answer that considers the health professionals involved in the care of the baby and mother and discuss what the parents should be doing during this time.

test is the thyroid function test as problems with the thyroid could lead to poor growth and possible learning difficulties.

Vitamin K given to the baby and the umbilical cord checked.

It is important for the mother to have a suitable diet and not get over tired. She should relax a little each day so that she has time and energy to feed, play with and talk to her baby and not worry about domestic chores.

This is a good aspect to the answer because it directly discusses what the mother herself needs to do in this period.

The mother should take part in postnatal exercises, to help regain her shape and therefore boost her self-esteem and overall health. She must attend the postnatal examination approximately 6 weeks after birth to ensure she is in good health and that the uterus has returned to normal state. At this clinic contraceptive advice will be given.

The father should be supportive and take paternity leave so that he can help and support mother by helping with household chores and taking care of baby so that she maintains her health and can rest. During this time it is also important for the father to bond with the baby.

If you are trying to produce a balanced answer and aim for top marks, then it would be good to have some mention of the father's role too.

Physical growth – becoming heavier

What will I learn?

- **How a child's body grows and increases in weight**

The growth of a child's body can be measured according to two characteristics: weight and height.

Weight

From birth onwards there is normally an increase in body weight. In babies with a healthy **diet** weight is gained through food which provides the child with the necessary **nutrients** to enable the body to grow.

The weight of a child can be measured using weighing scales. Birth weight of babies can vary considerably but the average weight is 3.5kg. By the age of 6 months most babies will have doubled their birth weight. And although after 6 months the weight gain is slower, by the child's first birthday the birth weight will in most cases have tripled. In general, boys tend to be slightly heavier than girls.

Remember, however, this is only a rough guide and individual babies will gain weight at different rates due to various factors such as health and level of activity. Because of this variation health professionals use centile charts to assess a child's actual weight gain linked to its age and gender. **Centile charts** are a good way

Key Fact

- Some babies, toddlers and young children have a food intolerance, such as an allergy to cows' milk, which may affect the weight gain. Health professionals can help with this problem and plan a change in the child's diet.

▼ **Boys' Centile Chart – Weight**

Weight in kilograms (kg)
91st percentile
50th percentile
9th percentile
Age in years

▼ **Girls' Centile Chart – Weight**

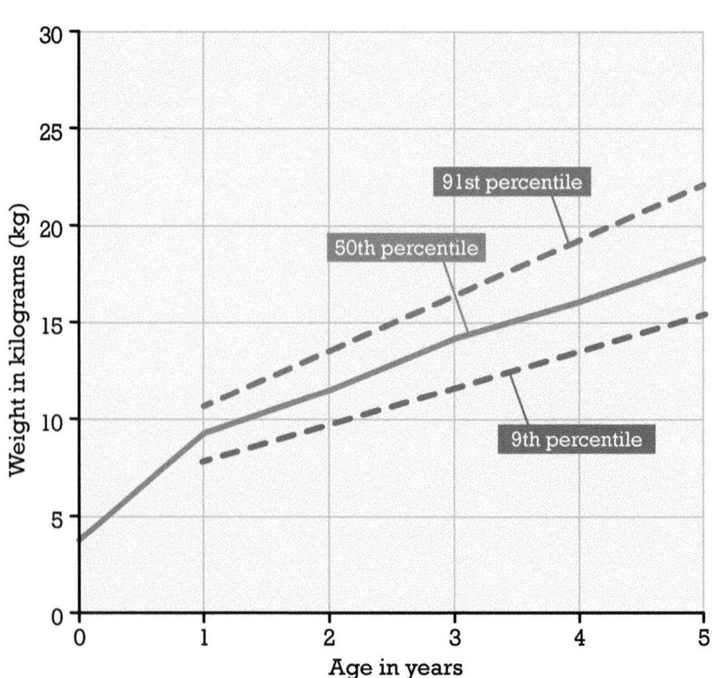

of quickly seeing how an individual child is developing compared with what a professional would expect to see.

In the Child Study on physical development you should record the child's weight at the first and last visits, compare them with the centile charts and discuss the findings.

- The 9th centile means that 9% of children will be below this weight.
- The 50th centile means that 50% of the children will be about this weight.
- The 91st centile means that 91% of the children will be below this weight.

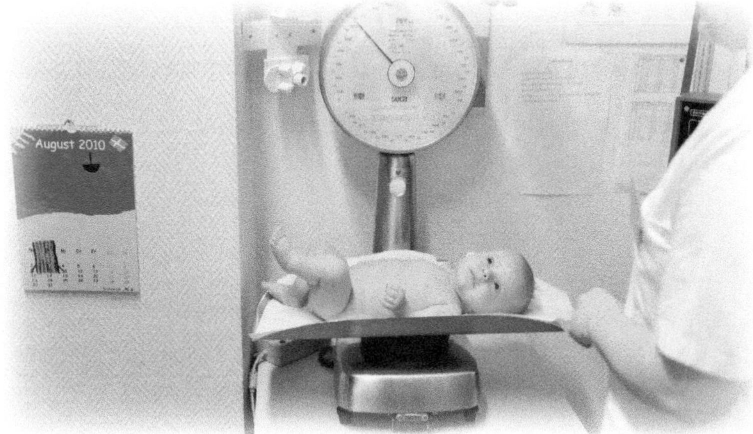

◀ **Weighing a baby**

If you have access to a young child, and with permission from the parents, measure the weight of the child. Using the relevant 'centile chart' assess the child's weight.

Factors that can affect the weight of a child

- A premature, small baby may be lighter in weight than a full-term baby.
- **Health** – there could be a loss of weight if the child has a serious illness or medical problem.
- **Diet** – there could be a large gain in weight if the child is given high fat and sugary foods. There could be a loss of weight if the child has a very poor appetite.
- Exercise – there could be a large gain in weight if the child does very little physical activity.

Weight – how heavy a baby is, measured in kilograms

Diet – the different food and drink given to a baby every day

Exercise – some physical activities for a young baby, such as crawling and playing on the floor with toys

Summary

- Growth is the physical change of a child's body.
- Growth can be measured by a gain in weight.
- The average birth weight is 3.5kg.
- Babies should have doubled their birth weight by age 6 months.
- Most children grow at about the same rate.

Make sure you understand how babies gain weight and the different factors which could cause weight loss or gain. You should be able to use the 'centile charts' to measure a child's weight.

Prove it!

1. **At birth a baby weighed 4.25kg. What might be the expected weight at 6 months?**
2. **Using the 'centile chart' for girls find out the 50th centile for a 2 year old.**
3. **Explain the factors which could affect the weight of young children.**

Physical growth – becoming taller

What will I learn? How a child's body grows and increases in height

The growth of a child's body can be measured according to two characteristics: height and weight.

Height

The average length of a baby at birth is approximately 50cm with the head being about 25% of the total length. Gradually the baby's body will develop and grow in length. During the first two years of life a child will grow quickly and limbs and muscles develop. Over this time the overall body shape changes slowly, as the head becomes a smaller proportion of the overall height. The muscles and **bones** of the arms and legs become stronger as a child becomes taller.

As with weight, health professionals use centile charts to assess a child's height linked to the age and gender of a young child.

Remember as with weight you should also record the height of the child at the beginning and at the end of the Child Study on physical development, use the centile charts and discuss the findings.

Key Fact

- When a child is examined and given developmental screening tests the health professionals will also measure the height of the child.

▼ **Boys' Centile Chart – Height**

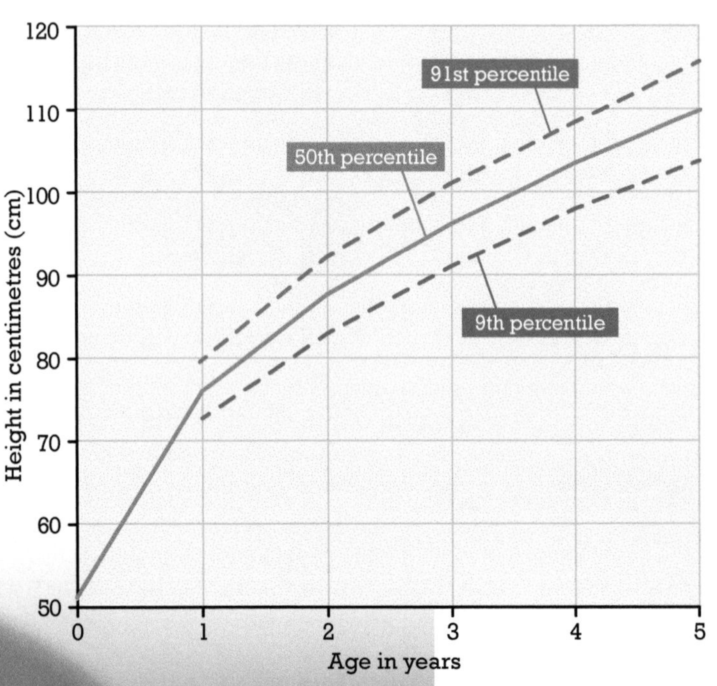

▼ **Girls' Centile Chart – Height**

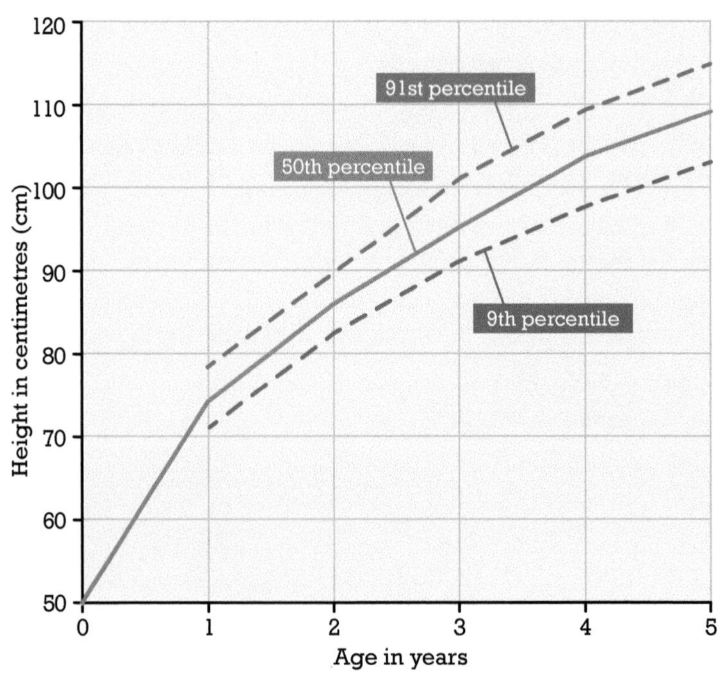

Make sure you understand how babies gain height and the different factors which could cause a slow rate of height. You should be able to use the centile charts to measure a child's height.

If you have access to a young child, and with permission from the parents, measure the height of the child. Using the relevant centile chart assess the child's height.

Genetic inheritance – the features that are passed from parents to child through the genes, such as the physical height

Growth hormone deficiency – when a child is lacking or has a very limited amount of the growth hormone which acts as a chemical messenger to make the body grow in height

- The 9th centile means that 9% of children will be below this height.
- The 50th centile means that 50% of the children will be about this height.
- The 91st centile means that 91% of the children will be below this height.

Factors that can affect the height of a child

- The **genetic inheritance** – the **genes** from the parents – will influence the height of a child. Tall parents will often have tall children and short parents will often have short children.
- A premature, small baby may be shorter in height than a full-term baby.
- If there is a **growth hormone deficiency** this will prevent the child reaching the average height. This can sometimes be corrected by medication.
- Poor health and a diet lacking in the essential nutrients could limit the height of the child.

▶ **How tall am I?**

Summary

- Height is related to genetic inheritance.
- The average birth length is about 50cm.
- The birth length and health in early life can affect how tall a child will become.

Prove it!

1. **Using the centile chart for boys find out the 91st centile for a 2 year old.**
2. **Using the centile chart for girls find out the 50th centile for a 5 year old.**
3. **Explain the factors which could affect the height of young children.**

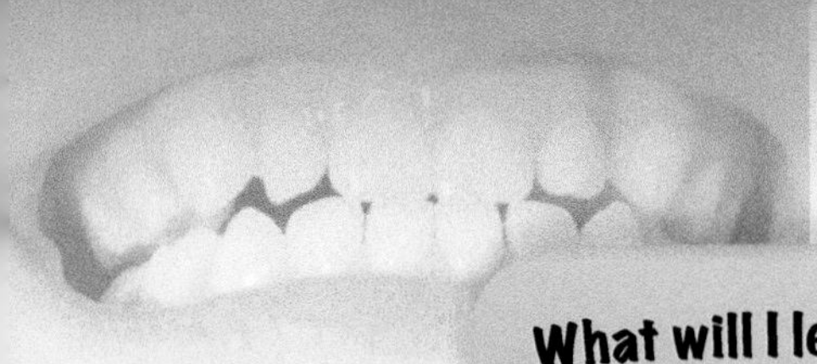

Dental development and care

What will I learn?

- **How a child's teeth develop**
- **The best way to take care of teeth**

Teeth are already developing in the gums in the mouth of a newborn baby. At about 6 months old the milk (or primary) teeth will begin to appear in the lower jaw, to be followed later by similar teeth in the upper jaw.

Key Fact

- Tooth decay is caused by the bacteria in the mouth coming into contact with sugar which produces acid. This acid can dissolve the enamel of the teeth and make holes in the teeth.

Teeth

Most children have a complete set of 20 milk teeth by the age of 3 years.

There are three types of teeth, each type performing a different task:

- Incisors – have sharp edges and are used for biting food.
- Canines – are pointed and sharp and are used to tear food into small pieces.
- Molars – have a flat surface and are used to grind down and crush food, making food easier to swallow.

These **milk**/primary **teeth** gradually fall out from the age of 5 years and are replaced with 32 **permanent teeth** which include an additional 12 molars.

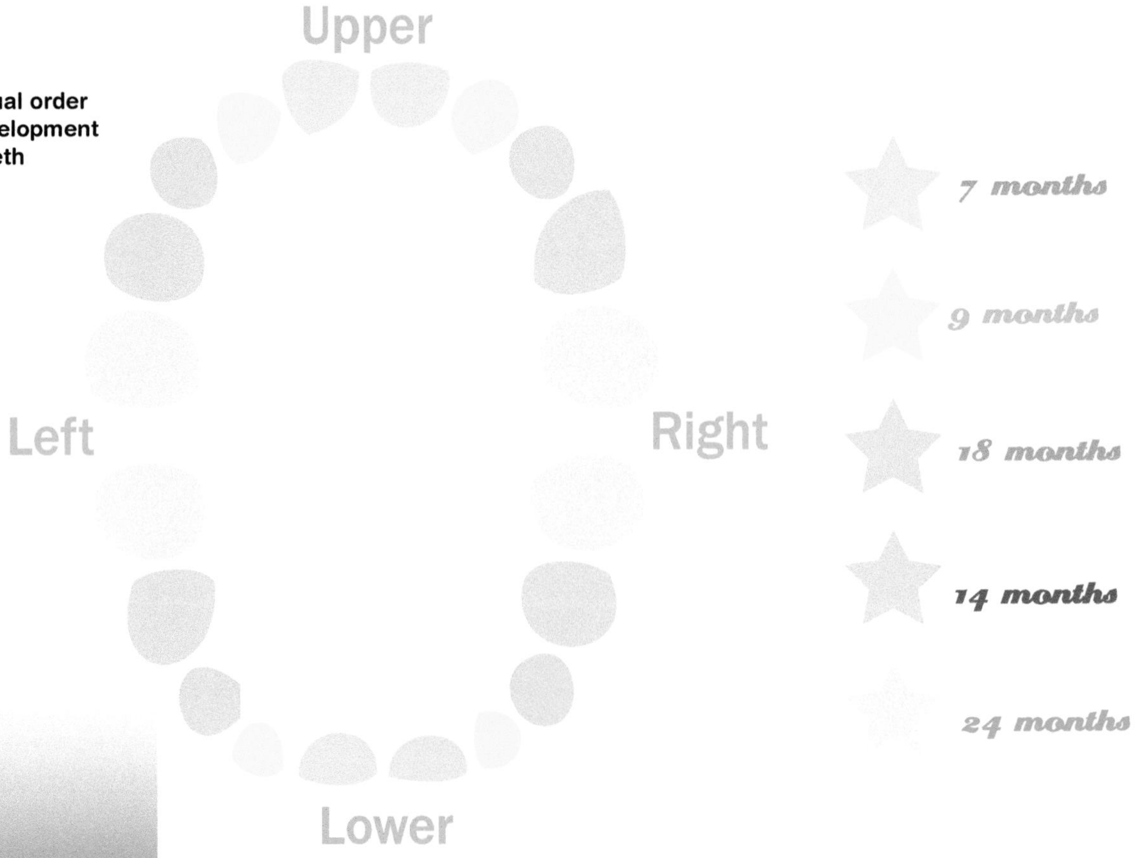

▶ The usual order of the development of milk teeth

Upper

Left

Right

Lower

7 months

9 months

18 months

14 months

24 months

Teething

Sometimes as milk teeth develop and are seen coming through, the gums can be sore and painful. This process is called teething, and it can cause babies to become very irritable and cross. They often dribble and chew their fists. A soothing teething ring or a baby rusk may help the general teething process. A child might be distracted from the teething discomfort by play or being given a different toy or activity. It would be a good idea to seek medical advice if the baby is frequently very uncomfortable and unable to sleep at night.

Diet

For a baby to have strong healthy teeth the diet must contain **calcium** and **vitamin D**, which work together to form the teeth. Milk is a good source of both calcium and vitamin D. Consuming lots of sugary foods and drinks will cause tooth decay. Children should be offered apples and carrot sticks as snacks which will encourage biting and chewing and help to maintain healthy teeth.

Fluoride, which is often found in the water supply or which can be given to a child as drops, also helps to strengthen teeth and prevent tooth decay.

Cleaning teeth

Children should be encouraged to brush their teeth from about the age of 1 year. A vertical action is best using short, gentle strokes. Young children should be taken to the dentist regularly so they become familiar with the check-up routine. The dentist can identify signs of decay and a build up of **plaque** on the teeth to prevent tooth decay and toothache. They can also advise on better ways to look after teeth at a young age.

Produce a leaflet explaining the development of the milk teeth and tips on caring for a toddler's teeth.

Summary

- Children have 20 milk teeth.
- These milk or primary teeth gradually fall out from the age of 5 years and are replaced with 32 permanent teeth.
- A diet rich in calcium and vitamin D will help to form strong healthy teeth.
- Good dental care and a diet low in sugary products will help to prevent tooth decay.

Prove it!

1. How many milk teeth will a child have? Describe the three different types of teeth.
2. What nutrients are needed to produce strong teeth?
3. Why should sugary foods and drinks be avoided in the diet of young children?

Key Terms

Milk teeth appear from about the age of 6 months; they are temporary and will fall out to make room for the permanent teeth from about the age of 5 years

Permanent teeth – develop in the gums below the milk teeth and will replace the milk teeth for the rest of one's life

Plaque – an invisible layer of bacteria and saliva on the teeth which can be removed by brushing the teeth regularly

You should have an understanding about how teeth develop, the need for calcium and vitamin D in the child's diet and how to care for them. In an answer about a toddler's bedtime routine remember to discuss the importance of cleaning the teeth. The development of teeth should be a feature of a Child Study on physical development.

Development and care of eyes

What will I learn?

- **How a baby's sight develops and possible visual problems**

When born, babies are short-sighted meaning they can only see faces and objects up to a distance of about 25 cm away. They will probably be unaware of any movement or shapes beyond this distance. Because of this limited vision it is important that the mother holds the baby close to her so the child can see her face clearly. This will enable the baby to begin to recognise the mother's features and maybe respond by smiling to the mother's eye contact.

Key Fact

- Colour blindness is more common in boys than girls. A child with this defect cannot distinguish red from green.

Vision

Babies are attracted to faces, patterns and movement such as colourful mobiles which are positioned close to them. They do not like bright lights and will react by closing their eyes. By the age of 3 months the baby's sight range will have extended with an ability to see further, and take much more interest in watching everything and everyone around.

▶ **Eye contact between mother and young baby**

Key Terms

Short-sighted – when close objects can be seen clearly but far away objects are blurred

Focus – the ability of the eyes to see objects clearly at various distances

Vision – the ability to see

Long-sighted – when far away objects can be seen clearly but close objects are blurred

In some young babies each eye works independently of the other, looking at objects in different directions. This is referred to as a squint. By the age of 6 months, as eye muscles develop, the eyes work together and are able to focus on the same object. The squint will have disappeared. Usually, by the child's first birthday long distance vision will have developed and a 2 year old should be able to see just as well as an adult.

Eye check-ups

The baby's eyes will be examined at birth and again at the 6-week check-up to identify any possible problems. Further check-ups will be carried out, probably at 18 months and when starting school. If at any time parents have concerns about their child's **vision** they should seek medical advice.

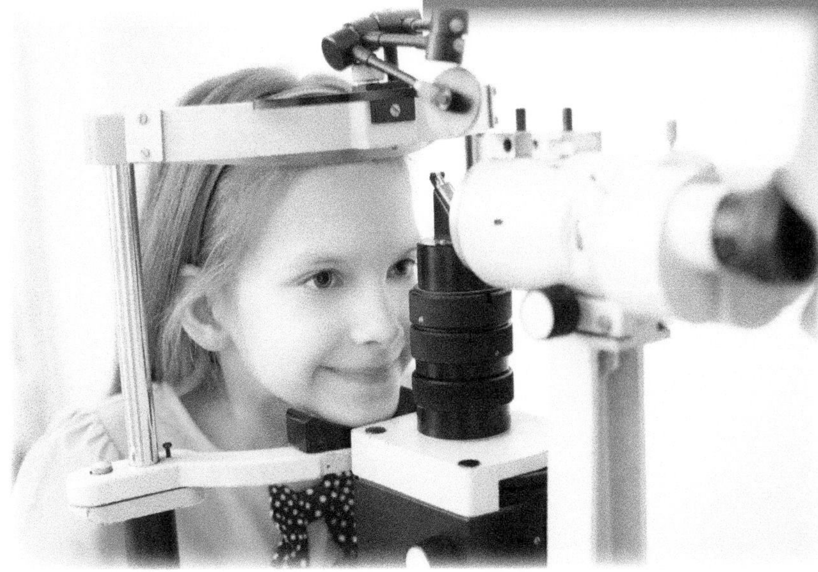

Examining a child's eyes

Vision problems

- Short-sighted – can see near objects clearly but everything in the distance will be very blurred and unrecognisable.
- **Long-sighted** – near objects will appear to be blurred, making it difficult to see words in a reading book.

Both of these vision problems can be corrected by wearing spectacles.

Visual Impairment

We generally refer to two levels of visual impairment:

- **Partial sight** – very limited sight which restricts the child's development.
- **Blind** – the child is unable to carry out any activity which requires sight and cannot make eye contact with people. Specialist help will be required to assist the child with this disability.

Summary

- Newborn babies are short-sighted and their vision will develop gradually so they are able to see further.
- In a young baby each eye works independently of the other, referred to as a squint. By age 6 months the eyes will be able to work together.
- A child's sight is developed fully by the age of 2 years.
- Some children have vision problems which can be corrected by wearing spectacles.
- Visual impairment such as partial sight and blindness require specialist medical help.

Design an attractive, colourful mobile for a 3 month old's cot, giving reasons for your choice of design and materials. Include instructions on where you think the mobile should be placed, and why.

You should be able to explain how baby vision develops and how both eyes are gradually able to work together to focus on an object. You also need to understand the possible sight problems that may occur and how they are treated.

Prove it!

1. **What is the distance a baby can see at birth?**
2. **What is a squint and why is it common in young babies?**
3. **Explain what is meant by being short-sighted?**

Development and care of ears

What will I learn?

- **How a baby's hearing develops and the problems of deafness**

Newborn babies are able to hear and are startled by loud noise. At about 4 months a baby will begin to recognise the sound of the mother's voice. Gradually the hearing ability improves and the baby will turn towards any sound in a room. By the first birthday the child will respond to being called by name.

Hearing

Parents should talk to the baby to encourage the development of hearing and speech. Being able to hear is an essential factor in speech development. A young baby will soon be able to identify different human voices and various other household sounds.

Hearing tests

A test for deafness will be given at the 6-week routine check-up. A sound is made which will cause the young baby to display the **startle reflex**. Sometimes a further test is carried out between 6 and 9 months, usually by the health visitor. Normally by this age the baby can sit up and control its head movements. The baby can sit on an adult's lap while a range of low- and high-pitched sounds are made behind the baby on both the left- and right-hand sides. If the baby hears these various sounds the baby's head will turn towards them. Further check-ups will be carried out, probably at about the age of 3 years and again when starting school.

▲ **Enjoying musical sounds**

Parents can carry out a simple hearing test within the home by standing behind a young baby and clapping their hands or ringing a bell, and then watching the child's response to the noise. If the parents are concerned about the hearing ability of the child they should seek medical advice.

Key Fact

- Hearing is linked to language development. A child needs the ability to hear words in order to develop speech and the means of communicating with other people.

Activity

Design and explain a simple hearing test that a parent could carry out on an 8 month old at home.

Examining a child's ear

Hearing – the ability to hear sounds

Temporary deafness – being deaf for a short time, often due to a health problem; recovery to full hearing ability will return

Partial deafness – lacking the ability to hear the full range of sounds such as high-pitched or low-pitched noises

Total deafness – lacking the ability to hear any sounds

Hearing problems

- **Temporary deafness** – young children may suffer temporary deafness due to recurring infections of the middle ear called **glue ear**. This is caused by a build-up of fluid in the middle ear and can be corrected by medicine or surgery.
- **Partial deafness** – the child is unable to hear some sounds such as either high- or low-pitched noises.
- **Total deafness** – the child is unable to hear any sounds.

Even slight levels of deafness can cause problems with the child's speech development. It is important to identify any deafness in a child by the first birthday. This will enable the child to have the correct training and treatment so that the child's communication skills can develop. If a child's deafness is not identified, the child will find it difficult to understand what is being said, have limited speech and will feel isolated. This deafness may possibly cause learning difficulties for the child.

You should understand how a child's hearing develops and the problems of deafness. When answering a question about language and communication skills remember to discuss that having the ability to hear sounds is vital for babies to copy and learn words.

Summary

- Newborn babies are able to hear and are startled by loud noise.
- A hearing test will identify any hearing problems.
- A one year old should be able to respond to being called by name.
- Some children suffer from temporary, partial or total deafness, which will require specialist medical help.

Prove it!

1. What is the startle reflex?
2. What is glue ear and how is it caused?
3. Discuss the problems of deafness in a young child.

Large muscle development

What will I learn?

- **What gross motor skills are and how a baby develops them**

Key Fact

- Gross motor skills involve the co-ordination of the brain and muscles. As the large muscles grow and develop the baby learns how to control them. Babies will achieve the ability to control these large muscles at different rates.

Gross motor skills mean the control of the large muscles in the body such as legs and arms. The development of gross motor skills involves the co-ordination between the brain and these muscles. These muscles begin to develop from the head downwards to the arms and legs.

Gross motor skills

Gradually children gain control of their large muscles and are able to crawl, walk, throw a ball and climb.

Different children gain the ability to use these muscles at different ages. Some children are able to walk by their first birthday while others master the art of walking much later. The **norms of development**, also called **developmental milestones**, are used as a rough guide to check the child's gross motor skills progress. These norms identify the age by which a child should have mastered a particular gross motor skill.

The progress of achieving gross motor skills can be affected by a child's health. Any physical disabilities may also hinder the development of the large muscles.

Learning head control

A newborn baby does not have any **head control** because the muscles that support the head are weak. When the baby is picked up from the cot the baby's head will fall backwards. To avoid this happening a newborn baby's head should always be supported with your hand.

By 3 months the baby has gained some head control and the head does not fall backwards as much. Care is still needed though when picking up and holding the baby. By 6 months the baby has gained full head control and can raise the head by itself.

▲ A baby able to control head movements

Activity

If you have access to a baby under the age of 1 year, and permission from the parents, observe the gross motor skills of the child.

Learning to sit

- A newborn baby placed in a **sitting** position will fall forward into a ball due to weak neck and back muscles.
- By 3 months the back muscles are becoming stronger and a baby can sit up with some support.
- By 6 months a baby can sit upright on the floor and use the hands to support the body for a short time.
- By 9 months a baby can sit unsupported for a short while.
- By the first birthday a baby can sit unsupported for a long time.

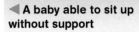

◀ **A baby able to sit up without support**

Child Study

In a Child Study on physical development you should observe and record your findings about these gross motor skills.

Learning to crawl

- A newborn baby lying on the stomach will fold up the knees under the body.
- By 3 months a baby can lie with the legs straight and use the arms to lift the head and shoulders off the ground.
- By 6 months a baby can raise the head and chest off the ground by using the arms. The baby will also have gained the skill of rolling over.
- By 9 months most babies can move along the ground by either using the hands or rolling over and over.
- By their first birthday most babies have learnt to either **crawl** using their hands and knees or move by shuffling the bottom along the ground.

◀ **A baby able to move by crawling**

Gross motor skills – the use of the large muscles in the body

Norms of development – a stage of development which an average child should have achieved according to age

Summary

- Gross motor skills are the ability to control the large muscles in the body, such as the head, arms and legs.
- Control of the large muscles starts with the head and progresses downwards.
- A young baby first gains control of the head and then the ability to sit unsupported.
- By their first birthday most babies will have achieved the skill of being able to move by crawling or shuffling along the floor.
- The age at which these skills are achieved can vary due to the development process and any health problems.

Prove it!

1. **Why is it necessary to support the head of a newborn baby?**
2. **Explain how a baby develops the skill to sit upright.**
3. **What are norms of development or developmental milestones?**

Development of gross motor skills

What will I learn?

- **How children use their large muscles to develop a range of gross motor skills**

By their first birthday most babies can stand, beginning by holding onto furniture or the hands of an adult. Gradually, as they learn to walk better, toddlers can walk by just holding one hand of an adult.

Development of the large muscles

By about 15 months, or possibly earlier or later, toddlers can walk alone. At first toddlers will be unsteady and hold up the arms for help with their **balance**. They will find it difficult to turn corners and will often fall down. Slowly their walking skills improve and children can walk steadily.

Once children have mastered walking they will develop other gross motor skills.

▶ **First steps, using the arms to help with balance**

Walking up stairs

- First a toddler will learn to crawl up the stairs and crawl backwards down the stairs.
- By about 18 months a toddler will be able to walk upstairs holding onto the handrail and place both feet onto each step of the stairs. The toddler will still probably crawl down the stairs.
- By their second birthday most toddlers can walk up and down stairs confidently placing two feet on each step. By the third birthday most children can walk up and down stairs confidently placing one foot on each step. When coming down the stairs children may still place two feet on each step.
- By their fourth birthday children can walk up and down the stairs in the same way as an adult.

▼ **Crawling up steps**

Key Facts

- A 2 year old will use the feet to move on a tricycle and by the age of 3 years will have gained the skill of being able to use the pedals. A 3 year old should be able to catch a ball with extended arms. Some 4 year olds enjoy good ball skills and using a bat to play team games. A 5 year old will be agile with well-developed gross motor skills.

Key Terms

Walking – the ability to stand upright and move one leg in front of the other to travel across the floor

Large muscles – found in the arms and legs and allow the body to perform various big movements such as walking

Running – being able to move quickly, such as walking at a fast speed

Climbing – being able to move vertically, such as climbing up a rope ladder in a play area

Learning other gross motor skills

Other gross motor skills using the **large muscles** will begin to develop once a toddler has the ability to walk. For instance:

- A 2 year old will be able to **run**.
- A 2½ year old should be able to walk on tip toe and also jump up and down.
- A 3 year old should be able to hop and throw a ball.
- A 4 year old should be able to **climb** and kick a ball.

Young children usually learn how to pedal a bike or ride a scooter. They often enjoy the opportunity to take part in activities in the swimming pool and begin to learn to swim. Babies and toddlers need to be able to control the large muscles in the legs and arms, and achieve a sense of balance and **co-ordination**, to acquire these gross motor skills. Parents should give toddlers as many opportunities to develop the large muscles as possible, such as by playing in the garden and visiting play areas.

A young child will gradually gain **confidence** and become more skilful with a range of movements.

Child Study

In a Child Study on physical development the gross motor skills of the child should be observed, compared with the norms of development and discussed. With the parent's permission, playing in the garden or park with a toddler or young child provides an ideal opportunity to participate in different activities.

Summary

- By using the large muscles in the arms and legs children have the ability to perform many large movements of the body.
- A toddler learns to walk and to walk up and down stairs.
- Young children develop greater control over the large muscles and are able to run, hop and also throw and kick a ball.
- Young children need to develop the sense of balance, co-ordination and confidence to perform these movements.
- The age at which these skills are achieved can vary due to the development process and any health problems.

You should understand how using large muscles develops many gross motor skills. Toddlers learn to walk and then extend the skills to their arms and legs. With balance and co-ordination, young children learn to run, hop, throw and kick a ball. In answering questions on gross motor skills, a common error is to ignore the use of arms. You should discuss how young children use large muscles in their arms to climb ropes and also throw and catch a ball.

Prove it!

1. **Where are the large muscles found in the body?**
2. **Describe how a 2 year old will walk up and down stairs.**
3. **Explain the importance of outdoor play in the development of the large muscles.**

Small muscle development

What will I learn?

- **What fine motor skills are and how a baby develops them**

Fine motor skills mean the control of the small muscles in the fingers, hands and feet. As babies grow, they develop fine motor skills and also hand–eye co-ordination. They can use the hands and eyes together to make movements and gradually learn to do a variety of tasks involving the small movements of the hands and feet. However, the age by which a child develops fine motor skills will vary.

Key Facts

- Babies learn to control movement firstly of their arms, then the hands and finally the fingers. Manipulative play, such as playing with a rattle and soft toys, involves the use of hands and will help with the co-ordination of the hands, eyes and brain.

Fine motor skills

The norms of development, or developmental milestones, give a rough guide to check the progress of fine motor skills by identifying the age by which most children should have mastered a particular skill.

The progress of achieving fine motor skills can be affected by the child's health. Any physical disabilities may also hinder the development of the small muscles.

Learning fine motor skills

At about 3 months a baby will begin to look at and play with their hands and fingers. If given a small toy, the baby can hold it for a few moments before dropping it. Gradually a baby will learn to clasp the hands together and begin to understand what hands can do.

Fine motor skills – the use of small muscles in the body

Hand-eye co-ordination – the ability of the hands, eyes and brain to work together to perform fine motor skills

▶ Exploring the fingers

By 6 months a baby can pick up and hold a toy using the whole of the hand. This is called the **whole hand palmar grasp**. The baby will pick up every object within reach to play with. Fingers are used to splash water at bath time. At the same time a baby will have discovered and play with their toes.

Enjoying play with a soft ball

Safety warning

It is very important that there are no small objects left near a baby. Babies who can pick up small objects will often put them into their mouth leading to a risk of choking.

Child Study

In a Child Study on physical development the fine motor skills of the baby should be observed, compared with the norms of development and discussed. You should play with the baby and watch how the toys are picked up and held.

By 9 months a baby can use the fingers and thumb to hold a toy. The index finger, next to the thumb, is used to touch and poke any object within reach. Using this finger and the thumb a baby will begin to learn to pick up small objects. This is called the **pincer grasp**. The baby will be able to open the hands and drop a toy onto the floor.

By their first birthday a baby will use the **index finger** to point to toys and people. The pincer grasp of the index finger and thumb will have improved to pick up slightly bigger objects

Summary

- Fine motor skills are using the small muscles in the fingers, hands and feet.
- As babies grow they develop fine motor skills and hand–eye co-ordination. Babies have the ability to use their hands and eyes together to make movements, such as clapping hands and picking up toys.
- The age at which these skills are achieved can vary due to the development process and any health problems.

You should now have an understanding of how babies develop the control of the small muscles which allow them to have fine motor skills of the fingers, hands and feet. The different hand grasps and the hand–eye co-ordination skill should also be discussed when answering a question on fine motor skills.

Prove it!

1. **Where in the body are the small muscles which provide fine motor skills found?**
2. **What is a palmar grasp?**
3. **Describe what fine motor skills should be expected in a 9 month old.**

Development of fine motor skills

What will I learn?

- **How children use their small muscles to develop a range of fine motor skills**

Key Facts

- Babies, toddlers and young children will be using and developing their sensory skills when playing with toys. The sensory skills of taste, touch, vision, hearing and smell are used to learn about the surrounding environment and can help to improve all areas of development. Vision is linked to fine motor skills and the development of hand–eye co-ordination.

By their first birthday most toddlers will be developing fine motor skills and be able to carry out more tasks involving small movements of the hands and fingers. These skills will make the child more independent and be beneficial when attending playgroups or nursery school.

Development of the small muscles

Being able to use cutlery

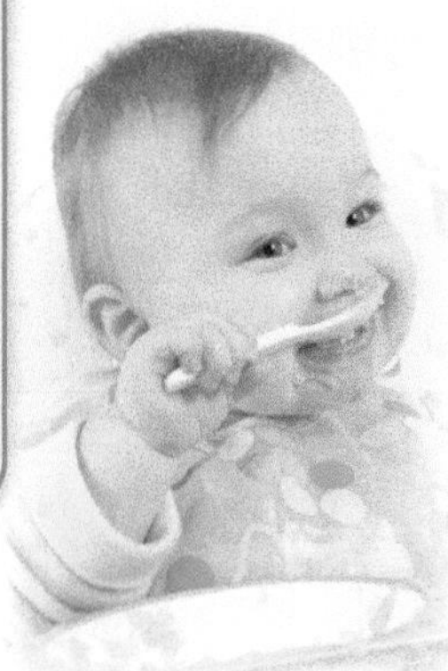

▶ Learning to use cutlery

From around the age of one, toddlers should be given opportunities to learn how to hold **cutlery** and practise how to feed themselves using a plastic cup and spoon. At first the toddler will not be very skilful in lifting the spoon or holding the cup to the mouth and some food and drink may be spilled. By 18 months, however, most toddlers will have gradually learnt the skill of eating with a spoon and drinking from a cup.

A 4 year old should be able to use a spoon and fork quite skilfully and a 5 year old should be able to eat food using a knife and fork in the same way as an adult.

Learning to dress

A 2 year old should be encouraged to learn to **dress** and undress without help, starting with trying to put on and take off shoes. Learning to dress and undress can be a slow process. A 3 year old should be able to dress and undress but may still require help with fastenings such as buttons. By the age of 5 years, most children should be able to dress and undress independently.

Key Terms

Small muscles – found in the fingers, hands and toes, which allow the body to perform small movements, such as picking up toys and holding cutlery

Cutlery – knives, forks and spoons used when eating food

Dressing – putting clothes and shoes onto the body

Child Study

In a Child Study on physical development, the fine motor skills of a toddler or young child, such as playing with a jigsaw puzzle, building bricks or board games, should be observed.

Child Focused Task

In the Child Focused Task you could be asked to make an activity to develop fine motor skills or hand–eye co-ordination. Remember the child should have to use the fingers as well as hands and eyes working together.

Other fine motor skills

One of the other fine motor skills that toddlers develop is that of balancing objects on top of each other – for instance by building a tower of bricks. At about 15 months a toddler will be able to place one brick on top of another. A 2 year old will build a tower of about 6 bricks and a 3 year old might build a tower of 8 to 10 bricks.

By about 2½ years a toddler should be able to thread large beads onto a piece of string or do a simple jigsaw puzzle.

◀ **Creating a tower with building bricks**

Which hand – right or left handed?

Very young babies initially use both hands and then gradually one hand may be used more than the other. By 18 months most toddlers will be using a preferred hand to carry out tasks and by the third birthday there will be a definite preference for either the right or left hand. Some children take a little longer to display their preference.

The brain controls which hand will be the preferred choice. Most children will be **right handed** with only about 10% being **left handed**. Children must be allowed to decide which hand they prefer to use for activities. A left-handed child must not be forced to use the right hand because research has proved that this can cause serious problems with language development and may result in the child stuttering.

A very few children can use either hand for tasks, such as writing, without any problems. These children are called **ambidextrous**.

Activity

If you have access to a toddler, and with permission from the parents, observe the child's fine motor skills by playing with the child such as building a tower of bricks.

Summary

- Children can perform many fine movements of the hands and fingers using the small muscles in the hands and fingers.
- Young children need to be given opportunities to practise these fine motor skills and should be given encouragement when practising these activities. Parents should allow toddlers and young children to feed and dress themselves. A range of toys and activities, which require fine motor skills, will be very beneficial for children. The age at which these skills are achieved can vary due to the development process and any health problems.

You should understand how toddlers and young children gradually learn how to use the **small muscles** of hands and fingers to carry out various activities and tasks. In an answer on the development of fine motor skills you should discuss how parents must allow toddlers to feed and dress themselves so they can practise these skills. Playing with jigsaw puzzles and construction toys, such as building bricks, should be mentioned as suitable ways of improving fine motor skills.

Prove it!

1. **Explain how a parent should start to encourage toddlers to feed themselves.**
2. **Describe some suitable toys which would help to develop the fine motor skills of a toddler.**
3. **Discuss why it is important to allow a young child to decide which hand to use when doing various activities.**

Learning hand control

What will I learn?

- **How a child's hand grasp improves through learning to draw**

From about the age of 1 year a toddler should be encouraged to draw. This will help the toddler to develop the hand grasp and also offer an opportunity to be creative. To begin with the toddler would need a thick pencil or crayon and a few sheets of paper or card.

Developing drawing skills

Learning to draw and develop a pincer grasp

At the beginning the toddler will hold the pencil using either hand in a palmar grasp. The drawing will be of backwards and forwards scribbles.

By 15 months the toddler may begin to show a preference for one hand. Some children may begin by using the primitive **tripod grasp** of the thumb and the first two fingers. Drawing skills will develop because the pencil can be lifted up from the paper and moved in various directions. A 2 year old usually has an improved primitive tripod grasp of the pencil. The drawings will include vertical lines and some circular scribbles.

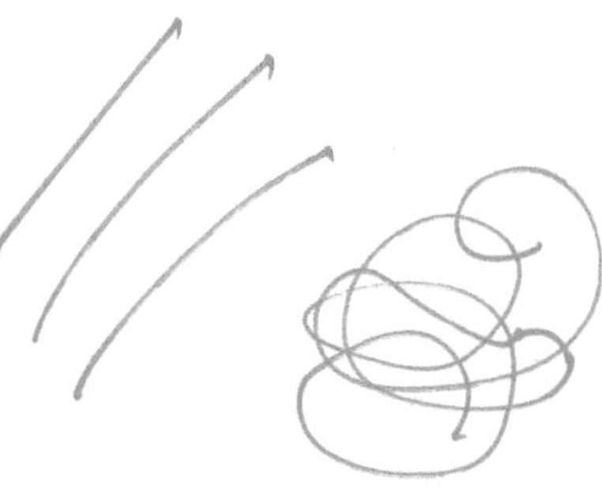

A 3 year old has usually identified the preferred hand, displaying quite good **control** of the pencil and can probably draw lines, dots, squares and incomplete circles. Sometimes there may be drawings of people who have a head and a few features.

Key Facts

- Toddlers and young children can express their feelings through drawings, allowing them to produce pictures of how they see their surrounding world. They can use their **imagination** and make a visual record of an event, such as a visit to the park or a family trip to the seaside. Young children like to explain their drawings to parents, which encourages communication skills. The self-esteem of young children will improve by receiving praise for their artistic skills and having their work put on display.

Key Terms

Tripod grasp – using the thumb and two fingers

Control – having the ability to make an item, such as a pencil, do what a person wants it to do

Child Study

In a Child Study on physical development the toddler should be asked to do some drawing and colouring to observe fine motor skills. Include the child's work in your study.

Child Focused Task

In a Child Focused Task on helping to improve the fine motor skills a suitable task would be an activity linked to drawing and colouring.

A 4 year old should be able to hold a pencil in a pincer grasp in the same way as an adult. With greater control of the pencil the child is able to colour in a picture, although not always within the outline of the picture. The child may be able to copy letters and draw a person with a head, arms and legs.

A 5 year old has good hand control and can produce more detailed and recognisable drawings of people. The child may have the skill to copy or write a simple word.

Another way in which the pincer grasp will develop is by giving a young child the opportunity to paint with a paint brush.

◀ **Practising the pincer grasp and being creative using paints**

Activity

If you have access to a toddler, and permission from the parents, spend some time with the child doing some drawings and observe the hand control of the child.

Summary

- By having the opportunity to draw, a child will use small muscles in the hands and fingers and develop a pincer grasp.
- Young children need the opportunity to be creative and use their imagination.
- Parents should encourage toddlers and young children to draw, as the ability to hold and use a pencil will be required in school.
- The age at which these skills are achieved can vary due to the development process and any health problems.

Prove it!

1. **What resources are needed for a 1 year old to draw?**
2. **Name the grasp a 5 year old uses to hold a pencil.**
3. **Explain the benefits for a 3 year old of being given opportunities to draw.**

Make sure you know and can describe the different stages of how a young child learns to draw. In a question about preparing a young child for school remember to discuss how parents should provide opportunities for drawing as children need to hold and control a pencil in the classroom.

Physical health and diet

What will I learn?

- **An understanding of how health and diet can affect the physical development of young children**

Key Fact

- An unbalanced diet containing too many calories and a lack of fruit and vegetables in early years could become the pattern for life with the risk of causing obesity and related problems, such as diabetes.

Babies may be born with or develop disabilities or illnesses. A well-balanced diet is important to physical development.

Physical disabilities

Some babies are born with **physical disabilities** which can hinder growth and limit their physical development. Other babies and toddlers may develop disabilities during their lives which can cause them physical problems. Problems with the major organs, such as the heart or the development of limbs, can cause the baby to fail to reach the expected norms of development. Parents of such children will be given medical advice about the most suitable types of activities for them to develop fine and gross motor skills.

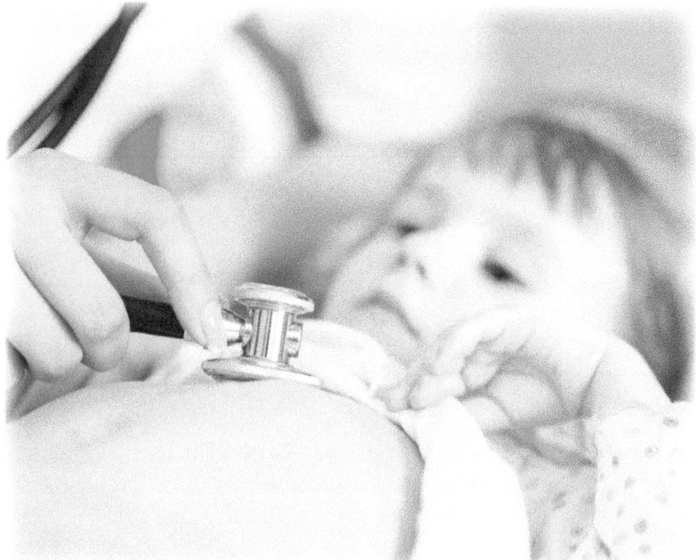

▶ Doctor examining sick child

Serious illness

A long-term **illness** might slow down the baby's growth and physical development, preventing the baby achieving the expected norms of development relevant to their age. If it is only a short-term illness, the baby will probably fail to reach the expected stage of development for a while but should catch up later.

Key Terms

Physical disabilities – can affect and sometimes prevent the development and growth of the body, such as the heart or limbs

Illness – when the body is not functioning properly due to an infection or virus such as a cold or tonsillitis

Child Study

In a Child Study on physical development you could discuss the health of the child with the parents. You could ask the parents to record the diet of the child for one week and then analyse and discuss the findings.

Child Focused Task

In the Child Focused Task on food remember to discuss how a well-balanced diet assists with the growth and development of the child.

Diet

Babies and toddlers must have a well-balanced diet in order to grow and develop. The following nutrients will help to promote growth as well as fine and gross motor skills:

- **Protein** is needed for body tissue to grow and muscles to develop. A diet containing milk, meat, fish, eggs and cheese provides the necessary protein. Cereals and pulses also provide some protein.
- **Calcium** is needed for bones and teeth to form and become strong. A diet containing milk and cheese provides the necessary calcium.
- **Vitamin D** is needed to help the body use the calcium for the formation of bones and teeth. A diet containing milk and margarine provides the necessary vitamin D.
- **Fat** is a very good source of energy. Toddlers need a high supply of energy as they burn up a lot of energy when using their gross motor skills. A toddler should have full fat milk because the fat provides some of the required energy. Other foods which provide fat are margarine, egg yolk and oily fish.

A diet containing too many sugary foods could cause a toddler to become overweight and even obese, which is harmful to health and could limit the development of gross motor skills.

◀ Meat provides protein for growth

◀ Cheese provides calcium for bones and teeth

Activity

Plan a day's menu for a 2 year old including the necessary nutrients for growth and gross motor skills.

Summary

- The state of health and any physical disability of a baby or toddler will affect growth and physical development.
- A well-balanced diet containing the necessary nutrients will help growth and physical development.

You should understand the need for a well-balanced diet to help the growth and physical development of babies and toddlers. When answering a question on diet and health, remember to name and discuss the important nutrients needed, giving examples of good food sources for each named nutrient.

Prove it!

1. **Give some reasons why a toddler may not achieve the expected norms of development.**
2. **Explain the function of protein in the body and name two protein foods.**
3. **Why should fat be included in a toddler's diet?**

Physical activities

What will I learn?

- **How exercise, new opportunities and a sense of freedom can affect the physical development of young children**

Babies and toddlers should be allowed to play in order to exercise the large and small muscles of the body.

Exercise

Exercise helps to develop and strengthen the muscles and the bones. Indoor play, such as playing with building bricks, jigsaws and drawing, helps to develop the small muscles in the hands and fingers. While playing with these toys toddlers also begin to learn about colours and numeracy.

Outdoor play such as kicking a ball, climbing trees or playground equipment and riding a bike all help develop the large muscles in the arms and legs. Outdoor play also provides toddlers with an opportunity to enjoy fresh air, helping to give them a **healthy appetite** as well as encouraging a **good sleep pattern**. Toddlers could run around and play with balls or ride bikes in a secure and safe garden at home, although this may not be possible in houses or flats without gardens. Play equipment, such as a swing or slide, if available, gives toddlers an opportunity to exercise the large muscles in the arms and legs.

Key Fact

- By having the opportunity to play outdoors toddlers and young children will be able to develop strong muscles and bones. This will help with the physical development of the body. Children will also be able to use their senses of vision, smell, hearing and touch.

Child Study

In a Child Study on physical development a visit to a play area with the toddler or young child can provide an opportunity to observe balance and co-ordination skills.

▶ **A child's play area encourages physical development**

Babies and toddlers enjoy visiting a **park** or **play area**, offering them a range of play equipment and more open space than at home. This different environment helps all areas of a toddler's development and should be a regular part of the toddler's life if the weather allows. Toddlers can shout, run about and enjoy the freedom of being able to 'let off steam' without disturbing any neighbours. By using different pieces of play equipment toddlers gain more confidence and learn to become more independent and, by using large play equipment, toddlers gradually develop balance and co-ordination skills. Parents should check carefully that the equipment in a play area is suitable for the age and the physical skill of the toddler.

Visiting parks and play areas also helps intellectual development. Social skills are learnt through meeting other children. Toddlers learn about the environment outside the home, looking at trees, flowers and birds. A family visit to a park gives an ideal opportunity for **quality time** as all family members interact with each other and enjoy the company of parents and any siblings.

Key Terms

Exercise – doing an activity which involves the movement of the large and small muscles in the body

Healthy appetite – eating a wide range of food and an adequate amount of food at mealtimes

Good sleep pattern – at night sleeping right through until morning or at least for 8 to 10 hours

Activity

Plan a visit to the local park with a 2 year old and discuss the physical activities you could do with the child.

◀ Enjoying a run in the park

Summary

- Exercise helps the development of the small and large muscles and offers opportunities to improve other areas of development.
- Different types of toys and play equipment will allow the toddler to learn different motor skills.
- Outdoor activities give toddlers the opportunity to run about and meet other children. Children may be able to play on large pieces of play equipment, such as a slide, which is often not available in the home.

Revision Tip

Make sure you understand how different activities for babies and toddlers can be beneficial to physical and other areas of development. When asked to discuss suitable activities for a toddler, remember to include an outdoor play session so that there is an opportunity to use the gross motor skills and have the benefits of fresh air.

Prove it!

1. Suggest some activities that would help develop a toddler's small muscles.
2. Discuss the benefits of taking a toddler to a play area.
3. What are the health benefits of outdoor exercise to a toddler?

Protecting the body

What will I learn?

- **How different types of clothing are needed for various physical activities of young children**

Clothes provide protection to the baby's body. A baby needs a variety of clothes for indoors and outdoors as well as hot and cold weather.

Clothes

Clothes must allow the baby or toddler to move easily and not be tight fitting. Clothes should be easy to put on and take off and also **hard wearing** and easy to launder. Young children grow quickly so it is important to buy large-size garments but not too large that they are uncomfortable to wear. Garments made from **stretch fabrics** allow movement and should have easy fastenings such as zips, popper studs or Velcro.

Key Fact

- All children's nightwear must have passed the test for slow burning fabrics so do not need to carry the LOW FLAMMABILITY label.

Indoor play

Toddlers enjoy playing with toys on the floor in a warm indoor environment. Suitable clothes would be T-shirts and shorts or, in colder weather, sweaters and trousers or dungarees. When a baby begins to crawl, protect the knees with suitable clothing to avoid any unnecessary injuries.

Outdoor play

Opportunities to play outdoors depend on the weather and a suitable safe environment. Toddlers and young children need a range of clothes for the various types of activities.

In hot summer weather a toddler would need to wear a cotton T-shirt and shorts to help keep cool. On hot sunny days a long sleeved T-shirt would protect the arms from the sun. A hat is a vital piece of clothing to protect the child from the danger of sunstroke. Ideally a sunhat should also protect the neck and ears.

The baby or toddler should have sun block applied regularly to the skin to avoid the danger of sunburn. A young child's skin should be covered by a sun protection lotion with a factor of 30 plus which must be applied frequently. Great care must be taken at the seaside as the strength of the sun is often underestimated because of a cooling sea breeze. Young children should be kept out of the sun between 11 o'clock and 3 o'clock to avoid the risk of sunburn. A sun umbrella is an ideal way to protect a baby or toddler.

◀ Applying sun block

Wrapped up warmly against cold weather

In cooler weather a few layers of warm clothing are needed. If the toddler gets too hot a layer of clothing can be removed. A sweater and a fleece with hard-wearing trousers are suitable garments for playing in the garden. In really cold weather quilted clothing would provide additional warmth and hats, gloves and scarves should be worn to keep the body warm.

In wet weather a young child should have **waterproof** clothing with a hood. The hood should be fastened with a popper stud or Velcro and not with a drawstring because this could cause a young child to choke if it became caught on any play equipment.

Key Terms

Protection – helps avoid any injury to the body

Hard wearing – a strong tough fabric which can last for a long time

Learning to dress

Toddlers gradually begin to want to dress themselves. At first it is a very slow activity and the clothes are often put on back to front or inside out. However, toddlers will be using the fine motor skills and will slowly become more skilful. Parents should allow toddlers to gain this physical skill, which will be required when attending school, so they become more independent.

Activity

Sketch or collect pictures of a selection of clothing for a 2 year old to wear for the following occasions, giving reasons for your choice:

(a) a summer visit to the seaside,
(b) a winter walk in the park.

Summary

- Clothing helps to keep the body protected and allow for body movements.
- Clothing should be suitable for the type of weather and the activity to be undertaken by the child. Babies and toddlers grow quickly so parents should consider room for growth when purchasing clothes.

Revision Tip

Make sure you understand the need for a variety of clothing for different occasions and climates. Remember to mention how a box of dressing up clothes gives toddlers an ideal opportunity to practise the fine motor skills.

Prove it!

1. **Suggest some suitable clothes for a 9 month old who is beginning to crawl.**
2. **What are the suitable fastenings for a toddler's coat? Give reasons for your choice.**
3. **Why should parents encourage toddlers to dress themselves?**

Protecting the feet

What will I learn?

- **How young children need different types of footwear for various physical activities**

Babies do not need footwear until they begin to walk.

Key Facts

- The upper part of the shoe should be made from leather which is hard wearing. Leather will stretch to the shape of the foot and also allow moisture to escape. Plastic uppers do not do either. Shoes with anti-slip soles are much safer for toddlers and young children. Light and flexible soles are able to bend with the movement of the feet and so are easier for walking.

Footwear

It is recommended that babies should be allowed to go barefoot when in a safe environment because this will allow the bones and muscles to grow naturally. This is the best way to form strong healthy feet. The bones of a baby's foot are very soft and can easily become damaged if the feet are in shoes or socks which are too small and tight, resulting in the feet becoming deformed and possibly causing problems in the future.

Shoes provide protection to the toddler's feet. Toddlers' shoes must **fit well** to support the feet and not damage them. The shoes should allow the soft bones and muscles to grow correctly. As the child becomes older the bones will begin to harden. Feet grow quickly so a toddler will require new larger shoes quite often, possibly needing a new pair of shoes about every 3 months. Feet increase by about 2 to 2½ sizes each year until about the age of 4 years after which the rate of growth slows down.

A child's feet must be measured by a trained shoe fitter using special equipment in order to obtain the best possible fit. New shoes must allow **room for growth** with about 12mm to 18mm of growing space. A variety of designs are available in whole and half sizes, and in different widths, to fit different size feet.

Points to consider when buying shoes for a toddler

1. **The shoes must be well fitting with space for the toes to move.**
2. **There must be room for the feet to grow.**
3. **The design of the shoes should give the feet support and protection.**
4. **The material should be smooth with no hard seams.**
5. **There should be an adjustable fastening.**
6. **The uppers should be flexible to allow the feet to bend easily.**
7. **The soles should be light, flexible and non-slip.**
8. **The heel should be well fitting and not allow the feet to slip up and down.**
9. **The shoes should have a low heel to avoid the feet slipping forward.**
10. **The shoes must be the correct width for the feet.**

Other types of footwear

Toddlers and young children will require some other types of footwear depending on the activity or weather. Lightweight sandals or canvas shoes can be worn in warm summer weather because these allow air to reach the feet. Trainers are often worn when playing in a play area or with a ball because they are sturdy and hard wearing. At home in the winter and at bedtime slippers are worn to keep the feet warm. When out walking in the rain, or playing on damp grass or in snow, wellington boots are required to keep the feet dry. Thicker warm socks should be worn because wellington boots do not keep feet very warm.

Activity

Sketch or collect a selection of pictures of footwear needed for a 3-year-old boy who enjoys outdoor activities giving reasons for your choice.

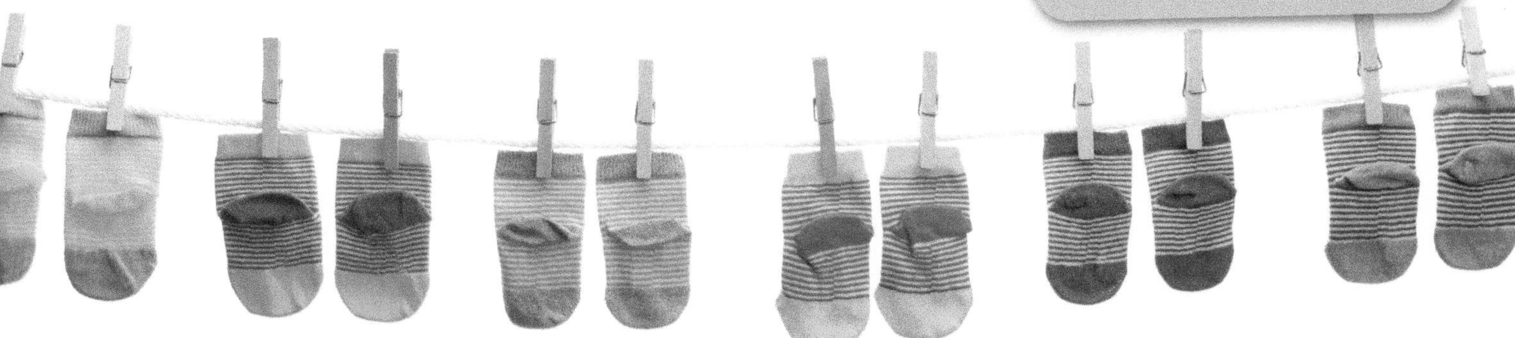

Socks and tights

Socks and tights must also be the correct size for a toddler's feet. Socks which are too small could damage the development of the feet but socks which are too big will be uncomfortable and could make the shoes too tight to wear.

Key Terms

Well-fitting – the shoes are the right size and shape to allow the bones and muscles of the feet to develop correctly

Room for growth – having some space for the growing foot to occupy in the future

Revision Tip

Make sure you understand the need for toddlers and young children to have well-fitting shoes and socks. Remember that, due to fast growth, toddlers and young children need to have their feet measured regularly to avoid them wearing shoes that are too small and which could damage the feet.

Summary

- Footwear – meaning shoes and socks/tights – helps to keep the feet protected and must allow for growth of the feet.
- The footwear should be suitable for the type of weather and the activity to be undertaken by the child.

Prove it!

1. **Why should a mother let a baby go barefooted as long as possible?**
2. **How often should a toddler's feet be measured?**
3. **Discuss the points to remember when buying shoes for a toddler.**

Indoor safety

What will I learn?

- **How to protect babies, toddlers and young children from injuries caused by accidents inside the home**

Babies and toddlers are very curious about their surroundings. As soon as babies can crawl and move around they begin to explore their environment. To them the surrounding area is like an adventure playground to investigate and enjoy.

Key Fact

- During the first 18 months of life children do not have any understanding about danger and must be supervised closely. A 2 year old will begin to learn about some dangers, such as hot or sharp items which cause pain when touched. Parents must teach and explain about the dangers to toddlers and young children so they gradually learn to protect themselves.

Babies and danger

Babies have no sense of danger and, as they grow older and stronger, they become more adventurous which brings with it the increased risk of having an **accident**.

There may be people of different ages at home carrying out various tasks using a wide variety of equipment. It is impossible to make the home completely safe for children. However, there are many ways in which parents and carers can create a safer environment. Babies and toddlers must be supervised closely to reduce the chance of an injury. Parents must think one step ahead of babies and toddlers and spot a potential **hazard** before an accident happens. Any dangerous objects should be kept out of reach. All equipment within the area where the child is playing should be checked to ensure that it will not cause the child to have an accident. Children should not be allowed to be in a dangerous situation which could result in an **injury**.

Indoors safety check

- Every room in the home should be checked carefully to make sure there are no avoidable dangers and that all the necessary safety **precautions** are in place.
- Floors should not be polished or have loose rugs which may cause a fall.
- Electric sockets should be covered and there should be no loose electric cables on the floor.
- Windows, cupboards and drawers should have safety catches to prevent them being opened.
- Any electric, gas or open fire should be fitted with a guard.
- Ornaments, small objects and plastic bags must be kept out of reach as babies often place things in their mouths which can cause choking.
- Medicines and tablets must be kept in childproof containers and stored well away from babies, toddlers and children.
- In some rooms, such as the kitchen and the bathroom, many more precautions are needed. All cleaning materials must be locked away. Cookers must not be left unattended when in use. Kitchen tools such as scissors, sharp knives, and sewing equipment like needles and pins, must always be kept away from toddlers and young children. When using equipment, such as an iron or food mixer, babies and toddlers should not be allowed to play nearby.

Activity

Produce a leaflet stating some safety rules which should be in place within the home.

▲ An accident about to happen

- The kitchen floor should be free from children's toys as these could cause an adult to trip over when carrying hot saucepans or dishes, causing a spillage and possibly a serious injury, such as burns, to a toddler.
- When preparing food, it is a good idea to place a baby in a playpen with some toys, so avoiding the risk of accidents.
- Never leave toddlers and young children **unsupervised** at bath time due to the risk of drowning. If a baby falls forward and the water covers the mouth and nose, they can drown in just a shallow depth of water.
- Closing doors between rooms will restrict the toddler's movements and also fence off access to any stairs.
- Always keep the front and back doors locked to prevent toddlers going outside unsupervised.

Key Terms

Accidents – happen due to hazards in the home, such as a loose electric cable on the floor, and also children being very adventurous and exploring their environment without considering the possible risks to themselves

Hazards – potential causes of accidents and injuries, such as a plastic bag left on the floor or toys covering the kitchen floor

Unsupervised – a child being left alone without the company of an adult

Summary

- Parents and carers are responsible for the safety of their children.
- Babies and toddlers enjoy exploring and do not understand that there are dangers within their home which can cause them serious injuries.
- Babies and toddlers must be supervised closely to avoid any accidents.
- Safety precautions must be put in place to prevent accidents.
- Safety checks must be carried out frequently within the home to provide as safe an environment as possible for children and to prevent injury.

You should have knowledge about safety precautions within the home to prevent accidents to toddlers and young children. In an answer on safety within the home, remember to discuss all hazards and the safety precautions necessary. Also mention the need to supervise toddlers and young children closely.

Prove it!

1. **Explain why babies are at risk of having accidents in the home.**
2. **Discuss how parents can make the home a safer environment for a toddler.**

Outdoor safety

What will I learn?

- **How to protect babies, toddlers and young children from injuries caused by accidents in:**
  - **the garden**
  - **play area**
  - **a car**
  - **on the road**

Babies and toddlers enjoy opportunities to go outside to play. This offers them a new environment to explore and the chance to play with larger toys and play equipment than indoors.

Outdoor play

With outdoor play there are many risks to toddlers and young children so parents must check the surroundings carefully for any possible **dangers**.

In the garden

The garden must be **secure** with any gates locked and no holes in fences. There should be no plants with sharp thorns or any poisonous plants. Garden tools, equipment, plant fertilisers and chemicals must be locked away. Toddlers should not be able to reach into any waste or recycling bins. The garden must be free from broken glass and dog faeces.

Garden ponds should be covered with a tight fitting fine net and if possible children kept away from it. If the garden has adequate space for large toys such as a swing, slide or trampoline, they must be positioned securely to prevent the possible danger of becoming unstable. Toddlers and young children should be **supervised** when playing with such large toys to avoid the danger of a child walking into a moving swing.

Key Fact

- Toddlers and young children enjoy the chance to be independent and explore the outside world and do not consider any possible dangers. Parents should reduce the risk of accidents, by not allowing children to play with gardening equipment, eat plants, pick up pieces of litter or run with sticks.

Key Terms

Dangers – situations and things which could cause a child to have an accident resulting in an injury

Secure – something which is safe and often gives protection such as a child lock on the car

Supervised – a responsible adult looking after the care and safety of children

Child Study

In a Child Study on physical development remember, when going to a play area, to supervise the child very closely and be aware of any possible dangers to the toddler or young child.

Activity

Carry out some research on the different types of car seats available for children from birth to 5 years old. Produce a leaflet to give to parents using the information obtained.

In the play area

If possible parents should choose a play area which is fenced in to keep out any stray dogs. Here also parents should ensure the ground is free from any dangerous items such as broken glass, cans, dog faeces and litter. Parents need to check that the play equipment is safe and secure with a soft surface beneath, such as rubber, which would reduce any possible injury. Parents should only allow a toddler to play on equipment which is suitable for that toddler's age and physical ability. Play areas can be very busy places and toddlers must be closely supervised to prevent them getting lost or injured.

▼ A toddler wearing safety reins

On the road

Young children should never play on the pavement or on the road. An adult must hold the child's hand. With toddlers the use of a wrist strap or rein offers additional safety. When crossing the road always use pedestrian crossings where possible. Tell young children about the dangers of the traffic and teach them **road safety** rules.

In the car

Never leave a child unattended in a car. Make sure that child locks are fitted on the rear doors. The child must be strapped into a secure **car seat** of the correct size for the child's weight. Never allow children to put their hands out through open windows.

◀ A baby safely strapped into a correctly sized car seat

Make sure you understand the need to take safety precautions and check carefully for possible dangers when taking children outdoors. When answering a question about outdoor safety remember to discuss various locations, such as walking along the pavement and crossing the road, travelling in the car, visiting the park or play area. A common error is to just mention only one or two situations and offer few safety precautions.

Summary

- Babies and toddlers must be supervised closely to avoid any accidents.
- When outdoors, parents and carers are responsible for making sure that babies, toddlers and young children are in safe surroundings.
- Risk of injury is present in most outdoor situations and, whilst this does not mean parents should avoid going outdoors, it does mean they have a responsibility to be aware of, and alert to, potential dangers and accidents.

Prove it!

1. **Explain what precautions a parent should take when visiting a play area with a 2 year old.**
2. **Suggest some ways in which parents could make the garden a safe environment for a toddler.**

Home environment

What will I learn?

- **An understanding of how the home environment can affect the physical development of children**

During the early years of life babies and toddlers spend a lot of time within the family home. Parents should therefore aim to provide the best possible home environment for the family.

Key Fact

- Being a parent is very demanding and having children is a long-term responsibility. Caring for babies and children is hard work both day and night and also restricts the parents' free time for leisure activities.

A clean and warm home

The home should be clean to avoid the danger of bacteria and other pests causing any infection to the child. In the kitchen, food should be stored in the correct conditions, prepared on clean working surfaces and cooked thoroughly to avoid the danger of food poisoning. Floors should be cleaned regularly and any spillages cleared up so that there is no build-up of dirt.

It is also important that the home should be kept warm and comfortable for children. If the environment is cold and **damp** then there is a risk that babies may develop chest infections that could become serious.

No smoking

Parents, other family members and visitors should not smoke within the home where there are babies and young children. If someone is smoking a cigarette, the child becomes a **passive smoker** by inhaling the smoke in the atmosphere. These children are at risk from having chest infections and developing asthma and bronchitis.

A baby living in a smoky home is twice as likely to die from **Sudden Infant Death Syndrome** (SIDS).

Keeping the house clean

Activity

Carry out some research and produce a fact sheet about Sudden Infant Death Syndrome.

Caring parents enjoying family activity

Caring and responsible parents

Becoming parents is a full-time commitment, especially when children are very young, as they rely totally on the parents providing all their needs. Parents have to undertake many tasks in order to provide a safe environment and loving care and attention. At all times parents must make sure that they are acting responsibly, looking after the baby or toddler. They must not consume an excessive amount of **alcohol** or take any **illegal drugs** which would make them unable to carry out the role of caring parents and could endanger the life of the child.

Key Terms

Damp – feeling slightly wet

Passive smoker – a person inhaling the smoke from another person's cigarette

Sudden infant death syndrome – the sudden and unexpected death of a young baby when asleep

Summary

- The home environment and care provided by the parents can affect the health and well-being of babies and young children.
- If the home is dirty and does not provide adequate warmth and comfort then babies might become unwell and develop a serious illness affecting their physical development.
- There are serious health risks, in particular chest infections, for babies and children living in a smoky environment.

Make sure you understand what conditions the home environment should provide to care for babies and young children. In a question about the home environment, remember to discuss the health risks to children which can affect their physical development.

Prove it!

1. What is a passive smoker?
2. Discuss the dangers to the child if a parent takes illegal drugs or excessive amounts of alcohol.

Toys

What will I learn?

- **How toys can help the physical development skills of babies, toddlers and young children**

Toys are an essential part of childhood. Babies, toddlers and young children learn and develop new skills and extend their knowledge and understanding by playing with toys.

Key Fact

- Toys can be described as being educational because they give children the opportunity to learn new skills in all areas of development. Parents and carers must check that the toys are suitable for the age of the child and that they provide plenty of long-term interest and **enjoyment**.

The benefit of toys

A selection of toys both indoors and outdoors provides a child with enjoyment whilst at the same time helping all areas of development. Toys should be suitable for the age of the child and the stage of physical development. It is very important that the toys are safe for the child and should display the **CE symbol** or the **Lion Mark**, meaning they have been tested for safety.

Toys from birth to 1 year

From a few months old a baby will begin to use their hands to hold toys, and everything is explored by placing it in the mouth. There should be a selection of toys for the baby to hold and feel such as a rattle, an activity mat and some large plastic bricks. These toys must be easy to handle and safe for the baby to put into the mouth.

Toys from 1 year to 2 years

From the first birthday the fine and gross motor skills will begin to develop more quickly so the toys should encourage the use of the small and large muscles. Toddlers enjoy a swing and slide as well as a 'push and pull' toy to develop the large muscles. A large-piece simple jigsaw, a shape sorter and crayons would encourage the fine motor skills.

Key Terms

CE symbol The toy has met the requirements of the European Union's Toy Safety Directive.

Lion Mark The toy has been made by a member of the British Toy Manufacturers' Association

Child playing with push and pull toy

Toys from 2 years to 3 years

Toddlers enjoy having a 'sit and ride' toy or a tricycle which help with the development of the large muscles. Playing with a large ball is also a popular outdoor activity. To help the fine motor skills toddlers could have some dolls or teddy bears to dress up, and interlocking building bricks to grasp and fix together.

Toys from 3 years to 4 years

As the fine motor skills will have developed further a young child would enjoy simple construction toys as well as the opportunity to play with modelling materials. A climbing frame can help to strengthen the large muscles of the arms and legs.

Toys from 4 years to 5 years

At this stage of physical development young children have quite good fine motor skills. They can play board games and do more difficult jigsaw puzzles and craft activities. Having better co-ordination skills with good gross motor skills, children enjoy playing bat and ball games, flying a kite as well as riding bikes and scooters.

Child Study

In a Child Study on physical development, using different toys and games with the study child will allow you to observe both the gross and fine motor skills.

Child Focused Task

In a Child Focused Task, which requires you to make an item to help with fine motor skills, remember to consider the toys used by the toddler or young child in the observation sessions of the Child Study.

Activity

Carry out some research on children's toys to help gross and fine motor skills by visiting stores and websites. Remember to look for the safety regulations, such as the CE symbol and Lion Mark, found on children's toys, so you can recognise the logos and understand what they mean.

Make sure you understand that children learn through play and should be provided with a range of safe toys to help develop their fine and gross motor skills. In a question about benefits of playing with toys, remember to discuss how toys help with the development of both gross and fine motor skills. You could also mention how playing with large toys can help to improve muscles and strengthen bones.

Summary

- Toys are the **learning tools** to help the baby or toddler to develop both fine and gross motor skills.
- Toys must be suitable for the age and stage of the child's physical development and also safe to use.
- Babies, toddlers and young children should always be encouraged to play with their toys.
- Parents should make an effort to join in with the activities.

Prove it!

1. **Suggest suitable toys for a 6 month old, giving reasons for your choice.**
2. **Discuss which outdoor play activities would enable a 4-year-old boy to develop his gross motor skills.**

Prevention of home accidents

What will I learn?

- **How sensible use of safety equipment can help prevent accidents to toddlers and young children**

Key Facts

- The home should be a safe and secure environment. However, it is the place where many serious accidents occur. Each week on average three children die from an accident in the home. The most serious accidents occur in the kitchen and boys are likely to have more accidents than girls as they are often more adventurous.

The only way to prevent toddlers and young children from ever having an accident is to supervise them closely at all times. However, this is impossible as all parents and carers have many different tasks to do within the home and cannot watch the children constantly.

Safety equipment

There are many different pieces of safety equipment available for parents to buy as manufacturers develop and design new products. It may also be possible to borrow suitable equipment from other parents whose children have gained a safety understanding and no longer require such equipment.

The following pieces of safety equipment can be used within the home to help keep toddlers safe.

A safety gate

A **safety gate** restricts the movement of a toddler, helping to keep the child in a safe environment and often within the sight of an adult. The gate can be fitted in the doorway of a room, for example to prevent access to the kitchen. A gate can be fitted at the bottom of the stairs during the day and then at night time moved to the top of the stairs.

Safety catches on fridges and freezers

A toddler may be able to pull open the fridge or freezer door and then explore the contents. A plastic safety catch can be fitted onto the side of the fridge. The door cannot then be opened without releasing the **safety catch**, which a toddler would be unable to do.

Window locks

Having safety **locks** fitted to **windows** prevents the risk of a toddler falling out.

Cupboard and drawer locks

Locks can be fitted to kitchen **cupboards** and drawers to prevent toddlers opening them. Kitchen cupboards and drawers contain many pieces of sharp and breakable equipment which can be very dangerous.

Table corner protectors

The corners of both dining tables and coffee tables are very sharp. When learning to walk a toddler could fall against the corner of a coffee table and suffer injury to the face or head. The risk of injury will be reduced by placing **plastic covers** over the **corners**.

Safety harness

A toddler should wear a **safety harness** when sitting in a highchair. Without a harness a toddler may attempt to stand up or climb over the side of the chair and could overbalance, fall and receive a very nasty injury.

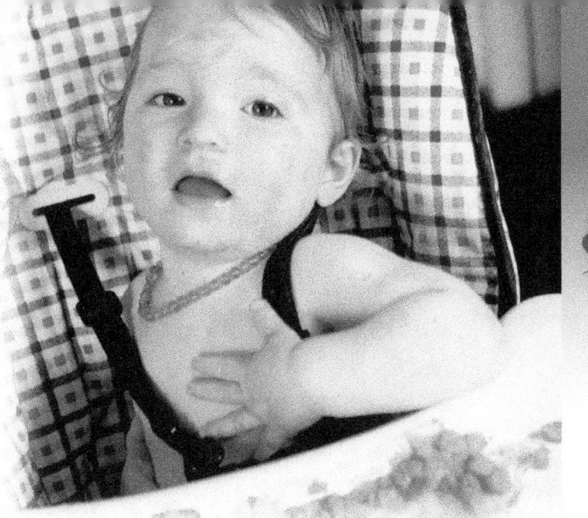

Socket covers

Toddlers enjoy poking their fingers or pencils into every small hole, including electric sockets. To prevent this, a flat plastic **cover**, which a toddler would be unable to remove, can be put into the **socket**.

Fire guard

All **fires**, including gas, electric or wood, should be protected by a **guard** fixed firmly into position. Toddlers are attracted to the colours of the fires and could easily receive a serious burn.

Safety caps on household cleaning products

Household cleaning products, such as bleach, must be stored out of the reach of toddlers and childproof **safety caps** must always be put back onto cleaning containers after use.

Locked bathroom cabinet

All lotions, creams and medicines in the **bathroom** should be stored in a **locked cabinet** with the key out of a toddler's reach. Toddlers are very inquisitive individuals. They like to explore and often taste everything they find and do not understand the health risks.

Cooker guard

The controls on the cooker should be out of the reach of a toddler. A **cooker guard** could be fitted around the hob, preventing a toddler reaching up to the saucepans. Remember saucepan handles must be turned inwards so they are out of the reach of a toddler and also adults walking past cannot knock the saucepans over.

Summary

- Safety equipment can help parents keep toddlers and young children in a safe environment.
- Safety equipment must be in good condition and fitted correctly.
- Parents and carers must always check that all the safety equipment is in place within the home to prevent any accidents to children.

Prove it!

1. Discuss the use of a safety gate within the home.
2. With a toddler in the family explain how the kitchen could be made into a safer environment.
3. Explain why parents should be very careful when storing toiletries, medicines and tablets.

Activity

If you can talk with parents of toddlers, ask them what safety equipment they have within their homes.

Key Terms

Safety gate – prevents access, for example placed at the bottom of the stairs

Window lock – prevents the opening of the window

Cupboard lock – prevents the opening of the cupboard door

Socket cover – covers an electric socket

Cooker guard – placed around the hob to prevent children reaching up to touch saucepans

Table corner protectors – placed on the corners of a table to prevent injury

Revision Tip

Make sure you understand how safety equipment can help prevent accidents to toddlers. You should be able to identify different types of safety equipment and describe how they can prevent accidents. When answering a question on home safety, remember to include **all** of the rooms. A common error is just to mention the kitchen and bathroom.

Dealing with accidents

What will I learn?

- **The risks of accidents to children and the need for a first-aid box in the home**

Toddlers do not understand the dangers in their environment, such as the home, park or playgroup. Parents should make young children aware of the risks and the possibility of them becoming injured.

Risks of accidents

There will always be risks in everyday life and parents should teach young children how to handle them. Children should be encouraged to become independent and, gradually over time, become better able to take care of themselves. Unfortunately, sometimes toddlers and young children will have accidents resulting in an injury.

Major accidents

Serious accidents need medical help. If the injury results in a great loss of blood, serious damage to a limb, a severe knock to the head, or the child is unconscious then either an ambulance should be called or the child taken to the Accident and Emergency department at a hospital. Remember if there is **severe bleeding**, pressure should be applied to the wound using a clean cloth while waiting for medical assistance.

Minor accidents

Many **accidents** are often very **minor**, such as a toddler falling over and grazing a knee. Everyday bumps and bruises, which toddlers receive when they are learning to walk or playing in the garden, can be treated by the parents or carers. Every home should have a **first-aid box** and all adults, including babysitters, should know where it is stored. A high cupboard in the kitchen or bathroom might be a suitable place to store it.

▶ **Treating a grazed knee**

Key Fact

- As well as a first-aid box within the home, it would be a very good idea to have a similar one in the car. Some organisations offer first-aid courses for parents of young children, providing relevant knowledge, skills and how to treat injuries.

Activity

Carry out some research on the range of first-aid materials available to parents.

First-aid box

The box should be labelled and the contents checked and replaced whenever necessary. The following items should be included in a first-aid box:

Disposable plastic bag – to hold all waste materials.

Disposable plastic gloves – to prevent any risk of infection through contact with blood.

Antiseptic wipes – very useful for cleaning grazes and wounds.

Cotton wool and paper tissues – to absorb blood.

Sling – to support a damaged arm.

Safety pins – to hold bandages in place.

Scissors – to cut the tape and bandages.

Cream – to treat insect bites.

Adhesive tape and bandages – to hold dressings in place.

Eye bath – to use for washing the eye.

Gauze dressings – to place over a graze or wound.

A selection of various sized plasters – non-allergic ones, which can cover and protect cuts and grazes, are best for children.

Tweezers – to remove splinters.

Calamine lotion – to treat sunburn.

First-aid knowledge

Parents and carers must know how to give first-aid treatment. Parents should carry out some research about possible accidents, and the recommended treatments, to be able to give the correct first-aid treatment if needed.

Serious accidents – where there are serious injuries, which may be life threatening, medical assistance must be sought

Minor accidents – where there are slight injuries which can be treated by the parents

Summary

- Parents should make toddlers and young children aware of possible dangers.
- Adults must be able to assess the injury and, if it is serious, get medical help.
- There should be a first-aid box in the home to help treat minor injuries.

Make sure you understand how important it is to assess the seriousness of any injury and the need to have a first-aid box in the home to treat minor accidents.

Prove it!

1. Why is a first-aid box an important item in the family home?
2. Explain how to deal with a toddler who has a serious wound and is losing a lot of blood.

First aid treatment

What will I learn?

- **How to give first aid and treat minor accidents**

The following information gives some basic first-aid knowledge and instructions for dealing with minor injuries to toddlers and young children.

Treating minor accidents

Remember – if the injury causes the child a lot of pain and discomfort, medical advice should be obtained.

Cuts and grazes

Toddlers can easily lose their balance and trip over or sometimes fall off their bike or scooter. Often the knees can become **cut** or **grazed** and need to be treated. The injured skin should be washed with clean water, checked for any foreign bodies, such as grass or gravel, and patted dry with a clean tissue. If necessary a clean dressing or plaster could be used to give some protection. A very small cut or graze can be left uncovered as a scab will form which helps the healing process.

Bruises

When the skin is knocked a bruise may appear, caused by bleeding beneath unbroken skin. A cold compress, such as damp cotton wool or a bag of ice cubes or frozen peas, will help prevent the bruise developing.

Burns and scalds

- A **burn** is caused by touching dry heat, for example a hot saucepan or an iron.
- A **scald** is caused by contact with moist heat, for example very hot water, steam or hot fat.

The damaged skin must be placed under running cold water for 10 minutes and then patted dry and, if necessary, covered with a gauze dressing. Do not rub any ointment or cream onto the skin or cover the area with a plaster. Never prick any blisters that may form as this could lead to an infection. The skin of babies and young children is very delicate and, if the area of damaged skin is larger than a 50 pence coin and the skin is broken, medical help should be obtained.

Key Facts

- As toddlers and young children frequently have minor cuts and grazes, it is very important that they have received their immunisation for tetanus as bacteria are found in soil and dirt.
- When treating minor injuries of toddlers and young children, remember to stay calm and reassuring as some children become very upset at the sight of blood.

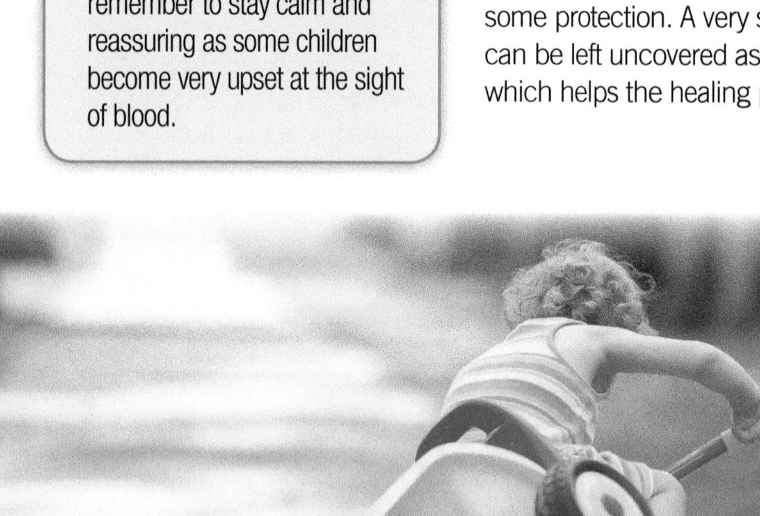

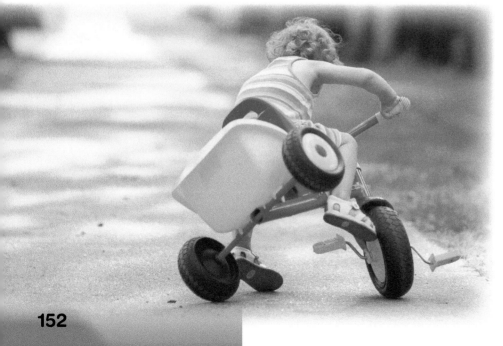

◀ **Heading for a fall**

Nose bleeds

A **nose bleed** can be treated by sitting the child down and bending the head slightly forward and at the same time pinching the soft part of the nose. Tell the child not to blow the nose for a few hours.

Choking

Choking happens when a large piece of food or an object gets stuck in the throat. Place the baby over the knees of an adult keeping the head low then give about 5 sharp slaps between the shoulder blades. A toddler can bend over an adult's knees.

Insect stings

A bee sting will need to be removed from the skin using tweezers and the affected area covered with a cold compress. Other types of **sting**, such as a wasp sting, can be treated using calamine lotion or anti-histamine cream to help to reduce the discomfort.

Poisoning

If a child has swallowed medicine, tablets or household cleaning liquid, try and remove any trace of the substance from the mouth. Do not attempt to make the child sick. Seek medical help and take a sample of the substance with you.

Foreign body in the eye

Grit or dust will irritate the eye and cause discomfort. The head should be tilted back and water poured into the inner corner of the eye which should remove the foreign body. If the eye is still very painful, medical help should be obtained.

Key Terms

Cuts and grazes – when the skin is broken and there is some bleeding

Burn – from contact with dry heat and the skin becomes red, sore and may form blisters

Scald – from contact with moist heat and the skin becomes red, sore and may form blisters

Nose bleed – when blood runs out of the nose, sometimes as a result of a fall

Activity

Produce a leaflet setting out detailed first-aid advice for any four minor injuries children might suffer.

▲ Treating a foreign body in the eye

Summary

- Parents should be able to give simple first aid for minor injuries of babies, toddlers and young children.
- Remember that if the injury is more serious then medical help must be obtained.

Revision Tip

Make sure you understand how to give first aid for minor injuries. When answering a question on a child's injury, remember to give detailed information about the necessary treatment and comment on the need to give comfort and reassurance to the child.

Prove it!

1. **What is the difference between a scald and a burn and describe the first-aid treatment for both?**
2. **Explain how to deal with a toddler who has some dust in the eye.**

Childhood infections

What will I learn?

- **An understanding of childhood infectious diseases**

This topic provides some basic information about infectious and contagious diseases and their treatment or prevention.

Infectious diseases

Infectious diseases are caused by both bacteria and viruses. Bacteria are found everywhere in the environment, in the air, soil and on humans. Only a few bacteria can cause diseases in humans. Each bacteria cell multiplies by dividing in two very rapidly. Bacteria can damage the tissues of the body and some produce poisonous toxins which can travel in the bloodstream.

Viruses are very small and they quickly feed and grow when inside some human cells. The cells then burst and the virus spreads causing damage and disease. There are many infectious diseases and some are very common in childhood, for example measles, mumps, whooping cough, German measles (Rubella) and chickenpox.

Key Fact

- Vaccines contain a very small, weak amount of the bacteria or virus. This makes the body produce antibodies and provides protection against the infectious disease.

- Many infectious diseases cause visible spots to appear on the body. If a child is feeling ill, parents should be on the look out to see if any spots have developed on the body and, if so, seek medical help.

▲ Young girl suffering from chickenpox

Tetanus is only contracted if you have a cut or graze and then come into contact with earth in the garden or park. The bacteria found in soil and dirt enters the body through the cut or graze.

Contagious diseases

Contagious diseases spread from one person to another person by direct contact. This can be through touching or kissing another person. These types of disease can also be spread through coughing and sneezing when tiny infected droplets from the nose or throat travel into the air and reach other people. This is called **droplet infection**.

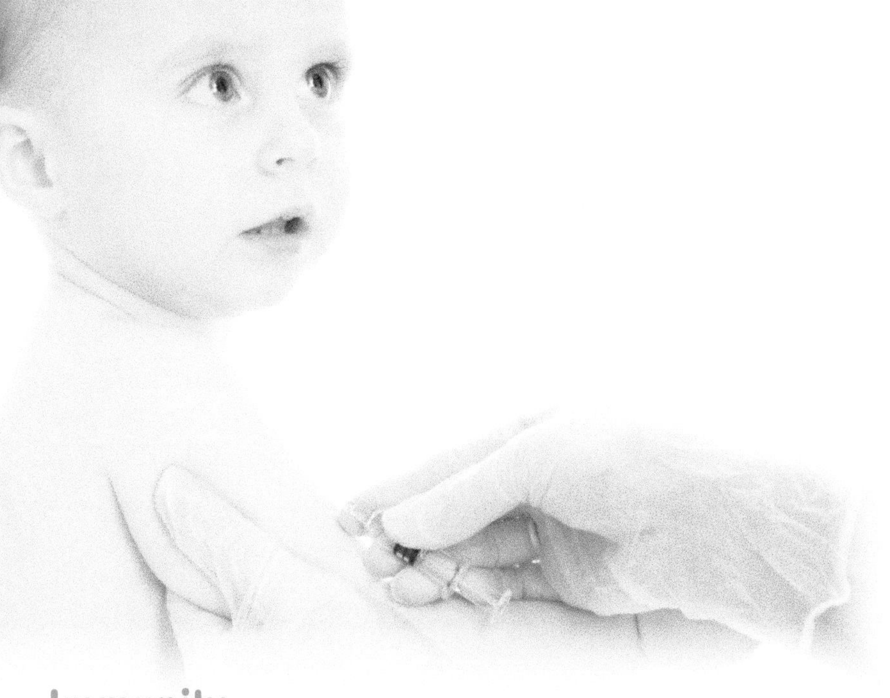

Baby receiving vaccination

Activity

If you can talk with parents of babies and toddlers, discuss childhood infectious diseases and vaccinations.

Immunity

Immunity is the ability of the body to resist infection. When the body has an infection it naturally produces antibodies to fight the developing infection. These antibodies will also provide protection from that disease in the future.

Immunisation can be given to a person by an injection (**vaccination**). A very weak amount of either the bacteria or virus is given, causing the body to produce the required antibodies for that disease which then protect the body in the future.

Chickenpox is the only childhood disease for which there is no vaccination available.

It is the parents' choice of whether or not to have their baby vaccinated. The risks of any harmful side effects or complications are very small and much lower than the health risks of the disease. There may be a few situations where the vaccination may not be advisable due to other health problems. Another benefit of immunising many people is that these infectious diseases become less common and prevent epidemics. Children have better health and do not have the risk of catching diseases which sometimes can cause serious health problems.

Infectious diseases – are caused by harmful bacteria and viruses

Contagious diseases – spread from one person to another by contact, such as by touching or using the same towel

Summary

- Infectious diseases can be caught by direct contact or droplet infection.
- Vaccination can prevent children having infectious diseases.

Make sure you understand how infectious diseases spread and the different types of immunity.

Prove it!

1. What is a contagious disease? Explain how it can spread.
2. Explain the health benefits of vaccinating a baby.

Immunisation programme

What will I learn?

- **What the immunisation programme for childhood infectious disease is and why it is important**

Immunity means having protection against an infectious disease. This topic provides some basic information about immunisation.

Immunity in newborn babies

Very young babies will rarely catch any of the childhood infectious diseases as the mother's **antibodies** give them protection. During pregnancy the placenta will have carried these antibodies from the mother's blood to the baby's blood. If the mother has had all the recommended **immunisations** then the baby will have the same protection. If the mother breastfeeds the baby, further antibodies will be passed to the baby in the milk. At about 2 months old the baby will be able to begin having vaccinations.

Before a vaccination

The health of the baby should be discussed with the medical professional. If the baby has a fever, has been taking medication or has had a fit, these should be mentioned.

Key Fact

- There are many benefits from being immunised against infectious diseases, such as a long-lasting protection and no further health problems linked to those diseases. The diseases will also become less common as more children become immunised.

Key Terms

Immunity – the ability to resist infection

Antibodies – substances produced by the body to destroy the disease and prevent the person catching the disease in the future

Activity

Carry out some research and produce a leaflet on the following childhood infectious diseases: whooping cough, mumps, measles, chickenpox and German measles.

Child Study

In a Child Study on physical development you could discuss the immunisation programme for the study child with the parent/carer.

The immunisation programme

2 months old

- A 5-in-1 single vaccination which gives protection against diphtheria, tetanus, whooping cough (pertussis), polio and Hib (a bacterial infection which can cause meningitis).
- A vaccination against pneumococcal infections such as pneumonia.

3 months old

- Second dose of the 5-in-1 vaccination.
- A vaccination against meningitis C.

4 months old

- Third dose of the 5-in-1 vaccination.
- Second dose of the vaccination against pneumococcal infections.
- Second vaccination against meningitis C.

Between 12 and 13 months old

- Measles, mumps and Rubella (German measles) vaccine, referred to as the MMR.
- Third dose of the vaccination against pneumococcal infections.
- Booster vaccination for meningitis C and Hib.

3 years 4 months old

- 4-in-1: Diphtheria, tetanus, pertussis and polio (DTaP/IPV) pre-school booster
- Measles, mumps and rubella (MMR) second dose

After an immunisation

There should be no side-effects from having an immunisation, other than perhaps a little redness and swelling in the area of the injection. Occasionally the baby may be a little irritable and have a slightly raised temperature for a day or so. Very rarely there may be a severe **allergic reaction** to a vaccine.

Summary

- Immunity in newborn babies has been obtained from the antibodies in the mother's blood.
- Immunisation gives protection against infectious diseases.

Prove it!

1. **Name the five diseases against which the 5-in-1 vaccination gives protection.**
2. **What is the MMR vaccination?**

Make sure you understand the immunisation programme for babies. In an answer on immunisation, remember to discuss the health benefits to children.

Examination questions

Such as sight, or hearing.

1 Children learn through the use of all their senses.
List the **five** senses. (5)

2 **(a)** State the average birth weight of a baby. (1)
(b) State the average birth length of a baby. (1)
(c) State **three** factors that can influence physical development at any age. (3)

3 Good dental care should be a daily routine for children.
(a) Complete the chart below: (4)

Nutrient for strong teeth	*Food source*
(i)	(ii)
(iii)	(iv)

(b) Suggest **three** ways to help prevent tooth decay. (3)
(c) Discuss the importance of taking young children to the dentist regularly. (4)

4 **(a)** What are gross motor skills? (2)
(b) Discuss **two** activities which two year olds are able to do that show the use of gross motor skills. (4)

5 It is important to have the correct footwear.
(a) Identify **four** features parents should look for when choosing shoes for a three year old. (4)
(b) Explain how babies and toddlers develop the skill of being able to walk. (6)

Tip When answering a question about how babies develop, think about all the stages of development and mention them in time order, i.e. starting at an early age and progressing as the child gets older. In this answer, notice how the student does just this, starting with the first reference at 9 months age and finishing several stages later at the 18-month development point.

At about 9 months most babies will be able to stand up for a short time by holding onto furniture and take a few steps, also by holding on to the two hands of an adult.

At about 1 year most babies can walk by just holding one hand of an adult. They may often take steps in different directions and sit down a lot.

At about 15 months most babies have mastered the skill of walking unaided, although some babies walk sooner and others much later. At the beginning they are unsteady on their feet and will hold up their arms to help with balance. They will be unable to turn corners and will fall down often.

At about 18 months toddlers will have become much more stable on their feet and will have learnt the skill of walking and turning corners. They become quicker at walking and begin to learn the skill of walking up stairs.

6 Discuss how parents can make the home a safe environment for young children. (6)

People of different ages share a home and they have lots of possessions, some of which can be dangerous for children. Parents should make sure that young children are protected and cannot accidentally go where there are dangers. Doors and windows which a young child might reach should be locked. The kitchen, hall, stairs, and bathroom can all have danger areas for young children. Safety gates should be used to restrict where a young child can go.

There should not be any uneven carpets or electric wires trailing across the floor which might trip up a small child. Electric sockets should be covered. All medicines, plastic bags, detergents, breakable ornaments and sharp objects, such as scissors, must be kept out of reach of children. Babies and toddlers must be kept out of the kitchen when parents are preparing food and cooking. Sharp knives and other kitchen tools and hot areas, such as the oven or hob, are all things which might injure a young child. Tools and any dangerous chemicals used in the garden and the garage must all be put away after use and placed out of reach of children. The garden shed, any garden gates and the garage door should be locked. There should be no holes in any garden fence or wall which might enable a young child to get out.

Tip This student has done well and remembered a key point with this sort of question: when the question says the word 'home' you should think of two immediate points – firstly, mentally make sure you go round every likely room in the house and describe the risks in each, and secondly don't forget to also mention the garden.

7 Children enjoy playing with toys.

(a) Suggest some suitable toys for a three year old to help develop the fine motor skills, giving reasons for your choice. (6)

Suitable toys to help develop a three year old's fine motor skills should make the child use the fingers. Building bricks that lock into each other are very popular. They make good use of fine motor skills and allow the child to be creative because a wide variety of items can be created. Jigsaw puzzles also make the child use their fingers and can be done with the parent or siblings as a team effort if the puzzle is a bit difficult for a three year old.

Dressing up games not only help teach the child how to put on and take off clothes but also how to use different types of fastenings, such as zips and buttons, all of which helps develop fine motor skills. Using paints and crayons allows a child to be creative and helps them learn how to hold a pencil and begin to learn to write. Drawing on a blackboard with chalk or playing with modelling dough all make the child use fingers and develop fine motor skills. Hand and eye co-ordination will also develop by doing activities using fine motor skills.

When answering a question about fine (or gross) motor skills, make sure your answer deals only with the type of motor skills mentioned in the question. In this case it is fine motor skills, hence the student's answer restricts itself just to detailing those.

If the question refers to a child of a particular age, your answer must be relevant to that age.

(b) What safety symbols should a parent look for on toys to avoid the risk of injury to children? (4)

8 A visit to the park and play area is an enjoyable experience for both children and parents.
Discuss how a four year old's physical development would benefit from such a visit. (8)

A visit to a park and play area allows a child to do physical activities that cannot be done at home. There will be more space than in the garden at home and the child can run around, play with a ball, let off steam and have more freedom. The child will benefit from fresh air and exercise, which will help avoid obesity, strengthen bones and can help the sleep pattern and appetite.

A play area will have a wide range of large play equipment not available at home, such as swings, slides and climbing frames. These give the child new challenges and provide good opportunities to help develop the larger muscles. Activities such as climbing up the steps to the top of the slide and stretching arms to reach ropes on a climbing frame all help develop the gross motor skills. Development of the fine motor skills is also helped when the smaller muscles in fingers are needed, for example when holding onto the chains of a swing or the ropes of the climbing frame.

If a question refers to a park or a play area, think about all the things you would find there and include some examples in your answer.

If the question mentions physical development, make sure you refer to both gross and fine motor skills in your answer.

9 Approximately 2½ million children are injured or killed by hazards in the home each year.
Explain the types of accidents a child might have in the home. (6)

Babies, toddlers and young children are very curious about their surroundings and are not aware of any dangers. They can easily fall over due to uneven or cluttered floors and might fall down stairs or from climbing onto furniture. Children might be scalded or receive burns by touching hot items, for example kettles, irons, mugs of hot drinks or from reaching and pulling over saucepans on the hob in the kitchen. Touching sharp items, such as scissors and knives left on a working surface, could cause cuts.

There is a risk of suffocation and choking from plastic bags, small toys or coins if these are left within reach of babies who will be tempted to put them in the mouth. Children can be poisoned by drinking household cleaning liquids or medicines and eating tablets if these are not kept in childproof containers. Young children can drown in even small quantities of water and must not be left unattended in the bath. Very young children can drown in paddling pools or uncovered ponds in a garden and there must be adult supervision.

When answering a question about accidents try and think of as many different types of accident as you can. If the question refers to the home, think about every room in your house and do not forget the garden. Remember the kitchen is the most dangerous room in the house.

10 Infectious diseases can be a serious health risk for children.

(a) Name **three** childhood infectious diseases. (3)

(b) What do you understand by the following terms?

- **(i)** Droplet infection (2)
- **(ii)** Immunity (2)
- **(iii)** Antibodies. (2)

(c) Discuss **two** benefits of the immunisation programme for children. (4)

11 **(a)** List **three** items found in a first-aid box. (3)

(b) Explain how to treat the following injuries:

- **(i)** a bleeding nose (2)
- **(ii)** a grazed knee. (2)

(c) A variety of environmental factors can affect the health and safety of children.

Discuss the possible environmental factors in both the home and the garden that may affect a child's well-being. (8)

A child will spend many hours at home. If the house is in a poor state of repair and is damp and lacks proper heating this could cause chest infections. Children could have skin infections if there is a poor standard of hygiene in the house and a lack of clean clothes. There is a risk of food poisoning if food is not stored correctly, for example milk not kept in a fridge, or if food such as meat is not cooked thoroughly.

The child's safety may be at risk if the parents have not taken precautions to make the home safe, for example by locking doors and windows, guarding stairs and electric sockets and putting out of reach or locking away medicines, sharp knives, tools and other pieces of equipment that might cause a child injury.

If adults in the home smoke, a child will become a passive smoker – possibly causing the child health problems such as asthma and chest infections, which could lead to a high risk of death and Sudden Infant Death Syndrome. Should the adults in the home use illegal drugs or drink excessive amounts of alcohol, they will probably not be able to provide adequate care and supervise the children properly, putting them at a greater risk of injuries.

An untidy garden can also affect the health and safety of children. There is a high risk of injury from garden equipment, fertilisers, broken glass, tins, plastic or animal faeces left lying around in the garden. These can cause health problems due to serious cuts or infections. Insecure fences and gates could allow a young child to get into the road and have an accident.

If the question mentions health and safety, remember to concentrate on these aspects in your answer. As this question did not state any particular age of child, you should think about the well-being of all ages from babyhood to age 5 years.

Tip In your answer remember to give examples to show your knowledge of the topic. When discussing food poisoning, this student mentioned the need to keep milk in the fridge and to cook meat thoroughly. There were also several examples given of some precautions parents could take to make the home and garden safe.

Stages of intellectual development

What will I learn?

- **What intellectual development is**
- **How children learn**
- **The concepts children need to understand**
- **The milestones for intellectual development**
- **The role of parents and carers**
- **Factors affecting learning**

Key Terms

Object permanence – begins at about 8 months. At this stage babies begin to be aware that objects and people they cannot see still exist. This is why younger babies do not look for an object they have dropped

Echolalia – making repetitive sounds like da-da, bab-bab but without real meaning

Intellectual development is also known as cognitive development. It is the development of the mind: the child's ability to recognise, reason and understand. Language development is very closely linked to intellectual development because we need words to help us make sense of what we see and hear. Language skills are learned in much the same way as thinking and reasoning.

How do children learn?

- By using their senses: even very young babies take in information about their environments by looking, touching, listening, smelling and tasting.
- By exploring: children will find out about objects by playing with them and finding out what happens when they are turned around, moved, banged, shaken, etc.
- By copying: children observe what other people do and imitate their behaviour.
- By asking questions: when children are able to talk they start asking questions. They want to know 'what', 'who', 'where', 'why', 'when' and 'how'. Sometimes these questions can be hard to answer or are repetitive, but the child is trying to make sense of their world, not trying to be naughty.
- By playing and doing: trying out new things and repeating actions enables children to find out about concepts and practise things they have learned.

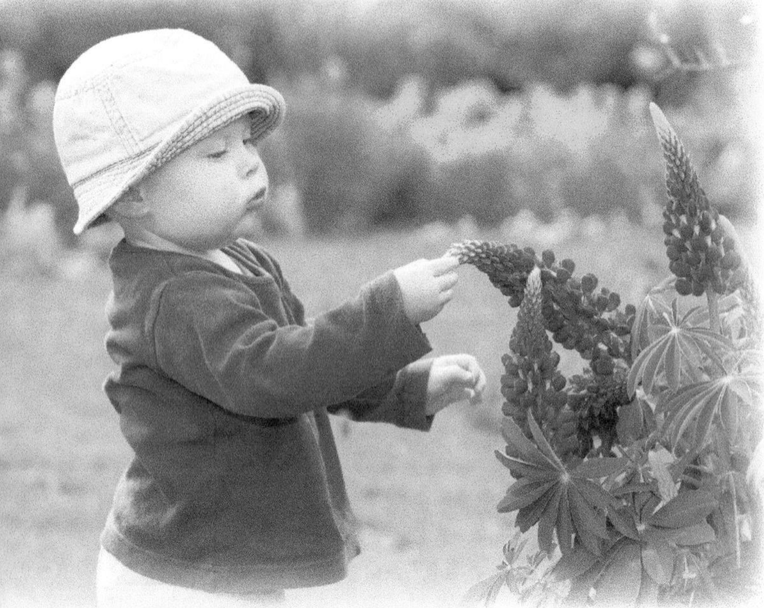

Children learn by exploring their world

Concepts

Concepts are ideas which help us to organise knowledge and information. Some concepts are easier to understand and explain than others. Concepts that children need to learn include: colour, size, shape, numbers, letters, temperature, speed, time and opposites.

The milestones for intellectual and language development

Children are unique and develop in their own way and at different rates. However, it is possible to identify the average age for the different stages of intellectual development. The table shows the main intellectual and language skills children will develop between birth and five years old.

Newborn–6 months

Intellectual milestones

- Listens to sounds and voices.
- Cries for assistance.
- Imitates facial expressions.
- By 4 months: repeats enjoyable acts, reaches for objects, appearing to be able to judge size and distance.
- By 5 months: recognises and responds to name.
- By 6 months: studies objects intently.

Language milestones

- Makes some sounds other than crying.
- By 3 months: begins cooing.
- By 4 months: makes first consonant sounds.
- Babbles.
- By 6 months: laughs and squeals in play.

6–12 months

Intellectual milestones

- Understands signs (e.g. bib means food is coming).
- From 8 to 9 months: finds hidden objects, and looks for dropped items (**object permanence**).
- Repeats actions that get a response, e.g. throwing a toy that gets given back.
- Enjoys looking at pictures in books.
- Waves bye-bye.

Language milestones

- Babbling sounds more like the intonation of the language they hear.
- Uses **echolalia**.
- Takes turns making sounds in 'conversation'.
- Puts together long series of syllables.
- Responds to name.
- Recognises words for common items.
- By 7 months: gestures to communicate, e.g. nodding head for yes.
- By 9 months: responds appropriately to a few specific words such as 'no'.
- Speaks a few recognisable words (e.g. mama, dada).

12–18 months

Intellectual milestones

- Can point to body parts.
- Identifies family members in photographs.
- Uses toys or objects to represent things in real life (e.g. doll = baby).
- Begins to scribble on paper (see learning to draw).
- Can make choices between clear alternatives, e.g. two flavours of drink.
- Begins to solve problems.
- Understands how familiar objects are used (e.g. spoon).

Language milestones

- Uses 4–10 words by 13–15 months and 10–20 words by 18 months.
- Can listen to and respond to simple commands.
- Listens to simple stories.
- Repeats overheard words.
- Uses **holophrases** which express an idea in one word.
- Enjoys trying to sing and joining in action songs.

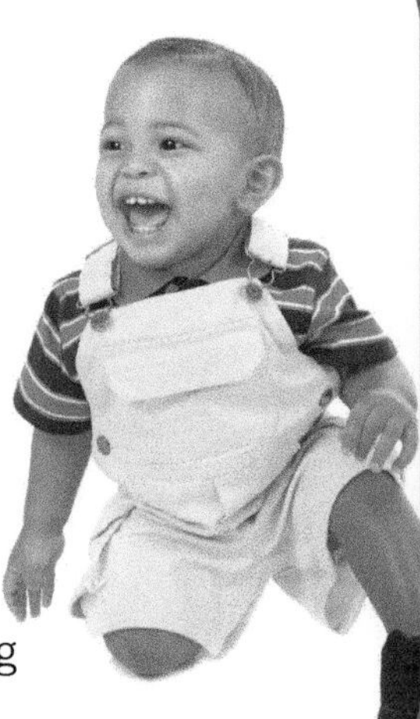

18 months – 2 years

Intellectual milestones

- Sorts shapes and colours.
- Attempts simple 2–3-piece puzzles.
- Begins make-believe play, e.g. feeding a doll.
- Enjoys nursery rhymes.
- Points to and names objects.
- Starting to learn concepts such as size, shape, weight.

Language milestones

- Expressive vocabulary of 20–25 words.
- Uses **telegraphic speech** – two-word sentences.
- Begins to use please and thank you, but may need reminding.

2–3 years

Intellectual milestones

- Can name and match 2–3 colours (usually red and yellow).
- Can sort objects into groups.
- Can complete simple 3–5-piece puzzles.
- Can stack beakers in order.
- Understands size in terms of bigger, smaller.
- Knows main parts of body and can point to them if not name them.
- Beginning to understand time (e.g. before lunch).
- Uses everyday objects in pretend play.
- Beginning to think about consequences.
- Able to concentrate for longer periods.

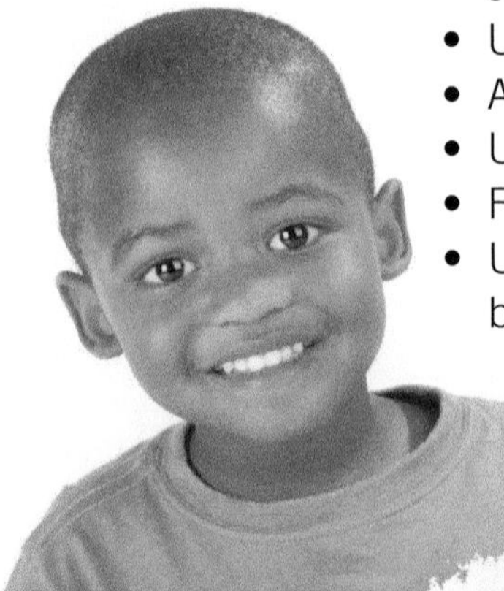

Language milestones

- By 2 years: uses 50+ words and combines words to form short sentences.
- Uses plurals.
- Answers routine questions.
- Understands some pronouns.
- Follows 2-step instructions.
- Uses size words correctly, e.g. big, little.

3–4 years

Intellectual milestones

- Can trace a square, copy a circle.
- Understands time concepts such as today, tomorrow, yesterday.
- Recognises and names simple shapes.
- Recognises some letters and numbers.
- Can say which of two objects is heavy/light, bigger/smaller.
- Will wonder what will happen if.... This is problem solving and hypothesis making.

Language milestones

- Correctly names some colours.
- Uses sentences with 4 or more words.
- Tells simple stories.
- Understands position words (in, out, under).
- Asks what, where, when, who questions.
- Speaks clearly enough to be understood by strangers.

4–5 years

Intellectual milestones

- Can count 10 or more objects.
- Can name 4 or more colours.
- Can complete a 6–8-piece puzzle.
- Beginning to understand time concepts such as morning, afternoon, night, day, later, after, while.
- Understands simple maths concepts such as simple addition and subtraction.
- Recalls the main details of a story.
- Beginning to understand the difference between fantasy and reality.
- Can understand and follow simple rules in games.
- Can match pictures in simple games.
- Understands measurements such as weight and height.
- Recognises their own name when written and may be able to write it themselves.

Language milestones

- Has 2000-word vocabulary.
- Joins sentences together.
- Accurately relays information.
- Uses past, present and future verbs.
- Uses negatives.
- Asks why and how questions.
- Can answer how, when, who questions.
- Uses possessives (mine, hers).
- Uses the third person.
- Follows up to 4-step instructions.
- Tells simple jokes.
- Can count up to 20 by rote.

Activity

Design and make a game for a four year old to help develop their intellectual skills.

Key Terms

Holophrase – express an idea in one word, for example 'cat' might mean any four-legged animal, 'cup' could mean 'where is my cup?', 'I want a drink'.

Telegraphic speech – uses the important words in a sentence without the joining words, e.g. 'want cake', 'where daddy'.

The role of parents and carers in intellectual and language development

Children naturally show a great interest in new things and new activities. They will learn best when the adults who care for them provide plenty of opportunities to learn new skills and practise the skills they have already acquired. Children need a range of toys and activities which will stimulate their imagination and make them want to try new things. Trips and visits provide new environments to discuss, and even tasks such as shopping and household chores can be used as opportunities to help children to understand new concepts and develop language skills. Allowing the child to be involved in planning what will happen and talking to them to help them recall past events will help them understand concepts such as time and make predictions about what might happen.

Children need praise and encouragement when they attempt something new as this will give them confidence to keep trying. Adults should not interrupt play by telling children what to do or taking control (unless the child is in danger) as children will have more fun learning by finding out for themselves.

Children need to be spoken to slowly and clearly using open questions that encourage conversation. They need to be given time to organise their thoughts before expecting an answer. A child's sentence should not be finished for them. Children who are in a secure and loving environment will ask questions endlessly and these should be answered as often as possible, in sufficient detail for the child's level of understanding. Patience and a sense of humour are often important in this stage of a child's development!

Activity

Identify the intellectual and language skills the child could practise while on a visit to the seaside. What other areas of development could be helped while they are there?

Child Study

In a child study about intellectual development, you would need to identify the child's thinking and language skills and compare them with the norms. Look at what you would expect a child of their age to be able to do so you can plan to play simple games and ask suitable questions.

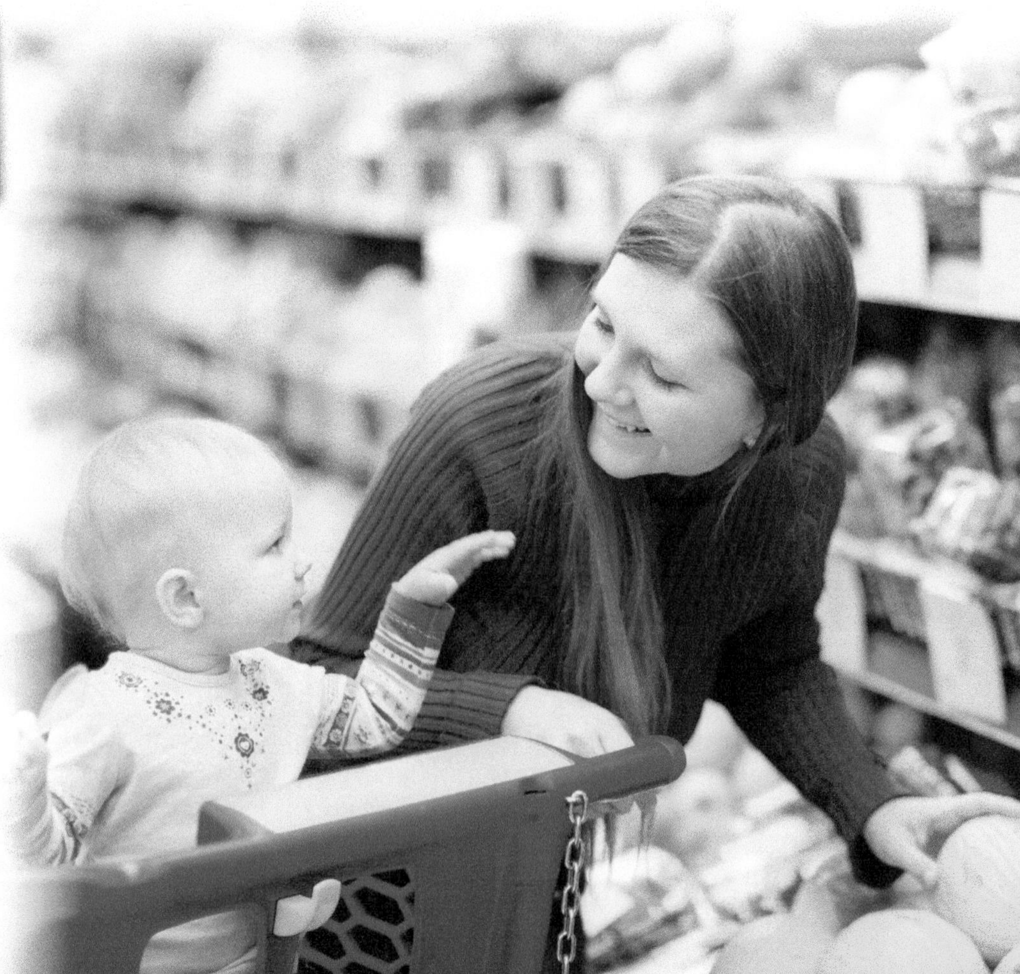

Everyday activities help children to learn new concepts and language

Factors affecting learning

There are several factors which may influence a child's intellectual development. The genes they inherit control the natural intelligence the child has, but how this is developed depends on the environment in which they grow up. A child who grows up in a secure, loving and supportive environment and who has a wide range of opportunities to learn and develop skills will thrive and develop more fully than one who is shown little attention.

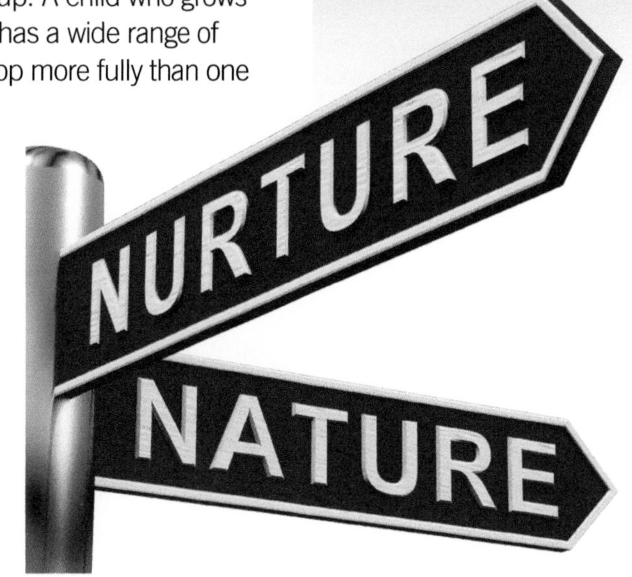

A child's state of health may also affect their intellectual development. A child who is frequently ill is likely to have fewer opportunities to practise new skills. Children who have a visual or hearing impairment or other physical or learning disabilities will develop cognitive and language skills at a different rate from children without these difficulties.

The **nature** versus **nurture** debate describes the ideas about what affects a child's intelligence. Nature refers to the child's genes which have been inherited from their parents and nurture refers to the environment a child grows up in.

Summary

- Intellectual development is the development of thinking and language skills.
- Children learn by absorbing everything around them.
- The adults caring for them need to make sure they provide a wide range of experiences.
- Children need to learn a number of different concepts which we take for granted.
- The nature/nurture debate refers to the impact of genes and the environment on intelligence.

Try to learn *at least* one intellectual and one language milestone for each age group.

Prove it!

1. **Define intellectual development.**
2. **What is a concept? Give two examples of concepts children need to learn.**
3. **List the intellectual and language skills you would expect the following children to have developed:**
   a) a one year old.
   b) a four year old.
4. **Identify and explain eight things parents and carers can do to promote a child's intellectual development.**
5. **What are the factors which affect a child's ability to learn?**

Learning through play

What will I learn?

- **What play is**
- **The different types of play**
- **The relationship between play and learning**

If children are not able or encouraged to play, they will become bored, irritable and destructive. Children who are not used to playing will find it difficult to learn.

What is play?

Play is how children spend much of their time. They play naturally because it is fun and makes them happy, but play is also an essential part of learning. Through play, children can become creative, practise gross and fine motor skills, develop dexterity as they manipulate new toys, learn how others behave and how to respond to that behaviour, learn to co-operate and use their imagination. Play enables children to learn new words, practise language skills and understand concepts such as numbers. By playing, children learn to organise their thoughts, feelings and ideas. Play also helps children to make sense of the world around them.

Different types of play

There are **SIX** main types of play:

1 Physical	4 Imaginative
2 Creative	5 Manipulative
3 Discovery	6 Social

1. Physical play

This takes place when a child is moving around and using their large muscles. It often takes place outside and involves running around, balancing, climbing, jumping or riding bicycles. Physical play helps to develop gross motor skills and fine manipulative skills, balance and co-ordination. It also helps to develop strong muscles and bones. It can help to develop concepts such as size and speed and develop new vocabulary. It helps to let off steam and relieve stress, build confidence and by playing with others, learn to share, take turns and respect others.

2. Creative play

3. Discovery play

This involves using the senses to find out how things work, how things are made and what can be done with them. Children engage with objects and by handling, throwing, banging or mouthing, assess its properties and possibilities. Playing with water and sand using different sized containers is an example of discovery play, where children can learn mathematical concepts such as weight and volume.

4. Imaginative play

This involves the child pretending to be someone or something else, or invent make-believe people or pets. The child can go on adventures and use everyday objects to represent entirely different things. Simple items such as cardboard boxes can be used to make cars and dens. Imaginative play is a good opportunity for children to develop language skills. It also helps children to understand other people, and acting out situations helps them to work through new situations, or help them express feelings that they may be unable to put into words.

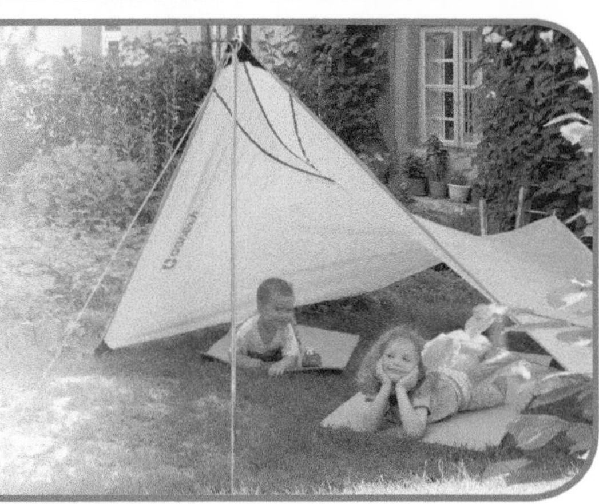

This takes place when children use their imagination and different materials to make something original. Examples could be using paint, play-dough, making a collage or using construction toys such as building blocks. Creative play helps a child to express ideas and emotions, learn about colours, textures, and how things go together. It also helps to develop fine manipulative skills and hand–eye co-ordination. Creative play is often messy but needs to be encouraged so that creative abilities can be developed.

5. Manipulative play

This is using the hands to build or fit things together. It helps children to develop fine manipulative skills and hand–eye co-ordination. Manipulative play starts as soon as a baby can hold a toy. Babies may play with activity centres and find that pushing or pulling things make something happen. Older children may play with shape sorters, puzzles and building blocks, etc., that encourage problem solving and logical thinking.

6. Social play

This is about playing with others. By playing together, children learn social skills such as sharing, taking turns, waiting and co-operating with others. There are several stages to social play as children develop the skills to play happily with each other. Social play is explored in more detail in Topic 6.

◀ **What type of play is taking place here?**

Many play activities involve more than one type of play; for example, making sandcastles at the beach could involve physical, creative, manipulative and social play.

Children enjoy playing alone, with other children and with adults. Adults need to provide a safe and secure environment and suitable equipment for play but should avoid giving too much direction and taking control.

> **Link**
>
> **Topic 4:** *Safety in and around the home*

Children often enjoy singing games and making music. These are play activities which have many benefits and require little equipment so can be valuable when outside the home. From a young age children enjoy listening to singing and objects that make sounds, such as musical mobiles. Through singing games and nursery rhymes, children can learn new words and develop memory skills. They can develop co-ordination and motor skills while clapping in time or joining in action songs.

Play and learning

Play helps to extend skills in all areas of development (**PIES**). For example:

- **P**hysical development – improving balance and co-ordination, fine manipulative skills and exercising muscles, using senses.
- **I**ntellectual development – language skills, memory and concentration, understanding concepts, imagination and creativity, counting and solving problems, learning about cause and effect.
- **E**motional development – feeling happiness, having a sense of control, preventing boredom, letting off steam, developing confidence and independence, acting out roles and feelings, increasing self-esteem.
- **S**ocial development – learning to share, take turns and co-operate, following rules, getting along with others, understanding and caring about others.

> **Link**
>
> **Topics 4, 5 and 6 (milestones of development):** *when studying all areas of development, think about how play activities help children to develop skills.*

You may find a question about play or a specific activity which asks you to identify how the activity helps all areas of a child's development. It doesn't matter if you haven't studied that particular activity – think about the list above and use your common sense. Remember to mention all the PIES though.

Child Study

Observe your study child playing and identify the skills they are developing. Plan a play activity to help them practise skills you have not seen.

Activity

Complete a table like this showing an example of each type of play and the physical, intellectual, emotional and social skills the activity could develop.

Type of play	Example	Physical	Intellectual	Emotional	Social
Physical	building sandcastles	fine manipulative skills using the bucket and spade	understanding how to get the sand to stick together	successful building develops confidence	team work when building with others
Creative					
Discovery					
Manipulative					
Imaginative					
Social					

Summary

- Children play because they enjoy it and they do not realise that they are learning.
- There are six main types of play, but children may be engaged in more than one type at a time.
- Children need to experience a wide range of play activities both playing alone and with others.
- Parents and carers should encourage children to decide how they play and not take control by telling them what to do.

Activity

Make a book containing simple games and nursery rhymes that could entertain a young child on a long car journey.

Prove it!

1. Why is play important?
2. Why do children need opportunities to play alone and with others?

Learning aids

What will I learn?

- **What to consider when choosing toys**
- **Safety considerations**

Children will use their imagination to turn objects they find in the home into things to play with and will happily play for hours with simple items such as cardboard boxes, twigs and pieces of fabric. Toys that are made for children are not essential, but have an important part to play in stimulating the child's imagination and helping them to develop new skills.

Safety symbols

The 'Lion mark' is only found on British-made toys and can only be used if the toy meets all relevant safety standards.

The Kitemark confirms that the British Standards Institution has tested the product and it meets a particular standard.

The CE mark shows that the toy has been made in the European Union and the manufacturer states that it conforms to the safety requirements agreed by the EU. It does not prove the toy has been tested.

Choosing toys

There are a variety of factors that need to be considered when choosing toys:

- **Is it safe?** Toys sold in Britain must meet strict safety standards. The toy and/or its packaging may display the symbols on the left to show that it meets specific standards. There should be no sharp corners or loose parts that could be swallowed. Colouring materials should be labelled as non-toxic. Toys for babies should be easy to keep clean as they will put them in their mouths.
- **Is it suitable for the child's age and stage of development?** Toys must be suitable for the child's age and ability. Children will quickly get bored with toys that are too simple, and frustrated with those that are too complicated. Giving a child a toy which is designed for older children is potentially dangerous as it may have small parts which the child could choke on or the toy may break easily. Manufacturers label toys with an age guide to give advice about its suitability.
- **Is it versatile?** A toy that can be used in many different ways will be good value for money and will be longer lasting than one which has limited uses.
- **Is it interesting?** A toy which is colourful and fun will be played with much more than one which merely has educational value.
- **Is it durable?** Young children are not always careful and toys can get broken easily.

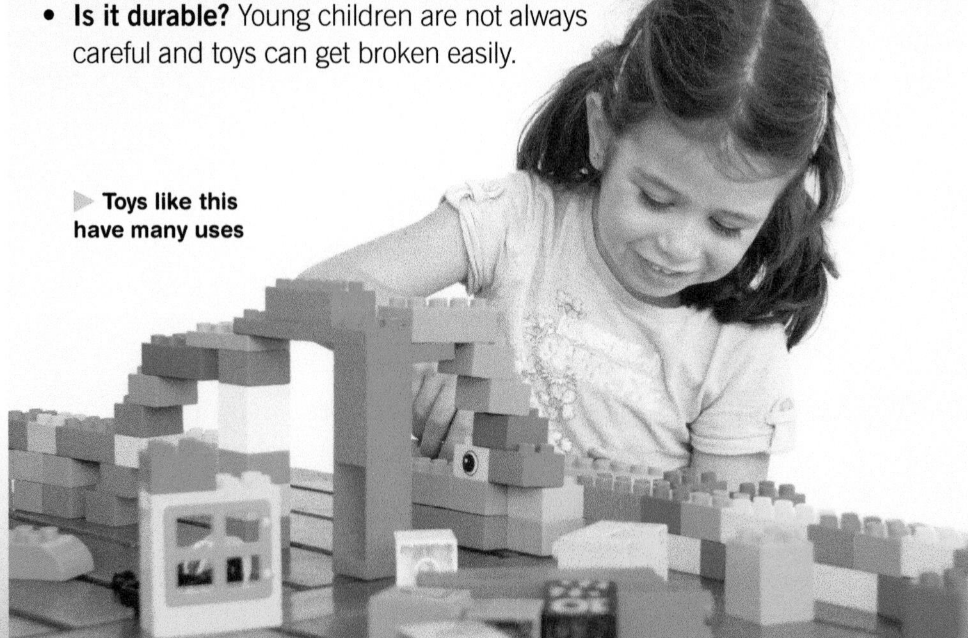

Toys like this have many uses

Toys can be expensive and manufacturers spend a lot of money advertising their products in a way that appeals to children. Children will use '**pester power**' to try to persuade parents to buy toys, and many parents do not want their child to miss out on the latest products. Spin-offs from children's television programmes and films also create demand for toys. Some neighbourhoods have toy libraries, where families can borrow toys. These give access to a wider range of toys and can provide an informal support network for parents.

It is not always necessary to spend a lot of money on toys. Many household objects can be used for play and allow a child to develop their imagination:

- Empty boxes, bottles and pots can be used for models, musical instruments and for playing shops.
- Larger boxes can become cars, boats and dolls' beds.
- Old clothes and jewellery can be used for dressing up.
- Sheets and blankets can be used for making dens, with a bit of help from furniture.
- A bowl of water, washing-up liquid and plastic containers can provide opportunities to learn about concepts such as bigger and smaller, floating and sinking.
- Rolls of cheap wallpaper lining can be used for painting and drawing.

Link

Topic 2: *Fast food outlets use free toys from films, etc., to advertise their products. This has implications for healthy eating, although these foods are fine to eat occasionally.*

Link

Look at the milestones for physical development in Topic 4 and intellectual development in this topic for information about children's abilities at different ages.

Toys for different ages

Age	Development	Toys and activities
Newborn to one year	Babies learn by using their senses, exploring with their hands and mouths. As they get older they are more mobile. Toys need to be easy to hold, unbreakable and safe to be put in the mouth.	Rattles, activity gyms, soft toys, squeaking toys, blocks and card/fabric books.
1–2 years	Children of this age are much more mobile. They need toys that will help develop balance, co-ordination and fine manipulative skills.	Shape sorters, threading and stacking toys, push and pull toys, simple books, simple jigsaws, small slides and swings, paddling pools, painting and drawing.
2–3 years	Physical skills are developed enough that children can handle toys with confidence. Language skills are developing fast, but concentration span is still quite short.	Soft toys and dolls, jigsaws with more pieces, play dough, toys for making music, dressing up toys, books, basic shape matching toys, picture dominoes, tricycles, simple climbing frames, swings and slides, balls.
3–4 years	Children at this age are very independent. They will be able to run, skip and climb confidently. They often like to pretend to be someone else and are starting to show empathy with others. They need toys and games to stimulate imagination and understanding of concepts.	Construction toys, small world toys (e.g. doll's house, play kitchen, etc.) and many of the toys suggested above, in more complex versions.
4–5 years	Intellectual skills develop quickly at this age and children are very curious. They are usually able to take turns and follow rules.	Paints and crayons, modelling toys, more complex jigsaws and construction toys, story books, skipping ropes, bats and balls, obstacle courses, bicycles.

Key Fact

- Any play involving water must be closely supervised as children can drown in only 5 cm of water.

Key Term

Pester power – the phrase used to describe how children influence their parents to buy advertised or fashionable items by repeated nagging

Toys for children with special needs

Children with special needs, like all children, learn through play. They need toys which are appropriate for their ability and developmental stage, which may not be the same as their chronological age. Toys intended to help overcome a difficulty will be more successful if they are also fun. The best toys will have bright colours, make noises and have some parts that move. Children with a visual impairment will benefit from toys which are brightly coloured, have different textures to explore and make noises in response to actions. Hearing-impaired children will need toys to stimulate language such as matching words to pictures. They may also enjoy toys with lights that flash to attract their attention.

Key Facts

- Even very young children quickly develop the skills to play games on computers, tablets and smartphones. Children must be carefully supervised and care must be taken to ensure children cannot access inappropriate material on the Internet or run up huge bills for data use or online games. Children need to be taught about Internet safety as soon as they are old enough to understand.
- Many television programmes and films, even if scheduled during the day, are not suitable for young children. Care must be taken to check the advice given to ensure the content is appropriate.

Activities

1. Collect pictures of toys from catalogues or the Internet. Identify the skills the child could develop by playing with them.
2. Produce a fact sheet for parents giving ideas on how to provide inexpensive play opportunities.
3. Find recipes for homemade play-dough. Try them out and evaluate them. Could they be made any better?

Audio-visual media and computer games

Computers and **audio-visual media** play a significant role in all our lives. Children often enjoy playing computer games and these have the potential to develop a wide range of skills. Watching television or DVDs can provide much needed quiet time and opportunities for children to find out about things they would not otherwise have the opportunity to experience. They have benefits to a child's development, but do also have some potential difficulties. If a parent or carer is involved in the computer game or television programme, then there are opportunities to discuss what has been seen, which will help to develop language skills and understanding of concepts.

Advantages of technology

Technology can help with the following:

- Developing fine motor skills through using a mouse, keyboard or touch screen
- Practising hand–eye co-ordination
- Understanding cause and effect
- Learning about numbers and words
- Developing concentration
- Improving observation skills

Disadvantages of technology

If used too much, technology can slow down the development of:

- Social skills
- Language
- Asking questions
- Gross motor skills
- Drawing, writing and creativity
- Reading skills
- Problem solving

Computer games and other visual media can provide too much stimulation because they have so many loud sounds, flashing lights, etc. Children can get irritable after using them and may need distracting. Children who become dependent on the stimulation may find it harder to focus on other activities. These games and television programmes do have many benefits, but it is important to provide a variety of activities so that children can develop skills in all areas.

Child Study

Find out what the child's favourite toys are and assess how they contribute to the area of development you are studying.

Summary

- Toys must be suitable for the child's age and ability.
- It is important to consider safety when choosing toys.
- It is not necessary to spend a lot of money on toys.
- Children need to be provided with a range of toys so they can develop skills in all areas.
- The best toys are those that give the child a variety of play opportunities.

Activity

Watch at least two television programmes aimed at young children. Write a review commenting on the entertainment and educational value.

Prove it!

1. **What criteria would you use when choosing a new toy for a child?**
2. **Identify two safety symbols to look for when buying a new toy.**
3. **Suggest suitable toys for the following children. Give reasons for your answer.**
   a) a six month old
   b) a two year old
   c) a four year old.
4. **You are looking after a three year old for a day. Plan how you will spend your time and explain the reasons for your choice of activities.**
5. **Discuss the positive and negative factors of playing with computerised toys.**

Learning to read

What will I learn?

- **How children learn to read**
- **Factors to consider when choosing books**
- **The role of parents and carers in helping children to read**

Reading is one of the most important skills children need to learn. A child who can read can use books to find out a wide range of information by themselves and discover things that are outside their own world.

Reading

Books can be used to prepare children for new experiences in a safe and fun way. Reading also helps children to develop memory skills and concentration, stimulates their imagination and gives pleasure. Children who can read are more independent and find it easier to entertain themselves.

In order to learn to read, children need to have acquired a number of **pre-reading skills**:

- They need to understand that symbols on paper have a meaning and to be able to recognise and match shapes. This develops into matching letters and then whole words. Games like snap and dominoes will help to develop these skills. Magnetic letters can be a fun way of helping children to recognise letters and words.
- Children also need to learn the sounds that letters can make. Word games such as 'I spy' and pointing out letters such as those in the child's name will help the child become familiar with letter sounds.
- Children need to be familiar with using print, understanding that we begin at the top of the page, read from left to right and turn the page form right to left.
- Practising writing letters and words will help with recognition. Learning to write also involves fine manipulative skills (see pages 126 and 130).

Key Fact

- Research shows children who enjoy books with their parents or carers usually have better understanding of language, wider vocabularies and higher cognitive skills than children who have not been introduced to books and reading at home.

Being familiar with letters helps children to read

When children have mastered these skills, they will go on to start to read with help. Many children who are read to regularly will appear to 'read' their favourite story because they have learnt it. True reading involves being able to decode words in an unfamiliar context and understand their meaning.

Each child will learn to read at their own pace. Children should be encouraged to read without being forced. If reading is not an enjoyable experience, the child will resist and this can cause reading difficulties as the child gets older.

Children are taught to read in different ways.

Phonics are used to teach the child the relationship between the shape of a letter and the sound it makes. As children learn the individual sounds, they are taught to match these sounds to objects through games and activities such as 'I spy'. Once a child knows all the initial sounds then they can be taught to blend and combine these sounds to make simple words such as 'can', 'dog'.

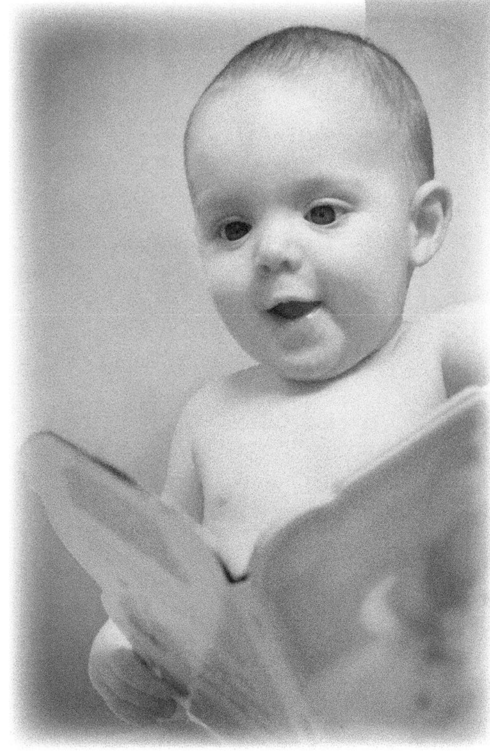

Children enjoy books from a young age

However, because not all words in the English language can be read through using phonics, children also have to learn to read a number of **high frequency words.** These are words which occur often in English, such as 'they', 'was'. These words are taught by repeatedly showing the children the word on a flashcard and saying the word, so that they learn to match the word with its shape. Most children learn to read more difficult words by combining these two methods.

Key Terms

Pre reading skills - the skills children need to have acquired before they can begin to learn to read

Phonics - learning about the sounds that are made by letters or combinations of letters

High frequency words - the words that occur most often in English. When children can read these, making sense of a whole sentence is much easier

Looking at books with an adult encourages children to try to read

The role of parents and carers in helping children to read

Children of all ages enjoy being read to. Sitting and reading stories, looking at the pictures and talking about what has been read are important parts in getting children interested in books and reading. Regular story time helps to establish a habit of reading as well as being valuable quiet time during the day or before bed. Story time can be made entertaining by the use of different voices, puppets and interactive books.

Key Fact

- Bookstart is a programme that offers free books to all children, in their first year and at 3–4 years old. There are special versions of the books for children with visual or hearing impairments. It is run by the Booktrust, a charitable organisation, supported by children's book publishers and funded by national government.

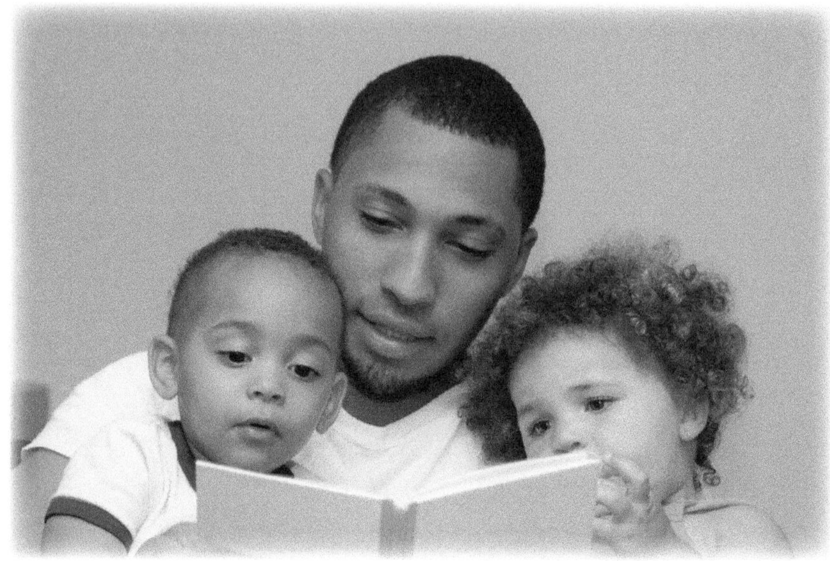

Adults should make sure a variety of appropriate books are always available. Books can be given as presents and rewards. Visits to the library can be an enjoyable experience which gives children the opportunity to experience more books than may be possible at home. Many libraries also offer 'story time' for children.

Parents and carers can also encourage children to read by being good role models and reading themselves.

Research shows that children who are regularly read to have a wider vocabulary than those who are not. Having an ability to read with confidence can support learning, develop confidence and improve employment chances as an adult.

Tips for reading to and with children:

- Try to have a regular reading time.
- Encourage the child to choose the book they want to read – even if it is the same story for several days.
- Let the child help to turn pages and point to the pictures.
- Talk about the illustrations and the story – ask open ended questions so the child can come up with their own ideas.
- Give the child chance to finish sentences and join in with rhymes.
- Remember you can read to a child even if they are not sitting with you – even if they are playing with something else, they can still benefit from hearing stories read to them and this may be less of a battle than trying to get an active toddler to sit still.

Choosing books

There is a huge variety of books available and the choice depends on the age and stage of development of the child, as well as their own interests and the cost.

Books for babies and toddlers should:
- be colourful
- have large, clear pictures and print
- be about everyday objects and events
- be uncluttered with only a few words on each page
- be easy to hold
- be strong and well made – cloth, cardboard and plastic books are ideal.

Books for older children should:
- have print which is easy to read
- match the child's interest
- be colourful
- have interesting characters and storyline
- be of a suitable length.

Activities

1. Make some flash cards which would help a child to learn letters and letter sounds.
2. Visit your local library and investigate the range of books available. Write a review of one book, commenting on its suitability for a pre-school child.

Summary

- Reading is a skill that all children need to develop.
- Forcing children to read before they are ready may make them reluctant to try.
- Parents and carers must set a good example by reading and making story time part of the child's routine.
- Books should be part of a child's world so that they become used to looking at them.

Children who enjoy reading will be able to find out things and entertain themselves

Prove it!

1. **Why are books important for a child's development?**
2. **How might books improve a child's:**
   a) fine manipulative skills?
   b) emotional development?
   c) social development?
3. **What factors would you consider when choosing books for children?**
4. **How can parents/carers encourage a child to have an interest in reading?**
5. **Describe the pre-reading skills children need to develop before they begin to learn to read.**

Learning to draw and write

What will I learn?

- **How children develop drawing and writing skills**
- **The role of parents and carers in encouraging children to draw and write**

Key Facts

- Children's drawings will vary with their mood. Sometimes a child who can draw and colour quite well may not do so, perhaps because they are rushing, tired or bored.
- Always try to be positive about a child's art work. It is better to praise what you can see, for example their choice of colours than to ask what it is.

Children love to draw and paint from a young age, making on paper marks that have meaning to them even if they are not clear to others. In order to learn to write, children not only need pencil control and hand–eye co-ordination to form the letter shapes, but also to be able to write in a straight line with letters and words spaced neatly. In addition they need to be able to spell and to use grammar and punctuation correctly.

Drawing

Drawing helps a child to express feelings, be creative and develop fine manipulative skills. Practice will develop good pencil control which will form the basis of writing skills. Children are ready to draw as soon as then can hold a pencil or crayon, usually between the ages of 12 and 18 months. Most children begin to draw using both hands and will start to show a preference for either their right or left hand by about 18 months old. Most have a clear preference by about 3 years old.

12–15 months	18 months	18 months to 2 years	2–2½ years	2½–3 years
The child uses a palmar grasp and scribbles by moving the hand backwards and forwards.	The pencil is lifted from the paper to make separate lines in different directions.	The child scribbles in circles.	The child draws separate circles using a primitive tripod grasp. Can copy letters T and V.	The circle begins to represent a face, with eyes, mouth and nose added. The tripod grasp is improving.

Key Terms

Palmar grasp – uses the whole hand to hold an object

Tripod grasp – uses the thumb and first two fingers. (See section on physical development.)

There are several stages to learning to draw and write. These overlap so children may show more than one stage in the same drawing. As they develop control, they will begin to form letters shapes as well as pictures. The ages given are an approximate guide.

Learning to write

The skills of pencil control and hand–eye co-ordination to form the letter shapes, writing in a straight line with letters and words spaced neatly as well as spelling and using grammar and punctuation correctly need a lot of practice and will develop gradually. Looking at books and reading will help children to develop an understanding of spelling, punctuation and grammar.

The role of parents and carers

Parents can encourage children to draw and to write by making it fun and praising the child's efforts. Displaying pictures develops the child's self-esteem and gives them the confidence to continue. Art should be a regular play activity and children need access to a wide variety of drawing implements, such as crayons, pencils and chalk as well as plenty of cheap paper.

A suitable chair and table encourages a child to develop the correct posture for writing. A black/whiteboard or easel can help children to draw and paint comfortably without leaning on their work. Colouring books and activity books containing dot-to-dot pictures and patterns to copy will help to develop pencil control. Children should be allowed to use their preferred hand as trying to make a left-handed child be right handed can cause difficulties in learning to read and write.

Child Study

Plan and carry out an art activity with your study child. Observe the child and identify how they are holding the pencil/paintbrush, etc. What stage are their drawing skills and what does this tell you about the child's development?

Summary

- Learning to draw or write is a fine manipulative skill (physical development) as well as an intellectual skill.
- Drawing can help children to express feelings that they are unable to explain in words.
- Children need to be praised and encouraged in their attempts at drawing and writing.
- Parents and carers should provide a range of materials for children to draw and write with.

Activity

Collect drawings from a range of children (or try looking on the Internet). Compare the drawings with the stages shown here and try to identify the probable age of the child.

2½–3 years

Lines are added around the circle.

3 years

These lines are grouped together to represent hair, arms and legs. Can copy letter H.

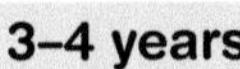

3–4 years

Small bodies are now added, with legs at the bottom and arms coming out of the head. The child will begin to trace letters, numbers and shapes formed by dots.

4–5 years

The body is more in proportion, legs have feet and arms have hands. The pencil is held in an adult fashion with quite good control. Circles, triangles and squares are copied, as are the letters C, A, U and Y.

5–6 years

Other features such as clothes, houses, trees and pets are included.

Prove it!

1. Why is it important to encourage a child to draw?
2. When are children ready to start drawing?
3. What are early drawings like?
4. When do drawings become more realistic?
5. How can parents and carers encourage a child to draw and write?

Learning about numbers

What will I learn?

- **How children learn about numbers**
- **The role of parents and carers in helping children to understand numbers**

Numeracy is a vital skill so it is important to introduce numbers from an early age. Numbers occur in conversation, stories and games, so children gradually become aware of numbers. Number skills can be developed through songs, rhymes, games, stories and everyday activities such as cooking and shopping. Children's use of their toys introduces them to the concepts of number, size, volume, capacity and weight.

Learning about numbers

There are various stages in which children learn about numbers:

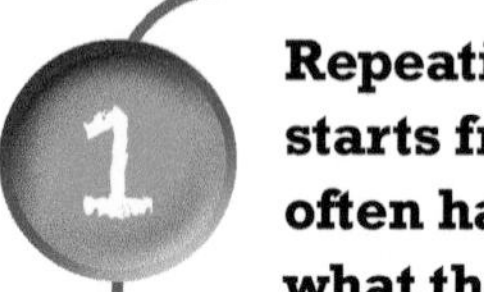

Repeating number words. This starts from about age 2, but children often have little understanding of what the words mean and get the words in the wrong order.

Matching number words to objects by counting them.

Understanding that numbers have a fixed order: one is followed by two, etc.

Learning about ordinal numbers.

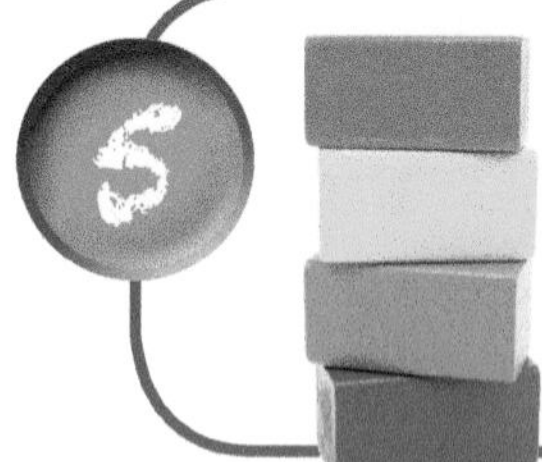

Comparing numbers: children learn about more than and less than in relation to numbers, e.g. 8 is more than 4.

Understanding that numbers are constant and are not related to position or size, e.g. larger size does not mean a bigger number.

Learning to recognise the shape of numbers and write them.

Learning to use numbers, e.g. add, subtract, share and measure.

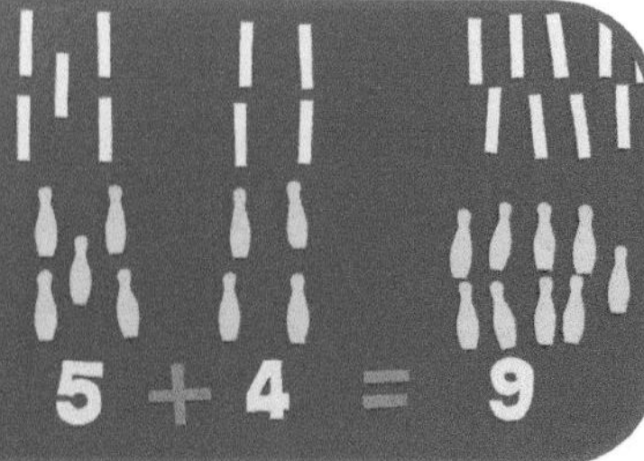

Children also need to understand other concepts associated with numbers, such as size, weight and volume. This happens naturally through play and other activities. When children are engaging in water or sand play using different sized containers, they are learning about volume and comparative size, by marking their height to see if they have grown they are learning about height and measuring and by cooking they are learning about weighing and proportion.

Learning about numbers should be fun

The role of parents and carers in helping children to understand numbers

Numbers can be used in many activities to help children understand the words and concepts in a fun way:

- Songs and nursery rhymes often contain numbers and are useful in helping children to understand the order of numbers.
- Counting and matching games such as dominoes and using dice help children to recognise and use numbers.
- Adults can talk to children about the things they see around them, pointing out numbers on houses, birthday cards and in books.
- Children can be encouraged to count items in the house.
- Magnetic numbers and colouring books with different numbers can be used to familiarise children with number shapes without needing to use them to count or manipulate numbers – this can come later.
- Painting and making handprints can be used to develop an understanding of bigger and smaller.

As children become more familiar with the meaning of numbers and the language associated with numbers they will gain the confidence to use numbers to solve problems.

Ordinal – number that describes position, e.g. first, second, third, last, etc.

Activity

Produce an activity book that could be used to help a child to develop an understanding of numbers.

Summary

- Children learn to use number words before they understand what they mean.
- Games, rhymes and songs make learning about numbers fun.
- Parents and carers need to make numbers useful in everyday life so children are comfortable using them.

Prove it!

1. **Identify and describe the stages in which children learn about numbers.**
2. **Suggest activities that adults can provide to help children understand and use numbers.**

Examination questions

1. Language is an important part of a child's development.
   (a) Explain what you understand by:
      (i) holophrases [1]
      (ii) telegraphic speech. [1]
   (b) Discuss how a parent or carer may encourage and promote the language development of their child. [5]

2. **(a)** Identify the **four** stages of play. [4]
   (b) Discuss the value of play in the development of a child. [6]

3. **(a)** Identify the different stages of social play. [4]
   (b) Explain how play progresses from one stage to the next as the child develops. [4]

4. **(a)** What do you understand by the term *imaginative play*? [1]
   (b) At what age would you expect imaginative play to start? [1]
   (c) Discuss the value of imaginative play to a child. [4]
   (d) Explain the role of the adult during imaginative play. [2]

Tip For question 5, say why children would like a variety of toys. Give examples of different types of toys and explain the skills they can help to develop, e.g. Lego: fine manipulative skills, language and number, understanding of colour, size and shape, emotional development (pride in their achievement) and social development if playing with others.

5. Discuss the importance of providing a child with a range of toys. [8]

6. Numbers are an important part of a child's world.
   (a) Give **two** examples of how a child may learn numbers. [2]
   (b) Identify the stages children go through in order that they fully understand the concept of number. [6]

7. Going shopping provides excellent opportunities for children to learn many skills.
   Explain how this activity can encourage children's:
   (a) mathematical skills [3]
   (b) language development [3]

8. Books provide a child with enjoyment and pleasure.
   (a) Suggest **three** factors that parents/carers should consider when choosing books for their child. [3]
   (b) Discuss ways in which parents/carers may encourage their child to enjoy books. [5]

9. Children's toys and games have changed greatly in the last ten years but remain an essential part of a child's learning process.
   (a) What is meant by *cognitive development*? [1]
   (b) State three cognitive tasks that you would expect an average 4–5 year old to be able to complete. [3]
   (c) Discuss the effects that the introduction of electronic and computerised toys have had on all areas of a child's development. [8]

Remember to think about positive and negative things.

10. Intellectual development is the development of the mind and brain.

(a) What is meant by the term '*nature*'? [1]

(b) What is meant by the term '*nurture*'? [1]

(c) Identify the ways in which children learn, and discuss the role of the parents/carers in promoting their child's intellectual development. [8]

11. How intelligent a child becomes depends not only on genes but also the environment in which they grow up. Discuss this statement. [10]

The answer to Q11 might give you some ideas on how to tackle this one, but remember it's not exactly the same question.

Genes are the basics of human life that a child inherits from both their parents. Genes control the amount of natural intelligence a child is born with, but how this intelligence is used and developed will be influenced by the way the child is brought up and the experiences they have.

Introduction shows understanding of the key words in the question: *genes* and *environment*.

Children learn by playing, by copying others and by asking questions. They will develop well when adults provide plenty of chances to learn skills appropriate for their stage of development. A range of activities both in and outside the home provide ideal learning opportunities. Children can develop language skills and understanding of concepts such as numbers through everyday activities and visits to places such as the seaside, providing they are encouraged to ask questions and talk about what they are doing. Having conversations with the child, asking and answering questions and explaining what they can see will help the child to understand and remember information and ideas. Giving the child chance to plan activities and predict what might happen helps the child to develop more complex thinking skills.

Play should be encouraged and not controlled or interrupted.

Explain why.

Appropriate toys and books will also help a child to understand the world around them. A loving and encouraging environment, where the child feels confident to ask questions and make mistakes, is vital. If mistakes are laughed at, the child will be reluctant to take chances and to try new things.

What makes them appropriate?

Adults should set a good example by reading and being willing to learn. They also need to ensure that the child has a healthy diet and that their eyesight and hearing are not impaired so that the child is healthy enough to concentrate and take part in activities.

Tip This answer would get 8 marks. It is well organised and shows understanding of the nature/nurture debate, but some parts could have more explanation.

12. Books, stories and rhymes play an important part in a child's intellectual development.

(a) What is meant by the term *intellectual development*? [1]

(b) Suggest three ways in which 'story time' can be made varied and interesting. [3]

(c) Discuss how 'story time' can promote children's learning. [8]

Answer for part (c)

Story time makes reading become part of the child's routine and establishes a habit of reading regularly, which is the best way to improve reading skills. (1) Books can help children to concentrate and listening to the story and looking at pictures gives them opportunities to learn to observe and notice things. (2) Reading and discussing stories encourages communication skills and helps children to learn the meaning and pronunciation of new words. (3) By looking at a variety of different types of books, children can learn to recognise colours, textures and shapes in the illustrations. (4) They can also begin to recognise the shape of letters and numbers and become familiar with the way books are used, for example reading from left to right and turning pages from right to left. (5) Stories give children chance to find out about people and places that they might otherwise not have chance to experience, so they can have a better understanding of the world. (6) Stories can also be used to explain everyday events in a way that is easy to understand (7) and can prepare children for changes that might happen, for example moving house. (8) Being able to read is a vital skill when children are in school and it will be easier for them to learn if they are familiar with books from a young age.

Tip This answer has 8 points, all of which explain something about why stories are important in helping children to learn so would get full marks.

13. Children's experiences are very important in their development of language. Discuss this statement considering:
(i) the influence of the home, and
(ii) the pre-school environment. [10]

Language is a skill that has to be learned. Development of language skills begins at birth when babies cry for attention and adults respond. Even though babies cannot communicate with words, they will respond when someone speaks to them and will begin to take turns in a 'conversation'.

Introduction shows understanding that language skills develop gradually.

Children need to be spoken to slowly and clearly using open questions that encourage conversation. They need to be given time to organise their thoughts before providing an answer. Adults need to be patient, so a child's sentence should not be finished for them because this stops them thinking for themselves. Mistakes should be corrected without interrupting the flow and without laughing at the child. If a child is interrupted, it is hard for them to remember what they were trying to say. Laughing at mistakes will stop the child wanting to try.

Children learn by copying, so it is important that adults use appropriate language and are good role models for the child, or the child may repeat words that are not acceptable, without understanding their meaning.

Praise and encouragement are important because children who are praised feel more secure and willing to practise. Children need to be given opportunity to practise language skills. Daily activities such as cooking and visits provide ideal occasions for conversation about what is happening and what can be seen. This gives children the chance to learn new words, ideas and ways of expressing themselves.

These three paragraphs say what adults should and shouldn't do when talking to the child, with reasons

If children are exposed to different forms of language by spending time with adults and other children, both in the home and in pre-school settings, they will develop a wide vocabulary. Introducing children to books also gives children experience of different forms of language and helps to develop their imagination and storytelling skills. Re-telling stories helps children to practise putting their thoughts into a logical order and give explanations for events. All adults working with children can help them to develop confidence in using language.

This final paragraph suggests ways to encourage language development, mentioning that it is everyone that the child meets that can have an influence.

Tip This answer could get full marks because it shows understanding of how children develop language skills and how the people involved with the child can affect them.

Social development

What will I learn?

- **How a child learns social skills in the family and society**

Socialisation

This is the process of learning a range of acceptable **social skills** and behaviour in order to live with other members of society.

A newborn baby does not have any knowledge about the acceptable social skills of society. **Socialisation** begins during the early years of childhood. Children have to learn many social skills, including behaviour, being able to communicate with others, learning to share, personal hygiene, manners, self-control, following rules and becoming independent.

Young children learn by watching other people and copying their social skills. It is important that from a young age children are given lots of opportunities to have the company of other people within the home and their community.

Key Fact

- Parents and carers have a very important task to make sure that young children copy acceptable social skills within the home. This enables children to have these skills and enjoy the company of other people in society.

Primary socialisation

Parents, other family members and child carers will be the main influence on a baby's social development. A baby will watch and gradually begin to copy behaviour and social skills. This is called **primary socialisation.**

Child Study

For social development you should observe the child and note what behaviour and social skills are copied from family members.

Activity

Talk with mothers about how they teach babies and toddlers social skills and discuss the different social activities they do as a family.

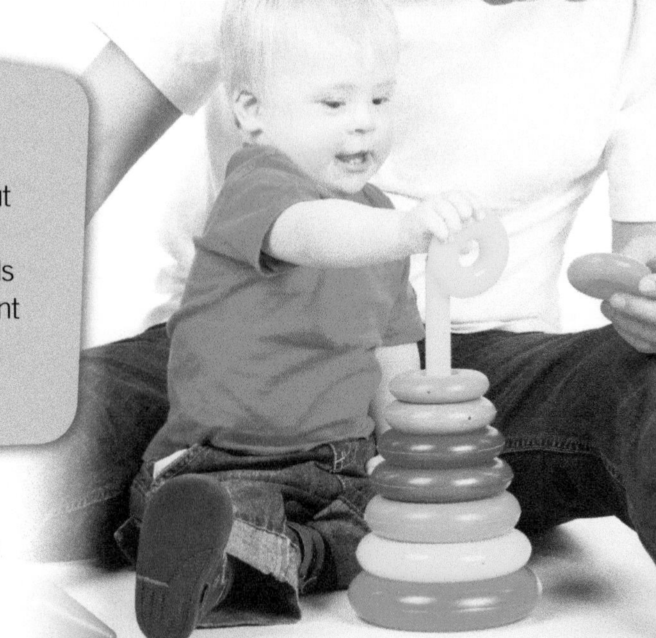

▶ Primary socialisation: parent and toddler playing together

Secondary socialisation

Babies and toddlers should have opportunities to meet other members of society to help develop and extend their social skills. It is important that babies and toddlers are taken out into the community and take part in a variety of activities. This can be achieved by attending parent and toddler groups, visits to parks and leisure centres, shopping trips, story times at the library and having meals out and day trips.

In all these situations babies and toddlers will meet and interact with people of different ages, cultures and those with disabilities. These experiences are called **secondary socialisation** as they take place outside the family home.

▲ **Secondary socialisation: in the company of other mothers and babies**

▲ **Secondary socialisation: shopping trip**

Key Terms

Social skills – having behaviour which is acceptable to other people

Socialisation – the process of learning social skills and behaviour which enable an individual to live with other members of a community

Summary

- Socialisation is the process during which young children learn acceptable social skills and behaviour.
- Socialisation takes place within the home and also in the community.
- Children are born without any knowledge of social skills and learn them during the early years of life.

Revision Tip

Make sure you understand how babies and toddlers develop social skills. You should have an understanding of the wide range of social opportunities for babies and toddlers that can help the socialisation process. In an answer on socialisation, remember to discuss the primary socialisation skills learnt within the home environment. You should also mention secondary socialisation, which helps to extend the social skills of young children.

Prove it!

1. **What is primary socialisation?**
2. **What is secondary socialisation? Give some suggestions of different secondary socialisation opportunities for babies and toddlers.**

The pattern of social development

What will I learn?

- **To gain an understanding of how a newborn baby begins to socialise with the family**

Key Fact

- The pattern of social development has to be learnt as children are born into a world where everybody has to share and live together.

From birth babies gradually develop social contact with other people.

Developing socialising skills

Newborn babies are aware of other people around them, and so **contact** with people is a very important part of their daily life. Babies are comforted by being nursed and cuddled, which makes them feel happy and secure.

Activity

If you have access to a baby under the age of 1 year, and have permission from the parents, observe the social skills of the child.

2 weeks

At about 2 weeks old a baby will begin to **watch** the mother's or father's face at feed times. On these occasions the parents should talk and slowly the young baby will be able to **recognise** the parents.

6 weeks

At about 6 weeks old a baby will start to smile at family members who talk to the baby.

3 months

By 3 months a baby will start to **communicate** with people, responding with noises and gurgling sounds.

6 months

At 6 months a baby is much more aware of people and sometimes can attract their attention by making noises, for example if the baby wants a particular toy. A baby will now enjoy playing simple games with parents and older siblings, such as clapping hands and having rhymes and songs sung to them.

Child Study

In a Child Study on social development you could observe how a toddler will join in activities with parents, siblings or yourself.

◀ **Waving bye-bye**

9 months

By 9 months a baby can recognise familiar people, such as parents, brothers, sisters and grandparents. A baby is aware of being part of a family and **smiles** and laughs with the family. A baby enjoys being in the company of other family members and the various activities taking place. Sometimes, at this age, a baby becomes aware of strangers and can become upset in their company.

12 months

From the first birthday a baby will have a much better awareness of people and begin to start talking. Usually babies start by saying a few words such as 'mum' and 'dad-dad'. Sometimes babies will be able to follow simple instructions and commands given by the parents, such as waving the hand and saying 'bye bye'.

Toddlers enjoy being part of the family and getting involved with household tasks. They watch their parents doing various housework chores, or doing work in the garden. If there are older siblings, toddlers enjoy watching them playing with their toys and games.

Contact – being nursed and cuddled by family members, which makes a baby feel loved and secure

Recognise – being able to see and know important people, such as a baby knowing their parents

Make sure you understand how babies begin to make social contact with the parents and family. Remember, it is important to discuss that young babies should be nursed, cuddled, played with and spoken to, as this helps in the first stage of socialisation.

Summary

- From birth, babies learn how to socialise with the parents.
- Socialisation skills develop gradually as a baby gets older and becomes more involved with the family.
- A toddler enjoys helping with household tasks.

Prove it!

1. **Why is it important that newborn babies are nursed by the parents?**
2. **Explain how a 1 year old communicates with the family.**

Social play

What will I learn?

- **To gain an understanding of how play can help the development of social skills**

Key Facts

- Children's social skills benefit from playing with other children.
- A young child learns many social skills through the various stages of play.

Children should be encouraged to play as it provides many opportunities to learn and develop social skills.

Social play

Babies, toddlers and young children learn many life skills through play. Play is a vital feature of childhood and should be part of everyday life. Social play is learning how to play with others, being able to share and accept the rules of a game. It is through play that toddlers learn these skills of social play. It is important that there are many opportunities allowing toddlers to develop these skills. A young child will be able to enjoy a variety of games, and the company and friendship of children, by having acceptable social play skills.

Key Terms

Solitary play – playing alone with toys

Parallel play – playing alongside another toddler but not playing together or sharing toys

The stages of social play

There are **FIVE** stages of social play and a child will normally achieve the fifth stage by age 5. Each young child will gain social skills at a different rate, due to the family background and the opportunities available to play with other children. Babies begin by playing alone and gradually involve other children as they become older.

Stage 1: Solitary play

This type of play takes place from birth to the age of 2 years. A baby plays alone with toys. Of course solitary play can also take place throughout childhood. Sometimes children enjoy playing alone with toys and using their imagination to create a play scene.

Stage 2: Parallel play

This type of play takes place from age 2 to 3 years. The toddler will play alongside another toddler but they do not try and play together. The toddlers play with their own toys and do not share them.

Stage 3: Looking-on play

This type of play takes place at about the age of 3 years. The child will watch with interest other children playing but stay a short distance away. Sometimes the young child will try to copy the play activity of the group. The child does not yet have enough confidence to become a member of the group.

Key Terms

Looking-on play – watching, from a short distance, other children playing together

Joining-in play – playing with other children in the same activity

Co-operative play – playing as a member of a team, sharing toys and roles

Stage 4: Joining-in play

This type of play takes place at about the age of 3½ years. The child will play with a group of other children and they all join in the same activity. This could be an outdoor activity, such as running around with a ball, or playing with dolls or cars. Young children will begin to have an understanding of **sharing** and allowing others to play with their toys. There can often be squabbles and tears because children are still learning how to become team members and consider other people's suggestions and ideas.

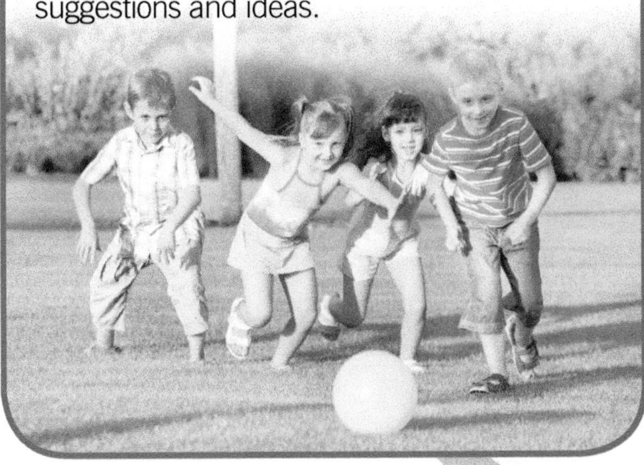

Stage 5: Co-operative play

This type of play takes place at about the age of 4 years. The child will play as a member of a group working on the same activity such as playing house or with toy cars. Young children will have learnt to work together as a team, to share the toys and play roles such as being doctors and nurses. Sometimes a team member may suggest different ideas which others do not like and arguments and tears can result. Gradually as children become older they will learn how to accept different ideas. Now children can participate in playing board games which can be a family activity, providing an opportunity for quality time, and involving different ages such as grandparents. When playing board games children gain an understanding of the rules that each competitor has to follow, learn about **taking turns** and that cheating is not allowed during the game.

Friends

From about the age of 3 years young children will begin to enjoy the company of other children when playing together during social play and will start to form friendships with a few other children. By age 4 most children will have formed some firm friendships with children of the same gender. They will discuss play ideas together, enjoy each other's company and learn how to share.

There will be occasions when disagreements will lead to tears and upsets, which can sometimes result in a breakdown of the friendship. However, some friendships made by young children can last a lifetime and provide much pleasure and enjoyment in later years.

Key Facts

- Young children can form firm friendships which may last a lifetime.
- Spending excessive time alone watching television programmes, some of which may be unsuitable for their age, can hinder young children's social development.

▶ Enjoying the company of my best friend

▼ Watching the television on my own

Loneliness due to a lack of social contact

Parents should make sure that babies and toddlers are able to experience a variety of social contact. Some young children may spend a lot of time alone in front of a television watching programmes, many of which may be unsuitable for their age, or sitting for several hours playing games on the computer screen. Although children can benefit and learn much from watching television and using computers, excessive time spent on both of these activities can have a negative effect on all areas of children's development.

Having only a few opportunities to interact in person with other people, and thus learn the social skills necessary to enjoy play and friendship, can slow down and hinder social development of young children. They could develop feelings of loneliness and boredom which will make them unhappy and sad.

This situation could also make the parents feel frustrated and upset, if they have purchased expensive computer software, but parents sometimes fail to realise that the young child is being starved of human company which is a vital element for social development. It is the responsibility of parents and carers to make sure toddlers and young children do not suffer from a lack of company and the opportunities to interact with other people.

Helping social play

Parents and carers should aim to provide babies and toddlers with a variety of different situations for social play. Some babies will attend a nursery or a childminder on a daily basis, while the parents are at work maybe, and so will be able to play with other young children. In some homes there may be two young children and both siblings will have a playmate. Inviting neighbours and friends with their young children into the home provides playmates for a toddler and an opportunity for parents to socialise. Parents can take toddlers to parent and toddler groups, soft play sessions and, in fine weather, visit a play area. All these situations provide a toddler with opportunities to help develop social skills while enjoying the company of other children and experiencing different play ideas.

If you have access to a group of toddlers or young children, and have permission from the parents, observe their pattern of social play.

Child Study

In a Child Study on social development you should aim to observe the study child in the company of other children to see what stage of social play has been achieved.

Child Focused Task

In a Child Focused Task on helping to improve social skills you could consider an activity which involves other children in order to develop the social skill of sharing.

Make sure you understand the five stages of social play as this is an important part of a child's social development. You should be able to discuss the various stages of social play and remember to highlight the parents' role of providing different opportunities for the child to experience social play.

Summary

- All children learn their social skills through the five stages of social play.
- It is important that parents and carers give babies, toddlers and young children many opportunities to play with other children.
- By providing a range of different play situations, toddlers and young children will gradually understand how to treat other individuals and learn various social skills. Also by doing this the child will have developed self-confidence and would welcome opportunities to participate in different games.

Prove it!

1. **What is looking-on play?**
2. **Describe two ways in which a parent could help a 3 year old develop social play skills.**

Learning manners

What will I learn?

- **To gain an understanding of how a toddler learns manners and self-control**

Young children should be taught an acceptable range of manners and behaviour. They learn many of these social skills by watching and copying the actions of other people.

Key Fact

- Social skills allow young children to become acceptable individuals within society. With a good understanding of why it is important to be polite, and to treat people with kindness, a child will become popular as a friend. The benefits are also that the child can fit in easily to various social environments, such as visiting friends or attending birthday parties.

Learning social skills

Babies and toddlers are very curious and interested in the surrounding environment. They develop social skills through watching the activities taking place around them and hearing the speech of parents, siblings and other adults. A toddler will attempt to copy the **actions** and words of the parents. The toddler does not know what is, or is not, acceptable and will **copy** the behaviour and **language** of parents, family and friends. It is very important that parents behave in a correct manner and do not fight or swear in the company of a toddler. Parents should act as a good role model so that the toddler learns acceptable social skills. With good social skills children will be well placed when they start school.

Please and thank you

A toddler should be encouraged to say thank you when someone gives them a gift or helps with putting on a coat or a pair of shoes. Parents should ask for toys with the word **please** and similarly receive toys with **thank you** when playing with babies and toddlers. Gradually toddlers will copy this pattern of social skills and they should be praised for their **politeness**.

▲ **Learning to say thank you**

Child Study

In a Child Study on social development you should aim to observe the child's social skills, such as table manners and saying please and thank you.

Child Focused Task

In a Child Focused Task on social development, the activity produced could help in the development of the social skill of self-control by allowing other people to have a turn playing a board game.

Table manners

A toddler in a high chair can join the family around the dining table for meals. This will allow the toddler to watch how the family use their cutlery, eat in a neat manner and do not speak with a mouthful of food. Opportunities should be given to toddlers to practise using cutlery and to make them understand that food should be eaten neatly and not played with or thrown onto the floor. Toddlers should be praised when they eat their meals in a pleasing manner but not rewarded by receiving sweets. By having acceptable **table manners**, a toddler will be able to join the family and friends having meals out in restaurants and everyone will be able to enjoy the occasion.

▲ **A toddler watching the family's table manners**

Self-control

Toddlers do not consider other people's feelings and thoughts. They only think about themselves and what they want. Sometimes toddlers can be very selfish and unkind to other young children by refusing to allow them to play with the toys or join in a game. This can lead to squabbles and disagreements. Occasionally these squabbles may develop into fights. Parents must step in to calm down the tension and make toddlers aware that such behaviour is unacceptable. Parents and carers must aim to teach toddlers and young children to treat other people in the same manner as they would like to be treated. Toddlers must be taught to show **kindness**, politeness and **respect** towards other people. Toddlers have to learn that their actions are not always correct.

Self-control should be learnt by age 4 to 5 years and will be required as part of normal behaviour within the school.

Talk to mothers of toddlers and young children and discuss how they teach their children manners and self-control.

Key Terms

Actions – doing different tasks, such as holding open a door for another individual

Copy – doing the same as another individual, such as placing the toys back into the toy box

Language – the way of communicating by speech

Politeness – saying please and thank you, taking turns in a game, sharing toys and not being selfish

Respect – treating other people with kindness and thoughtfulness

Summary

- Toddlers watch, listen and then copy the actions and speech of parents and other adults.
- Parents should teach toddlers the social skills of saying please and thank you, table manners and how to treat other people with kindness, politeness and respect.

Make sure you understand how parents should teach babies and toddlers manners and self-control, which are important social skills. These social skills should be discussed in an answer about learning social skills, or on preparing a young child for school.

Prove it!

1. **Discuss why it is important that parents should be good role models for their toddler.**
2. **Explain how a parent could teach a toddler to say please and thank you.**

Independence and personal hygiene skills

What will I learn?

- **How a child learns to follow rules and become independent**

It is important that from an early age children learn that rules have to be followed and are a part of society. Young children should be encouraged to learn how to care for their own personal needs.

Key Fact

- Both parents and also any carers should have the same set of rules. Children faced with different sets of rules often become confused and also learn which parent is less strict and allows them more freedom.

Learning to follow rules

Throughout life everyone has to follow rules. For example, a car driver has to stop at a red traffic light. Babies and toddlers should be taught to follow rules set down by the parents. Rules provide a set of instructions that a toddler should follow. These can be safety rules within the home, such as not touching the television screen or opening the bookcase. Other rules might be cleaning teeth after mealtimes and putting toys into the toy box before bedtime. It is very important that both of the parents, carers and other family members give a toddler the same rules. If the rules vary between parents, toddlers will quickly learn who is the more lenient parent and, in their eyes, who is kinder to them. Young children need to be able to accept and follow rules as they are a part of life.

Learning independent personal skills

Slowly toddlers gain social skills enabling them to carry out more tasks for themselves. Parents should encourage toddlers to practise these skills, which will gradually improve.

Personal hygiene is a very important factor. Toddlers should be given opportunities to learn how to wash, bath and shower themselves under close supervision. **Hand washing** should be done before mealtimes and after using the toilet. Toddlers should also be instructed in how and when to clean their teeth. These are frequent activities so a toddler should soon be able to carry out these tasks independently with some adult supervision.

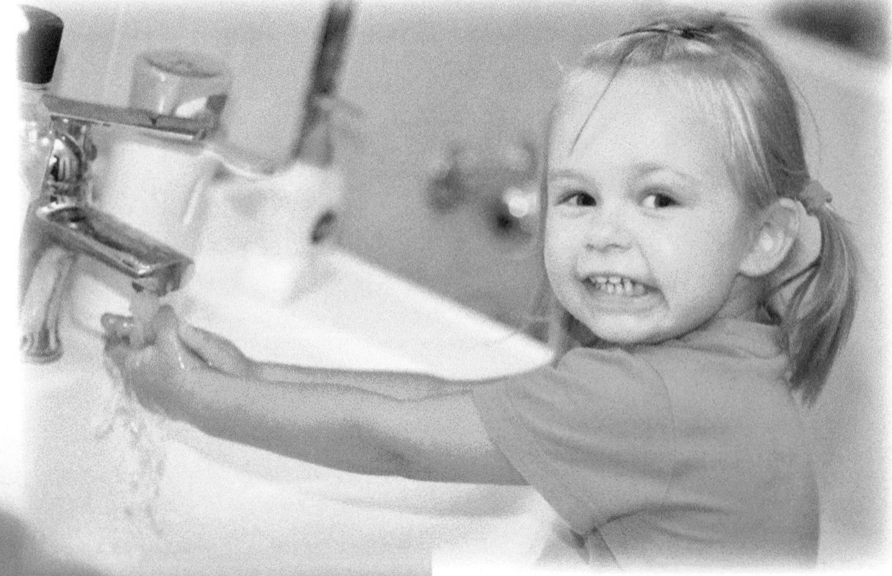

Hand washing is a vital part of personal hygiene

Learning to dress oneself can be made easier if clothes are easy to put on and have simple fastenings. Parents should encourage and praise a toddler's efforts to dress and undress independently. This skill of **dressing** can take quite a while to achieve and it is essential for school, for example when doing games or physical education.

Toilet training can begin from about the age of 18 months. At first toddlers will indicate to the parents that they are about to wet or soil themselves. Gradually a toddler will be able to give more advance warning and the parent can place the toddler on a potty. Most toddlers achieve control over the muscles of the bladder and the bowels by the age of 3 years, although this can vary greatly. It is important parents teach young children how to use the toilet and the need to have good personal hygiene standards. Toddlers usually stay dry and clean during the day before becoming dry overnight. Toilet training can take some toddlers a long time to achieve and parents must have patience and praise success.

◀ Toilet training

Child Study

When studying social development you should aim to observe the independent personal skills of a toddler or young child, such as the use of the toilet and hand washing.

Child Focused Task

In a Child Focused Task on social skills, remember one skill is the ability to dress oneself. This could be helped by creating an activity involving dressing a doll or designing an activity linked to different fastenings.

Make sure you understand why toddlers must learn to follow rules and become capable of carrying out personal hygiene tasks. Personal hygiene is often forgotten when social skills are discussed, so remember to include it in your answer.

Design a poster displaying some rules about personal hygiene to be placed in a young child's bedroom.

Summary

- Toddlers should follow instructions and rules.
- Parents and carers should teach toddlers the personal skills of washing hands, dressing, and using the toilet, in order that children can carry out these tasks independently when in school.
- It can be quite hard work for parents to train toddlers and young children to learn to follow instructions and rules.

Rules – instructions which have to be followed

Personal hygiene – being able to keep oneself clean

Prove it!

1. Why should toddlers learn to follow rules?
2. Explain how parents could encourage a toddler to learn personal hygiene skills.

Personal characteristics and the family situation

What will I learn?

- **How a child's personality and family structure can affect social development**

A person's genetic inheritance and the family, friends as well as the neighbourhood can all influence the social characteristics of an individual. An individual's personality is made up of a combination of all these influences, which means everyone's personality is unique.

Key Terms

Genes – inherited from parents and contain instructions which help to create an individual with some characteristics similar to the parents and grandparents

Nature – personal characteristics inherited from parents

Nurture – the influences on a person's character from the home environment and upbringing

Personality

Everybody has a unique **personality** created by the characteristics inherited from the parents through the **genes**, as well as the upbringing and environment in which a person lives. The personality of an individual is a mixture of **nature** and **nurture**. These are two important influences in everyone's life. Even two children of the same parents may have quite different personalities. One may be very lively and adventurous whilst the other might be comparatively quiet and cautious.

The social skills of a young child are also formed from the characteristics of the parents as well as the upbringing of the child in the home environment. If the parents are fairly **shy** and quiet then it is likely that the children may have similar social characteristics. Some toddlers become very shy when in unfamiliar surroundings or in the company of people they do not know. They can feel frightened and insecure, staying very close to a parent, or a close relative such as grandparents, where they feel safe.

▶ Ready for adventure

▲ Feeling nervous and scared

Forcing toddlers to do something against their wishes can make them upset and possibly cause a scene, making them more nervous and shy in the future. For example, sitting with other children at the table for a birthday tea party or taking part in playing games. It would be much better to allow the toddler to decide whether or not to take part in the activity. One option might be for the toddler to stay with the parents or grandparents and watch the activities. The toddler would feel secure and happy and at the same time have the opportunity to watch and, maybe, participate a little in the occasion. Gradually over time the toddler will gain more confidence and feel able to join in.

Activity

Talk with mothers about how they deal with the shyness of toddlers.

Parents should never criticise toddlers about their shyness, or talk about any shyness problem within earshot of the child, as this could cause the child to feel rejected and unhappy. Remember some young children take a while to gain the social skill of being able to mix and enjoy the company of other people.

Family structure

In society there are many different family structures. The structure of the family, and contact with other family members, can affect the child's social development. If a toddler is the youngest of several children there will be daily opportunities to watch, mix and play with brothers and sisters. The toddler will see their **siblings** sharing toys, playing board games or being members of a team and will see a range of social skills being used. On some occasions there might be friends of the siblings visiting the home and joining with the family for a meal. The toddler will become accustomed to seeing new people who may be playmates for a short period of time.

An only child does not have this ready-made social contact and may take a little longer to develop social skills. However, close family members, such as grandparents, aunts, uncles and cousins as well as family friends, may visit the family frequently. On these occasions the toddler would be able to play with the family members and enjoy their company. Grandparents are often very willing babysitters and enjoy spending time in the company of their grandchildren.

Family celebrations, such as birthday parties and weddings, provide ideal opportunities for toddlers and young children to develop their social skills. Visits to other people, such as neighbours and family friends, will also help with the development of the toddler's social skills.

You should consider the personality of the child, such as shyness or enjoying the company of other people. Remember to look at the family structure. There may be older siblings or close family members, such as grandparents and cousins, living nearby who might influence the social development of young children.

▶ **A family enjoying each other's company**

Summary

- A toddler's social personality is a mixture of genetic inheritance and their upbringing in the home environment.
- Some toddlers take a little longer to overcome any shyness and should not be forced into taking part in any activities.
- Frequent contact with family and friends can help toddlers overcome shyness and help develop their social skills.

Revision Tips

Make sure you understand how to help toddlers overcome being shy in the company of people they do not know.

You should have an understanding of how family and friends can help a toddler learn social skills. Remember to mention how both nature and nurture can influence a child's social development.

Prove it!

1. **What are the influences that help to create an individual's social personality?**
2. **Discuss how a parent should support and help a shy toddler.**

Home location and family lifestyle

What will I learn?

- How the home location and the family's lifestyle can affect the social development of a young child

Key Facts

- A young child who has very limited social contact with other people can feel lonely and may become unhappy.
- It is helpful for a young child to have lots of opportunities to talk to people and play with friends. At the same time the parent can have the chance to talk to other parents and carers which will also help to provide company.

Key Terms

Rural – the countryside, which may offer few facilities, for example no local library, leisure centre or shops

Urban – towns and cities where there is a wide range of facilities, probably with nearby shops, libraries, leisure centres, childcare and schools

Childcare – when another person, not the parents, cares for and looks after the child

The location of the family home and the family lifestyle are important factors in the social development of children.

Home location

Family homes are located in different types of areas and this may influence a toddler's social development.

Rural

Home could be in a very **rural** setting in the countryside. There might not be any neighbours nearby and the nearest village could be several miles away. In such locations there may be few facilities for toddlers and young children and, therefore, few opportunities to meet other toddlers and their parents. Public transport is often quite limited in rural areas and it is helpful if a family has their own means of transport.

If possible, an effort should be made to attend any local activities for toddlers and young children to provide the opportunity for play and to develop social skills. There is also the advantage that parents can make contact with other families, which might lead to other play dates being arranged.

However, living in the countryside usually has the advantage of being closer to animals and nature. For example, living on a farm a toddler will see family members caring for animals and crops. The toddler will see how people work together and may be able to be involved with farm life at an early age.

▼ A home in the countryside

Play area squeezed under a busy city road

Child Study

In a Child Study on social development, you should discuss the home location and the facilities in the local neighbourhood which could help with a toddler's or young child's social skills. You should also consider the family lifestyle, such as employment and the use of childcare facilities.

Urban

Many family homes are in towns and cities with a wide range of facilities available, some usually within walking distance of the home. Parents can take toddlers and young children to various venues, such as the local park, leisure centre and regular activities such as parent and toddler groups. These activities are very useful as they give toddlers the opportunity to play with other children and improve their social skills.

Family lifestyle

There are many varied patterns of family life. In some households, one parent stays home to look after the child while the other parent is in employment. In others, both parents might work shifts or have part-time employment and, between them, care for the child. In many households the parents' employment pattern means they need to use **childcare**. This could be a **relative** such as grandparents, a **childminder** or a **nursery**. When babies are cared for in a nursery they are often in the company of other babies and toddlers. In these situations there are many opportunities for babies to develop social skills.

Activity

Talk with parents about the different childcare arrangements they use for their babies and toddlers.

Revision Tip

Make sure you understand how the location of the family home and the family lifestyle can affect the social development of a baby and toddler.

When answering a question about the social development of a child, you could include some discussion about the location of the home and the social facilities available in the area.

Summary

- Facilities to help with social skills of toddlers and young children depend on the location of the family home.
- In some families, where both parents are in employment, childcare facilities are used for babies and toddlers. These usually offer contact with other people which helps develop social skills.

Prove it!

1. **Discuss the differences between rural and urban home locations on a toddler's social development.**
2. **Describe the different childcare options which are available to parents.**

Facilities for social development

What will I learn?

- **An understanding of the different types of play facilities that help with the social development of toddlers**

Key Facts

- Attendance at a pre-school group will provide a toddler and the parents with the opportunity to make new friends and use a wide variety of toys.
- Some children would particularly benefit, such as an only child who might lack company, a child who has a limited number of toys or a child living in an overcrowded home with little space to play.

Activity

Carry out some research to discover what facilities are available in the local area for toddlers and young children that could help their social development. Write a report about your findings.

Giving children frequent opportunities to play will help the development of their social skills.

▲ Soft play area

Play facilities

Play facilities, where parents can take babies and toddlers, may be either indoors or outdoors. The range of facilities can vary. For some facilities a charge is made.

Outdoors

Outdoor facilities are ideal when the weather is dry and not too cold. Many are free to use.

A visit to the local **play area** is a popular activity. Play areas offer a range of physical activities and help social development. For example, toddlers may have to learn to wait in a queue to use the slide and take turns on the swings. They will learn that the play equipment does not belong to them and has to be shared with other children. They will learn to treat other children as they would wish to be treated so, for example, no kicking or fighting.

Visits to a **park** with family or friends provide another suitable outdoor activity, which could also involve a **picnic** and this will help with social skills. Ball games are ideal for family activities. They provide the opportunity for young children to learn how to be a team member and follow the rules of the game.

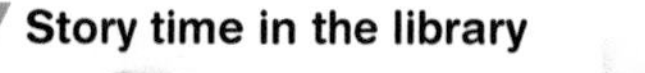

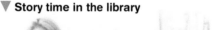

▼ Story time in the library

Indoors

Some indoor social activities can be very beneficial. There is often a charge made for their use.

Leisure centres offer soft play sessions for babies and toddlers. Toddlers can enjoy the freedom of playing with a wide range of different-shaped pieces of foam-filled play equipment to crawl and climb over and at the same time mix with other children. Some leisure centres provide a crèche for toddlers, where they can enjoy safe play under the supervision of the staff, whilst parents are participating in other activities.

There are other privately run centres providing a variety of play activities for young children. Some may also offer games sessions for older children. This makes these centres good for families as there may be activities for all ages. Some **libraries** hold regular story time sessions for the 'under 5s'. A member of staff reads a story and encourages the young children to make appropriate actions or sounds linked to the text. These sessions give young children the chance to participate as members of a group and also look through the range of books that could be borrowed from the library.

Child Study

Remember to ask the parents if the toddler or young child attends any pre-school activities and if these sessions are helpful in extending the child's social skills. If you have parental permission, a visit to a play area will give you an ideal opportunity to observe the study child's social skills in the company of other children.

There are many **parent and toddler groups**, usually held weekly for about 2 hours at venues such as community halls. These sessions enable toddlers to play with a different selection of toys and have the company of other children. While the children are playing, under the supervision of parents or grandparents, refreshments such as tea, fruit juice, biscuits and fresh fruits are prepared and served. These groups provide an ideal opportunity for parents to just have a chat with friends, exchange ideas and obtain useful advice from more experienced parents. Many friendships are formed in these sessions, amongst both children and parents, which may lead to further social events being arranged.

Playgroups are for young children from about 2½ to 5 years old. They are usually held in community centres or village halls and often last about 3 hours on a few occasions during each week. The parents do not stay with the children, who are supervised by qualified staff, some of whom could be parents. Playgroups provide an opportunity for children to play with other children, sing songs, listen to instructions and become more independent in preparation for school.

Key Terms

Play area – a fenced-in area containing large play equipment, such as slides and swings

Leisure centre – a place offering a range of exercise activities for all ages of people

Libraries – places providing a wide selection of books, which can be borrowed, and where staff may also offer story time sessions

Parent and toddler group – held in a hall for a few hours where parents can talk and toddlers have the opportunity to play with other children

Playgroup – allows an unaccompanied young child to attend for a few hours and play under staff supervision

▶ **Parent and toddler group**

Summary

- Outdoor and indoor facilities help with the social development of toddlers and young children.
- They also provide opportunities for parents to have contact with other parents, or possibly take part in another activity.
- By attending activity sessions, all areas of a child's development will benefit and this will probably help the child to settle into full-time education more easily.

Make sure you understand how outdoor and indoor facilities can help with the social development of toddlers and young children. Remember, giving toddlers and young children the opportunities to mix with others will help develop social skills and should be discussed in an answer on social development.

Prove it!

1. **Describe the opportunities for a toddler to learn social skills on a family visit to the park.**
2. **Discuss the benefits to both the toddler and the parent of attending a parent and toddler group.**

Nursery school

What will I learn?

- **How nursery schools can help young children with their social development**
- **The role of nursery schools in getting children ready for going to school**

Key Facts

- Nursery school education provides young children with vital learning skills for full-time education.
- Children will be given help with their language and numeracy skills.
- The nursery school environment will help young children with their social skills as there will be plenty of opportunities to play with other children and use social skills, such as sharing and taking turns.
- The nursery school will also provide a structured programme of activities so children will become more familiar with the school routine.

Providing the opportunity for young children to attend nursery school will help them have a better understanding of school life. Nursery school can help with all areas of a child's development.

Nursery school

A nursery school can be either:

- A **private school**, where the parents pay a fee for the child to attend and the child can stay for a full day.
- A **state school** linked to a primary school, where there is no fee and the child will be able to attend for half-day sessions.

Some private nursery schools take children from about the age of 3 years. State nursery schools accept children in the academic year in which they have their fourth birthday.

Young children have to understand that parents will not be staying with them at nursery school. Some children may become upset at first, especially if their parents have always stayed with them when attending other activities in the past. Many nursery schools prepare young children for this situation by giving them a few opportunities to visit the school, before they attend on a regular basis, so they are familiar with the surroundings. Initially young children may only stay for one hour to ease them into the routine of attending a school. Gradually the stay will be extended

▶ Young children enjoying an art session at nursery school

Talk with mothers about their children's experience of attending nursery schools.

Child Study

In a Child Study of a young child who attends nursery school, you should discuss the benefits linked to social development.

until they stay and attend the whole session.

All children attending nursery will be expected to have learnt personal hygiene rules. The staff will assist and encourage them to use the toilet correctly and will supervise hand washing. Attending a nursery school enables young children to become familiar with **school routine**, in preparation for compulsory full-time education at the age of 5 years. Nursery schools are usually on the same site as the primary schools and the young child will see older children attending school and playing together. Some young children will be familiar with the school if they have accompanied older siblings being taken to and from school each day.

The young children will usually be with children from other backgrounds and cultures. This helps them to become aware of various different customs and social habits. Trained and experienced nursery school staff will provide a structured programme of activities for each session, similar to the primary school routine. Children will be expected to listen and follow the instructions given by the staff.

Young children will have the opportunity to play with a wide range of indoor and outdoor play equipment as well as a variety of toys. The staff will aim to involve the children in the various activities, helping to extend all areas of their development. A young child's social development will be helped through the opportunities for play sessions with other children. By interacting with each other, children learn to play together in a friendly manner.

Nursery school – school for children between the ages of 3 and 5 where they attend for half-day sessions

School routine – the pattern of activities that happen during each nursery school session, such as story time, playing with toys and singing songs

Make sure you understand how nursery schools help a young child's social development as well as other areas of development.

In an answer on preparing a child for full-time education, remember to highlight the benefits of nursery education. You should discuss that, by attending nursery school, a young child has the opportunity to become familiar with the school routine and also learn new skills and knowledge.

Summary

- Nursery schools provide a young child with an environment that is similar to a primary school.
- A young child will become familiar with a school routine.
- Nursery school staff will encourage a child to interact with other children, listen to instructions and help all areas of development.

Prove it!

1. **What are the differences between a private nursery school and a state nursery school?**
2. **Discuss the benefits to a young child of attending a nursery school.**

Emotional development

What will I learn?

- **An understanding of how a child learns to have an acceptable standard of behaviour and gains the ability to control emotional feelings**

Key Fact

- All individuals will express a wide range of different emotions, such as fear, anger, sadness, shyness, affection or pride. These emotions are feelings due to personal inborn temperament, the health of the individual and the surrounding environment.

The skill of being able to control and express one's feelings is influenced by many factors, such as an individual's inherited characteristics from the parents, family lifestyle and contact with other people in society.

Emotions

When we talk about someone's **emotions**, we mean the expressions of their feelings, which are linked to a particular situation. There are two types of emotions: positive ones such as happiness, and negative ones such as sadness. These may then lead to a show of good or unacceptable behaviour.

The behaviour and the emotional feelings of individuals are a combination of nature and nurture, similar to that of social skills. The ability to be able to control one's behaviour and feelings is a skill which should be learnt during childhood. Children need to learn how to control their feelings, in particular negative ones such as spitefulness and aggression. Once toddlers and young children have a pleasing standard of behaviour they will be accepted by other children and enjoy their company.

I am happy

I am sad

Key Term

Emotions – the feelings of an individual

Child Study

In a Child Study on emotional development you should consider how both nature and nurture can influence a child's emotions.

Activity

Talk with mothers about the emotional feelings of their toddlers and young children.

Factors affecting a child's emotional development

Genetic inheritance – through the parent's genes, can be an important factor in the child's behaviour and feelings. If one parent has a short temper then possibly the child will have the same.

The **environment** and home – where the child grows up can affect emotional development. A child will see how other people behave and express their feelings and the child may copy these patterns of behaviour.

Guidance from parents or carers – a child's emotional development will be influenced by the guidance they receive about how to behave and control feelings. Other individuals, who young children meet during their everyday lives, can also influence the child's behaviour and emotional development.

Health – this can affect both behaviour and emotions. Illness will probably lead to feelings of sadness. A very tired child might behave poorly and be unco-operative towards the parents. However, when playing with other children, or being taken for a walk in the park, a child is likely to be enjoying the activity and will have happy feelings.

Each individual will experience unique emotional feelings and may show different styles of behaviour in various everyday situations.

Activity

Talk to mothers of toddlers and young children and discuss how they teach them manners and self-control.

Summary

- A child's emotional development is influenced by genetic inheritance and the environment.
- The training given by parents, and the child's health, can affect the ability of the child to behave acceptably and control emotional feelings.

Revision Tip

Make sure you understand how various factors can influence the emotional feelings and behaviour of a young child. In an answer on emotions remember to mention that young children may not have learnt the skill of being able to control their emotions

Prove it!

1. **What are the emotions of a young child?**
2. **Discuss the factors that can influence a child's emotional development.**

Bonding

What will I learn?

- **An understanding of the importance of bonding between a newborn baby and the parents**

Bonding is creating a very close two-way relationship between the newborn baby and parents.

Key Facts

- The emotional development of a child can be affected by how strong a bond of affection was created during the early months of life.
- A basic need of a child is to be loved and to feel wanted by the parents.
- A lack of love may mean children are unhappy and insecure and could have problems coping with their emotions.

Bonding

Bonding is the close relationship between a child and its parents. It is having strong feelings of **affection** for very important people, and so it can also mean the mother's and father's love for their child. The baby has the feeling of comfort and being safe and will gradually be able to show signs of pleasure such as smiles. A very close bond between parents and baby from birth will create a good foundation on which to build and develop a strong relationship in the future.

It is important that the feeling of bonding begins before the baby is born. The pregnancy should be planned and the parents should be in a stable relationship with the partner supporting and helping the mother-to-be during pregnancy. The partner should assist the mother with the breathing and relaxation techniques during labour as well as giving encouragement and support.

Creating a close bond

As soon as it is born the baby should be given to the parents and placed in contact with the mother's breast or skin. The newborn baby should be cared for by both parents so they are both able to create a close bond. The parents should hold and cuddle the baby, which will help to give a sense of **security** to the child. If the mother is breastfeeding the baby, there will be frequent skin contact between them.

Talking to and holding the baby close to the parent's face will enable the child to focus on the parent's eyes and gradually begin to respond with a smile. Soon the baby will be able to recognise the voices of the parents, in particular the mother, and respond by turning towards the familiar sound.

The bond of affection between the child and parents will strengthen by giving the baby plenty of love and cuddles.

◀ **Proud parents bonding with new baby**

Feeling happy with mother close by

By the age of 3 months babies show signs of pleasure, such as smiles and gurgles when given attention by adults and in particular parents, close family and the main carer. The baby becomes very attached to the main carer and is very contented and happy in their company as it gives the baby a sense of security.

Separation anxiety

At about the age of 5 months babies can become very upset if they cannot see their parents or main carer. Babies are unable to understand that the parents still exist and will return to them, even if they are only out of sight at the time. If parents walk out of the room, babies may cry and become upset because they think that they have been **abandoned** and lost their parents. Gradually babies learn that it is only a temporary absence and the parents will return to them.

Feeling upset because parents are out of sight

Another common emotional feeling is that some babies become upset and frightened of strangers, such as family or friends who are occasional visitors. Again this **fear** will gradually diminish as babies grow older.

Summary

- Bonding between the newborn baby and the parents is giving love and affection to the baby who will feel secure and safe.
- The baby should be held and cuddled by the parents. Gradually the baby will respond by smiling.
- Some babies become upset if they cannot see their parents as they do not understand that the parents are only out of sight and will return to them.

Prove it!

1. Explain how parents should bond with their newborn baby.
2. What is separation anxiety?

Activity

Produce a leaflet for parents-to-be on the importance of bonding with a newborn baby.

Key Terms

Bonding – close two-way feelings between baby and parent

Affection – a strong feeling of love

Security – a feeling of safety

Revision Tip

Make sure you understand the importance of bonding between parents and the newborn baby and the problem of **separation anxiety**. This aspect is often ignored in answers to exam questions about caring for newborn babies.

Love

What will I learn?

- **An understanding of the importance of giving love to children**

When babies, toddlers and young children are loved by parents and family they will feel happy, which will help with their emotional development.

Key Facts

- If a young child feels loved by the family then this will develop into a strong bond of affection.
- Children who are loved will show love to other people, which will help them make friends.

Key Terms

Love – can be shown by giving cuddles, kisses and spending time together with another individual such as a parent

Attention – having the complete interest of a parent or another individual, such as playing a game or reading a book together

Lonely – having no company, which can lead to feeling unloved and sad

Showing love

Being loved is an essential need of babies, toddlers and young children. Indeed it is needed by all individuals throughout life. A baby who receives **love** from parents and other family members will have a feeling of happiness and security.

It is important to show love to a baby by spending time together. The parent should frequently give the baby plenty of **attention** so the baby can enjoy the close company and feel wanted and loved. A parent can cuddle and talk to the baby, play together with toys or look at a book.

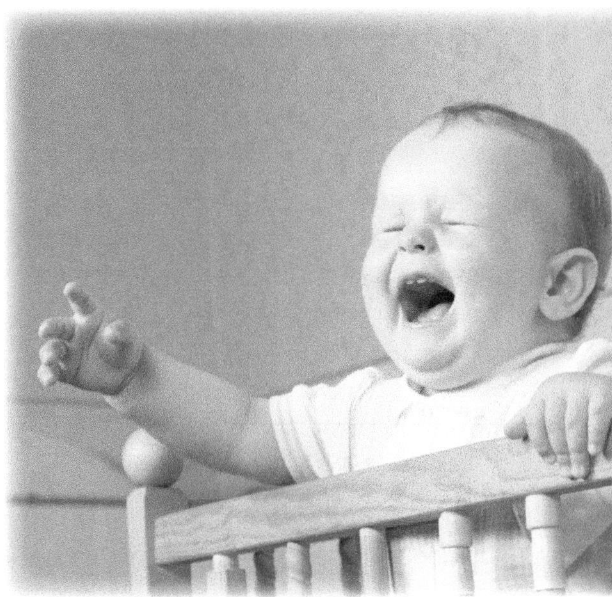

▲ Crying for love and cuddles

As the toddler grows there will be many opportunities to share time together and join in conversations such as playing games, doing household tasks, gardening and walking in the park. Such times spent with parents will help to show the toddler how to love other people and the child will respond by giving love to the parents by smiles, laughter, kisses and cuddles. Love is an essential part of a child's upbringing as it helps them develop the skill of showing love and affection to the close family, other family members and friends.

Child Study

When studying emotional development remember to observe how a baby, toddler or young child shows love to family members and favourite toys.

A young child unloved by the family will not have learnt the skill of how to love other people and will find it very difficult to form friendships with others. If a baby or toddler receives love, and can then learn how to love other people, this is an important factor in the emotional development of the child.

▶ My teddy always sleeps with me

Toys

Some babies are given a wide range of toys to play with alone but lack the company of parents and other family members to share in their activities. These babies can feel **lonely** and unloved.

By 9 months babies will enjoy the company of other people who play with them and show smiles and laughter, although babies may still be a little frightened of strangers.

Some babies show affection to one particular soft toy, such as a teddy bear, which becomes a constant companion and is taken to bed. This is referred to as a **comforter** and enables babies to express emotional feelings of love towards their toy.

Activity

Talk with parents about how they spend time with their child and show love and affection.

Smother love

Some parents become very anxious about all aspects of the child's development, even when there are no problems. Although it is important that babies, toddlers and young children are given love, they must also be given opportunities to develop **personal independence**. When old enough they must also be allowed to have some freedom of choice and decide how to play a game or an activity. This may lead to mistakes from which they will learn. Parents must not be overprotective or interfere in an activity and prevent a child from expressing individual ideas and showing personal independence.

Revision Tip

Make sure you understand the importance of love between parents and their child and the problem of **smother love**. In an answer on emotional development, giving and receiving love are very important features of helping a child become happy and friendly.

Summary

- Love is an essential need of babies, toddlers and young children as it gives them happiness and security.
- Parents should spend time with the baby, giving love and attention. This will help the child's emotional development.
- It is important to allow a child to have some freedom of choice in order to develop personal independence.

Prove it!

1. Discuss how parents should give love to their baby.
2. What is smother love?

Expressing emotions and happiness

What will I learn?

- **An understanding of how toddlers and young children express their emotions and the positive emotions of happiness and security**

Emotions can be spoken in words, giving facial expressions and by actions and are a part of everybody's behaviour.

Types of emotions

Everyone has emotions – these are your feelings about different people, items and situations throughout life. Toddlers and young children have a limited vocabulary and find it very difficult to say how they feel in words. They tend to **express** their **emotions** by actions. Expressions of happiness can be laughter and giving cuddles. Parents should always encourage the child's **positive emotions**.

Negative emotions are shown by hitting, crying, screaming and kicking. These display feelings such as anger and frustration. Negative emotions need to be handled carefully and parents should sometimes ignore the toddler's display of emotion. The situation could become very difficult to resolve if a parent becomes very angry with the toddler. It can be helpful to distract the toddler with another toy or activity.

The age at which a child displays the various emotions depends on many factors, such as the level of bonding with parents, any health problems, the position of the child within the family, if there are other siblings and opportunities to mix with other people. Remember each child will have a unique state of emotional behaviour.

Key Fact

- It is very important that parents and carers always make sure they praise and give plenty of encouragement to children, both when they succeed and also when they fail. This will help children to understand that it is quite acceptable to fail to do a task and they should not become angry or sad.

Key Terms

Expressing emotions – showing personal feelings

Actions – using movements such as giving kisses, cuddles or kicking

Remember in the Child Study to observe closely the various people and activities which make a baby or toddler show positive emotions.

▶ Showing positive emotions

Positive emotions of happiness and security

A baby expresses happiness in many different ways such as smiles, laughter and giving kisses. A baby will feel secure and safe when a firm bond is made with the parents. This baby will then enjoy the attention of the parents and be happy and contented.

From about the age of 1 year a baby will hold a parent's hand, as it provides a feeling of closeness and security, especially when in unfamiliar surroundings. This action remains throughout early childhood, giving a child the important sense of being protected and loved. At about the age of 3 years toddlers will begin to show kindness and concern for others, such as their soft toys as well as close family members. This is an expression of affection and wanting others to become as happy as they are. A happy toddler will gradually begin to show more independence and confidence, and be able to enjoy the company of people and different activities.

◀ **Loving and caring for my soft toy**

When a family gives a child care and protection the child will have a feeling of security and belonging to that family. At about the age of 4 years the young child will show love to younger siblings, and by the age of 5 years the young child will show concern and want to help any family member or close friend who is unwell or unhappy.

Talk with parents about how their young children express positive and negative emotions.

Summary

- The age at which different emotions are expressed depends on many factors.
- Toddlers and young children express their emotions by actions.
- Parents should encourage positive emotions and handle negative emotions carefully to avoid the situation becoming worse.
- Happiness and security are very important in children's lives to give them a sense of being protected and loved.
- A happy toddler will gradually gain confidence and become more independent.
- A young child will show love and concern towards family and close friends.

Make sure you understand the ways emotions are expressed and the importance of happiness and security to a child. When answering a question on emotional development you should discuss both positive and negative emotions. Do not forget to include the importance of parents giving plenty of love, praise and encouragement.

Prove it!

1. **Describe how a toddler shows positive emotions.**
2. **Why is it important to give a baby a sense of security?**

Negative emotions

What will I learn?

- **An understanding of negative emotions**

Some situations can make a child have negative emotions, which may be displayed in various ways of poor behaviour.

Key Fact

- Toddlers and young children often show negative emotions when various problem situations occur in their lives which they do not understand.

Egocentric toddlers

At about the age of 2 years toddlers can become very **egocentric**, which means being very self-centred. They consider that they are very important people, that the whole world revolves around them and they only see a situation from their own point of view. Often toddlers will not do as they are told and demand to have their own way all the time and do as they wish.

Looking after these toddlers can be a difficult task for parents and carers. When toddlers are prevented from having their own way this can result in **temper tantrums**. Toddlers may lie on the floor kicking, screaming and shouting as a protest for not being allowed to do as they wish. This can occur at home or when out and about – such as when out shopping or visiting a play area. Parents must try to remain calm and sometimes the poor behaviour will stop if the toddlers are ignored. Another approach is to attempt to interest the toddlers in another activity. Slowly toddlers will begin to understand that they cannot always have their own way.

If parents give in to their demands, toddlers will realise that this is the best way to get what they want and they will continue to have temper tantrums. The result is toddlers who will be very self-centred and demand that everybody does as they want. These toddlers will not have learnt how to behave and treat other people kindly and often they will not be liked and will have few friends. It is important for parents to make toddlers understand that they have to listen to instructions and do as they are told, in order that the toddlers grow up to be well-behaved and co-operative young children.

▲ Temper tantrum

Activity

Carry out some research work and produce a leaflet for parents explaining about the behaviour problems and the negative emotions of toddlers. Include some advice on how to cope with these difficult situations.

Feeling sad and insecure

Key Fact

- Children's reactions to problems are usually by actions which are visible to other people so can easily be noticed.

Negative emotions of insecurity, anger and regression

Sometimes parents do not give their children much love and attention. If toddlers feel unloved and unhappy, they may develop feelings of insecurity because they believe nobody cares for them. Toddlers can occasionally show bad behaviour and **anger** in order to gain attention, or become very timid and withdrawn which should alert the parents to the fact that there is a problem. Angry toddlers can become very aggressive and destructive with their toys and even household items. Although this sort of behaviour has the desired effect of attracting the parents' attention, it usually results in the toddler being told off. What the toddlers really want is love and affection from the parents.

If parents gave time and attention to the toddlers, by playing together with toys or reading a book, then gradually there would be a sense of affection and security and the toddlers would feel loved. The toddlers' behaviour would slowly improve once they are receiving frequent attention and do not need to show anger in order to have their parents' company.

Sometimes when toddlers feel **insecure** and unloved, they go back to an earlier stage of behaviour. This is called **regression**. It is a way of attempting to gain attention from the parents. For example, toddlers who have been toilet trained may start to wet their pants. Some toddlers might refuse to use a spoon at mealtimes and instead use their hands or throw food onto the floor. If parents give the toddler attention and cuddles, the child should feel loved and wanted and the poor standard of behaviour should stop.

Key Terms

Egocentric – being self-centred and only seeing things from their own point of view

Temper tantrums – a toddler screaming and kicking

Insecure – having a feeling of being unloved and not receiving care

Regression – a child showing the behaviour that might be expected from a child of a younger age

Child Study

In a Child Study of a 2 year old you should look out for any egocentric behaviour and temper tantrums. If studying an older child you should be aware of any negative behaviour such as jealousy.

Key Fact

- Toddlers and young children find it quite difficult to express their feelings in words due to their limited vocabulary. These young children have not yet reached the stage in emotional development where they understand how to control their feelings.

Jealousy

Everyone, including toddlers and young children, will experience **jealousy** during their lives. There are many situations where the actions of others can cause toddlers to become jealous and unkind. Toddlers can squabble over a particular toy when playing with other children and sharing a selection of toys. Toddlers have not learnt to share or be patient and take turns with the toys. One toddler may dislike another toddler playing with a particular toy and decide to take action to change the situation. Toddlers demonstrate their jealousy in a variety of ways. They may snatch the toy away from another child and also hit, kick and bite the child.

Revision Tip

Make sure you have an understanding about egocentric toddlers and negative emotions. In an answer on emotional development you must always discuss the negative emotions of toddlers and young children as these are a common feature in early childhood.

▶ **Unwilling to share the crayons**

Toddlers and young children may also become jealous when there is a new sibling in the family. A child, who previously had no brothers or sisters, now has competition for the attention of the parents, and can display signs of jealousy towards the new arrival. Parents must be careful to avoid this problem by giving the older child plenty of attention.

Fear

Everyone, including toddlers and young children, will experience being frightened during their lives. For a baby this might be something as simple as a sudden loud noise that might make them cry. By about the age of 9 months a baby starts to be aware of strangers and again may become upset and cry.

Between the ages of 2 and 3 years a toddler's imagination will be developing, although without a very good understanding of all aspects of life. Different fears may develop, such as fear of the dark, spiders or thunder. Parents must give the toddler comfort and reassurance that there is no reason to be frightened. The toddler's fears may gradually disappear if parents spend time giving a simple explanation about the fear. A nightlight in the bedroom should provide a solution to a fear of the dark.

Sometimes a young child will have a **nightmare** due to a frightening dream. The child may wake up screaming or may still be asleep and shout out in fear. Parents must go and comfort the child.

Key Facts

- Children can become unnecessarily fearful about possible dangers, such as house burglaries and fire.
- Adults should not discuss any dangers and threats in the company of young children.

Having a nightmare

Nightmares can occur for a variety of reasons, such as the beginning of an infection or watching a scary television programme. Nightmares may be caused by a problem within the home or being unhappy at school, which parents should aim to resolve. Parents need not worry about children having nightmares, although it might be a good idea to get medical advice if they occur every night.

Summary

- At about the age of 2 years toddlers can become egocentric and think they are the most important people in the world. They want their own way and can be very demanding.
- They have temper tantrums if they are prevented from having their own way. Parents need to remain calm and either ignore or distract the toddlers with an activity.
- Toddlers will have feelings of insecurity and anger when there is a lack of love and attention from the parents.
- Toddlers can become very aggressive and show bad behaviour in order to seek love and attention from the parents.
- Jealousy and hatred can be seen in many situations, such as squabbling over a toy as the toddlers have not learnt how to share.
- An only child may be jealous of the arrival of a baby into the family.
- Toddlers and young children could develop many fears, such as fear of the dark.
- Nightmares can occur for a variety of reasons such as an infection or being unhappy. Parents should not worry about them unless they occur every night.

Key Facts

- Being angry with an aggressive toddler will make a difficult situation worse.
- Parents should aim to handle the negative emotions of a young child carefully.

Prove it!

1. **Why are temper tantrums a common feature in a 2 year old's behaviour?**
2. **Describe the negative emotions of a toddler who lacks love and attention from the parents.**
3. **Describe how a parent could deal with a toddler who is afraid of the dark.**

Self-esteem

What will I learn?

- **An understanding of a young child's self-esteem and self-image**

The ability to interact with other people is closely linked to how individuals feel and think about themselves.

Key Fact

- Young children will copy the behaviour of close family members. Parents and family members should be careful about the type of image they show to young children, such as behaviour, attitude and speech. They should avoid any form of stereotyping: all household tasks should be shared by both parents to avoid any gender stereotyping.

Self-esteem and self-image

- **Self-esteem** can be described as the respect you have for yourself – how you value yourself as a person, compared with the ability and skills of people similar to you. It does not mean the things you can or cannot do compared with others, particularly older children or adults. Young children are able to undertake a variety of activities but clearly cannot do many of the things that older children can.
- **Self-image** is a mental image of how one sees oneself as an individual with a name, body and family.

Both the self-esteem and self-image of young children are closely linked to their social and emotional development, as well as other factors such as physical health and home environment. Babies should be allowed to feed themselves and toddlers encouraged to dress themselves because completing these tasks gives a sense of achievement, independence and being **self-reliant**.

Young children with high self-esteem have a positive self-image of themselves which will help them in all areas of their development. They will have **self-confidence** when meeting people, playing games with other children and visiting places, such as play groups and story time at the library. With encouragement, these children will become more independent and want to do tasks themselves. Young children with low self-esteem think they have few skills, **lack confidence** and may be too afraid to do any new tasks or mix with other children and make friends. They will have a negative self-image and they are often very timid and can feel sad and lonely.

Activity

Prepare a fact sheet on positive and negative self-esteem in young children.

◀ Showing self-confidence

Encouraging positive self-esteem in young children

Young children develop their self-esteem and self-image through contact with parents and adults. The way adults treat them will influence how they feel about themselves. If they are given love, talked to and encouraged to do tasks, children will grow up feeling loved and valued. It is very important that all adults give babies, toddlers and young children plenty of opportunities to play with toys, games and with other children. Allowing young children to do tasks by themselves, and occasionally make mistakes, will help them understand that sometimes failure is quite acceptable. Praising toddlers and young children for their achievements helps build up positive self-esteem.

Key Terms

Self-esteem – how a person feels about themselves

Self-image – a mental picture of oneself

I like myself

High self-esteem

Positive self-image

Not afraid of failing

Finds it easy to make friends

Willing to try new things

Confident

I do not like myself

Low self-esteem

Negative self-image

Afraid of failing

Finds it difficult to make friends

Not willing to try new things

Not confident

Summary

- Self-esteem and self-image are linked to social and emotional development.
- Self-esteem is how you value yourself as a person.
- High self-esteem will lead to a positive self-image. A young child will have the confidence to mix with others and become more independent.
- Low self-esteem will cause a young child to lack confidence, be timid and shy and afraid to mix with others.
- Parents should encourage positive self-esteem by giving praise and love.

Prove it!

1. Give three reasons why a young child with a negative self-esteem may have very few friends.
2. Describe how parents can encourage a self-reliant attitude in a toddler.

Make sure you understand the importance of how to create a positive self-esteem in a young child. This topic is often ignored in answers about emotional development, so remember to include some information on self-esteem.

Discipline

What will I learn?

- **Why discipline is important to help a child's social and emotional development**

The level of discipline given to young children will affect their behaviour as well as their social and emotional development.

How to discipline

Discipline could be described as a set of rules and instructions that we live by. It is needed so that young children understand what standard of behaviour is acceptable and what they can and cannot do. Some rules are essential because children need to be kept safe and away from harm. Gradually children understand how to behave correctly and learn the skill of **self-discipline**.

The level of discipline should be suitable for the age and understanding of the child. It is very important that both parents and carers have the same standard of discipline so as not to confuse young children. If there are variations in standards, children will quickly realise which adult is kinder – in their eyes – and will allow them greater freedom. Disciplining children can be a difficult task for parents. Frequently toddlers and young children do not want to co-operate and like to have their own way. If the parents' discipline is firm, **consistent** and kind, a young child will learn acceptable behaviour, will know what is safe and unsafe and have the feeling of being protected.

Discipline should be introduced as soon as the child has some understanding of what is expected of them. At the age of 1 year some babies understand the word 'no' and realise some of their activities do not please their parents. As children become older their understanding improves. A 2 year old should be able to follow more instructions, such as 'Wait' or 'Quiet', and by the age of 3 years a young child should have a good understanding of the discipline guidelines and how to behave.

Child Study

In a Child Study looking at emotional development you should obtain some information about the type of discipline used within the home.

There will be many occasions when toddlers and young children do not understand or do not wish to listen to instructions. Parents should then give some help to the children to make sure that discipline guidelines are followed. It can be beneficial to give toddlers time to sit quietly, in order to calm down and think about their recent misbehaviour.

Key Facts

- A lack of discipline will make young children very disobedient, always wanting their own way. They are often rude, selfish and sometimes get injured if they are not taught to be aware of dangers.
- Too much discipline with many rules can make young children very miserable due to frequent 'nagging' from parents. This may then cause some difficulties in creating a loving relationship between parents and child.

Activity

Make an attractive rules poster for a 3 year old to place in their bedroom.

Ways to discipline children

1. Set a good example

Children watch and copy both the good and bad actions of adults. Parents and carers must set a good example of behaviour and safety rules so the children learn and will copy.

2. Give praise

Giving **praise**, when children have shown good behaviour and followed instructions, will encourage them to do the same on future occasions.

3. Be consistent

It is important that everybody caring for a child follows and applies the same rules. Adults should not change the rules as the child will be confused and will not know what is right or wrong.

4. Follow the rules

When parents state a rule or instruction the child should follow it. It can be quite difficult for a child to learn rules if parents give a rule but allow the child to ignore it. A child without a framework of rules and instructions can become very demanding and have a feeling of insecurity.

Key Terms

Discipline – enforcing a set of rules and instructions

Self-discipline – being able to behave in a correct manner by having self-control

Make sure you understand the importance of discipline and how parents and carers should make sure children follow rules.

In an answer on discipline remember that the rules must be suitable for young children to understand.

You should mention that it is important for parents and carers to be consistent with the rules so the child will be able to learn an acceptable standard of behaviour.

Summary

- Discipline is a set of rules and instructions given to children to have good behaviour and to be safe.
- Parents should always have the same standard of discipline.
- Discipline guidelines must be suitable for the age of the child.
- Adults must set a good example, give praise, be consistent with the rules and make sure the child follows them correctly.

Prove it!

1. What is discipline?
2. Why is it important to be consistent with the rules for young children?

Stress in the early years of life

What will I learn?

- **How parents can help toddlers and young children cope with stressful situations in the early years of life and how children react to stress**

Key Fact

- It is very important that in a stressful situation parents and carers should aim to give their time, attention, love and support to toddlers and young children. A lack of care and comfort may have a long-term effect on the emotional well-being of young children.

Within families there will be problems and tensions which can cause children to experience some stressful emotions.

Stress

There will be occasions in life when events and situations become very difficult and cause a great deal of worry and distress. These situations can affect all members of a family including young children. Toddlers and young children may sense that there is a problem, due to a change in the behaviour of parents and close family. There may be some very tense situations, possibly leading to shouting, swearing and even domestic violence, which young children may witness. They do not have the ability to understand and appreciate all aspects of a difficult and unhappy situation.

▲ **Why are Mummy and Daddy always arguing?**

Although it can be very difficult, it is vital that adults attempt to maintain a stable and safe environment for young children. If a situation becomes very tense, young children could become extremely scared, frightened and upset. Toddlers and young children do not have the ability to know how to express or control their feelings.

If there is a very long and distressing situation within the home environment, young children could become emotionally unstable and display some unacceptable behaviour. If parents are aware that a **stressful situation** is likely to happen in the near future, it is essential that **explanations** are discussed with young children beforehand so that they have an understanding of what is likely to happen. Children will be more prepared for the event and it may reduce the level of their emotional stress. Make sure the child is given time to ask questions, or express any anxieties, to avoid the child feeling there are aspects of the situation which have not been discussed.

Child Study

In a Child Study on emotional development you should consider any stressful situations which have occurred within the family and their possible effect on the child's feelings and behaviour.

Unfortunately there will be unexpected stressful situations that families have to face. When these happen, family members must make time to give lots of love, affection and appropriate explanation of the situation to young children.

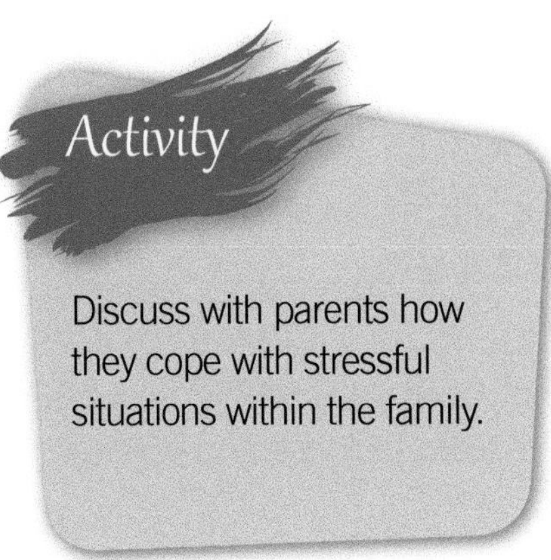

Activity

Discuss with parents how they cope with stressful situations within the family.

◀ **Upset and crying**

How toddlers and young children react to stress

Everyone has a different way of expressing the negative emotions caused by a stressful situation. Toddlers and young children can display their feelings in various ways. Often toddlers and young children will display **poor standards of behaviour** with temper tantrums, jealousy and anger. Children may also become aggressive and kick, hit and bite other individuals.

Regression is a common feature of stress shown by wetting pants or eating meals in a baby-like manner. Some children feel insecure, cry and become very reserved and quiet. Frequent nightmares and bed-wetting are also signs of stress. It is important that parents give toddlers and young children plenty of love and care to help reduce their level of stress.

Key Terms

Stressful situation – problem which causes arguments, unhappiness and sadness

Explanation – giving information in a simple way so that an individual is able to understand the situation

Summary

- Toddlers and young children find it difficult to understand a stressful situation.
- They do not have the ability to know how to express or control their feelings.
- Parents should spend time with toddlers and young children to explain the problem.
- Children express their negative emotions in various ways such as poor behaviour, regression and bed-wetting.

Revision Tip

Make sure you understand the problems caused by stressful situations and how toddlers and young children react to stress. Remember, when discussing stress within the family, you must mention that it is very important to give a simple explanation with plenty of love and comfort to a young child.

Prove it!

1. **Why should parents explain a possible future stressful situation to a young child in advance?**
2. **Describe how toddlers may express their feelings about a stressful problem in the family.**

Stressful situations for toddlers and young children

What will I learn?

- **An understanding of the stressful situations caused by a new baby or death in the family**

It is very important that parents and carers help and support toddlers and young children to cope with their feelings of stress, sadness and anger.

Stressful situations

There will be situations which can cause unhappiness and stress in every child's life. The individual's own emotional feelings can affect the level of stress felt, as well as the amount of support given by the family. Remember each individual will show a unique reaction to a stressful situation, as everyone views each situation differently.

Some common situations may cause most toddlers and young children to become stressed. One of these is starting school full time. Another may be the addition of a sibling to the family. Other stressful situations could be due to ill health, death and problems in family relationships.

Key Fact

- Experiencing a stressful situation can have a serious effect on all aspects of development of a toddler or young child. The parents and carers must aim to provide a lot of support and comfort in order to reduce the negative effects on the child's well-being.

The arrival of a new baby in the family

This is a very happy event for the family. However, some toddlers and young children see the new baby as a competitor for the love and attention of the parents. An only child will be especially aware of this threat as previously the parents have been able to give all their attention to one child. Now love and attention will have to be divided between the two children.

The new baby will probably be given some attention by the older curious sibling. There may be some jealousy shown as the older child feels threatened and possibly insecure. This is called **sibling rivalry** and may lead to poor behaviour and regression.

▶ **Why is my new baby sister getting all Mummy's attention?**

Parents need to prepare a young child for the arrival of the baby in order to prevent a stressful situation. Towards the end of the pregnancy the mother could explain to the young child about the developing baby inside her body and the need to go to hospital for the birth. It would be helpful for the young child to understand that the baby will have to be fed, will cry and will need quite a lot of help.

When the baby is born, the parents must spend time with the older child giving plenty of attention and love in order to reduce jealousy and bad behaviour. Young children can be encouraged to help with the baby by collecting the baby's clothes and stroking the baby's hand. The young child will have the feeling of being useful to the new baby and parents. This involvement can help the self-esteem and independence of a young child.

Sibling rivalry – being jealous of a sister or brother

The death of a family member or a family pet

This distressing situation can cause a great deal of grief in the family. When there is a serious illness and the death seems likely, it may be advisable to carefully explain the situation to young children in order to prepare them for what will happen. With an unexpected death toddlers and young children will find the situation very difficult to understand and will be very confused and upset. Parents should give them comfort and love to help them cope with the situation.

If it is the death of a parent, the family may benefit from receiving **professional counselling** advice to help with the emotional care of toddlers and young children.

Make sure you understand the possible stressful problems due to the arrival of a new baby and the distressing situation of a death in the family. When discussing stress in the family you should always mention the arrival of a new baby and offer some suggestions for how parents could prepare a toddler for this event.

Carry out some research work about voluntary organisations which offer advice and help to distressed families due to the death of a family member.

Summary

- It is important for the family to consider carefully the emotional feelings of toddlers and young children in stressful situations.
- Whenever possible it would be very helpful to young children if they are given some advance explanation about a stressful change in the family.

Prove it!

1. **Discuss why an only child may be jealous of a new baby in the family.**
2. **Describe how parents could help a young child to cope with the expected death of the family dog.**

Other stressful situations

What will I learn?

- **An understanding of other stressful situations in the lives of babies, toddlers and young children**

In the early years of life children experience many changes which may cause them to become emotionally upset. Parents and carers should aim to consider how to reduce the possible stress to the child.

Key Fact

- Many children experience a change in the family structure. It is very important that all children have a special relationship with parents and siblings as well as with any step-parents and step-siblings. This will help establish a stable upbringing as well as make them emotionally stable with a happy outlook on life.

Childcare arrangements

Many parents are in full-time employment and require childcare for their young children. Sometimes close family members, such as grandparents, are willing to carry out the task. If this is not possible then parents have to organise alternative childcare for their children. Parents should consider carefully the various options and study the facilities available. Information and advice can be obtained from other parents who already use childcare services for their children.

Once a decision about childcare has been made then the parents and child should visit together. Starting with several short visits, longer visits should gradually be introduced to give the child an opportunity to become familiar with the new surroundings, carers, staff and other children. Parents must aim to avoid any situation that will cause the child to become upset and stressed, so it is important to allow plenty of time for the child to become familiar with the childcare arrangements. When the child first starts to attend childcare, the parent could also stay there. This would help the child settle into the new environment more easily. Gradually the parent should leave the child unaccompanied and a regular routine will become established.

If there is a need to change childcare arrangements, the same pattern of short visits should be carried out to make the move to a new environment and new carers as stress free as possible. If children are very unhappy in childcare it may cause them to refuse to eat, become angry and have nightmares. This can create a very difficult problem for the parents to resolve and can cause a great deal of worry and tension in the family.

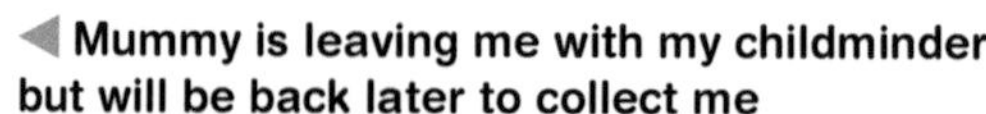

Mummy is leaving me with my childminder but will be back later to collect me

Produce a leaflet giving some advice to parents on how to help toddlers and young children cope with stressful family situations.

Starting school

◀ **Getting ready for my first day at school**

All children have to be in full-time education by their fifth birthday. Before then parents must make sure children have an understanding of what happens at school, and the main way of doing this is through going to pre-school. If young children have already enjoyed many opportunities to socialise with others, and gained some knowledge about school, the possible danger of stress and unhappiness when starting full-time education will probably have been reduced.

Children will be expected to be able to look after their own personal needs at school. Therefore parents should encourage the child to become independent. Children whose parents have not allowed them to do tasks themselves will find school stressful as they will have limited personal skills.

Meeting and mixing with people

Some children, who have been in full-time childcare from a young age, will be familiar with being left unaccompanied in the company of carers, staff and other children. Attending school may not be so stressful to them. For other children it is important that parents have provided many opportunities outside the home for them to meet and mix with other people. The parent and toddler could attend parent and toddler sessions providing opportunities to play with other children. Attending a playgroup, where the young child is left unaccompanied for a few hours, will offer a similar situation to attending school. As children get closer to full-time education they can usually attend a daily nursery session at the school and this provides an ideal introduction to school life.

In the home, parents should encourage young children to draw, and possibly practise writing their name, count and spend time looking at books and doing activities. Parents can also talk and play school with a young child to help develop an understanding of the school day and activities. Remember it is important that parents consider carefully how to prepare a young child for full-time education in order to avoid any unnecessary stress and unhappiness for the child. There may be occasions when children become upset and stressed during their school life and parents should aim to resolve these as quickly as possible.

Child Study

You should discuss with the parents any stressful situations your study child has experienced, such as starting nursery school, and enquire how they helped to prepare their child for this new situation.

Moving house involves the whole family

A patient in hospital

It is possible that a child could be taken to the Accident and Emergency Department of a hospital following an accident or be admitted as a patient to a hospital ward for a planned operation. Such situations can be extremely stressful and upsetting for both the child and the parents.

To prepare a young child for the possibility of being a patient, parents could read stories about children going into hospital. Role play as doctors and nurses, perhaps dealing with an injured teddy bear or doll, would allow parents to explain medical treatment. Taking a young child to visit a relative or friend who was a hospital patient, if such an opportunity arose, would be a good way of showing the child the inside of a hospital and the care given to patients.

Key Facts

- If parents choose to separate, this may be a relief for children if there have been frequent arguments and violence in the home.
- A single parent may struggle financially after a family break-up.
- Sometimes children have to move house as a result of the parents separating.

Moving house

Moving house can cause a sense of insecurity and stress as a child moves away from familiar surroundings. However, with some careful thought and planning, a house move for a family with young children can be achieved without causing too much stress and upset.

If the family plan to move house, it is important that any children are included in some of the discussions and visits to the new home. This will avoid the child suddenly being told to pack up their belongings. By talking about the planned move in a positive way the child will begin to understand and accept the proposed change.

Family break-up

The break-up of a family is clearly a very stressful time for all family members. Toddlers and young children cannot understand the problems between the parents and may become confused and frightened living in a tense and unstable environment. Children may show poor behaviour and distress, such as regression and nightmares.

Parents should not argue or show any aggression in front of the child. They should never criticise the other parent within earshot of the child. It is very important that each parent does not attempt to influence a young child's feelings and affection. Both parents must show love for the child despite their personal problems.

If the parents decide to separate, a toddler or young child will become upset and stressed due to the absence of one parent. In some cases one parent and the children may have to move out of the family home. This will be an extremely stressful situation.

Daddy doesn't live with us any more

The household's daily routine may have to change, causing further problems and tensions for children. This situation will need to be handled very carefully. To help reduce a child's stress, the parent must give love and spend time with the child enjoying each other's company. The **absent parent**, in agreement with the other parent, should be given opportunities to spend time with toddlers and young children in order to help maintain a bond.

Sometimes, if young children have witnessed parents arguing and being violent, the split-up may result in a more stable lifestyle. This will gradually help to reduce any emotional stress. However, in a **single parent family** the one parent may have less time to pay attention to a child because of the other demands of work and household tasks. Children may become upset and stressed if they feel neglected and unloved. A reduced family income may mean children have to be refused toys or day trips, which will also cause a feeling of anger and distress.

Many children become members of a **step-family**, also called a **reconstituted family**, when their parent has a new partner. This new partner may also have children, and sometimes they might all live together in the same home. It can take some time for everyone to adjust to the new family arrangement. Toddlers and young children may resent the arrival of a replacement parent who has other children. These are **step-siblings** and there may be tension and rivalry between the step-children, leading possibly to jealousy and aggression.

The standard and control of discipline may change. The step-parent may set new rules and be more, or less, strict. Again this can create a very stressful situation for all the children. Any new family arrangement must be handled with a great deal of care and thought in order to reduce any tension or stress.

Single parent family - in this family the child is brought up by one parent, often the mother. It is sometimes called a lone or one parent family

Step-family / reconstituted family - In this family one of the adult partners is not the birth parent of all the children. This type of family occurs when a single parent forms a new partnership with another single parent or a person without any children

Summary

- Every child will have to face various stressful situations during the early years of life.
- It should be the parents' aim whenever possible to reduce the negative feelings of a child caused by a change in the family lifestyle.

Make sure you understand the possible situations that can cause stress to toddlers and young children. When discussing a family breakup, remember to consider the positive issues, such as living in a home without any violence, as these issues are often ignored.

Prove it!

1. **Discuss how parents can help a toddler settle into a new childcare arrangement.**
2. **Explain the meaning of the term reconstituted family.**
3. **Explain how parents can prepare a young child for the possibility of being a hospital patient.**

Examination questions

1 Children learn through different types of social play.
(a) Describe parallel play. (3)
(b) Describe co-operative play. (3)

2 **(a)** What are the emotions of a young child? (2)
(b) State a positive emotion. (1)
(c) State a negative emotion. (1)

3 **(a)** Explain the term 'egocentric'. (2)
(b) How should parents deal with the temper tantrums of a 2 year old? (4)

4 Discuss the importance of parents bonding with a new child. (4)

5 How can parents encourage a young child to learn the following social skills:
(a) Sharing? (4)
(b) Taking turns? (4)
(c) Following behaviour rules? (4)

6 Mealtimes are an important feature of a child's day.
Discuss the social value of mealtimes for a child. (5)

Tip When answering a question like this, remember to concentrate on the activity stated in the question, in this case 'mealtimes'. Then try to think about as many aspects of that activity as you can.

Mealtimes provide a child with several opportunities to engage in social activities. The child will see and be expected to copy the manners of the adults, using cutlery correctly, showing courtesy and waiting in turn as food is placed on plates. The child will also see that hygiene is important where the handling of food is concerned. With other family members eating together at the same meal there will be a valuable shared social family experience. If others involve the child in discussions at the meal table, this will help the self-esteem of the child who will feel part of the family and its culture. If the child takes part in conversations involving others present at the meal, the child will learn the importance of listening to what other people are saying.

7 How can parents encourage a young child to have positive self-esteem? (6)

Parents should remember to praise the young child for being able to do a task such as putting on clothes and shoes. The child will feel pleased to receive praise and would be willing to do the same task again and also probably try other tasks in the future. A young child often likes to help with household jobs, such as unpacking the shopping, tidying the dining room or helping to lay the table. Parents should encourage a young child to help as the child will have a feeling of being helpful and useful to the family.

Parents should not criticise if the child cannot do a task or activity as that can make the child have negative self-esteem and be sad. Parents should encourage children to develop new skills, such as making and decorating cakes, making a model aeroplane or painting a picture. The young child will be very pleased to be able to learn new skills and make a new item. The young child should be praised by the family for the success. This will make the child happy and it will help to build the child's confidence. A young child who receives love and cuddles from parents and close family will feel happy and loved which helps the child's positive self-esteem.

Remember the key words are 'to give praise' for a child's achievements and love. Give examples of tasks and activities which can be praised and displayed, for example placing a child's art work on the fridge door.

8 Discuss **four** social skills that a young child should have achieved before starting full-time education. (8)

Beginning full-time education is a big step in a young child's life. Parents should make sure that the child is fully prepared for this important event. The child should already have been taught some social skills so that the child is able to settle into the new school routine. One important social skill is to be able to mix and play with other children and know how to share toys. Parents should have encouraged the young child to share toys with siblings and friends. By going to parent and toddler sessions and playgroups the young child would have had opportunities to learn how to share toys with other children. Visiting a play area, where the child has to take turns on the equipment, is another good way to teach this social skill.

At home the child should have had plenty of practice of dressing in the morning and undressing at night. Another idea is for parents to provide a box of dressing-up clothes so that the child is able to put on a coat or change for games when in school.

Parents must help a child learn the personal skill of being able to go to the toilet independently and also the hygiene rule of washing the hands. Children who have lunch at school should be able to eat correctly using cutlery. At home the parents should allow a toddler to learn how to feed themselves using a spoon, then with a fork and finally using a knife and fork. At first the toddler will probably make a mess but will slowly learn how to use the cutlery.

Remember how toddlers learn how to play with other children and learn how to take care of their own needs. Because this question refers to 'full-time education' and the 'key words' are 'social skills', think about these in the context of different school activities.

If the question asks for 'four social skills' make sure your answer includes at least that number of such skills. Give examples of activities which involve other children, for example sharing toys, taking turns. Then think about situations where children need to be able to do things on their own, such as going to the toilet, washing hands, dressing and undressing.

Correct use of cutlery is also a skill which can be learnt before a child reaches school age.

Parents need to phrase the news in such a way that the child will understand what is happening. The young child should not feel pushed to one side by the expected arrival of a new baby.

It is important to mention that parents must prepare the young child for the new arrival to reduce the risk of jealousy.

Getting the child involved with caring for the needs of the new baby gives the child a feeling of being helpful and useful to the parents.

9 Discuss how parents can prepare a 3 year old for the addition of a new baby to the family. (8)

Parents must think carefully about how to tell the young child that a new baby will be arriving in the family in order that it will not be an unexpected and possibly unwelcome surprise. After a few months of pregnancy the parents could explain that there is a baby growing inside the mother's tummy who will become a new brother or sister. Nearer the date of the birth the parents could get the young child to help prepare the nursery, such as placing baby clothes in a drawer and arranging the bathing equipment. Doing these tasks will improve the child's self-esteem because the child will have the feeling of being helpful. It is important to explain that the mother will probably be going into hospital for the birth and may be away for a few days. The child may have been able to go with the parents to ante-natal clinics so the hospital is already a familiar building. When the young child visits the mother and new baby in hospital for the first time it would be better if the mother was not nursing the baby. This may prevent the young child feeling ignored now the new baby has arrived.

Jealousy can occur if the older child sees the new baby as a rival for the parents' attention. The parents and close family should make sure that the young child is given plenty of love and affection in order that the child feels secure, even if there is bad behaviour. Explaining to the young child that the mother will need some help with the baby and getting the child involved by passing baby clothes and giving the baby a cuddle will help reduce the possibility of jealousy. Gradually the young child will hopefully accept the new baby and they will grow up to love each other and become playmates.

10 **(a)** Explain the following terms:

(i) Nature (3)

(ii) Nurture. (3)

(b) Describe how parents and carers should discipline a young child. (4)

11 Social development is an important aspect of a child's development. Evaluate the role of the parent or carer in the socialisation process of the child. (10)

It must be remembered that a young child does not know what social skills are acceptable and what are unacceptable. A child learns many social skills within the home. Parents and carers are the role models for a child. The child will copy both good and bad actions, behaviour and language of adults and older siblings. It is very important that only good behaviour is seen in the home and that swearing and bad language are not used in front of children. Young children will be very confused if they learn social skills from the family which are not acceptable in school, such as kicking and fighting. Parents, carers and other family members must make sure that young children learn good social skills so they will have good behaviour and be able to play well with other children.

Remember toddlers use their eyes and copy social skills. Parents must show good social skills.

Another important role for parents is to encourage the child to mix with other children as this will help with social play. Going to parent and toddler groups gives the opportunity for the child to meet and play with other children. Gradually young children learn how to play together and share toys. A visit to the local play area, where children have to queue to use the slide, will teach the child how to take turns. Arranging visits to the homes of other young children will also encourage the child to mix and learn what behaviour is unacceptable, such as fighting or throwing food around the room. Taking the child to different activities, for example soft play sessions, swimming lessons and story time at the library, will all help teach the child the social skill of listening to instructions and being a member of a group.

Think about the wide variety of social skills and remember social play stages.

Children need company to learn social skills and parents should provide opportunities for the child to mix with others. Give examples of some suitable activities and events.

Parents must also be the role model for personal social skills, such as teaching the child to use the toilet correctly and then washing the hands. The child should copy good manners from the parents, for example saying please and thank you. A child should be taught how to eat food in a polite way and be able to use cutlery.

Include examples of some of the social skills children need to learn at an early age.

So parents and carers have a very important role in the socialisation process of a young child. They should remember that children look up to them and copy their behaviour. Giving children opportunities to visit different places and attend events, where they can mix with other people, is a very important task which parents should do as it helps in the socialisation of a child.

Examination guidance

It is not enough to know a lot about Child Development to do well in the examination; it helps if you understand how the examination system works so you can get the most from your knowledge and maximise your marks.

Assessment process

There is one paper for the GCSE course which makes up 40% of the marks for your final grade. The other 60% of the marks come from the two controlled assessments. The paper lasts for one and a half hours. It is marked out of 80 and the actual pass mark for each grade will change every year.

The paper will consist of short-answer, structured and free-response questions drawn from all areas of the specification. There is space provided underneath each question to write your answer. The last question on each paper gives you a choice of two alternatives. Make sure you read these carefully and **do not** attempt to answer both questions. You will not have time to answer both properly and only marks for one of them will be added to your total for the paper.

Assessment objective	What it says on the specification	What this means in practice
AO1	Recall, select and communicate their knowledge and understanding of a range of contexts	You will be able to remember, choose examples and describe a variety of areas in child development
AO2	Apply skills, knowledge and understanding in a variety of contexts and in planning and carrying out investigations and tasks	You will be able to explain the value of a range of situations to children's development
AO3	Analyse and evaluate information, sources and evidence, make reasoned judgements and present conclusions	You will be able to explain factors affecting children's development and look at both positives and negatives of things they experience

Key Terms

Specification – the information put out by the examining board for teachers and candidates about the content of the examination

Mark schemes – the guide for markers to explain how to reward answers to questions

Assessment objectives (AO1, AO2, AO3) – what examiners are looking for in answers

Markers are trained to mark positively, this means that they will try to give you marks wherever possible and will not take marks off for mistakes.

In questions which involve extended writing you will be assessed on the quality of your written communication within the overall assessment of that question. Examiners will be looking for:

- Accurate spelling, punctuation and grammar
- Clear meaning
- How well you organise the information in your answer
- Your ability to select an appropriate style of writing. This means you need to write in a formal style, not using 'text speak'.

How do you improve your performance in the examination?

Here is a simple checklist of things that you should be doing to achieve your best under examination conditions:

1 Revise and understand your class notes. Examiners are looking for evidence of knowledge of child development such as subject-specific terms.
2 Look at the **specification**, which is on the WJEC website. Anything on the specification can form the basis of a question.
3 Read around the subject. The more you know, the easier it is to develop further understanding. Do not just rely on your teacher notes.
4 Do not be frightened by examinations. It is wise to learn relaxation techniques so that your approach to the paper is calm and collected.
5 Look at past papers, mock papers, **mark schemes** and candidate essays. You will have a clear idea of the standard expected and how you can achieve it.
6 Write in good English and use subject-specific language. If your writing is hard to read, ask for help from someone to sort this out.
7 Plan your time in the examination.
8 Answer the question. The question should tell you exactly what to do! If you do not answer the question, then no matter how good your writing, or how much you write, you cannot get the mark.
9 If there is a picture with the question, it has been put there to help give you ideas, not to make the examination paper look nicer.
10 Do not use bullet points for higher mark questions. You are unlikely to be awarded more than half marks as the examiner is looking for your ability to write an extended answer.

Answering the questions

The clue as to how much to write should come from the command words to the question, the space provided and the marks available. If there is only one mark for the question, there is no point spending time writing a long answer. No matter how relevant it is, you won't get any more marks. However, if the question is worth a higher number of marks, the examiner will be looking for a longer answer.

The typical commands are:

- ***Identify/ list/ state …*** a simple answer giving facts about, or names for, something in the question. Check to see how many points are needed (it will usually say in bold in the question).
- ***Suggest one (or two) reasons why …*** you will only be marked for one (or two) reasons. Anything more will be ignored, so don't say 'also' in your answer.
- ***Describe …*** give facts about whatever it is you are asked about.
- ***Discuss …*** these questions test a higher level of thinking and require you to include a number of points. Aim to provide a brief introduction, a main section giving your answer and a short summative conclusion.
- ***Explain …*** give reasons for something (usually how or why). Stick to the question, and keep referring back to what it is that you are explaining. You will gain marks for offering clear reasons for whatever it is that you are asked to explain.
- ***Evaluate …*** these questions are looking for more than one point of view, so try to include both positives and negatives in your answer.

Short answer questions usually have right or wrong answers. The parts of questions with 6 or more marks are usually 'criteria marked'. This means that there are a number of points that could be included but your answer also needs to show subject-specific language and understanding of the topic. You will need to give facts, some discussion and consider all aspects of the question to get the higher marks.

Some questions will ask you about the value of an activity for promoting aspects of a child's development (or learning). You will need to mention all four areas of development (physical, intellectual, emotional and social) even if there is more to write about for some areas than others. Don't worry if the activity is something you haven't thought about before: children learn or practise gross or fine motor skills, learn new words and concepts, develop confidence and social skills in almost every situation, so this is a good starting point from which you can develop your answer.

The Child Study

Coursework is an important element of the GCSE Child Development course and if done properly you can gain valuable marks, which will improve your overall total in order for you to achieve a good final grade.

Guidelines

* You should have been given a timetable showing when the controlled assessments are taking place. Make sure you are fully prepared with the necessary information and resources.
* You need to complete an individual time log for BOTH the Child Study AND Child Focused Task.

* **Time allowance:**
  - **15 hours classroom-based work;**
  - **6 hours contact time with child.**

* **This should be started in the Spring Term of the first year of the course.**
* **You need to be able to visit the study child regularly over a period of up to 6 months and conduct at least 6 visits.**
* **The length of the final study should be between 2000 and 3000 words.**

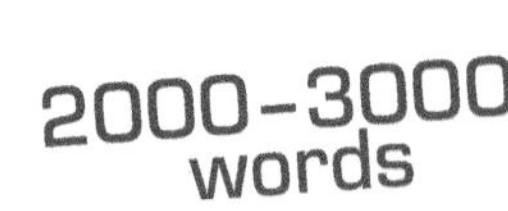

The Child Study counts for 30% of the final mark.

The aim of this section is to help you to get as many marks as possible, to help you structure your coursework and assist you in presenting it correctly.

This is where the fun starts! Unlike the first part of the book, where you're reading and learning about the development of a child, this section is where you spend time with just one child. You observe their development and write about your findings.

Quality is more important than quantity.

Throughout the Child Study you need to draw on the knowledge and understanding of the work you have covered in the classroom. You also need to show off your skills to:

a) **Carry out relevant observations and investigational work.**

b) **Record and analyse your findings.**

c) **Evaluate the evidence and make reasoned judgements with conclusions.**

Before you can start you need to select a child to be the focus of your study:

* **The child must be under the age of 5 by the end of your study.**
* **You need to have regular contact with the child so the nearer they are to where you live the better, as it will make your visits easier.**

Next you need to decide on an area of development on which to focus your study:

* **Physical development OR**
* **Emotional and social development OR**
* **Intellectual development (such as numeracy and verbal skills).**

Always try to protect the identity of child.

It would be much better to choose a development area where most changes occur in a 6-month period of time specific to the age of the child chosen.

Babies are cuddly and gorgeous but do sleep most of the time!

Now let's get started!

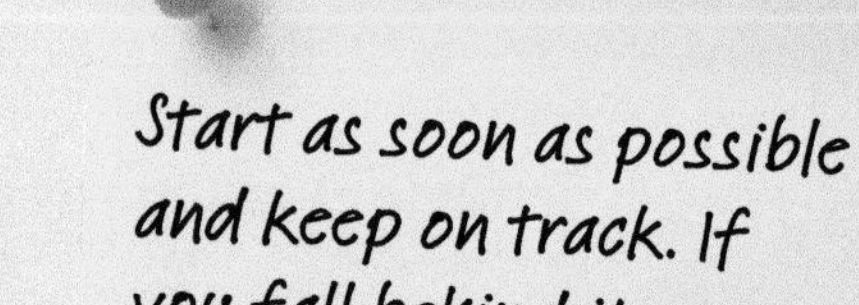

Start as soon as possible and keep on track. If you fall behind it can be hard to catch up.

Your initial plan of action and time plan:

1. **Write to the parents of the child you have selected and ask for their permission to observe their child in the home – and possibly outside – along with other siblings and other family members.**

2. **Devise a questionnaire for the parents to complete so you can get some background information on the child, and on the area of development you have chosen to focus on.**

Always save your work as you go along.

3. **Write a time plan for the whole of the study. Include a time plan for your visits – this is classed as unsupervised time. Also include one for the 15 hours supervised class time.**

4. **Make a list of resources you could use in your research.**

The introduction to your study

The first part of the study should really be a statement of your aims. You could explain the reason why you chose the child and the area of development. Give a definition of this area along with the 'norms' specific to the age of child. Next use your questionnaire from *Initial plan of action* (above) to compile a 'fact file' and collect some other information which could be useful on your first visit. Make sure you mention what the child looks like, their height, weight, etc.

Link

Topic 4 pages 112–114 for BMI charts.

Summarise the family background and type of family:

* **Do the parents work?**
* **Does child attend nursery, etc.?**

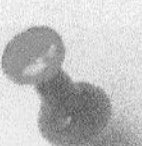

Keep asking yourself WHY this might have an effect on development.

Describe the home and local environment:

* **Does the child have their own bedroom?**
* **Is there an area to play in?**
* **Is there a supply of suitable toys available?**

Include your letter to the parents and their response in this section.

All information like this could be very useful when writing up your analysis and evaluation.

Planning and conducting research

Research is a way of collecting information and finding facts, and in this case it means about the development area you have chosen. Make sure that you conduct a specific search in the right age band. This will help you to understand the area better and will assist you in the completion of your study.

Remember that research can come in many forms: textbooks, magazines, TV programmes, DVDs, websites, questionnaires, surveys and personal experiences. Wherever possible, try to use books and magazines that are up to date. These will give the most recent information, and use UK websites so you will know the information is relevant.

Questionnaires

These are excellent ways of collecting information – besides simple background information – such as on health issues, routines, behaviour, eating habits. This makes them invaluable as a starting point. In questionnaires use both open – 'Describe the child's personality' and closed questions 'Have you got Sky TV at home?' where the answer is yes/no. Also make use of tick boxes as a way of giving a range of possible answers to a question. These are quick to answer but can be more difficult to analyse.

QUESTIONNAIRE

What is your child's full name:

What is his/her date of birth:

Parents' full name and date of birth:

Parent's occupations:

Does he/she have any brothers or sisters:

What was the pregnancy like:

What is his/her favourite:
- Toy:
- Colour:
- Food:
- TV programme

What was his/her:
- Height and weight at birth:
- Height and weight at present:

What hospital was he/she born in:

Doe you have any pets:

When did he/she start to:
- Crawl
- Walk

Does he/she suffer from any illnesses/allergies:

Make sure you record title, author, websites, etc., to include in your bibliography.

Remember to include a copy of your questionnaire.

Evaluating research

Use this information to highlight the normal developmental milestones that you should expect the child to have reached. As with all research it is important to analyse and evaluate thoroughly and carefully; select only the most important points that you have learnt, and say why they are important.

Pick out what you think is important and useful.

* **Ask yourself 'which was the best?' and 'why?'**
* **Then state how you will use this research to help you in the rest of the study.**

This will help you plan activities on your visits to observe if any progress has been made.

Planning visits

Plan of action	Method	Justification	Results
State the area of development you will be focusing on in the visit.	*Describe how and where the activity will take place and resources needed.*	*Write why you chose this specific activity, how you would observe it and monitor it.*	*Present your results in various ways, photographs, tick lists, graphs and where possible evidence of child's work.*

At least six visits should be planned and carried out over a period of six months. In each visit you need to carry out at least one task or activity that is suitable for the age and stage of development of the child, because this will show you the development of your chosen area. If possible, try to arrange your visits to take place in other environments besides the home, such as a local park, nursery or playgroup.

In your planning, give clear **aims** for each visit and **activity** and also **expectations** of what you expect to find. Refer back to the research you have gathered, as this information can be used for comparisons in your analysis and evaluation.

Here is an example:

During this visit I plan to do some painting with my study child. This will show me fine motor skills, hand-eye co-ordination and sensory development.

If you are clear about what you will be doing in the activity and what you expect to get out of it, then you know to be thoroughly prepared and have the necessary resources with you in order to carry it out. Make a checklist before your visits, relevant to your specific area and age, so you will know exactly what to look out for.

If you have time it could be useful to repeat a specific activity at a later stage and this would show if any progress in development had been made.

Activities that could be used to show development in all four areas: remember that you can use these activities in ANY of the areas that you've chosen.

Play is something that all children do. Different types of play improve a wide range of skills, in all areas of development.

Painting/ colouring/ dot to dot

Dressing up/ model making/ small world play

Reading/ playing card and board games

Park visit/ garden apparatus/ ball games

Cooking/ shopping

Water and sand play

Lego building/ shapes sorters/ jigsaws/ playdough

VISIT PLANNER

Visit no: .... Date: ....

Age at this visit: .... Time allowed for visit: ....

Place: ....

In this visit I aim to:

....

....

....

Plan of action:

....

....

....

I expect to discover from this visit (expected stage of development):

....

....

....

I observed that:

....

....

....

My evaluation of visit:

....

....

....

Plan what you are going to find out.

Know what you are going to do to record the information.

Carrying out visits

Visits should not last for more than 30 minutes. The purpose of the visit – in addition to conducting the activities or tasks – is to observe. As well as being one of the most important parts of the study, observations are also the fun bit where you watch and make notes. If possible – and with the parents' permission – use a camera to record evidence and include it in your study. It might allow you to spot something you otherwise would have missed, but it can also improve the presentation of your work and make it more interesting.

Keep the parents informed and involved because they can provide support and resources should you require it.

Observe everything that happened from beginning to end of each visit. What did the child do when you first met? What did the child say? What mood were they in? This information may have an effect on the responses you noted, or the results of how the activity goes.

You will learn many things from the observations during your visits:

These are all appropriate for whichever area of development you are focusing on.

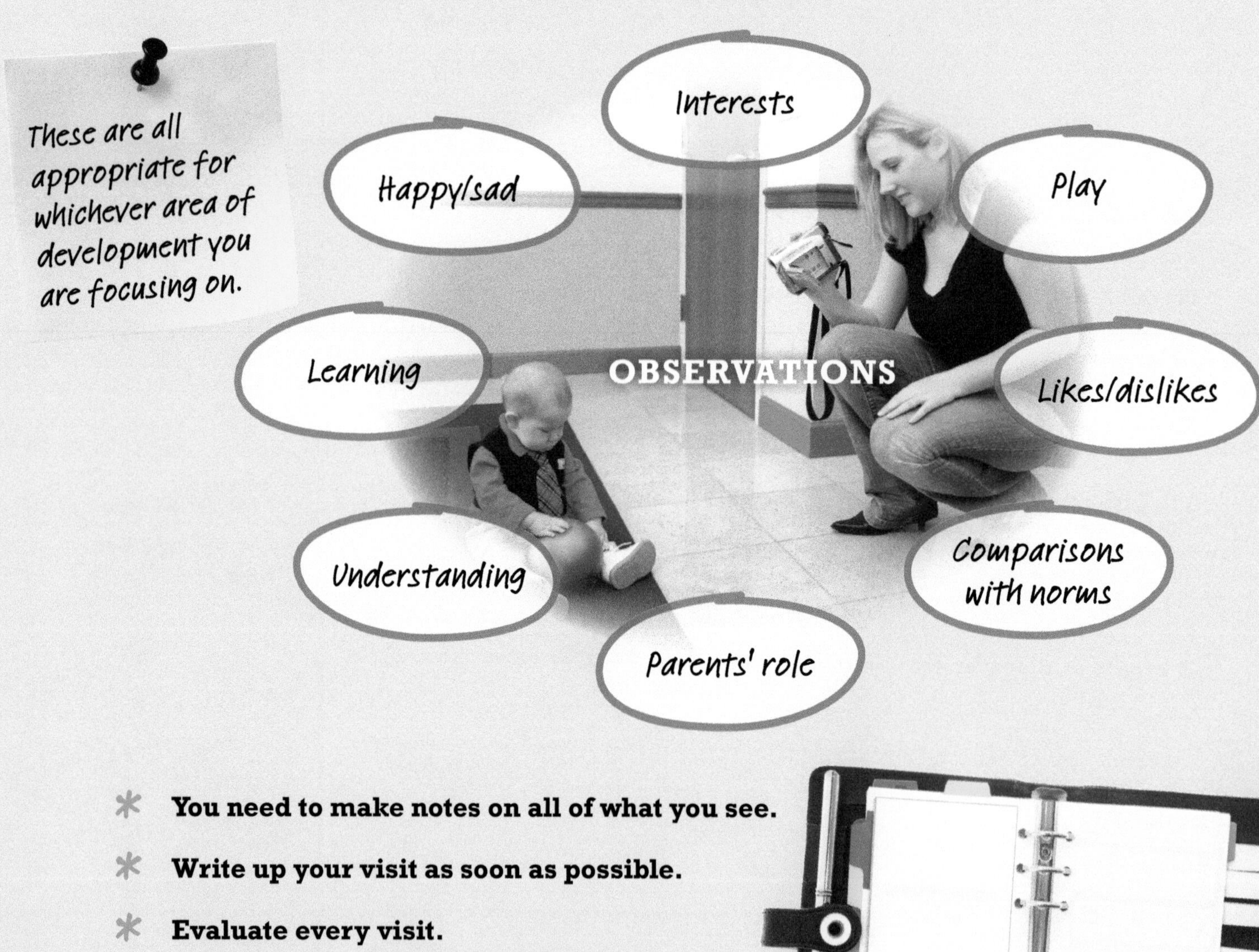

- **You need to make notes on all of what you see.**
- **Write up your visit as soon as possible.**
- **Evaluate every visit.**

Observing your development area

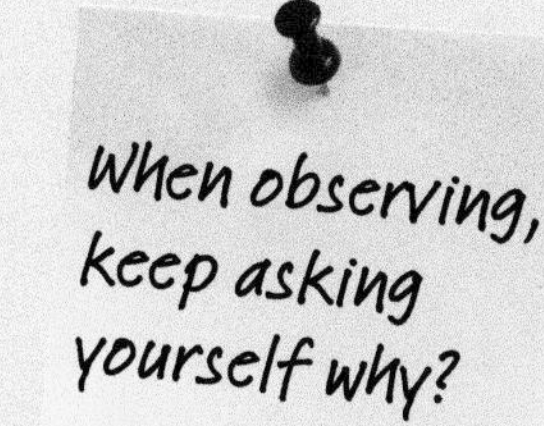
When observing, keep asking yourself why?

Physical

* **What gross and fine motor skills did you see? Were they quite developed?**
* **Did you have to help at any stage? If so, how did the child react?**
* **What indications of sensory development did you see, and did the child use any of these to explore and learn?**

EXAMPLE

Here's an example – if your child should be at the stage to walk up a couple of steps but found this difficult, it could be that the child lives in a flat or bungalow and has no access to steps!

If possible use photos and your own knowledge and research to give a personal comment on what your child is able to do at this stage and compare your evidence to the 'norm'.

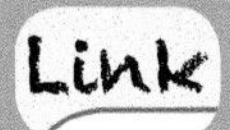
Link

Topic 4 pages 122–131.

Emotional and social

This area of the specification is about feelings – specifically about the child within the study and the ways in which they show their feelings. Remember that these feelings can be positive and negative.

Social development is the level of social skills the child has, for instance how they make friends, play, or how they get on with others. It is also about their behaviour: how do they behave, will they share willingly or not, or did you see any temper tantrums?

Some of the key things to keep in mind are:

* **What was the mood of the child?**
* **How did the child react when away from the parents?**
* **How did the child react with other children?**

And similarly, if the child was especially polite, it could be that parents proved to be good role models in instilling good manners and habits from an early age.

* **Did the child play with others and what type of play?**
* **Did sharing occur?**

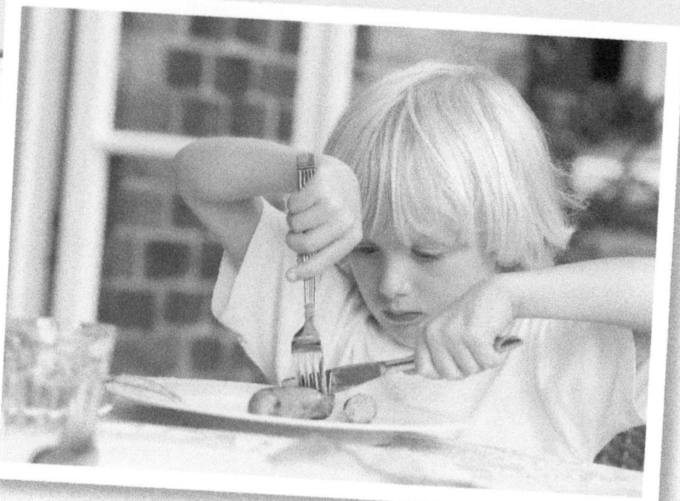

Also make a note of whether the child has the opportunity to meet others of their own age, can they feed themselves, are they toilet trained, and as far as you can tell could they dress themselves?

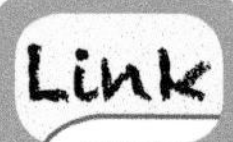

Topic 6 pages 190–195.

Other key questions that you can consider are:

* **Was the child pleased about the activity you did?**
* **What was their reaction and what was said?**
* **Can you say what a child of this age should be doing?**
* **What do you think about the child's emotional and social abilities?**

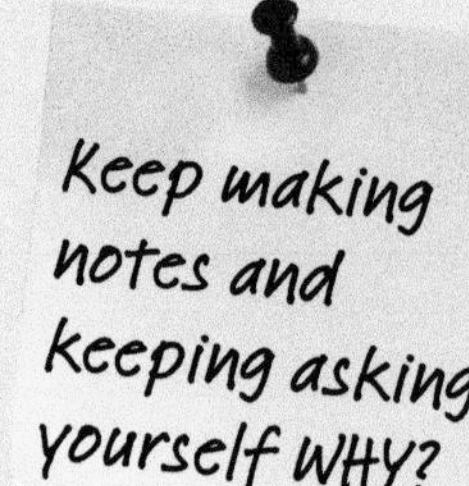

Keep making notes and keeping asking yourself WHY?

Intellectual

When thinking about **language skills** ask yourself if you think the parents encourage language development – for example, do they know simple rhymes or songs to sing or recite with the child? Could you give some examples in an activity of your own?

* **Did the child have any speech difficulties? Give examples of what they were.**
* **What was their speech like? Refer back to your textbooks and recap on what it says about types of speech. Is the type that you observed the one expected at this age?**
* **What was the child's memory like? What did you do to test it?**
* **Could the child follow instructions and if so, did they understand what to do? Again make sure you give specific examples.**

EXAMPLE

If the child's speech was below the 'norm' it could be that the parents did not communicate with the child regularly, or by simply answering the child's questions with yes or no. This would mean that the child's ability to learn new words and increase their vocabulary was very limited. In all these cases, where you give an example, you need to then follow on and try and give the reason for what you observed.

Link

Topic 5 pages 163–165.

You could make a list of words/phrases the child used at the beginning and end of the study to compare and discover how they have improved – or not – over that period of time.

When thinking about **cognitive skills**, make sure you know what this term refers to. It means how the child develops their thinking, reasoning and learning skills. So, for instance, some questions that you could consider include:

* **Could the child count?**
* **Do they know their numbers and if so how many? How do you know that they know them?**
* **Do they understand about colour, size, shape, opposites? Again, how do you know?**
* **Can the child read, write or draw?**

What do you think about the child's intelligence?

Setting activities or observing cognitive skills also includes the child's memory, concentration and ability to problem solve. So you'll need to include something that tests what their memory was like, or at the very least observe this. What could you do to test it?

Making notes

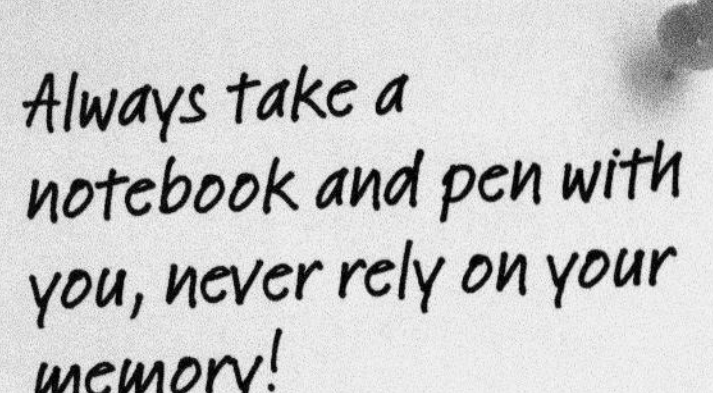

Always take a notebook and pen with you, never rely on your memory!

Make notes throughout each visit you make, and alongside them take simple checklists or tick charts of the norms/milestones that you have found out about during your research. Having them with you alongside the notes of your observation is a quick way of recording just the right information you need, and comparing it later with what you have observed.

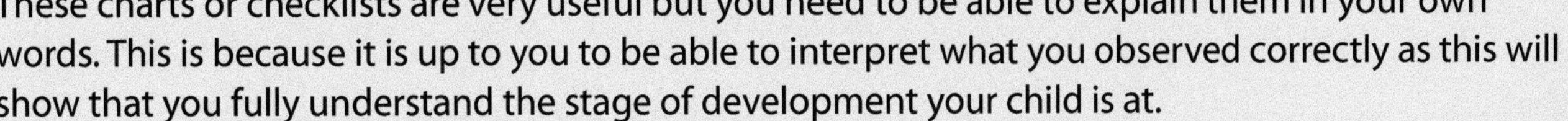

These charts or checklists are very useful but you need to be able to explain them in your own words. This is because it is up to you to be able to interpret what you observed correctly as this will show that you fully understand the stage of development your child is at.

Assess and evaluate the activities that took place on your visits and what you observed in each. Do this in order to:

1. **Identify how the child is developing and how it compares with the 'norm' of a child of the same age.**
2. **Allow you to compare development with previous visits.**

Keep asking yourself questions:

- Was it a good activity?
- Was it age appropriate?
- Was it interesting?
- Did I see what I hoped to see?
- Did it fulfill my aim and expectations?
- Was it difficult or too easy?

Analysis/interpretation

This stage of the assessment can at first appear a little daunting. From all the observations and visits you'll have quite a collection of facts that you have discovered, as well as all the results you have achieved through your questionnaires, research and checklists. You then need to interpret them, to see how the child is developing.

Write down what you have discovered from your visits and explain what your results mean. Using a chart to record both the norms of development AND the results from activities done with the study child can be a useful way to compare evidence. Think about what the child can do and make comparisons to what the average child is able to do.

If the child had elder siblings, their social development could be above the 'norm' as there were more opportunities for social behaviour.

If the child was taller than 'norm' at the same age it could be because one or both parents were over 6 feet tall, etc.

Link

Topics 4, 5 and 6 and your notes and use your research (for example, your charts) to compare the child's development with the 'norm' at the same age. Give your own personal comments of what results were found and discuss your findings.

Evaluation

This comes after the analysis of your results. You should draw up your own conclusions, using personal comments and opinions and also include **references** and **quotations** to back up your ideas.

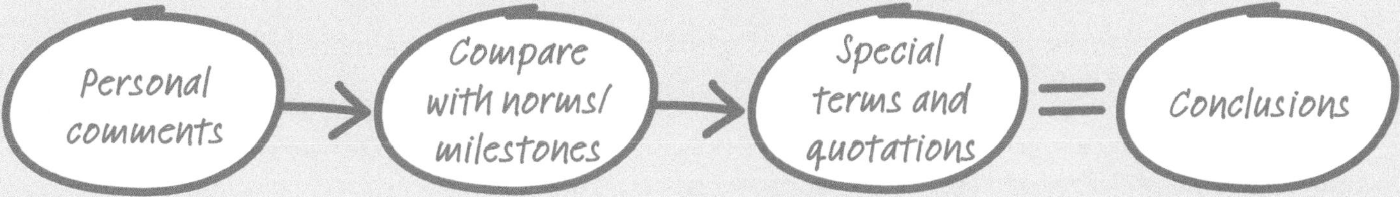

Analyse and evaluate the child's development at the end of the study and say how successful your planning and activities were. You need to consider how the activities you did encouraged any development.

Each section needs to be evaluated:

* ***Research* – was it really necessary, which aspect was most helpful and why?**
* ***Plan of action* – was having a plan a good idea? Did you follow it rigidly or not? What sort of problems cropped up along the way to make you review your plan? Make sure you mention if you made any changes as you were going along and explain why.**
* ***Visits* – were they informative, did each fulfill the aim, and were expectations realised?**
* ***Activities* – were they suitable and age appropriate, and did they provide evidence that development in chosen area had occurred?**

Use specialist terms, quotations and include references.

Gathering information and the presentation of results

This will show how the child developed since the beginning of the study.

* **Conclusions can be drawn up with personal comments and opinions included to back-up the findings.**
* **You could find quotations from textbooks to support your comments.**
* **Write a paragraph on your focused area and highlight any changes and progress.**
* **Remember not everything needs to have a positive outcome.**

Final evaluation of whole study

In this section you need to indicate how the child has developed over the period of time you have been observing. This could include when you became aware of changes and how the research and activities that happened during your observational visits helped any development.

This is the place to make your final comparisons with the 'norm'. Personal opinions and comments on comparisons would be a good idea, but always try to justify them.

Describe what you have gained by completing the study and whether your knowledge and understanding of the chosen area of development has improved.

Refer back to your original aims and comment on whether they have been achieved.

Use specialist terms, quotations and include references. Always include a bibliography.

Mention whether your research was successful and whether you feel that the activities during the visits were essential to discovering any development made, or even if they helped to develop new skills. What is your evidence for this?

You should evaluate the strengths and weaknesses of your complete study honestly and suggest ways to improve it. It is not a failing to be critical of your work – in fact it shows maturity and an ability to be aware how in the future work can be developed further and improved.

Presentation checklist

1. **Complete all parts of your study.**
2. **Use headings for each part.**
3. **Present your study neatly and in the correct order, as this shows good organisational skills.**
4. **Try to use a variety of methods to present your work and different ways of recording your findings.**
5. **Use your ICT skills and techniques to enhance the presentation of your study.**
6. **Label all photographs, charts, graphs, checklists.**
7. **Check your spelling, grammar and punctuation.**
8. **Include a colourful front cover which includes your name, candidate number, school and school number.**
9. **Check your spelling, grammar and punctuation.**

Technical terms and words

You could include some of these to improve your written work.

- Anxious
- Attentive
- Concentrate
- Concepts
- Confident
- Co-ordination
- Excitable
- Fine muscle control
- Friendly
- Frustration
- Genes
- Independent
- Inquisitive
- Joining in
- Knowledge
- Mature pincer grasp
- Moody
- Nature/nurture
- Palmar grasp
- Patience
- Physical movements:
  - crawling
  - sitting
  - walking
  - skipping
  - hopping
  - kicking
  - pedal
  - throw
  - catch, etc.
- Pincer grasp
- Polite
- Right/left handed
- Separation anxiety
- Shy
- Stimulate
- Temper tantrums
- Tripod grasp

- According to
- Although
- As a result
- Briefly
- Consequently
- Despite
- Eventually
- Finally
- However
- In conclusion
- In particular
- In summary
- Likewise
- Meanwhile
- Nevertheless
- On the whole
- Similarly
- Specifically
- Therefore
- Whereas

The Child Focused Task

Guidelines

* This task should be undertaken during the first half of the second year of the course.

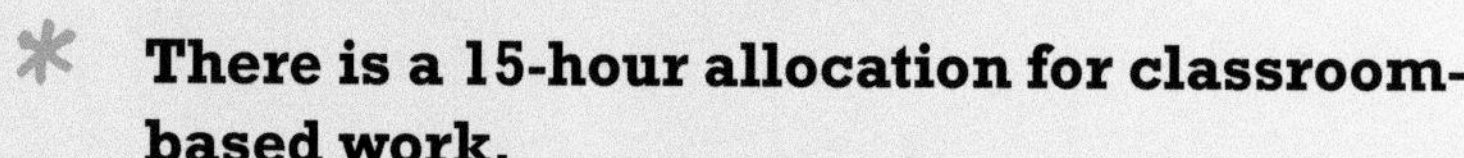

* There is a 15-hour allocation for classroom-based work.

Time is limited so it is very important to use it wisely.

* The target length for the work should be 8 pages of A3 or 16 of A4 – although this might sound a lot, you will probably find you have to be quite concise and keep your ideas focused, making reasoned selection and rejection statements on your final choices and how you would develop your ideas.

* You need to select one task from those set by the examination board. One task is designed to be completed through the medium of food (throughout these pages we'll refer to this as Task 1: Food); the other through the medium of material, e.g. fabric, wood, art (we'll refer to this as Task 2: Materials).

8 pages of A3
or
16 pages of A4

* In both tasks there will be opportunity to develop a wide range of skills:
  - Understanding and analysis of the task and identifying necessary resources.
  - Carrying out well-focused and relevant investigational work.
  - Selection and development of ideas, making reasoned choices/judgements.
  - Planning and making your idea.
  - Evaluating the work and offering reasoned judgements with conclusions.

The Child Focused Task accounts for 30% of the final mark.

The aim of the following pages is to help you get as many marks as possible and to assist you to structure your coursework properly and present it correctly.

Let's break these down into SEVEN steps as you can see in the flow diagram, and discuss each one in turn.

Pages 1 and 2: Interpretation and analysis of task

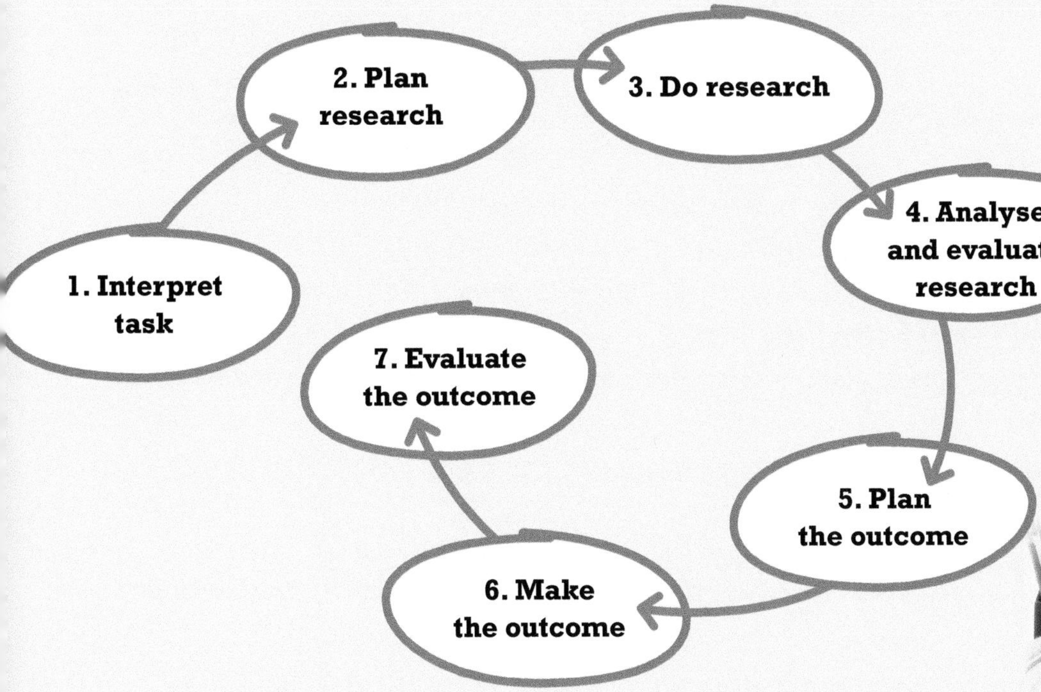

1. Interpret task
2. Plan research
3. Do research
4. Analyse and evaluate research
5. Plan the outcome
6. Make the outcome
7. Evaluate the outcome

1. Interpret task

First copy out the task chosen.

Then follow these steps:

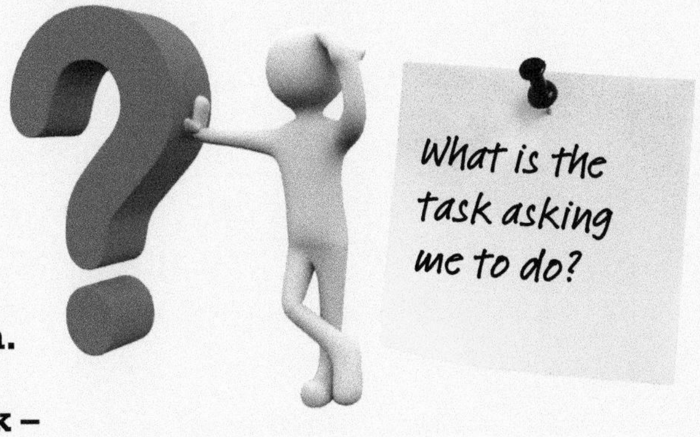

What is the task asking me to do?

1. **Highlight the key words.**
2. **Give a definition of each key word.**
3. **State what you understand by the task chosen.**
4. **Give a concise set of aims relevant to the task – ideally you should have between 6 and 8.**
5. **Work out a plan of action.**

On the following pages there are lots of examples of actual student work taken from the WJEC website. These have been retyped for legibility but have not been corrected in any other way. They are not meant to be copied but are an idea of how some students approached these tasks. Further exemplar materials can be accessed through the WJEC website.

Task 1: Food

Plan and make a selection of attractive food types that will encourage a child to eat a variety of foods.

Keep thinking to yourself – do I understand what this task is asking me to do?

SAMPLE 1

Key Words

Food refusal: As children develop more independence they become more fussy about what they eat. This can result in them not eating their food.

Fussy eaters: Children who are at a stage in their life where they don't want to eat certain foods sometimes even if they like them.

Balanced diet: A diet which contains the right amount of food essential for a healthy diet.

Malnourished diet: A diet where the child isn't taken in the right amount of nutrients and minerals.

Nutrients: There are 2 main types of nutrients, they are either known as macronutrients and micronutrients. Nutrients are essential for growth, development and energy.

Presentation of food: Making food more appealing to children who are fussy eaters and encourage them to try more new foods.

Definitions – this is where you have to define each key word that you listed beforehand.

SAMPLE 2

Aims

1. To research information on fussy eating and food refusal.
2. To investigate information on nutrients and balanced diets for 3 year olds.
3. To design and carry out a questionnaire with parents to find out what types of foods are unpopular with children.
4. To identify several dishes which may help encourage children to become less fussy eaters.
5. To select a range of foods to cook using the results from the questionnaire and research.
6. Prepare and make a selection of foods, taste and test them.
7. To evaluate the assessment task to see if I can make any improvements to my work.

Task 2: Materials

Plan and make an item that will help a child to achieve social skills.

SAMPLE 3

Keywords

Socialisation – is the acquisition of a wide range of social skills such as being able to interact with other people.

Social Play – is any play that is done with other children, where they are sharing and using their imagination.

Social Development – can be simply defined as a child's interaction and mixing with others.

Social Skills – e.g. Self care skills (Washing, Dressing), Good Manners, Sharing, Taking turns, Fair play and understanding rules.

Types of play – Creative Play, Social play, Imaginative Play.

What sort of information do I need to find out? Why is it important?

Definitions: this is where you have to define each key word that you listed above.

SAMPLE 4

Aims

- Investigate information on Social Development and Social Skills.
- Research the norms for Social Development and Intellectual Development for a child of 3 years.
- Research the views of parents and social development
- Investigate existing toys and activities available to help with Social Development.
- Design a selection of activities and toys to help a child's Social Development.
- Make an activity to help Social skills.
- Review and evaluate the work carried out for the Controlled Assessment Task.

2. Plan research

Make a list of the resources that you will need to use and the areas of research that will be required. Both resources and research should support your understanding and development of ideas. At least four sources should be used, relating to the keywords of the task.

Task 1: Food

SAMPLE 5

Balanced Diet

A balanced diet means that the child has to take in enough of the nutrients needed to grow and stay healthy. A child needs to have a diet containing the right foods, this is essential so that the child can maintain a suitable weight for its age and height.

Task 2: Materials

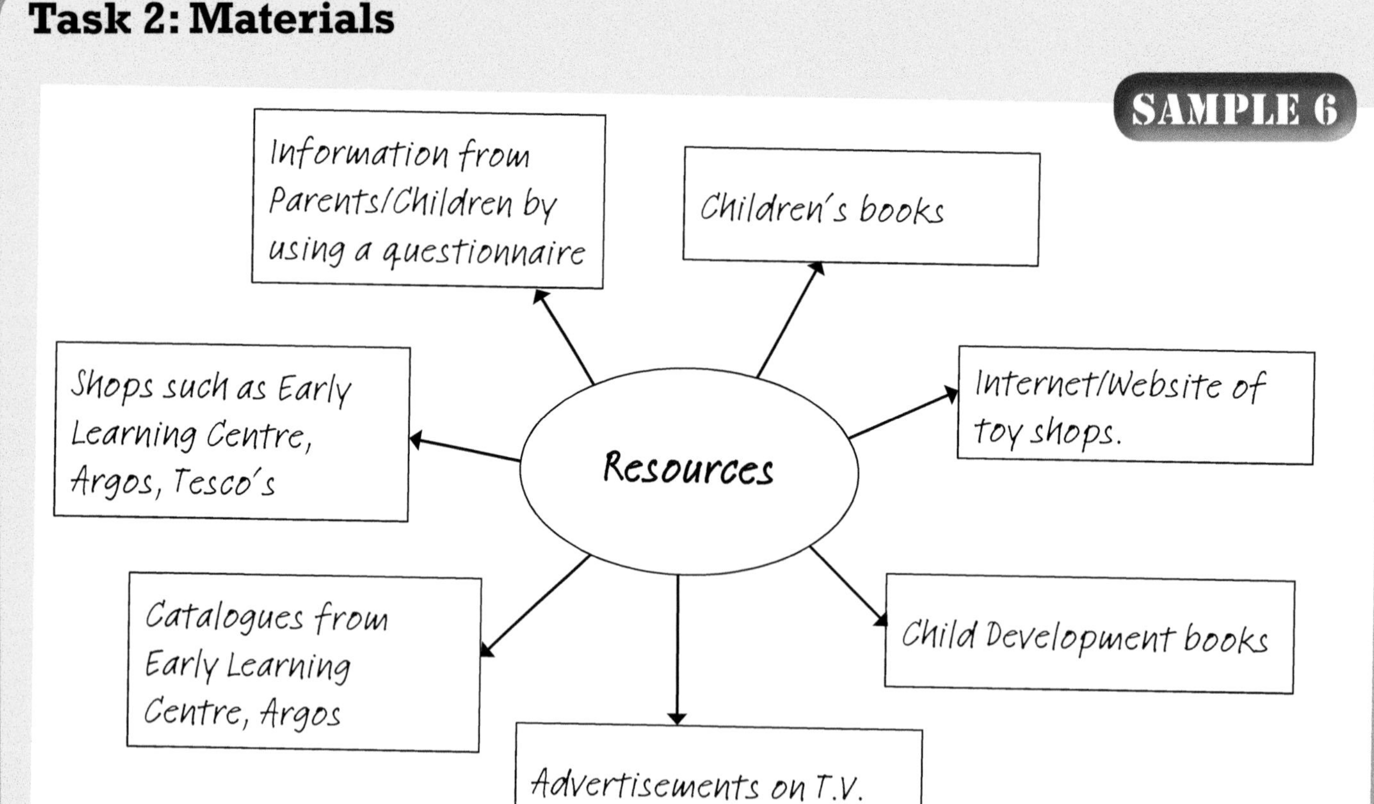
SAMPLE 6
Resources
Information from Parents/Children by using a questionnaire
Children's books
Internet/Website of toy shops.
Child Development books
Advertisements on T.V.
Catalogues from Early Learning Centre, Argos
Shops such as Early Learning Centre, Argos, Tesco's

3. Do research

Examples of the ways you can approach the research could include questionnaires (either following a standard type or making up your own), market research – i.e. visiting food or toy stores to find out what is already available – and interviews. All of these types of research (sometimes called research methods) will provide you with your own findings and results. This can sometimes be referred to as primary research. Secondary research is when you refer to textbooks, magazines, leaflets, teacher notes, websites (preferably British sites), etc.

There is no need to include every bit of research that you come across – you need to learn the art of being selective.

Task 1: Food

SAMPLE 7

A Healthy Diet for Children

- Needed for growth and development.
- A poor diet can cause health problems in childhood and later life e.g. diabetes.
- Tooth decay is caused by too much sugary foods.
- Obesity is caused from too much sugary and fatty foods.
- Too much salt can cause high blood pressure and increase the risk of heart disease.

Task 2: Materials

SAMPLE 8

Social Development or Socialisation – the process of learning the skills and attitudes which enable individuals to live easily with other member of the community. its is necessary for children to develop social skills so that they are able to interact and mix with others; successful social interaction leads to happier and healthier children.

Remember that it is a good idea to keep in mind why you are actually doing this research in the first place – it is how you are going to find the information you need to understand and complete your task. So, take the time to explain what you are trying to discover, and ask yourself why? Why is it important and what are you trying to find out? If you keep doing this and keep these questions in mind, it will make sure that the research stays on track and that you don't get side-tracked.

4. Analyse and evaluate research

How do I present my findings? Some of the best ways of displaying your research results are to use flow charts, tables, graphs or spider diagrams. All of them are good ways of showing information, and you could use one or two to give your research findings some variety. However, beware of using too many types of chart as it can get confusing to read or interpret.

Give a brief description of what you did and give references to show where you got the information from. Analyse your research, record your findings and make conclusions to finalise the specification for the practical outcome of the task.

Task 1: Food

SAMPLE 9

Questionnaire Conclusion

Having looked at my questionnaire and evaluated the results, I have found out that 20% of the parents I surveyed said that their child was a fussy eater. Also half of the parents said that their child started showing likes and dislikes at the age of 2–3 years. From the questionnaire I have found that fish and cheese were children's least favourite protein foods and children enjoyed chicken, eggs and meat the most. I also found out that half of the children's least favourite carbohydrate was rice, and bread was the carbohydrate that children enjoyed the most. From the questionnaire I have found out that children's least favourite vegetable were onions which had the highest result. Peas and salad were children's most enjoyed vegetable. Banana's were the least liked fruit from the 10 parents I surveyed, whilst plums and peaches were the children's most liked fruit. When I asked the parents if their child consumed 5 portions of fruit and vegetables a day a massive 80% said that their child didn't. The last question that I asked parents was which of the 5 drinks did their child least like and all parents said that their child enjoyed squash and pop but sadly the healthy drink e.g. water and milk were the least popular.

Task 2: Materials

SAMPLE 10

Conclusion

From the results of my parental survey, I found that while parents provided toys for Physical and Intellectual Development. They did not seem to find buying toys for Social Development as important. Of the toys bought to help Social Development, the survey showed that in joint first place was puzzles and balls, followed by Sand and Water Play. The activity less provided was card games.

From the surveys into children likes and dislikes. The most popular type of toys and activities wer first board games follower by puzzles and balls in second place but the least popular activities with children were card games and sand and water play.

Of the types of social development activities provided by parents before school age, the most popular were going to parties, visits to the park/swimming pool and nursery followed by playing at friends/family home. The least popular was playschool.

Most parent surveyed said that the age that their child started mixing and playing with others was between 2–3 years.

When you come to think about the specifications for the task you need to draw up a list of the requirements that the food dishes should meet.

You need to consider the specifications. For example, in Task 1 dishes need to be colourful, healthy, and be able to stay fresh. And for Task 2 Materials, they need to be safe to use and age appropriate.

Both of these are actually called specifications – the word literally means a detailed description of how something should be made, or done. So in this case, that means a description of the features the packed lunch food types should have.

Task 1: Food

SAMPLE 11

Specification

The foods that I make need to;

- Be healthy and contain protein, carbohydrates, vitamins and minerals.
- Contain unpopular foods with popular foods.
- Be suitable for 4 year olds.
- Made within 3 hours.
- Be easy to eat.
- Be served into small portions.
- Look appetising by being colourful.
- Be presented in a novelty way to encourage child to try them.

Task 2: Materials

SAMPLE 12

Specification

- *Will encourage social skills such as sharing, taking turns, using rules.*
- *Suits ability and age group of 3 years.*
- *Safe to use.*
- *Easy to use and play with.*
- *Colourful and attractive*
- *Keep children interested*
- *Must be able to be made in three hours.*

Finally don't forget all of these points need to be on your one side of A3 paper.

Pages 3 and 4: Selection and development of ideas

You need to give a wide range of ideas relevant to the task itself.

At least **eight** ideas should be given for Task 1: Food, whereas **four** will be acceptable for Task 2: Materials. These could be displayed initially in the form of a flowchart or spider diagram of a range of ideas. You can add more detailed information for each of the appropriate ideas at a later stage.

Task 1: Food

SAMPLE 13

Task 2: Materials

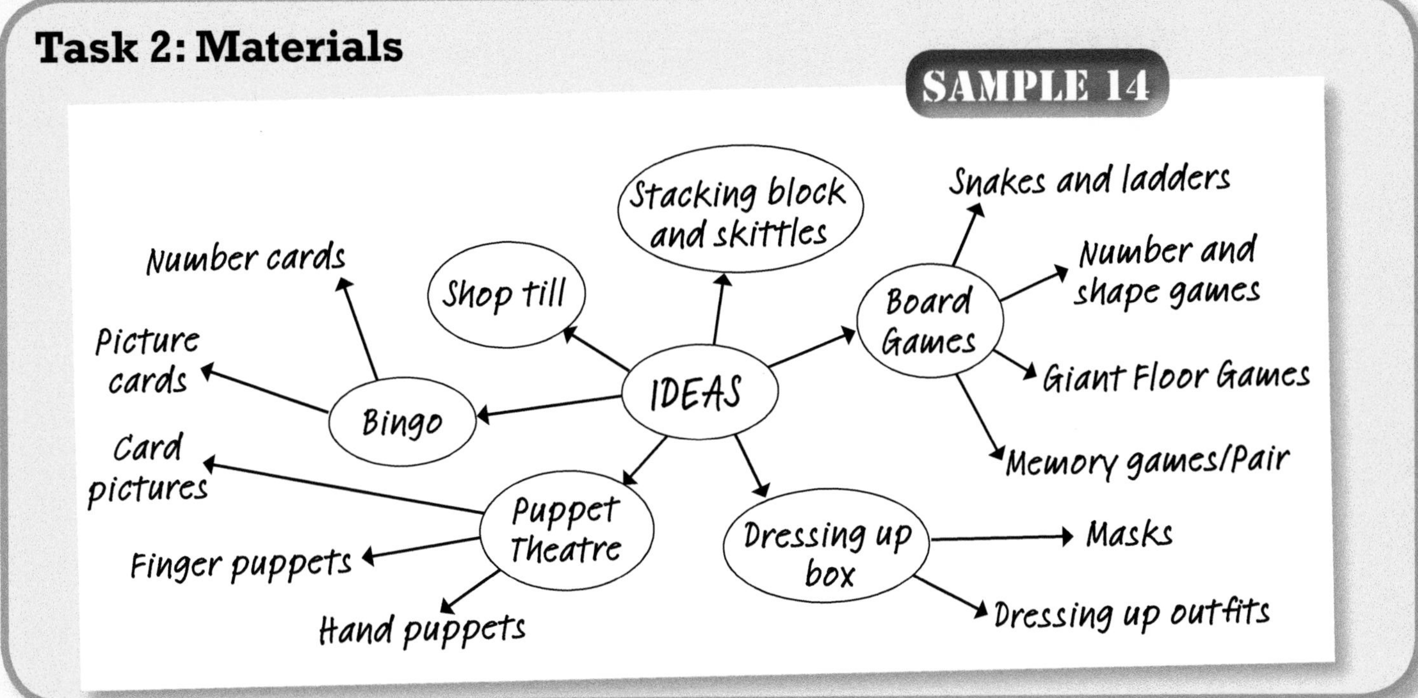

You could refer back to your analysis of the research that you had undertaken, to indicate how your ideas were influenced by results.

Then you need to select and reject your ideas referring back to the key words and research results. A **criteria chart** is a useful tool for this.

You could use the specifications that you have listed as headings in the criteria chart. So, for example:

- **Food**: attractive, healthy, appetising, easy to make, food allergies/intolerances, cost, time allocation OR
- **Materials**: attractive, safety, easy to make, plus meeting specific skills related to the task, time allocation, durability

Task 1: Food

SAMPLE 15

Criteria Chart				
Criteria	Cheesy Beef Burger	Fruit Skewers	Pinwheel Sandwiches	Banana + Strawberry Smoothie
Healthy		✓	✓	✓
Suitable for Children	✓		✓	✓
Easy for the child to eat	✓	✓	✓	✓
Made hygienically	✓	✓	✓	✓
Not too many complicated flavours	✓	✓	✓	✓

Task 2: Materials

SAMPLE 16

Criteria	Idea 1 (Finger Puppet)	Idea 2 (Puzzles)	Idea 3 (Skittles)	Idea 4 (Domino/Card Game)
Social Development	It helps Role plays, Imaginary play and Creative skills	Teaches about Rules and helps with Mixing	Helps with Taking Turns, Sharing, Rules	Involves 2 or more Players and Helps with Mixing
Age Group	Suitable for Child aged 3+	Suitable for Child aged 4+	Suitable for Child aged 3+	Suitable for Child Aged 4+
Cost to Make	Cost would be around £6.00	Cost would be around £3.00	Cost would be around £6.00	Cost would be around £4.50
Appeals to Children	Colourful	It is colourful and attractive	Colourful	Not very attractive
Teaches Physical Development	Teaches hand eye-coordination	Helps with Fine Manipulative Skills	Helps with hand - eye coordination	Helps hand – eye coordination
Teaches Intellectual Development	Helps with Creative Skills	Helps with Word Skills	Helps with Number Skills	Helps with Number Skills and Word Skills
Time	Will approximately take 2 hours to make	Will approximately take 3 hours to make	Will approximately take 2 and half hours to make	Will approximately take 3 hours to make
Safety	Has no sharp edges but has little pieces (the eyes)	Has no Sharp edges	Has no sharp edges or little pieces	Has no sharp edges or little pieces

Star diagrams can also be used

Develop a few basic star diagrams giving sketches, list of ingredients/materials and discuss how these ideas match the required criteria of the task. Discuss each fully so that a **final selection and rejection process** occurs. Then when you select the final chosen idea or ideas you will need to make sure you clearly state your justification for your choice.

Other techniques here could include pie graphs, block graphs or tick lists.

Task 1: Food

SAMPLE 17

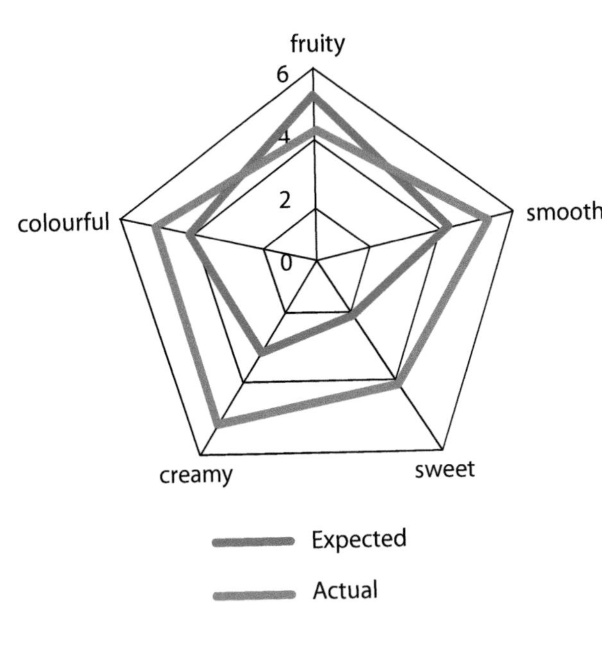

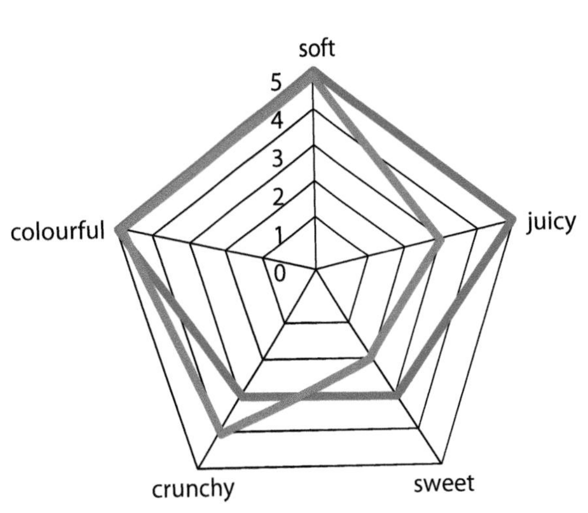

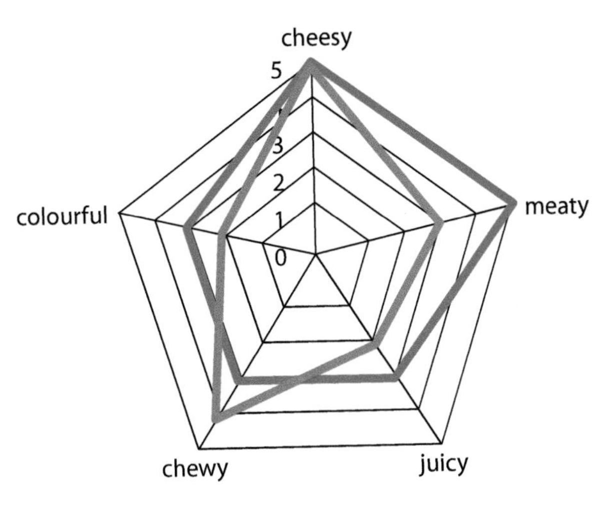

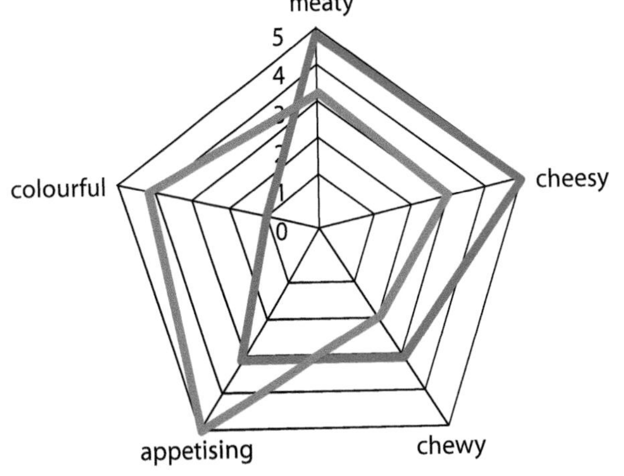

Task 1: Food

SAMPLE 18

Final Choice and Reasons for Choice

The items that I intend to make are strawberry + banana smoothie, pinwheel sandwiches, fruit skewers and cheesy beef burgers.

I have chosen to make a strawberry + Banana smoothie because it is a healthy drink for the child it is also tasty and a attractive colour.

I chose to make pinwheel sandwiches because they are quick and easy to make also because they are more appealing to a child as they are not as plain as a normal sandwich.

I also chose to make fruit skewers because they are healthy for a child and because they are colourful and more of a fun option for a child than putting the fruit in a plain bowl.

I have chosen to make cheesy beef burgers because they are easy to make and young children tend to like burgers but they are also getting calcium out of the cheese. I can also turn the cheesy beef burgers into faces.

Another reason that I chose these dishes is because they are quite cheap to make so if the child does not like the food then it will not be a big waste of money. Also if the child does not like the food because it is quick and easy to eat then it will not be a waste of time.

Task 2: Materials

SAMPLE 19

Reasons for Choice

The activity I have chosen for my final idea is the Domino Card game. I have chosen the game which I think will help with Social Development as the activity involves Taking Turns and Sharing. The game involves 2 – 4 players, Mixing and it also teaches about rules. The game also helps with Intellectual Development by teaching Number Skills. I think the game will be easy to use and simple to play for ages 3 – 4 years. It is safe to use with no small pieces. As well as showing numbers as figures. I will also show them as words. The game will have 28 large pieces which will be shared out between the players. Children will have to match the same numbers to the cards on the floor.

Finally, you need to list the materials or ingredients required to complete the final outcome, the specifications and any other relevant factors. Also list all of the skills that you will need to complete the task, and be aware of time restrictions, costs, and health and safety issues.

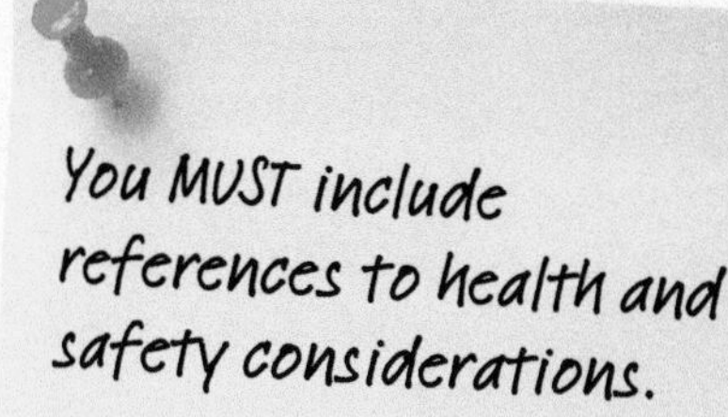

You MUST include references to health and safety considerations.

Page 5: Planning the outcome

5. Plan the outcome

List the materials/ingredients you could use and then select and reject the less appropriate ones, taking into account health and safety issues, or healthy eating guidelines, for instance. If you have the time, maybe you can attempt some experiments on a prototype to help in the selection process of ingredients/materials, different finishes (if a material) and also presentation styles.

A flowchart should be then compiled presenting your plan of action or order in which you will do the work.

Page 6: Making the outcome

6. Make the outcome

If you have completed all of the previous steps carefully then all that you now need to do is carry out your complete plan of action as far as possible – simple! However, remember that if in the actual carrying out of the plan, you make a change – even if for a very good reason – you must say so and say why. What were the reasons for your change? Use as many specialist terms throughout as you can, making sure you understand them and that they are the right ones. Also, try and use a range of appropriate skills and techniques to complete the final outcome.

Photographs can also provide excellent evidence to demonstrate this whole making process, and at the same time you can record your final outcome.

Pages 7 and 8: Evaluation

7. Evaluate the outcome

You should now move on to evaluate the completed task, which means evaluating the written supportive work as well as the practical work.

To make it easier divide the evaluation into **FIVE** sections:

1. **Understanding of task**
   - Did I understand the task?
   - Did I do enough research?
   - Did I use correct resources and methods?
   - How did my research help me to complete the task?

2. **Development of ideas; selection and rejection of ideas**
   - Were my ideas relevant to my chosen task?
   - Did I use correct criteria to select and reject ideas for final outcome?

3. **Planning and making**

- Did I have good understanding of how to plan correctly?
- Did I choose correct materials?
- Did I consider health and safety issues?
- Did I bear in mind the suitability for age specified in the task?
- Did I choose correct methods to make the final outcome?
- Was I organised?
- Did I have the skills to complete the outcome?
- Was the finished outcome relevant to the task?
- Did the outcome meet my expectations?

4. **Strengths and weaknesses**

- What were my best bits?
- Were there any areas that were weak?

Task 1: Food

SAMPLE 20

One of my strengths was that I organised myself well. I completed the questionnaire first of all and this was useful because I knew exactly what I had to do and it saved me a lot of time. Another strength was that I chose dishes that I was capable of making which helped me to complete in allocated time

One of my weaknesses was that some of the dishes weren't that attractive and may not have appealed to a 3 year old and also I used too much syrup in the biscuits which made it sickly and not very healthy.

Task 2: Materials

SAMPLE 21

I think the appearance of the game was good and the overall cost was small as I recycled a box to use and that I have good organisation skills and used my time well to finish in the time.

My main weakness was that I had trouble sticking down the coloured shapes because the glue I used was not suitable for shiny surfaces. Also I could have made more puppets that would have been useful for role play.

5. **Further developments**

- If I did this task again would I make any changes and if so what and why? Could I make any improvements? An example of this could be an expansion of the range of food you have made, or further development of your item for different age groups or mass production!

Task 1: Food

SAMPLE 22

If I did this task again I would look at special diets eg vegan or allergies, as that would be different and I would also get my study child to taste the dishes to see what a child would really think of what I had made. Also I would improve the overall appearance of the foods to make them more attractive, drizzling melted chocolate on the muffins or adding some small colourful sweets.

Task 2: Materials

SAMPLE 23

Another improvement I would make would be to have tested the glue first as I wasted a lot of time and it would have improved the appearance and also designed different characters from everyday life which would help a child use their imagination more through their own stories and plays.

Presentation

Make your piece of work colourful and easy to read. Try to include different methods to present and enhance your work, for example:

* **Wherever possible use specialist terms, quotes and references.**
* **Try to use your ICT skills and techniques, which will enhance the overall final presentation of your work.**
* **Think about layout, illustrations, sketches and photographs.**
* **And finally, make sure you put your name, candidate number and centre number on EVERY page and secure all the pages together.**

Include a bibliography – this is a list of all the external secondary sources of research that you consulted. Give the title, author, publisher and date of publication if you can.

Nearly finished – time for one final bit of good advice…

Don't waste lots of time making the final presentation too decorative, with lots of different coloured paper, cut out images or fold-out sections stuck all over the sheets of A3. It might feel like you're making the presentation even better by doing lots of colouring in of spaces, fancy borders or images stuck down that have been printed off – but the reality is that very little of this has any actual impact on getting a better grade. Make the final presentation as neat and colourful as you can, but don't go over the top with it – concentrate on making the actual facts and writing as good as you can.

Glossary

ABANDONED – baby thinks the parents will not be returning to care for his/her needs

ABSENT PARENT – a parent who does not live with the child

ADJUSTABLE FASTENING – found on the strap of shoes in order to allow sufficient space for movement and growth

ALCOHOL – a drink which if taken in excess can affect a person's ability to act responsibly, for example being unable to care for children

ALLERGIC REACTION – sensitivity to a particular food or medication, such as eggs and nuts, which does not affect other people

ALLERGY – an abnormal reaction to something, such as a type of food; symptoms may include rashes and breathing difficulties

AMBIDEXTROUS – able to write using either hand

ANAPHYLAXIS – a severe, potentially life-threatening allergic reaction

ANGER – a feeling of being very annoyed and upset

AUDIO-VISUAL MEDIA – technology using pictures and sound, such as television

BALANCE – the ability to keep the body upright and level

BLIND – has no sight

BONES – these form the framework of the body, known as the skeleton

CALCIUM – a mineral used to form strong bones and teeth

CAR SEAT – a special seat in which babies and young children can be strapped when travelling in a car

CENTILE CHARTS – charts showing the average weight and height of children according to their age

CHILDMINDER – a person who looks after other people's children in the childminder's own home

CHOKING – when an object is stuck in the throat and causes a problem with breathing

COELIAC DISEASE – a condition where someone has a reaction to eating gluten

COGNITIVE – another name for intellectual development

COMFORTER – an item offering the child security when separated from the parents, such as taking a soft toy to bed

COMMUNICATE – being able to interact with other people by smiling, laughing and talking

CONCEPT – an abstract idea that children need to learn, e.g. time

CONFIDENCE – having belief in oneself

CONSISTENT – always applying the same rules without making any changes from one day to the next

CO-ORDINATION – the ability to use two senses together, such as the hands and eyes

CRAWLING – using the hands and knees to move across the floor

CREATIVE PLAY – making something new

DEVELOPMENTAL MILESTONES – another expression for the norms of development used to describe the stage at which an average child should have gained a skill

DISCOVERY PLAY – finding out, e.g. what happens if...?

DRAWING – creative work using pencils and paints

DRESSING – being able to put on and take off one's own clothes

DROPLET INFECTION – droplets containing bacteria which can pass from one person to another when coughing or sneezing

ENJOYMENT – having fun and feeling happy

ENVIRONMENT – the area around the home, such as other homes, shops, schools and play areas, it is sometimes described as the neighbourhood

EPIPEN – a safe syringe in the shape of a pen which injects adrenaline; it is used when someone has a severe allergic reaction

FAECES – the waste material produced by the body when food has been digested

FAT – a nutrient which provides the body with energy and warmth

FEAR – feeling frightened
FINE MOTOR SKILLS – controlling and using the hands and fingers
FIRE GUARD – placed in front of a fire to prevent contact with heat and flames
FIRST AID BOX – a box containing a selection of equipment such as antiseptic wipes, plasters, bandages and plastic gloves
FLUORIDE – a mineral found in water which helps to form the enamel on teeth
FOLIC ACID – a B group vitamin essential in early pregnancy
FOOD INTOLERANCE – a reaction to eating a food, which usually starts several hours later, and causes cramps and bloating
GASTROENTERITIS – inflammation of the stomach and bowel, causing diarrhoea and vomiting
GENES – these are found in the chromosomes and are responsible for inherited characteristics, such as hair colour
GLUE EAR – a recurring infection of the middle ear
GLUTEN – a protein found in many types of cereal grains and the foods made from them
GUIDANCE – giving direction in order to help an individual follow the correct way, for example parents explaining to a toddler how to show thanks for a gift
HALAL – food and drink which has been prepared following Islamic law
HAND WASHING – washing hands in warm soapy water, especially after using the toilet and before eating food; important personal hygiene rule
HEAD CONTROL – the baby has the ability to hold the head upright and turn it to look around
HORMONE – a chemical released by the body that has an effect on other parts of the body
HYDROCEPHALUS – a build-up of fluid on the brain
ILLEGAL DRUGS – drugs which have not been prescribed by a doctor which, when taken, can affect a person's ability to act responsibly, for example being unable to care for children
IMAGINATION – having the ability to picture in the mind scenes, people and objects when they are not able to be seen
IMAGINATIVE PLAY – pretend play
IMMUNISATION – having a vaccination, usually as an injection, to give protection against an infectious disease
IMMUNITY – a person's ability to resist or fight off infection
INDEX FINGER – the first finger next to the thumb
INJURIES – damage to the body, such as a grazed knee or a cut finger
INSECT STINGS – stings, usually from bees and wasps
INSULIN – a hormone which controls the level of sugar in the bloodstream
INTELLECTUAL DEVELOPMENT – the development of the mind and thinking skills
JEALOUSY – a feeling of envy of another person, for example a young child feeling that the newborn baby in the family is receiving more attention than themselves
KINDNESS – being friendly and helpful to others such as a young child showing affection by cuddles
KOSHER – food and drink which conforms to Jewish law
LACK OF CONFIDENCE – being frightened to speak to people or take part in an activity due to the individual thinking they are not capable of doing it
LANGUAGE – using words to express ideas
LEARNING TOOLS – toys, books and activities which help toddlers and young children learn various skills
LEFT HANDED – a person who uses the left hand to write

LOCKED BATHROOM CABINET – used to keep medication and toiletries safely locked away out of the reach of toddlers and young children
MANIPULATIVE PLAY – using the hands
MENINGITIS – an infection of the protective membranes around the brain and spinal cord
MISCARRIAGE – the accidental loss of a pregnancy
NATURE – the genes a child inherits from their parents
NEGATIVE EMOTION – when an individual is feeling sad or angry
NIGHTMARES – during the night waking up very upset, crying and frightened due to a very unpleasant dream
NURSERY – a place where young children are looked after by trained teachers, usually for a half-day session
NURTURE – the way a child is brought up and the environment they grow up in
NUTRIENTS – these are found in a variety of foods and carry out different functions in the body, such as growth and providing energy
OESTROGEN – a hormone produced by the ovaries which regulates the menstrual cycle
PARK – an open space for the public to use for exercise and leisure which has grass, flower beds, picnic tables, often a play area and maybe a lake
PARTIAL SIGHT – very limited sight
PERSONAL INDEPENDENCE – being able to look after one's own needs, such as going to the toilet by oneself
PERSONALITY – a person's individual characteristics, such as being quick tempered or timid, as well as attitudes, such as being helpful and friendly
PHYSICAL PLAY – using the body
PICNIC – having a meal outside, such as in the park or at the beach
PINCER GRASP – using the index finger and the thumb to pick up an object
PLAY AREA – an area with a range of large play equipment, such as slides and swings, which help to develop children's gross motor skills
PLEASE AND THANK YOU – a social skill which shows politeness
POISONING – something taken by the mouth which is harmful, for example a child drinking bleach or eating painkiller tablets
POOR STANDARD OF BEHAVIOUR – showing behaviour which is not appropriate to the age of the child or is unkind and nasty behaviour towards other individuals
POSITIVE EMOTION – when an individual is feeling happy and cheerful
PRAISE – congratulating a child's achievement by, for example, saying 'well done' or giving a hug or kiss
PRECAUTIONS – taking actions to prevent accidents occurring
PREMATURE – a baby born before the 37th week of the pregnancy
PRIMARY SOCIALISATION – social skills which are taught within the home by the family
PRIVATE SCHOOL – a school which charges fees for education
PROFESSIONAL COUNSELLING – receiving help and advice from qualified and trained people
PROGESTERONE – a hormone produced by the ovaries which regulates the menstrual cycle and is needed for pregnancy
PROTEIN – a nutrient which helps with the growth and repair of the body
QUALITY TIME – when a parent and child spend time together talking, playing a game and enjoying each other's company
REGRESSION – going backwards to an earlier stage of behaviour, such as eating food with fingers and refusing to use cutlery
RELATIVE – a person who is related by blood or marriage, e.g. parent, brother, sister
RIGHT HANDED – a person who uses the right hand to write

ROAD SAFETY – understanding how to behave on the pavement and crossing the road

SAFETY CAPS – found on bottles of cleaning liquid and tablets designed so that children cannot open them

SAFETY CATCHES – placed on the doors of fridges and freezers to prevent them being opened by young children

SAFETY HARNESS – worn by a toddler when in a high chair, pushchair or walking with parents on the pavement, to avoid the child climbing out or running away

SECONDARY SOCIALISATION – social skills learnt from society, such as school and clubs

SELF-CONFIDENCE – believing that you are able to interact with other people and cope with different situations during life

SELF-RELIANT – having an independent attitude and doing tasks on one's own, e.g. dressing and feeding oneself

SENSES – taste, touch, sight, smell, hearing

SEPARATION ANXIETY – a baby feeling unhappy and being distressed when separated from the parents or carer

SEVERE BLEEDING – when an injury causes the loss of a lot of blood

SHARING – allowing other people to use one's own belongings, e.g. toys

SHY – a child who is unwilling to talk and mix with other children or adults, often staying very close to the parent or carer for support

SIBLINGS – brothers and sisters of the same parents

SITTING – the ability to sit in an upright position on the bottom once the back muscles are strong enough to support the body

SMILES – a baby's social reaction to a familiar person, e.g. parent, sibling

SMOTHER LOVE – when parents are overprotective of their child and will not allow them to become independent, for example by interfering with play activities, not allowing the child to play outdoors on large play equipment or worrying excessively about the child's health and development

SOCIAL PLAY – playing with others

SQUINT – when the eyes work independently of each other and appear to look in different directions

STARTLE REFLEX – when a loud noise makes young babies close their hands into fists, bend the arms up to the shoulders and often cry

STATE SCHOOL – a school funded by the government so parents do not have to pay any fees for education

STEP-SIBLINGS – children who share only one parent with you, e.g. you both have the same mother but different fathers

STRETCH FABRIC – this fabric has the ability to expand by stretching

SUCKING REFLEX – the baby's reaction to something touching the roof of the mouth is to suck

TABLE MANNERS – knowing how to eat food in an acceptable way, such as correct use of cutlery

TAKING TURNS – everyone is given the same opportunity to play, for example in a board game

TEAT – the soft plastic part of a baby's bottle that the milk is sucked through

TOILET TRAINING – having the ability to stay clean and dry and going to the toilet independently

UPPERS – the top part of shoes covering the feet

VACCINATION – an injection to give protection against infectious diseases

VITAMIN D – a vitamin which helps the body absorb calcium to make strong bones and teeth

WATCH – babies and toddlers watch the actions of adults and then copy them – this is how they learn many developmental skills

WATERPROOF – clothing which is able to keep the body dry when raining

WHOLE HAND PALMAR GRASP – using the whole hand to pick up an object

Index

U

V

W